FORGIVENESS and SPIRITUALITY in PSYCHOTHERAPY

FORGIVENESS and SPIRITUALITY in PSYCHOTHERAPY
A Relational Approach

EVERETT L. WORTHINGTON, JR.,
and STEVEN J. SANDAGE

American Psychological Association • *Washington, DC*

Published by
American Psychological Association
750 First Street, NE
Washington, DC 20002
www.apa.org

To order
APA Order Department
P.O. Box 92984
Washington, DC 20090-2984
Tel: (800) 374-2721; Direct: (202) 336-5510
Fax: (202) 336-5502; TDD/TTY: (202) 336-6123
Online: www.apa.org/books/
E-mail: order@apa.org

In the U.K., Europe, Africa, and the Middle East, copies may be ordered from
American Psychological Association
3 Henrietta Street
Covent Garden, London
WC2E 8LU England

Typeset in Goudy by Circle Graphics, Inc., Columbia, MD

Printer: Sheridan Books, Ann Arbor, MI
Cover Designer: Naylor Design, Washington, DC

The opinions and statements published are the responsibility of the authors, and such opinions and statements do not necessarily represent the policies of the American Psychological Association.

Library of Congress Cataloging-in-Publication Data

Worthington, Everett L., 1946-
Forgiveness and spirituality in psychotherapy : a relational approach / Everett L. Worthington, Jr., and Steven J. Sandage. — First edition.
    pages cm
  Includes bibliographical references and index.
  ISBN 978-1-4338-2031-1 — ISBN 1-4338-2031-5 1. Psychotherapy—Religious aspects.
2. Forgiveness. 3. Spirituality—Psychology. I. Sandage, Steven J. II. Title.
  RC489.S676W67 2016
  616.89'14—dc23
                            2015009341

British Library Cataloguing-in-Publication Data

A CIP record is available from the British Library.

Printed in the United States of America
First Edition

DOI:10.1037/14712-000

CONTENTS

PREFACE

This is a book based on research but aimed at mental health practitioners. If you want to know more about how people deal with transgressions, especially when religion and spirituality get mixed up in them, then this book is for you. If you do research on forgiveness or spirituality or are an undergraduate seeking an application-focused, research-informed understanding of forgiveness and spirituality, or if you are a curious and thoughtful reader with expertise in another area, we hope you will be enriched by this book, too. We have tried to stay close to the research while writing this book directly for those who struggle to help clients through their difficulties.

Most writing for clinicians and researchers about the topic of forgiveness has been done since 1998. Research on how forgiveness and spirituality relate to each other has developed more recently (for a meta-analytic review, see D. E. Davis, Worthington, Hook, & Hill, 2013). Little new theory has guided that study, especially in interventions (for a meta-analysis, see Wade, Hoyt, Kidwell, & Worthington, 2014). In the past few years, we believe, that has changed. We aim at theory- and research-informed clinical applications.

Much of our theorizing grew from a research grant awarded by the Fetzer Institute to Dr. Worthington, with Dr. Sandage and with Dr. Michael McCullough of Miami University as coinvestigators. The three of us met in 2005 in the midwinter Miami steam heat, and we cooked up this theory of how people with interpersonal problems, which often include grudges and vengeful motivations, could forgive. And because most people in the United States consider themselves spiritual, religious, or both, we included religion and spirituality in our thinking about how forgiveness and spirituality might change with time. We planned three longitudinal studies—one for each of us—and a host of smaller studies to test our theorizing. Some of this Fetzer-funded research piggybacked on existing grants (Lilly Foundation, to Sandage; National Institute for Mental Health, to McCullough), and other research has piggybacked onto it (John Templeton Foundation grant to Worthington and later to Dr. Don Davis at Georgia State University). The three of us formulated the basic theory of forgiveness and relational spirituality together—the pyramid that you will see in Chapter 4. However, McCullough was completing a large National Institutes of Health grant and could not participate as a coauthor in this book. So we cite his work, but we (Worthington and Sandage) tell the story of the research, place it in the broad context of their theorizing and other research, and most important, make it clinically and personally relevant.

We do not emphasize a particular religious or spiritual tradition. We highlight the importance of clinical sensitivity to various traditions. We recognize that forgiveness is sacred to some people but is not religious or spiritual for others. In 1997, the three of us published *To Forgive Is Human: How to Put Your Past in the Past* (McCullough, Sandage, & Worthington, 1997), a trade book whose thesis was captured by the title. Forgiveness does not belong to any religion. It is a *human* enterprise. We affirm that position in this current book.

We do not consider spirituality as an aspect of religion. Spirituality can be religious or nonreligious. Although some people might associate the topic of forgiveness with certain religious traditions, we find a diversity of expressions of forgiveness in various traditions. Some individuals have experienced negative or abusive experiences with spiritual and religious communities, and their forgiveness struggles can be complicated by traumatic associations with the sacred.

We want to make this book usable. We have included many cases, adapted with masking or by synthesizing a composite client, and we have conformed to ethical guidelines in disguising at least five identifying characteristics of individuals. We believe you will enjoy this read regardless of whether you share our theoretical perspectives. We hope you find this book stimulating.

ACKNOWLEDGMENTS

We wholeheartedly thank the Fetzer Institute, which initiated this project. Program Officer Wayne Ramsey was our contact with the Institute from the beginning. He challenged us to find a project and kept after us to bring it to fruition. Through Grant 2266, the Institute not only funded personnel time to collect data, analyze it, and write but also provided the lens that kept our separate projects converging on a single image. Dr. Worthington received another grant from the John Templeton Foundation (Grant 14979) to complete his data collection and to consider new variables (namely, humility). Dr. Sandage's research was also supported by Lilly Endowment, Inc., Grant 2078 and the John Templeton Foundation Grants 10987 and 29630 on relational spirituality and humility that informed this book.

From a personal standpoint, we want to acknowledge the many wonderful collaborators in this research. Listing all the names of participants since the project began in 2006 would be tedious, but we are not any less grateful. The acknowledgments of those collaborators are authorship on the many publications that came from these three projects (you can peruse the references and see their names). Also, numerous workers within each lab were crucial to the success of the research, even though their contributions might not have risen to the level of publication credit. Thank you to all. A special thanks go to Sarah Hassen for graphic design and to Sajel Patel and David Paine for their research support.

Writing this book has consumed three weeks of each of three summers for me (Ev), and I am so grateful that my wife, Kirby, has been so generous in allowing me to retreat to Florida for writing and to Wayne Canipe for providing the condo. I (Steve) want to thank my wife, Danielle, and daughters, Kate and Camille, for sharing the journey of learning about relationships, forgiveness, and spirituality. I am also grateful to my primary clinical mentors, Jim Maddock and Noel Larson, for showing me the possibilities for integrating attachment and differentiation.

FORGIVENESS and SPIRITUALITY in PSYCHOTHERAPY

INTRODUCTION

Luisa has a problem—several, really. She and her partner—"We're not married, but we've been together for 14 years"—are embedded in deep conflict that has recently gotten worse. They hurt each other often, and they are bitter toward each other. Their 13-year-old son (Jamie) and 10-year-old daughter (Maria) are being affected, and the 13-year-old is demanding more independence and playing off Luisa against her partner, Carlos. Jamie was recently suspended from middle school for looking at pornography on the school computer and, as subsequent school investigation showed, exchanging naked pictures of himself with several young women in his class. Below is an exchange between Luisa and her psychotherapist.

> *Luisa:* Carlos is in denial. He just goes to work and leaves it to me to deal with Jamie and Maria. He flat-out refused to get family therapy or come to see you. We have huge fights over what to do about Jamie, and they end

http://dx.doi.org/10.1037/14712-001
Forgiveness and Spirituality in Psychotherapy: A Relational Approach, by E. L. Worthington, Jr. and S. J. Sandage

with Carlos throwing up his hands and storming out. We are like John Gottman's "Four Horsemen of the Apocalypse." (Yeah, I saw that on a television program about troubled marriages one night.) We have gone beyond criticism and defensiveness and contempt. We are now in a battle, and he stonewalls me. It's no wonder I'm depressed and anxious all the time.

Psychotherapist: You are certainly dealing with many problems that seem impossible to solve. I sense your hopelessness. I also feel your anxiety about what might happen in your son's life, your family, your own relationship with Carlos, and your own emotional life.

Luisa: I don't know what to do. I've tried everything.

Psychotherapist: What have you tried?

Luisa: I've been on the Internet. I've talked with my priest. I've talked with my mother and sister for hours. Mama really understands. My dad abandoned all of us when I was 5, and she had responsibility of raising the six of us for most of my life. We needed Dad, but he wasn't there. But Mama had the courage and strength to get through her own problems. She didn't have much insight on my problems other than, "Hang in there." I keep thinking that if I just find the right person to help and get the right information, I'll be able to turn everything around.

Psychotherapist: But so far?

Luisa: So far, nothing I've learned, nothing I've tried, has done any good. In fact, Carlos gets upset when I bring up suggestions. If I mention God, he goes crazy. He doesn't believe the church can be trusted. He seems to have given up on his faith. He's right in some ways—Father Ramirez couldn't help. He's overwhelmed that the youth group has come unglued. There was the nude-picture scandal at school, and the parents are upset with him for not being keeping their kids from such disgusting things as sending naked pictures to each other.

Psychotherapist: So, the kids in the youth group were involved in Jamie's problems at school?

Luisa: Yes, the problems apparently *started* within the youth group! The kids just got busted at school. How can that happen? In church?! I knew Jamie was drifting

	from God, but I didn't think the youth group would *add* to the problem.
Psychotherapist:	So, you are really most upset that Jamie could get into this kind of behavior through church.
Luisa:	Well, I don't know if I'm the most upset over that. But I'm really, really upset. I'm disappointed. I'm disillusioned. I'm hurt. I feel betrayed. And Father Ramirez not only couldn't help me, he seems unwilling to do anything. The church should be solving these problems. But instead it's causing problems and then denying responsibility.
Psychotherapist:	And Carlos isn't engaged in trying to help?
Luisa:	He's doing the same thing. He has caused a lot of problems by not being the family man we need. He's neglected his faith. And now that problems have come up, he denies responsibility: "Luisa, you solve it. Luisa, take care of your son." As if Jamie wasn't his son, too.
Psychotherapist:	You resent it.
Luisa:	Big time! And rage. And I feel powerless to do anything about it all. Basically, I'm stuck. And the sources of strength in my life have become the sources of my destruction. God has always been a help in my trials. Now I feel like God—if he even exists—is not around. I have prayed for help but nothing. *That's* despair.

WHERE DID LUISA'S PROBLEM SEEM TO WORSEN?

Luisa unfolded her problems to a psychotherapist whom a friend had recommended. She presented multiple problems, ending in her self-diagnosis that she was depressed and anxious. Her narrative emphasized that she had too much to cope with and did not have adequate resources to deal with all of the threats to survival—to her, her son, and her and Carlos's relationship.

Furthermore, Luisa's problems involve God, the church, and the sacred. She described how Carlos "goes crazy" when she mentions God; she expected Father Ramirez to solve the problems but he could not; and the problems started in the church, where she believed the solutions to lie, and yet that added to the problems.

The introduction of spiritual dimensions seemed to make the problems more serious and disillusioning. As the psychotherapist continued to direct Luisa to talk about the problem, she revealed a parallelism between her perceived failure of the church and her perceived failure of Carlos. Luisa ended by voicing a profound thought—that a God on whom she had relied for spiritual strength, courage, and perhaps care and comfort was at best not around, and at worst, nonexistent. A bedrock foundation of her existence was eroding or being undermined, and it seemed to be tumbling into the abyss. One senses that, like her mother, she might have been able to cope and have courage and strength, but that the undermining of her faith has damaged her coping ability.

In the months to come, Luisa would revisit many of the themes she introduced in those first few minutes with her psychotherapist. They would work on her coping repertoire and the relationship of different coping attempts to her feelings of strength, competence, and relational comfort. They would deal at length with her unforgiving feelings toward both Carlos and the Roman Catholic Church and their relationship to each other. They would explore the connections between her mother, who was courageous and strong; the father, who abandoned the family in a time of need; and her conception of God (and of the church) as doing the same thing—abandoning her in a time of need. And they would consider ways Luisa could encourage parenting collaboration with Carlos even though they were in different places spiritually. Finally, she started to reflect for the first time on her own implicit assumptions about the relationship between sexuality and spirituality and ways this was affecting her stance toward her son's emerging sexual development.

It is not surprising that Luisa brought her own relational expectations and conflicts into her relationship with her psychotherapist. Establishing and then later maintaining a therapeutic relationship with her male psychotherapist was even a challenging issue, especially during a rough patch when she was not feeling like any progress was being made in psychotherapy. As with Father Ramirez, Carlos, her father, and God (whom she perceived in male terms), she started to become disappointed in another male. However, this time she experienced her psychotherapist showing empathy for her disappointments and struggles. He did not rescue her, but he also did not counterattack nor abandon her. According to dynamic psychological theories, some of those old *attachment templates*—working mental models that had presumably been established through Luisa's interactions as a child with her father or other significant male and were used as patterns for current relationships with males today—were being reshaped. The psychotherapist stayed with her in the heat of the psychotherapeutic desert, in the wilderness of wandering and seeking a new way of understanding her spiritual past, present, and future. That stability of her psychotherapist invited Luisa into an authentic relational process that could hold her tension and frustration and provide space for honest dialogue. Psychotherapy was mostly about relationships and the way they played into religion and spirituality, stress and coping, and justice and forgiveness.

What's more, Luisa did not leave psychotherapy in complete psychological control with her problems "fixed." In fact, psychotherapy helped her profoundly reorient her direction in life and set the stage for a period of over a year of spiritual wrestling and searching. She did not enjoy that year. Yet, when she emerged from that process, she had renewed her attachment and commitment with God. However, her experience of God had become less anxious and more secure, and this affected her relationship with Carlos, her relationship with her children, and her engagement in her church and community. The psychotherapy relationship became, as several therapists have described it, a *crucible* (Napier & Whitaker, 1978; Schnarch, 1991, 1997, 2009; Wallin, 2007).

An effective crucible is a resilient yet incredibly strong container that can hold intense heat and pressure without reacting to the materials being contained in the crucible. As it holds the pressure, a catalyst (i.e., the psychotherapeutic interactions) provides the equivalent of the chemical reaction sites at which the materials of Luisa's internal and external life can react, give off heat and light, and eventually produce a transformation of the old materials into a material with new properties. The crucible of the therapeutic relationship provided a balance of support and challenge that eventually formed a secure attachment between Luisa and her psychotherapist (Schnarch, 1991; Wallin, 2007). This provided a corrective relational experience for Luisa that shifted her relational templates about conflict and forgiveness and offered a holding environment (Winnicott, 1986) for her own relational healing and development.

In this book, we describe how to create a therapeutic relationship that facilitates spiritual transformation to help clients forgive—a relationship that will heal and also permit the effective use of evidence-based treatments. Our approach can be applied to brief or long-term psychotherapy, as well as therapy with various client configurations (individuals, couples, families, and groups). In addition, we hope this to be broadly applicable by integrating conceptual ideas into other therapeutic approaches and by informing other approaches to forgiveness and spirituality or religious issues.

Because spirituality and religion can either facilitate or impede forgiveness, our work identifies not only spiritual and religious factors that are positively associated with forgiveness but also those that are negatively associated with forgiveness. (Examples of the latter include perceived desecration, spiritual grandiosity, and anger at God.)

We use a relational approach to religion and spirituality that we have called *relational spirituality*. This term, which might seem unusual to some readers, reflects the way that religion and spirituality are embedded in relationships, including perceived relationships—relationships between an offender and victim, relationships between victim and the sacred, the victim's perception of the relationship between the offender and the sacred (and whether it is similar to or different than the victim's perception of this relationship), and even the relationship between the offense and the sacred. It is the nature of those relationships that governs whether people can forgive.

Although neither of us trained personally with Schnarch or Wallin and do not presume to be experts in the therapies they teach, we draw from their ideas. Notably, we draw from a Bowen-informed approach to long-term psychotherapy and from their writing about the nature of a psychotherapeutic crucible for instigating change. Those ideas are congruent with our own experiences.

In short, we want to help psychotherapists effectively use relational dynamics and constructive coping strategies in helping clients deal with the inevitable interpersonal conflicts in life. We especially seek to help you treat the very hot and energetic reactions that involve (a) deep interpersonal wounds that might (depending on the psychotherapy and the person's reactions to it) either form chronic knots of resentment and bitterness or might be forgiven and (b) deep spiritual disruptions that might result in defensive retreat or transformation. We hope to help by facilitating your understanding of the complex natures of these problems. We want you to see how transgressions trigger a stress-and-coping process that draws out interpersonal templates like one's attachment schemas and also often activates religious and spiritual templates that seek to provide meaning. These all fit together. With that understanding, we offer practical suggestions about how to apply that understanding in the lives of your clients. Reviews of much research have clearly shown that if clients can forgive with authenticity, there are benefits to the clients' physical health (Worthington, Witvliet, Pietrini, & Miller, 2007), mental health (Griffin, Worthington, Wade, Hoyt, & Davis, in press), relationships (Riek, & Mania, 2012; Waldron & Kelley, 2008), and spirituality (D. E. Davis, Worthington, Hook, & Hill, 2013).

In the remainder of this chapter, we elaborate on how you can benefit from this book, present background information about why forgiveness matters and common misconceptions about forgiveness, and provide an overview of the book's major themes and a road map of how we navigate those themes.

HOW YOU CAN BENEFIT FROM THIS BOOK

Most psychological problems are strongly influenced by interpersonal issues, and most people in the United States consider themselves religious or spiritual or recovering from spirituality or religion "gone awry." Thus, numbers alone suggest that this could be a very pertinent book for you and your clients.

Psychotherapy tends to deal with problems that occur in interpersonal contexts. Often, people hurt or offend others. Think about your own week and how many times people have hurt or offended you—intentionally or not. When people stop and look, they see offenses everywhere—the colleague who makes a snide remark, the spouse who is critical, the friend who fails to show for the long-planned appointment. When people are well functioning, many of those transgressions roll off. But clients are not usually functioning that well. Stresses leak into and magnify the daily hassles, often rendering the clients depressed, anxious, angry, or even traumatized.

Thus, this book will help you spend time thinking about some very prevalent human problems and dilemmas. It will help you sort out religious and spiritual issues and practical issues. It will help you guide your patients to make better decisions about their lives.

Despite findings that few graduate programs train psychotherapists to discuss religious and spiritual issues in counseling (Delaney, Miller, & Bisonó, 2007; Sauerheber, Holeman, Dean, & Haynes, 2014), it has been our experience that most psychotherapists are quite good at dealing with these issues. If they were not, there would, we believe, be a public outcry demanding more competence. But the more pertinent question is this: Might *you* want to improve your ability to sensitively discuss these topics in ways that can help religious and spiritual clients?

Most clients endorse some type of religion or spirituality (The Pew Forum on Religion & Public Life, 2008). In addition, most say that they would like to discuss matters of their faith with their physician or psychotherapist (Richards & Bergin, 2014). Yet, surveys show psychotherapists are often less religious than the general public (Aten & Leach, 2009). Even psychotherapists who are themselves religious or spiritual might lack knowledge and confidence in dealing with clients who hold different religious or spiritual beliefs and practices. Many psychotherapists—whether religious or not—must treat clients who are either explicitly religious or who consider themselves spiritual but not religious. Some clients have also experienced negative or abusive experiences with religious or spiritual communities, and their painful experiences of relational spirituality can also inform their dynamics related to forgiveness. Psychotherapists—whether they treat individuals, couples, families, or groups—must treat people for whom religion or spirituality is important and usually differs to some extent from the practitioner's religion or spirituality or even others in the same therapy. Even when the religion or spirituality of a client is similar to the practitioner's, the practitioner may not necessarily know how to use religion and spirituality effectively in his or her practice. In this book, we seek to provide such help for mental health practitioners.

There is a lot of interest in this topic. Although religion and spirituality might not be personally important to all psychotherapists, their dedication to their professional competence has led to increasing interest in seeking more training than they already have. Webinars, conference presentations and workshops, articles, chapters, and professional books that deal with religious and spiritual psychotherapy have arisen to meet this interest (e.g., Aten & Leach, 2009; Aten, McMinn, & Worthington, 2011; Aten, O'Grady, & Worthington, 2012; Miller, 1999; Pargament, 1997, 2007, 2013a, 2013b; Richards & Bergin, 1997, 2000, 2004, 2005, 2014; Shafranske, 1996; Sperry & Shafranske, 2004; Worthington, Johnson, Hook, & Aten, 2013).

We are not advocating that the psychotherapist force-feed overconcern for forgiveness or religion to clients. Yet, we wish to show how you can open that doorway and let people discuss the things that they might not ordinarily bring into psychotherapy because they are afraid that religion, spirituality, and forgiveness might not be "proper" to discuss in psychotherapy. Religion and spirituality are not roadblocks for clients' progress, nor are they a panacea. They can be an opportunity to enter the client's personal existential world so that he or she can undergo a transformation that would not have been possible had the psychotherapist given religion and spirituality short shrift.

In short, through this book, you will have, we hope, a more nuanced understanding of religion and spirituality and their roles in interpersonal problems. In particular, this book will help you deal better with aiding religious and spiritual people consider forgiveness sensitively.

WHY FORGIVENESS MATTERS IN PSYCHOTHERAPY

Interpersonal conflict is inevitable (McCullough, 2008), and in national probability samples, most people admit to holding some unforgiveness (Toussaint, Williams, Musick, & Everson, 2001). People wrong and are wronged. Boundaries need to be maintained and defended—and people continually step into others' private psychological space. Subjective perspectives on various issues collide as people get to know each other. When people do wrong during conflicts, almost everyone wants to be forgiven for their transgressions. Many people want to forgive those who have hurt or offended them, particularly if they care about the relationship. Sometimes they do not believe they can or should forgive. When they are unable to be forgiven or to forgive, people are usually stressed (Worthington, 2006). They become emotionally distraught, experience a release of stress hormones, might have physical symptoms of such stress, experience relationship upheaval (which adds another layer of complications), mobilize numbing defenses against painful affect, and may feel disconnected from God or their sense of the sacred. Unforgiveness has a way of becoming contagious. Resentment leaks into tense interactions with someone else who may further pass along this chain of estrangement.

Repairing conflicts is also often just as inevitable (McCullough, 2008). When transgressions occur, human communities often use socially evolved methods to reduce the volatility of unforgiveness and to restore violators to the group. If that were not the case, group members would be cast adrift and would not survive for long. Human societies simply cannot hold together if massive unforgiveness is the norm.

Is there hope that people can get over grudges by themselves or with the help of a friend? Of course. Counseling and psychotherapy have been around only a little over 100 years, but people forgave for centuries before psychotherapy became common. But many people do not get over grudges. One might suspect that the rate at which grudges are maintained might be worsened by the chronic stress of dealing with a psychological disorder or chaos in one's life. Some people are bitter and develop stress disorders. Some are passive-aggressive and experience relational discord. A few take up weapons and act out in the violence of a righteous jealous lover or religious or antireligious terrorist.

DiBlasio and Proctor (1993) surveyed a variety of types of psychotherapists and concluded that forgiveness is often addressed in psychotherapy. Almost one half of the cases were reported to be forgiveness-relevant. It is important to note that DiBlasio and Proctor's study was done in 1992, before psychologists were attuned to the importance of forgiveness. For example, research and writing on forgiveness within psychology only began in 1984. But after puttering on with only a few devotees, it took a huge step jump upward in 1998 when the John Templeton Foundation funded a competitive request for proposals to study forgiveness. Now, the number of empirical articles published in 2014 exceeded (by far) the total number of publications on forgiveness in the 15 years between 1984 and 1998. One survey 10 years after the DiBlasio and Proctor work found that a majority of mental health professionals agree not only that unresolved and unforgiven harms arise often in psychotherapy but also that forgiveness can be therapeutic for some clients (Konstam, Marx, Schurer, Lombardo, & Harrington, 2002).

How good are psychotherapists at dealing with forgiveness? The answer is, we do not really know. We do know that psychotherapists deal with it a lot. They meet the challenge of the client, but they might not feel confident that they are really giving good help to the client on forgiving. This book will help.

Professionally, vast resources are available to help psychotherapists become better at helping clients forgive. Books are too numerous to list, although many are cited in our references; here are a few from the leading writers for practitioners: Enright (2012), Enright and Fitzgibbons (2000,

2014), and Worthington (2006). One cannot typically attend a large conference without some presentations on forgiveness. Experts in forgiveness (e.g., Abrams, DiBlasio, Enright, Hargrave, Luskin, and Worthington are a few) provide workshops for clinicians. Websites provide resources (e.g., http://www.EvWorthington-forgiveness.com, http://www.forgiveself.com, http://www.internationalforgiveness.com). In the present book, we provide another resource to help you more competently deal with forgiveness issues.

MISCONCEPTIONS ABOUT FORGIVENESS

Despite the easy availability of the abovementioned resources, many misconceptions about forgiveness exist. Some psychotherapists hold views about forgiveness that might not be helpful to clients. In fact, some psychotherapists hold views that do not agree with the scientific understanding of forgiveness. They might have the following beliefs:

- Forgiveness is a purely religious rather than psychological topic.
- Forgiveness is not complete as long as the forgiver does not have emotional peace.
- Forgiveness requires telling your offenders you forgive them.
- Forgiveness means that one must reconcile with the offender.
- One must forgive to heal.
- Forgiveness is always beneficial to the forgiver.
- A forgiven person is more likely to reoffend than an unforgiven person.
- Forgiveness means that you return the offender to the pre-offense state and essentially reboot the relationship.
- If one remembers the offense, and especially if one remembers or feels any negative emotions toward the offender, forgiveness is not complete.
- Apology and repentance by the offender is always necessary if one is to forgive.
- If the offender does not make restitution, forgiveness will encourage repeat offenses.
- If an offender asks for forgiveness three times, one is duty-bound to forgive.

These beliefs are not held by everyone. Certain spiritual or religious traditions might teach some of the perspectives above, and clinicians certainly need to be sensitive to their clients' traditions and values. However, the scientific study of forgiveness has shown that none of these is believed by most forgiveness researchers today nor are they always descriptively true

(Enright & Fitzgibbons, 2000, 2014; Worthington, 2006). Worse, they usually are not helpful for a forgiver. If you found yourself agreeing with some of the assumptions above, it might be valuable to reflect on (a) the sources of influence on your own moral, spiritual, or religious perspectives on forgiveness and (b) the empirical counterevidence we present in the chapters that follow. That evidence paints a different portrait of interpersonal forgiveness. Injustices are stressful, and forgiveness is one of many possible coping responses to transgressions and unforgiveness but differs from reconciliation.

IDENTIFYING OUR THEMES: ESSENTIAL TENSIONS

Throughout the book, we emphasize six tensions that occur when religion, spirituality, and forgiveness collide. One might think of these as poles between which people oscillate. One might see them as conflicts that show up countless times in individual adjustment and in societal interaction. One might see them as dialectics that people do not resolve but hold in dynamic tension. Each is like two elephants balancing on a teeter-totter. One cannot get off without wrecking the other and disrupting the playground. These tensions within forgiveness and relational spirituality will be elaborated throughout the book, but let us mention them now.

First, there is the tension between conflict, which tears relationships apart, and restoring relationships. This has to do with defending (psychological, physical, and social) boundaries against assault and violating others' boundaries. Forgiveness is at the center of this tension. Many clients come to therapy depressed, anxious, angry, guilty, and ashamed. Most emotional struggles are embedded in interpersonal conflicts. Those often involve unforgiveness or self-condemnation over acts done to others.

Second, there is tension between attachment and differentiation of self. In the same way that societies must hold together in tight bonds and yet provide freedom for members to expand outside the boundaries, individuals must experience appropriate stable and secure attachments and yet be able to act as a differentiated individual within the context of relationships.

Third, there is tension between emotion regulation and emotion processing. People are emotional creatures—much more, we believe, than they are rational (Kahneman, 2011). They experience emotion and must regulate its expression without overcontrolling it. But just keeping emotions tamped down does not let them understand their meaning. They can best benefit if emotions are revealed and people process their experiences to gain understanding and reconstruct meaning.

Fourth, there is tension between hope and humility. When people are troubled, they may hope that someone can rescue them. But reality has taught most people that life happens, and they must also have the humility to endure and live through troubles and not just hope they will go away. Mature hope involves the desire to move forward, and humility helps people learn from conflicts rather than remain trapped in toxic cycles of shame.

Fifth, there is the tension between spiritual dwelling in a safe or familiar place in regard to the sacred and spiritual seeking. All people at times become unmoored and drift away from their spot of existential security. Other times, they may intentionally seek new meaning or spiritual experience. They need to be able to negotiate those destabilizing, stretching times of spiritual seeking, grow from them, and come into another place of spiritual dwelling. That stands in contrast to becoming lost in spiritual seeking, becoming like Ahab obsessed by the white whale, wandering the seas in search of it, and yet knowing that it is likely to eventually be one's undoing.

And sixth, there is tension between justice (which may require things beyond our control, such as the offender's willingness to atone) and the emotional and physical benefits of releasing resentment. Should I demand restitution? Should I forgive? How can justice be served if I forgive and mercy be served if I demand unremitting justice?

Forgiveness often ends up at the center of these tensions. Forgiveness helps people negotiate between defending boundaries and restoring relationships, know when to hold closely to attachments and when to differentiate, sense when emotional processing is possible and when emotional regulation is prudent, experience hope when they feel disempowered and humility when they seek to reconcile justice and mercy, live in the moment but with a sense of deep inspiration, and experience the pain of unmoored spiritual seeking without giving in to perpetual spiritual wandering.

Many of the centrifugal and centripetal tensions—forces that sling people outward or seek to implode them inward, respectively—are powered by religious beliefs and religious communities and by the closeness or distance people experience with things they treat as sacred. Where religion and spirituality come together with justice and forgiveness, deep cultural and evolutionary pressures are at work. They form a knot. The nature of a knot is that it has at its nip—its center—a point of friction and pressure. Without the friction and pressure, the knot will not, in fact it cannot, hold. Thus, we should expect to feel the heat of friction and the push and pull of pressure when counseling people in which forgiveness and justice and religion and spirituality are coming together. We want to help you tie a strong, healthy knot that will bear the clients' weight of healthy living.

THE REACH FORGIVENESS MODEL

In addition to addressing the aforementioned tensions, this book emphasizes a treatment model that both of us use in psychoeducational and therapy groups, in individual counseling, and in couple counseling to help people forgive others. We also use an adapted version of this model to help clients forgive themselves. Over the course of the book, you will see it placed into use both as a formal model and as the source of long-term psychotherapy or group therapy. Let us describe the model now.

In the REACH forgiveness model, spelled out below, each letter of REACH cues one step to reach emotional forgiveness of others.

- R: *Recalling* the hurt differently than as a source of rage or woundedness. Some degree of emotional maturity, of differentiation of self, is needed to disentangle one's emotions from the hurtful event.
- E: *Emotional* reprocessing. We often call "E" *empathy*, though empathy is only one of four emotions that can be used to replace unforgiveness (i.e., resentment, bitterness, hostility, hatred, anger, and fear). The others are sympathy, compassion, and love.
- A: Giving an *altruistic* gift of forgiveness—one that is predicated on blessing the offender who is a needy person.
- C: *Commitment* to the emotional forgiveness experienced.
- H: *Hold* onto the forgiveness when doubts occur.

Although REACH has primarily been applied to help clients forgive others, we have also adapted it to help clients forgive themselves. When we deal with self-forgiveness, we find that the five steps of the REACH forgiveness model recur as a subpart of the self-forgiveness process. Self-forgiveness is one response to self-condemnation that one feels because one has either done something he or she considers to be wrong or feels that he or she is failing to live up to his or her standards. Thus, in the Afterword, we present six steps to responsible self-forgiveness. We briefly name them here.

1. Restore a right relationship with humanity, nature, or God.
2. Repair relationships.
3. Rework one's unrealistic standards and reduce rumination (obsessing self-condemning thoughts and feelings).
4. Use the REACH forgiveness steps toward forgiving the self (see above).
5. Seek to accept oneself as being less perfect than one had previously felt.
6. Seek not to fail in the same way again.

OVERVIEW OF THIS BOOK

In Part I of the book, we explain why and when forgiveness and spiritual transformation might be appropriate therapeutic goals. To do this, we introduce four interlocking models that guide our understanding of forgiveness and relational spirituality and we summarize the research evidence supporting the models. These models are described below.

1. *How forgiveness helps people cope with stress.* Making a decision to forgive and experiencing an emotional transformation from bitter grudge-holding to more peaceful acceptance are healthy targets that many patients aim for. Chapter 1 presents this first model.

2. *How spiritual transformation occurs.* People tend to seek a stable sense of dwelling comfortably with their religious and spiritual beliefs and practices, which we call *spiritual dwelling* (after Wuthnow, 1998, 2000). Yet, life kicks them out of those dwelling places into often chaotic *spiritual seeking*. That pattern can lead to either (a) finding a new dwelling place, (b) returning (albeit changed) to the previous dwelling place, or (c) getting stuck in seeking. Spiritual transformations can lead to reexamination of prior hurtful relationships and surface forgiveness issues. Or current difficulties in forgiving—often a life-changing event like in a divorce or traumatic loss—can lead to spiritual struggles and crises. Chapter 2 presents this second model.

3. *How people's relations with significant attachment figures affect their relations with the sacred.* We see spirituality as being embedded in relationships, so we tackle attachments in current and past relationships. We introduce the idea of a *relational template*, the way or ways people learned to relate emotionally in early emotion-charged relationships that serve as unconscious models for current emotion-charged relationships. Chapter 3 presents this third model.

4. *Why spiritual transformation may be needed before people can forgive their perceived transgressor if (a) they perceive that someone else has transgressed against them and (b) our current relations with the sacred prohibit them from forgiving.* Chapter 3 also presents this fourth, and cumulative, model, which links stress and coping with spiritual dwelling and seeking.

In Chapter 4, we examine a large amount of research evidence supporting the models. We seek to give you a good sense of the scope, depth, and power of the research supporting the various models we use in the book. Yet we also seek to make this a user-friendly account of the research, not a full-on dry and boring review of massive study after study.

Although Part I is about theory and evidence that ground our clinical applications, Part II is about applications. It is filled with cases, psychotherapist–patient dialogues, techniques, and references back to the theoretical grounding. By the end of the book, we think you will know what to do in psychotherapy, how to do it, and why to do it.

In Chapter 5, we describe generally how one can help someone change his or her personality. This is the basis for subsequent chapters on applying the theory and these general thoughts in brief and long-term individual, couple, family, and group psychotherapies.

We next describe (Chapter 6) and illustrate (Chapter 7) how people can be helped with forgiveness issues regarding religion and spirituality in a brief psychotherapy format. We recognize the practical constraints of having to practice in agencies that set time limits on psychotherapy, with managed care and employee assistance programs, and with patient personal preferences that require psychotherapists to use brief, hopefully evidence-based, practices. In these two chapters, we describe how to accomplish the maximum possible short-term change and long-term personality transformation within a brief format.

In the next two chapters, we describe (Chapter 8) and illustrate (Chapter 9) how people can be helped with forgiveness issues regarding religion and spirituality in a long-term, systems-theory-informed psychotherapy format. This long-term format can be a luxury for some patients and psychotherapists in today's fast-paced world. However, it might also be highly desirable by or explicitly requested by patients.

In Chapter 10, we consider the presence of multiple people in the psychotherapy room—in couples and family therapies. Although the principles are the same as those we applied throughout Chapters 5 to 9, the methods can differ.

In Chapter 11, we examine applying the theory and methods described in the book to groups. We apply the ideas in both psychoeducational and therapy groups. These groups include methods we have developed and adaptations and additions to treatments like mindfulness-based training and dialectical behavior therapy.

In the Afterword, we wrap up our journey through the book. We consider how clients renarrate their lives with the help of the treatments we have described. We conclude by considering your noble role as a guide for clients through a sacred reconsideration of their lives.

CONCLUSION

We believe you will find this book enlightening and helpful in conducting your psychotherapy. It is not a detailed step-by-step instruction manual. Rather, it offers general principles that can be adapted to your specific cases.

Similar to being on the battlefield, the psychotherapist is like a general, helping an emotionally involved and emotionally distraught client battle for a fulfilling way of life in the battlefield of the psyche. The battle for the psyche requires all of the preparations that an actual battle requires—planning, knowing your opponent (the problems) and your own officers (the client), mapping a winning strategy, making bold decisions, and knowing yourself—and your tendencies to act well and to yield to pressures that take you in unproductive directions. It also requires flexibility. Do not lock yourself into a treatment plan or treatment approach from which you cannot escape. Adaptation is always necessary. Change is necessary. What worked with the previous client might not work with the present one: "Thus, one's victories in battle cannot be repeated—they take their form in response to inexhaustibly changing circumstances" (Sun-Tzu, *The Art of War*, 4th century BC).

There will be tensions, which are, as we said, essential. They are part of a relational dialogue you can have with each client about the stresses he or she confronts and the ways he or she can cope with those stresses—within the context of religion and spirituality and of forgiveness and justice.

I

THEORY AND EVIDENCE

Theory cannot equip the mind with formulas for solving problems, nor can it mark the narrow path on which the sole solution is supposed to lie by planting a hedge of principles on either side. But it can give the mind insights into the great mass of phenomena and of their relationships, then leave it free to rise into the higher realms of action. There the mind can use its innate talents to capacity, combining them all so as to seize on what is right and true.

—Carl von Clausewitz, *On War*

We are products of our past, but we don't have to be prisoners of it.
—Rick Warren, *The Purpose-Driven Life:*
What on Earth Am I Here for?

1

HOW FORGIVENESS HELPS PEOPLE COPE WITH TRANSGRESSIONS

When people experience injustice or offense, it is easy to hold a grudge or seek vengeance. Not doing so is stressful. But pursuing payback is also stressful. In fact, over the years, there has been some general agreement that forgiveness could be conceptualized within a stress-and-coping theory (Strelan & Covic, 2006; Worthington, 2006). In this chapter, we present the first of three interlocking models—the stress-and-coping model of forgiveness—to help you understand unforgiveness and forgiveness and how to help people respond effectively to injustices. We begin with definitions and then walk you through the stress-and-coping model of forgiveness. In doing so, we show the key roles of both relationships and religion and spirituality in understanding forgiveness. We begin to talk about psychotherapy when relationships and religion impinge on forgiveness.

http://dx.doi.org/10.1037/14712-002
Forgiveness and Spirituality in Psychotherapy: A Relational Approach, by E. L. Worthington, Jr. and S. J. Sandage

GETTING DEFINITIONS STRAIGHT

Let's be clear what we mean by forgiveness of another person. For the moment, let's put aside forgiving oneself or what some people refer to as "forgiving God." We also bypass forgiveness by God, or feeling forgiven by God.

There are a host of lay definitions of forgiving others, and (unfortunately) many people define forgiveness in ways that lead to social and mental health problems for the people following those definitions. For example, virtually all psychological scientists who study forgiveness agree that it occurs within the forgiver's skin—it is intrapersonal. Yes, it occurs in interpersonal and social contexts. That is, most forgiveness is because people have been actually (or perceive they have been) harmed or offended by someone. They experience a *transgression*, which violates psychological or physical boundaries. They might deal quickly with the felt injustice—by seeing justice done, accepting the transgression as minor and not worthy of paying more attention to, or lowering their sense of injustice.

If people are not able to deal with the harm or offense productively, they might become unforgiving. *Unforgiveness* is a stress response. It involves emotions like resentment, bitterness, hostility, hatred, anger, and fear. Linked to the emotions typically are motivations like avoiding the transgressor, seeking revenge, and devaluing the person. When people are unforgiving, they usually *ruminate* about the transgression, the transgressor, the conditions that led to the transgression, how the transgression occurred, their response to it, and perhaps their later attempts to deal with the transgression that might have or usually did not work. *Rumination*, like a cow who chews her cud, continually spitting it up and wallowing it around in the mouth, is continuing to bring up old thought patterns. They might think, "If only . . ." or "What if I had. . . ." Rumination can be angry (e.g., "I am so pissed that I cannot even concentrate"), vengeful (e.g., "I'll get her back"), anxious or fearful (e.g., "If I respond at all, he might beat me"), or depressed ("There is nothing I can do about this. I'm so depressed that I don't even feel like going to work").

Exline, Worthington, Hill, and McCullough (2003) identified two types of forgiveness. One is *decisional forgiveness*, which is making a behavioral intention statement to treat the transgressor as a person of value, to forswear revenge, and to act in ways that forbear expression of anger about the transgression. Decisional forgiveness is not a behavior. One might never carry out the intended behaviors. For instance, imagine that you are robbed. You might never find out who robbed you, and yet you could make a decision to forgive the robber. Or imagine that an offender moves away. You might decide to forgive the person but can never carry out the forgiveness because you no longer have contact with the offender. Or you might intend to treat the offender more positively, but he or she newly offends you, so you cannot carry out the intensions to treat the person better because of the new untrust-worthy offense of the offender.

One might decide to forgive and carry out those intentions success-fully for the remainder of life, and yet might still feel resentment, bitterness, hostility, hatred, anger, and fear—in short, emotional unforgiveness. This suggests that there is a second type of forgiveness. *Emotional forgiveness* is the emotional transformation from negative unforgiving emotions to some improved state: (a) less negative unforgiving emotions (i.e., an improve-ment, but with lingering emotional unforgiveness), (b) emotional neutrality (balanced valence of emotions surrounding and attributed to the offense), or (c) emotional positivity (one has subdued negative emotions to the extent that positive other-oriented emotions are dominant).

In this chapter, we present Worthington's (2006) stress-and-coping model of forgiveness (see Figure 1.1). The model proposes an emotional replacement hypothesis—that negative unforgiving emotions were replaced gradually until the net feeling might (or might not) become positive toward the offender. The gradual nature is important—it is to be differen-tiated from a sudden activation of defenses, such as reaction formation (in which a person threatened by feelings of unforgiveness, suddenly professes profuse forgiveness to minimize the anxiety), and involves an integrative process of emotion transformation. This overall hypothesis was supported by neurobiological, hormonal, cognitive, emotional, and behavioral evidence (see Worthington, 2006, Chapter 4). A metaphor used to explain emotional replacement was chemical titration, in which negative acid (representing unforgiveness) is titrated by dropping in a positive-pH base, bringing the pH back to neutral. Note, of course, that this is a metaphor and is not a literal explanation of what happens neurochemically. In some cases, rather than replace negative emotions by positive, the positive is built alongside of the negative and ambivalence is experienced. Positive and negative emotions are not the opposite ends of a single continuum but are two different experiences involving some overlapping and some distinct physical systems (Watson & Clark, 1997). Nevertheless, positive emotions seem to stand against negative emotions.

Forgiveness and Justice

Forgiveness is paradoxically related to justice. Forgiveness and justice often seem contradictory, but they can become integrated in various ways. To forgive presumes the guilt of the wrongdoer even as it relieves the guilty party from some of the consequences of the guilt (which, at a minimum, are those that the offended party might impose). Thus, forgiveness is intimately tied up with justice (Worthington, 2009). This can be seen in the mental

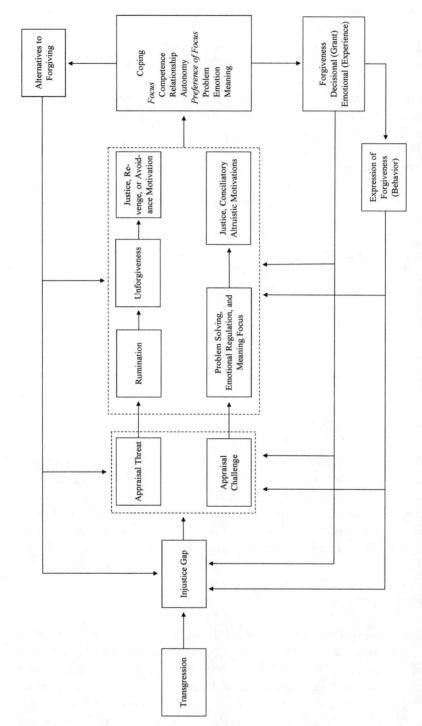

Figure 1.1. Stress-and-coping model of forgiveness. From *Forgiveness and Reconciliation: Theory and Application* (p. 30), by E. L. Worthington, Jr., 2006, New York, NY: Brunner-Routledge. Copyright 2006 by Brunner-Routledge. Reprinted with permission.

computations (conscious or unconscious) by people who perceive themselves to have been unjustly treated. Their perceived *injustice gap* is roughly the subjective difference between the way an offended victim would like to see the injustice resolved and the way the victim perceives the situation to stand at present (Exline et al., 2003; Worthington, 2003, 2006, 2009). Big injustice gaps are hard to handle; small gaps, easy to handle or even ignore.

Perceived justice can narrow the injustice gap. For example, if an offender does something costly, such as making a sincere apology, offering restitution, or making amends (see Fehr & Gelfand, 2010), then the injustice gap may be narrowed or closed. The victim can thus absorb the harm or offense because the injustice gap has been reduced.

In some cases, just actions by offending parties may make it easier to forgive them. For example, if (from the example presented in the Introduction) Carlos told Luisa that he knew it was unfair to avoid his parenting responsibilities and if he offered to go to counseling with her, Luisa might forgive more readily. The reverse can also be true—forgiveness by an offendee sometimes paves the way for less hostile discussions about justice. This is the lesson offered by spiritual leaders such as Gandhi and Martin Luther King, Jr. In fact, trait forgiveness has been positively correlated with a commitment to social justice (Jankowski, Sandage, & Hill, 2013). We return to this forgiveness and justice dialectic in the chapters that follow.

Forgiveness and Relationality

In a different sense, relationships among people in the client's network seem also to be crucial (Lazarus, 2006). Most people learn about life in early relationships (Bowlby, 1969/1982, 1980, 1988). They live out those approaches in relationships. In relationships, they feel disappointment, grief, discord, and distress. Problems arise from relationships, even relationships long past.

But healing also occurs in relationships. People can learn through valuable present relationships that all relationships are not like the early disappointing ones. People and lives can be redeemed through relationships. Thus, it is not surprising that we consider that forgiveness, spirituality, and psychological and social functioning can be profoundly influenced by the relationships between client and psychotherapist. Forgiveness might be an internal act of an individual, but it is manifested in the client's relationships. And forgiveness is often stimulated in relationship with the psychotherapist. Even though there are excellent evidence-based treatments to lead clients to forgiveness (for a meta-analysis, see Wade, Hoyt, Kidwell, & Worthington, 2014), those treatments need to be delivered within healing relationships involving a good working alliance, empathy, frequent feedback from the client on his or her progress, and matching of treatment and psychotherapeutic style to client (for reviews, see Norcross, 2011).

Attachment theory is a valuable relational framework for understanding interpersonal transgressions and forgiveness (for meta-analyses of the effects of attachment in psychotherapy, see Bernecker, Levy, & Ellison, 2014; Diener & Monroe, 2011). Attachment security is related to positive psychotherapy outcomes (Levy, Ellison, Scott, & Bernecker, 2011). Attachment and forgiveness, specifically, have recently been associated in a growing body of research. Securely attached individuals have been found to be higher in state and trait forgiving than are insecurely attached individuals (e.g., Burnette, Davis, Green, Worthington, & Bradfield, 2009; Burnette, Taylor, Worthington, & Forsyth, 2007; Hall, Fujikawa, Halcrow, Hill, & Delaney, 2009; Jankowski & Sandage, 2011; Lawler-Row, Younger, Piferi, & Jones, 2006; Mikulincer & Shaver, 2007; Webb, Call, Chickering, Colburn, & Heisler, 2006).

Interpersonal transgressions involve anxiety and stress, which activate neurobiological attachment templates about self and other. Attachment theorists suggest that forgiveness requires (a) an effective capacity for emotional regulation (i.e., not "popping off" with uncontrolled emotional expression but sifting emotions and expressing them maturely) and (b) a well-developed capacity for empathic responses rather than frequent self-protective or aggressive responses to internal representations of the other (Burnette et al., 2007; Karen, 2001; Lawler-Row et al., 2006; Sandage & Worthington, 2010). Empathy requires the ability consistent with a secure attachment style to care about others without being overwhelmed by emotional distress or remaining entrenched in defensive postures. Thus, securely attached individuals have likely internalized calm, empathic relationship experiences or repair following conflict, which provides internal resources for emotional regulation and forgiveness following painful events. In addition, security about being forgiven by key attachment figures may result in the capacity for empathy and forgiveness toward one's own offenders. Attachment security has been empirically associated with both empathy and forgiveness following relational betrayals and conflicts (for a review, see Mikulincer & Shaver, 2007).

Stress and Coping and How Attachment and Religion Play a Part

Life is composed of a series of challenges, and often those challenges come at the same time—in parallel with each other rather than in series. In the 1950s, when Hans Selye (1956) was formulating basic ideas about stress, University of California, Berkeley, psychologist Richard Lazarus (see 1997 for a historical analysis), put forth what would today be called a cognitive and behavioral theory of stress and coping. Lazarus and Folkman (1984) updated the theory, and Lazarus (1999) later incorporated more attention to emotions.

Stressors

The essence of the model is that demands for change occur in life, called *stressors*. Stressors can be changes in the physical or interpersonal environment or in one's body, behavior, cognitive, or spiritual world. Stressors do not automatically produce stress reactions.

Appraisals

Rather, stress reactions are caused by *appraisals* of stressors as either challenges or threats. Challenges command attention, but they are not necessarily perceived as harmful. Appraisals that the stressor is likely to result in danger or harm upon initial appraisal are potentially threatening. Under a secondary appraisal, if the person does not believe he or she is capable of coping with the threat, strong stress reactions occur.

Stress Responses

Challenges and threats activate *stress response systems*—involving an immediate release of the parasympathetic vagal brake and subsequent activation of the sympathetic nervous system through direct means and through release of hormones along the hypothalamus–pituitary–adrenal axis. Emotions such as fear and anger focus one's attention on relief from danger but unfocus one's cortical problem solving and rational thinking. The emotions narrow attention to the immediate freeze–flight–fight behaviors.

Another system is prevalent as well. Some species, when threatened, pack tightly together. Strength in numbers is their motto. Thus, besides freeze, flee, and fight, humans at times practice tend-and-befriend—a relational stress response.

Coping

People try to deal with stress by *coping*. Just because a person tries to cope does not mean he or she succeeds. In coping, people try to modify some aspect of the stress response system; appraisals; or situational, bodily, or psychological stressors. The person experiences feedback about how the coping attempts are or are not working, and the person might institute more or different coping mechanisms. Coping can be broadly classified as problem-focused coping, emotion-focused coping, and meaning-focused coping.

Problem-focused coping tries to solve the problems as they are understood. Thus, problem-focused coping might try to change the situation that is making the demands. *Emotion-focused coping* involves efforts to control or modify unpleasant emotions and might involve deep slow breathing, progressive relaxation, meditation, calming self-talk, singing, or prayers for calm.

Emotion-focused coping aims to control emotions for their own sake, not as a means to solve problems. However, emotion-focused coping could clear the way for problem-focused coping efforts once the emotional arousal has been reduced. *Meaning-focused coping* (Park & Ai, 2006; Park & Folkman, 1997) seeks to change one's stress by changing the meaning of the stressor or response. Thus, one might reappraise whether a demand might be harmful, or whether one can cope with it. One could also try to put the situation into a broader frame—perhaps thinking that the stress is beneficial, stimulates learning, or builds moral character.

Religious coping is often one type of meaning-focused coping. However, religion can also be used to solve problems and manage emotions so it does not have to be meaning-focused coping (Pargament, 1997, 2007). Religious-focused coping can be adaptive or maladaptive. Religious-focused coping can be *conservative*—aimed at maintaining familiar beliefs and practices. It can also be *transformative*—aimed at finding a new system of religious or spiritual belief or behavior that works better than an old system. How one moves from conservative religious coping to transformative religious coping can be quick, but it most often involves a time of religious or spiritual seeking and wandering, unmoored from one's prior religious (or nonreligious) position. Religion can look relatively stable for many people over the life course, but their *religious spirituality*—that is, the nature of their relationship with the sacred (e.g., closeness or distance and types of connection)—might swing hugely from periods of stable dwelling to chaotic seeking and back to stability (Shults & Sandage, 2006; Wuthnow, 1998).

Feedback

Coping is aimed at affecting the stress-and-coping process. Coping can affect the stressor. Problem-focused coping might strive to reduce the stressor. Similarly, coping can affect appraisals. Both emotion-focused and meaning-focused coping can affect elements of the stress-and-coping response that feed back into further coping efforts.

Mediation Both of Attachment and of Religion or Spirituality

When religion or spirituality is salient for a person, both attachment and religion or spirituality are involved in every step of the stress-and-coping process (Granqvist & Kirkpatrick, 2008). They mediate—become a causal link between—the way that appraisals of stressors are affected by transgressions. That is, they become at least one pathway through which a stressor yields a particular appraisal for a person (i.e., because of one's attachment patterns or one's religious or spiritual beliefs and practices). Once appraisals are made, secure or insecure attachment and religion or spirituality are mechanisms through which unforgiving emotions, motivations, and behavioral intentions are either activated or shut down. Once unforgiveness is experienced, whether one can make a decision to forgive and experience emotional forgiveness is influenced by attachment and by the religious and spiritual structures and processes. Finally, attachment and religion and spirituality affect all of these experiences through feedback loops, in which experiences build on prior experiences.

Forgiveness as Relationally Formed Coping

Worthington (2006) and Strelan and Covic (2006) have conceptualized processes leading to forgiveness as one instance of stress-and-coping theory (see Figure 1.1). We have (as we have explained already) now begun to integrate attachment as well as religion and spirituality as mediators in this model.

Stressor—the Transgression

Transgressions are violations of boundaries—physical, psychological, or moral—and are conceptualized as stressors, events that demand a response from the person. The same comment, slight, or tone of voice that would be overlooked from strangers can be devastating if one is emotionally invested in a relationship. We might then see the stressor within a triangular contextual relationship among victim, offender, and transgression. Furthermore, cultural dynamics and relationship history make big differences in the way the transgression is experienced and thus how much and what kind of a stressor it is. A thoughtless remark that calls attention to one's inadequacy might be experienced uncomfortably in Midtown USA, but if the same lack of social sensitivity occurred in Japan, it would be a great insult. A thoughtless comment might sting in a happy stable couple. But in a couple who have been making, at best, fragile progress in couple counseling, a similar comment could signify (or could be interpreted as) death to the relationship.

Some of the most stressful interpersonal transgressions betray or threaten the attachment security in an important relationship. For example, sexual abuse or partner infidelity often result in emotional injuries but also assault the security of one's relational attachments in life. S. M. Johnson (1996) called these *attachment injuries*, which can be traumatic and shift the "default setting" on one's *internal working model* (or, as it is also called, *relational template*) of relationships from trust to mistrust.

Researchers now know that neurobiological attachment processes shaped by relational experiences are involved in the activation and deactivation of stress-regulatory systems in the orbitofrontal cortex, which influence emotional regulation (Diamond & Hicks, 2004). Interpersonal transgressions are registered as attachment-related stress, and this activates the limbic system—that system of emotion-processing structures in the middle of the brain under the cortex—along with the release of stress hormones.

In addition, Greer, Worthington, Van Tongeren, et al. (2014) found that transgressions by one who is religiously similar (i.e., a fellow member in one's congregation) were extremely hurtful—much more hurtful than when an offender was an outgroup member. This might be because ingroup transgressions violate not only one's boundaries but also one's sense of attachment and one's sense of the sacred.

Appraisals of Transgressions

Individuals *perceive* stressors (i.e., the transgressions) within the framework of their relationships with offenders and their internal working model of relationships (i.e., attachment style). As people perceive the meaning of the transgression through their own internal working model of relationships, they also make other appraisals. First, people evaluate the degree of injustice experienced, the *injustice gap* (Exline et al., 2003; Worthington, 2003, 2006). The injustice gap is the difference between the way one would like to see a transgression resolved and the way on currently perceives it. A primary appraisal of the transgression (i.e., Is this potentially harmful to me or to my sense of self or relationships?) is followed by a secondary appraisal (i.e., Can I cope with it? Can I do so in such a way that it does not disrupt my relationships?). More than 40 empirical studies have shown that attachment styles influence appraisal processes and patterns of coping with interpersonal stress (for an overview, see Mikulincer & Shaver, 2007).

Insecurely attached individuals tend to appraise stressors as more threatening than do securely attached individuals. Those with anxious–ambivalent internal working models of relationships not only make distress-intensifying appraisals, but they also tend to perceive their own coping capacities as much lower than those with secure internal working models of relationships. Individuals with avoidant internal working models of relationships show a more complicated pattern of results by (a) often appraising interpersonal stressors as highly threatening while (b) often consciously perceiving their own coping resources as adequate. However, avoidantly attached individuals overuse emotional distancing and repression or basic deactivation of the attachment system, so they may consciously register their coping resources as strong because they are avoiding awareness of their underlying anxiety and emotional distress.

Thus, individuals generally seek to make attachment-congruent appraisals of dangerous or threatening social situations (Ein-Dor, Mikulincer, & Shaver, 2011). So, interpersonal stress exerts bidirectional influence on internal working models of relationships, which in turn, interact with appraisal processes and activation of various forms of coping (including forgiveness).

Unforgiveness as Stress Reaction

When people experience a transgression and appraise it as a threat, they often feel unforgiveness. Unforgiveness is thus a stress reaction (Worthington, 2006). Evidence includes several observations that are supported by research: (a) unforgiveness feels stressful; (b) unforgiveness creates similar physiological states as does stress—including patterns of sympathetic and parasympathetic activity that are similar to stress reactions (for a review, see Worthington & Sotoohi, 2010), similar hormonal patterns, similar neurohormonal (cortisol) release (Berry & Worthington, 2001; Tabak & McCullough, 2011), similar brain activity patterns (Farrow et al., 2005, 2001), and similar blood chemistry (Seybold, Hill, Neumann, & Chi, 2001); (c) unforgiveness can create moods and mental states similar to stress; (d) unforgiveness can put people's relationships under strain (Riek & Mania, 2012); (e) unforgiveness can place a strain on people's spiritual relationship (D. E. Davis, Worthington, Hook, & Hill, 2013); (f) unforgiveness triggers similar coping mechanisms as does stress (Worthington, 2006); and (g) unforgiveness may be responsive to the same interventions (e.g., relaxation) as is stress (Hook et al., 2010). After reviewing this research, Worthington (2006) concluded that unforgiveness is one type of stress reaction.

Coping With Transgressions Can Involve Many Types of Efforts, Including Forgiving

Victims might deal with an injustice gap in many ways (Worthington, 2006). These include seeing justice enforced by an external agent (Worthington, 2009), seeing the offender reap the just desserts from the act (Worthington, 2009), explaining away the transgression by excusing it (i.e., focusing on mitigating circumstances for the wrongdoing) or by justifying it (i.e., finding that the wrongdoing was, in itself, a balancing of justice from a wrong that one earlier perpetrated), turning the matter over to God for divine judgment later, turning the matter over to God out of humility, forbearing, seeking points of learning and meaning, seeking restitution, or accepting and moving on with one's life. One might also forgive the offense. Virtually all happen in relational context and are affected by one's internal working models of relationships and one's connections to the sacred.

A Closer Look at Internal Working Models and Relational Spirituality

Internal Working Models of Relationship

Internal working models of relationship are mental representations shaped by relational experiences. Early attachment experiences with caregivers are particularly powerful. Yet other significant relationships can also affect one's internal working models of relationships. Internal working models of relationships provide a default template encoded neurobiologically in the brain, which comes "online" during times of interpersonal stress, threat, vulnerability, illness, and risk of loss (Cozolino, 2006). A vast empirical literature has reliably identified individual differences in attachment styles or internal working models of relationship, which influence a host of relational and stress-related outcomes. Generally, these styles are secure attachment and insecure attachment, which consists of anxious-ambivalent, avoidant, and disorganized styles of attachment.

Religion and Spirituality

Worldwide, most people are religious (Berger et al., 1999). Virtually all religious and spiritual traditions value forgiveness and provide mechanisms and rituals by which adherents forgive (McCullough, 2008). Religion and spirituality are powerful influences on behavior, especially moral behaviors. They are at the core of many individuals' belief and practice systems, and they also form the core of communal experience and support systems.

Religion and Spirituality Defined

Religion is a system of beliefs or practices endorsed by a community of like-minded people. *Spirituality* is a set of patterns in how people relate with the sacred. People treat many objects as sacred—God or a divine being, humans, nature, rituals, or a sense of transcendence. A person can thus be religiously or nonreligiously spiritual. The nature and quality of people's relationships to their sacred objects affect much of their behavior and their interpretations and appraisals in life. Hill et al. (2000) described *spirituality* as a search for the sacred. Such a search, they argued, typically occurred within a religion or religious community, and that community that contextualized the search continues to exert an influence on one's spirituality even when the community and its beliefs and practices are explicitly rejected. In other cases, the search for the sacred may be influenced by nonreligious sociocultural and relational contexts.

Relational Spirituality

Shults and Sandage (2006) translated the definitions of spirituality offered by Hill and Pargament (2003) to fit a relational theoretical orientation by defining *relational spirituality* as "ways of relating to the sacred" (p. 167)—and those ways could be salutary or pathogenic. In the Chapter 2, we outline Shults and Sandage's theory. In a research program of numerous studies, Worthington and his colleagues have focused on the emotional valence of the person's relationship with the sacred. They talk about spirituality as emotional closeness that one feels—or does not feel—toward the sacred. In this book, we keep the definition of relational spirituality within the broadest frame—relating to the sacred—to provide the most general theory. However, as we focus on whether people forgive and the role the sacred plays in that experience, we note the strong importance of emotion, affect, and feelings of closeness or connection. Attachment bonds (which can be highly emotionally charged), emotion-focused coping (which can include seeking to deal with stressful unforgiveness by emotional forgiveness), and the response of emotional forgiveness itself all place emotional processes (of course, accompanied by cognitive, motivational, and behavioral changes) in the forefront of forgiving. Often, people's similarity in emotional valence of their respective relationships with the sacred is at the emotional core of whether forgiveness occurs.

Relational Spirituality Affects How People Experience Unforgiveness. Relational spirituality can play a big role in how people experience unforgiveness (i.e., forgiving others or feeling forgiven by others) and in whether and how, as a method of coping with injustice and unforgiveness, they forgive or seek forgiveness. Our theoretical model suggests that the dynamics of relational spirituality can affect each dimension of the overall process that connects transgressions, appraisals, stress reactions, coping, and attachment templates. In the chapters that follow, we describe research supporting this model.

Relational Spirituality Affects How People Cope With Unforgiveness Through Relationships—Now, in the Past, and With the Sacred

Relational spirituality is a useful framework for understanding forgiveness because the psychological processes related to interpersonal conflict and repair are influenced by neurobiological relational templates (Cozolino, 2006). People establish attachments early in life. Those attachments can become templates for adult attempts to reestablish similar relationships with close people or to avoid particularly toxic relationships. Either way, the early attachment relationships might still be guiding interpersonal relations years later.

Psychologists of religion also provide substantial empirical evidence that those same early attachment relationships can shape a person's God image or view of the sacred and one's relationship with those sacred objects (E. B. Davis, Moriarty, & Mauch, 2013; Kirkpatrick, 2005). One might have either a close or disappointing relationship with his or her primary caretaker and see, in God or the sacred, a correspondence or recapitulation of that relationship. This is called the *correspondence hypothesis*. Another person could have an insecure attachment to his or her primary caretaker. That relational template can lead to seeing God or the sacred as everything that the parental caretaker was not. This is known as the *compensation hypothesis*.

Attachment dynamics with the sacred influence individual differences in ways of coping with stress (Pargament, 2007). These links between attachment, spirituality, and coping are central to our overall model of forgiveness and relational spirituality.

It might seem obvious to apply attachment theory and other relational frameworks when individuals believe in a personal deity or spiritual beings. For example, the Islamic sage Imam al-Haddad (2010) wrote, "To love God the Exalted is for the servant to feel inclination in his [sic] heart, attachment, and passion for that holiest and loftiest of presences" (p. 250). However, some might question whether relational spirituality applies to traditions such as Buddhism, which are nontheistic. However, we suggest that language and metaphors about relational dynamics tend to emerge within all spiritual traditions. For example, in his work on managing anger through compassion and forgiveness, Buddhist teacher Thich Nhat Hanh (2001) invoked attachment imagery by suggesting that people are "mothers of our anger, and we have to help our baby, our anger" (p. 165). He suggested, "The mother is the living Buddha, an internal figure that is a source of mindfulness energy that one needs to recognize and keep alive" (p. 169).

Relational Spirituality Can Affect the Coping Response of Forgiveness. Relational spirituality can influence forgiveness both positively and negatively. And religion and spirituality certainly play a large part in whether many people experience forgiveness. This is true in national tragedies for which people hold grudges against terrorists (i.e., think of the September 11, 2001, terrorists attack on New York and Washington, DC). This is also true of offenses that occur closer to home, in contentious workplace or school decisions where hurts and offenses may have religious dimensions as complicating factors, or in disagreements and splits in churches, mosques, synagogues, and temples. This is true in people's closest relationships. Couples disagree over religious issues in marriage or parenting and may end their relationship.

Although many spiritual and religious communities offer teachings, practices, and resources to encourage forgiveness, emerging research suggests that some communal practices and resources may be more effective than others in actually promoting interpersonal forgiveness, such as small groups (Wuthnow, 2000). This invites the question of whether certain forms of relational spirituality are more conducive to forgiveness than others.

Empirical studies also suggest that some ways of relating to the sacred might actually be unfavorable to forgiveness (Sandage & Jankowski, 2010). For example, those who relate narcissistically to the sacred (i.e., so that they feel elevated above others and "special" in the eyes of the sacred) may be less forgiving than others. Their particular form of relational spirituality might work against the development of a forgiving character.

PSYCHOTHERAPY: WHEN FORGIVENESS AND RELATIONAL SPIRITUALITY COME TOGETHER

In this book, we try to help you deal with cases that involve many of our clients, those who have (a) religious and spiritual issues involved in their problems, (b) unforgiving attitudes within their interpersonal relationships, and (c) religious and spiritual issues and unforgiving attitudes that are related to their presenting problems. Most of us psychotherapists were not trained to deal with these problems, so it is easy to neglect them or decide that they are not important to dealing with the presenting problems. We may focus on treating depression, anxiety, and personality problems, which we were trained to handle. Yet, we might thereby miss opportunities to engage struggles with forgiveness and religion or spirituality as pathways toward improving emotional and relational functioning. Sometimes those are the very pathways that will lead patients to the most lasting and profound changes.

Ask About Religion, Spirituality, and Issues With Unforgiveness

It is easy to avoid asking clients about religious or spiritual issues. This is especially true if the psychotherapist is not personally religious or spiritual. It is also true if the psychotherapist holds strong opinions or beliefs about religion that differ from the client's beliefs and opinions. Because clients will never share every feature of our worldview, even if we as psychotherapists are drawing from a limited referral base, dealing with religion and spirituality is difficult for all psychotherapists at least some of the time. Yet, we may benefit from wading into unfamiliar and muddy waters even if we know there are risks requiring sensitivity and clinician humility.

It is easy not to ask about whether a person is being eaten up by unforgiveness. We treat the case—often successfully helping the clients improve in their mental health symptoms but leaving them in the stew about their religious or spiritual lives or their struggles to forgive. Later, it is not surprising, those difficulties have fallout. Clients, initially satisfied with the relief of symptoms, might conclude that we did not help with the *real* problems. They are troubled later by the spiritual problems or recurrent bitterness.

To help you become more capable and comfortable dealing with religious or spiritual issues and forgiveness, we have melded together four concepts: relationships, relational spirituality, stress and coping, and forgiveness.

SUMMARY

We have just begun to construct a model of how to understand forgiveness through 3-D glasses. Like the red and blue 3-D lenses in cinema, this depth viewing of forgiveness also has two lenses, one relational and one religious-and-spirituality lens. We have three steps left to consider. First, we discuss exactly what we mean by relational spirituality, which we will tackle in Chapter 2. Second, in Chapter 3, we synthesize the full model. Third, in Chapter 4, we look at some experimental evidence for it.

In Chapters 5 through 11 (i.e., Part II), we describe how to use the model to promote changes in people who seek our help using various modalities of psychotherapy. We examine personality changes, brief psychotherapy, long-term individual psychotherapy, couple and family therapies, and group therapy. In the Afterword, we draw our ideas together.

2

HOW SPIRITUAL TRANSFORMATION OCCURS

When people come to psychotherapy, they are suffering, usually because they have experienced wounds in relationships. Their souls have been damaged, and that damage tends to shut off spiritual relationships, at least for a while. People must then decide: Will I let the estrangement languish, or will I seek to move into and through the suffering to spiritual growth and maturity? This chapter is about the cycles that most humans pass through several times over their lives, cycles in which their spirituality is transformed.

In the present chapter, because relationships and religion and spirituality are crucial, we begin by defining and explaining relational spirituality. We show that relational spirituality is embodied, developmental, hermeneutical (i.e., interpretive), and intercultural. We then examine the goal of spiritual maturity, not just spiritual comfort or spiritual happiness. To set the relational context, we examine the first of the tensions we identified in Chapter 1: attachment and differentiation of self. Then, we look to the process of spiritual

http://dx.doi.org/10.1037/14712-003
Forgiveness and Spirituality in Psychotherapy: A Relational Approach, by E. L. Worthington, Jr. and S. J. Sandage

transformation, involving times of peaceful spiritual dwelling and other times of seemingly chaotic spiritual seeking. By the end of the chapter, we believe you will have a good idea of what we mean by relational spirituality and how it can play into the lives of your patients.

DEFINING RELATIONAL SPIRITUALITY

Spirituality is notoriously complicated to define. There are more than 100 definitions offered in scholarly literature. Popular understandings of spirituality may be even more wide ranging. In Googling "spirituality is" one quickly sees this incredible plethora of meanings and learns that spirituality is "transcendence," "meaningful purpose," "compassion," "laughter," "following Jesus," "the Buddha within," "ecological activism," "tantra sex," and a dizzying array of other options. Perhaps most interesting, one of the first subject options that can pop up online is "spirituality is bullshit," with a host of sites dedicated to a dismissive or even hostile posture. Clearly, the topic of spirituality evokes many definitions and emotional reactions.

Roots of Relational Spirituality

Hill and Pargament (2003) offered a psychological definition of *spirituality* as related to "a search for the sacred." They use the term *sacred* to signify "a person, object, principle, or concept that transcends the self" (p. 65). The sacred can include "a divine being, divine object, Ultimate Reality, or Ultimate Truth" that is "set apart" as holy and beyond the ordinary (p. 65). The term *search* implies an active quest for the sacred (Pargament, 2007). By defining spirituality in relation to whatever a person considers sacred, this phenomenological orientation enables individual differences and wide-ranging diversity in understandings of the sacred. Clinically, it orients attention to ideals, to whatever may be deeply important to a client. Clients who may not consider themselves "spiritual" often hold certain ideals or values they care about deeply or that seem ultimate, such as a client of mine (Steve) who was an atheist but described being moved to a sense of awe and profound respect for the processes of evolution.

Shults and Sandage (2006; Sandage & Shults, 2007) adapted the definition of *spirituality* offered by Hill et al. (2000) to fit a relational theoretical orientation by defining *relational spirituality* as "ways of relating to the sacred" (Shults & Sandage, 2006, p. 161; see also Hall, 2004; Hill & Hall, 2002). In theistic spiritual traditions, the sacred includes personal divine beings and spirits with whom humans can relate. Yet, as we discussed in Chapter 1, spiritual traditions that are not theistic also offer rituals and practices for relating with the sacred and, thus, can be viewed through a relational framework. In this sense, people can relate to God and the sacred in a variety of ways, including love, avoidance, trust, disappointment, questioning, anger, submission, and many other relational categories.

We Are Tapping a Long-Standing Tradition

William James (1902/1958) defined *personal religion* as the "feelings, acts, and experiences of individual men [sic] in their solitude, so far as they apprehend themselves to stand in relation to whatever they may consider divine" (p. 42). The second part of that definition ("to stand in relation") refers to the relational dynamics of what we mean by spirituality. Spirituality emerges as people *relate* to the developmental and existential challenges of making meaning in the midst of the ambiguity of life (Fowler, 1981).

Why Do We Insist on Calling It *Relational*?

Besides the obvious point we made in the previous chapter that the birthplace of religion and spirituality is the primal relationships in which one is reared, there is another important reason for emphasizing its relational aspect. Dualistic frameworks tend to view spirituality as "all good" and as a singular substance of which individuals have a quantitative amount. Our relational model draws attention to the variety of ways people relate to the sacred and ways those relational dynamics may change over time—not just in quantity but in quality. We find that exploring relational dynamics in spirituality can deepen the understanding of the complex and conflicting motivations people bring to relating to the sacred, including both healthy and destructive motivations.

Religion Versus Spirituality

The differentiation of *spirituality* and *religion* can also be confusing. Again, we find the approach of Hill and Pargament (2003; Pargament, 2007) helpful, as they defined both religion and spirituality as involving the "search for the sacred" (p. 65) but made spirituality the broader construct that can potentially be expressed through religious (social and institutional systems) or other contextual channels. They argued that the "polarization of religion and spirituality into institutional and individual domains ignores the fact that all forms of spiritual expression unfold in a social context" (p. 64). Pargament (2007) suggested, "We cannot decontextualize spirituality. This dimension of life does not unfold in a vacuum, but rather in a larger religious context, even if it is a context that has been rejected" (p. 31). Thus, for most people influenced in some ways by religious traditions and contexts, spiritual and religious development can be broadly understood as interactive and overlapping (Hay, Reich, & Utsch, 2006). Pargament (2007) reported survey findings in the United States, showing that about 74% self-define as "spiritual and religious"; 19%, as "spiritual but not religious"; 4%, as "religious but not spiritual"; and 3%, as "neither spiritual nor religious." So, religious contexts influence the self-definition of 81% of survey respondents, and we assume that religious contexts have influenced (negatively or positively) the experiences of many who do not claim to be religious. Even when religious contexts have not been influential, other social contexts influence relational spirituality and the dynamics of forgiveness and unforgiveness in ways we illustrate in the chapters ahead.

This relational and contextual emphasis on spirituality also allows the flexibility to move beyond the individualistic notions that do not fit well with some collectivistic cultural or religious traditions. For example, Paris (1995) described a communal spirituality of African peoples. He explained that links with both living and ancestral communities are essential to relational spirituality. It is the strength and healthy vitality of communal spirituality that shapes African and African American approaches to forgiveness (Paris, 1995, pp. 148–152), and this communal emphasis is common to many cultural and religious traditions.

CONTOURS OF RELATIONAL SPIRITUALITY

Four key assumptions organize the contours of our model of relational spirituality.

Relational Spirituality Is Embodied

All human spiritual experience is mediated neurobiologically. Regardless of what one believes about metaphysical realities of spirituality or the sacred, human spiritual experience involves the brain and physiology (Bland & Strawn, 2014). On the one hand, some spiritual and religious communities promote a dualistic worldview that sharply distinguishes spiritual or human realms, the sacred and the profane. Yet most spiritual and religious traditions have at least implicitly acknowledged the role of embodiment in developing spiritual practices and rituals that engage mental processes and the body, including bowing, meditating, deep breathing, dancing, signing, speaking in tongues, sweating, eating communion bread, counting prayer beads, making hand gestures, and many others. The vast and growing empirical literature on religion and spirituality that has emerged in the past two decades offers valuable resources for understanding potential connections between spiritual practices, forgiveness, and healthy embodiment.

Some contemporary theologians and religious scholars are also moving beyond substance dualist views and promoting models of human personhood in which the complex connections among factors such as neurobiology, bodily health, immune system functioning, and social interaction cannot be separated from "spirituality" (Brown & Strawn, 2012). These approaches fit with our relational framework in drawing attention to the constitutive embodied and relational dynamics involved in spiritual experiences and the processes of change.

A relational approach to spirituality also finds rapprochement with the emerging field of interpersonal neuroscience, which suggests that early relational experiences of attachment with caregivers begin to imprint schemas or templates about relationships within the deep-seated emotional limbic brain (Cozolino, 2006). These templates shape self–other relational configurations and images of God and the sacred. Relational templates can be transformed but not without relational experience. As Lewis, Amini, and Lannon (2000) explained, "When a limbic connection has established a neural pattern, it takes a limbic connection to revise it" (p. 177).

Neuroscientists are also documenting neurobiological processes related to spiritual and religious experiences, including forgiveness (Newberg & Waldman, 2009). Azari, Missimer, and Seitz (2005) mounted neuroimaging evidence of cerebral blood flow that religious experiences of Buddhists and Christians are mediated through prefrontal structures involving social–relational cognitive processes. They suggested that religious experience involves the neurobiology of a "perceived relationship" with the sacred (p. 275). Clearly, this has important implications for the influence of neurobiological functioning on individual differences in forgiveness and relational spirituality and the challenges some individuals may have in forgiving.

Relational Spirituality Is Developmental

Spiritual experience emerges in the contexts of human development and in conjunction with other developmental processes (e.g., cognitive, emotional, social, moral, intercultural). Although our focus in this book is largely on working with adults, it is important to be cognizant of spiritual development across the life span and developmental differences in working with children, adolescents, and adults. Some of the important early empirical research on forgiveness by Enright (1996) investigated developmental differences in reasoning about forgiveness using a cognitive moral development framework. This research showed, for example, that some individuals might understand the rationale for forgiving others out of a preconventional fear of spiritual punishment if they did not forgive, a conventional ethic of duty or obedience to the social or religious codes of one's community, or a postconventional and internalized commitment of wanting to be a loving and forgiving person. Processes of forgiveness were influenced by underlying developmental factors, and individual motivations for forgiveness often shifted with maturity.

We are particularly drawn to relational models of development, such as attachment theory (Bowlby, 1969/1982) and differentiation-based family systems theories (Bowen, 1985). In addition to the formative influence of parents and caregivers, relationships with people who serve as spiritual mentors, teachers, or admired role models can be highly influential on psychosocial and spiritual development. These influential relational figures can model examples of seeking or granting forgiveness (or not). Moreover, experiences of interpersonal conflict and the ways those conflicts are handled in sacred contexts (spiritual or religious communities or relationships) can be particularly influential on relational spirituality templates related to forgiveness. In the best case scenarios of relational development, individuals experience healthy adult exemplars of authentic forgiveness and repair of conflict both personally and in their wider social networks. This is an important part of secure attachment relationships and the holding environments that foster emotional intelligence and the integration of challenging emotional experiences. (*Holding environments* are, in the theorizing of Winnicott, 1986, psychological spaces that follow a model set up by a positive mother–baby bond established when the mother held the baby.) In contrast, when families or spiritual communities hold ideals of forgiveness but model either inauthenticity or chronic unforgiveness, it creates a psychological split between ideals and relational realities, which can impede the healthy development of forgiveness.

A relational approach to spiritual development can also move past a common tendency to view spirituality in exclusively positive terms. An idealistic view of spirituality obscures efforts to understand spiritual pathology or maladaptive ways of relating to the sacred. A relational framework can invite consideration of relational discrepancies even within spiritual leaders and communities, such as priests, gurus, clergy, or other leaders whose actual interpersonal behavior is destructive and in severe conflict with their stated spiritual ideals. As one example, the Mennonite scholar John Howard Yoder (1994) wrote a widely influential pacifist theology (*The Politics of Jesus*) emphasizing forgiveness. He was later disciplined by his church for sexually abusing women. Misconduct or abuse by spiritual leaders can complicate the topic and the practice of forgiveness for those who have been disappointed, injured, or traumatized by such radical discrepancies in relational spirituality.

Aside from major conflicts or traumatic disappointments, the relational spirituality of a given individual can also undergo developmental changes over time. Most spiritual and religious traditions describe periods of struggle, questioning, or spiritual darkness, which can ultimately formative but may temporarily involve reductions in spiritual and emotional well-being. We consider the ways in which spiritual struggles might emerge from interpersonal conflicts and also influence how those conflicts are handled. In some cases, spiritual struggles can potentiate a transformation that results in new experiences of forgiveness.

Relational Spirituality Is Hermeneutical

Spiritual experience is interpreted through a worldview that is formed by sociocultural and often religious traditions. Although spiritual experiences can transcend words, the brain interprets and translates experience into language and other symbols of representation. These "rules" of meaning-making are *hermeneutics*. The human brain processes experience using the hermeneutical or referential activity of attempting to integrate verbal, symbolic, and subsymbolic levels of information processing (Hall & Porter, 2004). This is an attempt to integrate experiential and conceptual forms of knowledge, which is a process we take seriously in our model of relational spirituality. Implicit relational knowledge based on interpersonal experience informs this process of interpretation. In philosophy, the school of ontological hermeneutics affirms these neuroscientific discoveries—who we are influences what we know and vice versa (Sandage, Cook, Hill, Strawn, & Reimer, 2008). This is why it is potentially transformative to integrate conscious theological reflection with growing awareness of one's "unconscious theology" that is shaped by relational experiences with one's family of origin and wider social network (Duvall, 2000).

Hermeneutical perspectives in philosophy, religion, and theology are also helpful for understanding interpretive connections between relational spirituality and forgiveness. Within any spiritual or religious community, there will be individual differences in how traditions or ideals are interpreted in terms of spiritual practices and virtues. For example, it has been suggested that many spiritual and religious traditions have a stream emphasizing purity or in-group boundaries and another stream emphasizing compassion toward all people. Individuals within the same tradition or community may differ in whether they focus more on moral purity or compassion, and some individuals find creative ways of integrating the two. Although this contrast between purity and compassion is probably an oversimplification, it does point to ways in which equally committed individuals may draw on different streams of interpretations of the same tradition in seeking to understand ideals of spirituality. Emotional forgiveness seems easier to integrate with a hermeneutical focus on a relational spirituality of compassion, but a purity or duty ethic might also promote decisional forgiveness.

Extremely stressful or painful experiences can be particularly difficult to understand within one's prior interpretive horizons. Again, traumatic experiences typically fragment one's ability to make meaning out of those events. In the previous chapter, we discussed appraisal processes related to stress, which essentially involve interpreting the causes and meaning of a given set of stressors. So, *hermeneutics* refers to this bidirectional interpretive process of seeking to make sense of both (a) one's experience and (b) one's spiritual and cultural traditions of meaning and virtue. In some cases, individuals can experience great dissonance, for example, between their interpretation of spiritual ideals in their tradition ("I must immediately forgive everyone or I will not be forgiven by God") and their own experience ("I am deeply angry at my perpetrator, despite repeatedly praying for God to release me from these feelings"). Clinicians may find themselves working with clients experiencing such spiritual and hermeneutical dissonance. They will need to be cognizant of the influence of their own interpretive frameworks related to forgiveness and other virtues and resist an urge to quickly remove all dissonance.

Relational Spirituality Is Intercultural

We have suggested that relational spirituality is always influenced by contextual factors and processes of interpretation in relating with the sacred. Systemically, this means spirituality not only involves relating with one's own sense of the sacred but also the sacred of others. Thus, relational spirituality is intercultural in the sense of relating to the diverse cultural frameworks of others. This means a relational dimension of spirituality is *alterity*, which means that there are ways, developmentally set into a pattern, of relating to the differentness of others. There is a natural stranger anxiety and in-group preference among humans that can challenge spiritual hospitality and relationship across various sociocultural differences. In fact, Griffith (2011) argued, on the basis of evolutionary psychology, that one of the primary sociobiological functions of religion has been to promote kin recognition and peer affiliation within a group. Generosity or compassion toward out-group members is sometimes realized among spiritual and religious communities, but this represents a more challenging evolutionary achievement. Yet, intercultural development, or the capacity to relate empathically and competently across cultural differences, is a key characteristic of spiritual maturity in many spiritual and religious traditions (Sandage & Harden, 2011; Shults & Sandage, 2006). Emmanuel Levinas (1969) suggested that ethics begins in the "face of the other," or our perceptions of the humanness of others who challenge people with their difference, and the same might be said about spirituality.

Deficits in intercultural development and mature alterity can result in forms of relational spirituality characterized by several different problems, such exclusionary defensiveness and out-group hostility, shame about one's social identity, or anxiety-driven efforts at serving others that are more rescuing and exploitive than empowering. In fact, dispositional forgiveness has been negatively correlated with intercultural defensiveness (Sandage & Harden, 2011). Some cases of unforgiveness are clearly embedded in the dynamics of alterity and fear of the other who is perceived as dangerously different. The process of forgiveness in such cases will often involve spiritual growth in intercultural competence and mature alterity.

SPIRITUAL WELL-BEING AND SPIRITUAL MATURITY

A relational approach to spirituality can also use the lens of human development to consider the range of ways of relating to the sacred. These stretch from the immature and even pathological to higher levels of spiritual maturity.

Spiritual Well-Being Does Not Equal Spiritual Maturity

One important tenet of the relational spiritual model is that spiritual well-being and spiritual maturity are different goals. Together, they form a complex relationship (Sandage & Shults, 2007; Shults & Sandage, 2006). A parallel case has been made differentiating psychological well-being and maturity based on empirical findings that show measures of well-being do not necessarily correlate with measures of cognitive or emotional complexity that characterize psychological maturity (McAdams, 2006). Psychological well-being, particularly in self-report, can sometimes reflect use of defense mechanisms or positive illusions about oneself and the world that do not authentically account for complexities. A person might feel happy or satisfied with life while remaining oblivious to the relational impact on those around them. From our relational model, both psychological and spiritual maturity involve well-developed capacities for relational attunement and self-awareness, along with skills in emotional regulation, which are typically conducive to well-being and tolerating suffering needed for growth.

Spiritual Well-Being

Spiritual well-being has been defined in various ways using several different measures but generally refers to a state of positive connection with the sacred that contributes to a sense of meaning and purpose in life (Unterrainer,

Ladenhauf, Wallner-Liebmann, & Fink, 2011). Ellison (1994) is one of the most prolific researchers of spiritual well-being and based his definition on the Jewish understanding of *shalom*, which is a multidimensional concept referencing an integration of personal and communal wholeness and flourishing. In the Hebrew Bible, *shalom* involves fidelity to covenant and forms of relational spirituality that promote both harmony and social justice through love of God and neighbor. In this tradition, spiritual well-being (or *shalom*) involves ongoing authentic processes of forgiving and being forgiven.

Spiritual well-being has been empirically associated with many indices of psychosocial and physical well-being (Jankowski & Sandage, 2011) and has predicted happiness over and above other personality factors (Gomez & Fisher, 2003). Forgiveness has been positively associated with spiritual well-being (Strelan, Acton, & Patrick, 2009), and forgiveness has also been included as a subdimension of two different scales measuring spiritual well-being (Unterrainer et al., 2011). Lawler-Row, Hyatt-Edwards, Wuensch, and Karremans (2011) found that forgiveness either fully or partially mediated the relationships between religiosity and health across three studies, suggesting forgiveness may be a key dimension of salutary ways of relating with the sacred.

Yet, individuals can experience reductions in spiritual well-being, either temporary or chronic, for various reasons. Traumatic events, life transitions, serious illness, busyness or distraction, and various other stressors can make it challenging to sustain spiritual well-being. Interpersonal conflicts can be a great threat to spiritual well-being (Taylor, Chatters, & Levin, 2004) for several reasons. Such conflicts in one's spiritual community can rupture a sense of *shalom* and distract from connecting with the sacred or even promote avoidance of spirituality. Interpersonal conflicts can take many forms, such as a power struggle within a spiritual community, feeling spiritually abandoned or disappointed in people, encountering spiritual judgment or coercion, or even experiencing abuse by spiritual leaders or community members. In some cases, stressors may lead an individual to experience an intense relational conflict with God or the sacred, taxing the person's spiritual trust in the midst of their suffering.

There is a growing literature on *spiritual struggles*, which have been defined as "efforts to conserve or transform a spirituality that has been threatened or harmed" (Pargament, Murray-Swank, Magyar, & Ano, 2005, p. 247). That research suggests such struggles can either impair one's relational spirituality or become pathways toward spiritual development.

Spiritual Maturity

Spiritual maturity has received more limited theoretical and empirical consideration among social scientists than has spiritual well-being (Shults & Sandage, 2006), but it seems clear to us that one part of spiritual maturity is a resilient, self-regulating capacity to cope with spiritual struggles, including those involving interpersonal conflict (Bonanno, 2005). Precise definitions of spiritual maturity will differ across traditions; however, we propose that spiritual maturity involves relational capacities for secure attachment and high levels of differentiation of self (described below), which impact both interpersonal and spiritual functioning. And, spiritual maturity involves complexity in cognitive, emotional, and relational functioning (Albright, 2006) or what Fowler (1981) called "conjunctive" forms of faith, which can (in the same way that a conjunction holds together two clauses in writing) hold dialectic tensions between seeming contradictions (e.g., law and grace, justice and forgiveness, grief and hope).

Spiritual Well-Being and Spiritual Maturity in Suffering

Suffering does not necessarily lead to complexity or spiritual maturity, but spiritual maturity cannot be developed without some suffering. A spiritually mature person has likely developed self-regulatory spiritual practices and ways of relating to the sacred that help recover spiritual well-being following stress. Some people will report high spiritual well-being but are characterized by "spiritual bypass" (Cashwell, Bentley, & Yarborough, 2007) or "illusory spiritual health" (Edwards & Hall, 2003), both of which describe unconscious attempts to use spirituality as a defense against internal conflicts or injustice in the world in contrast to developing spiritual maturity.

Attachment and Differentiation of Self—Similarities and Differences

In Chapter 1, we briefly discussed theoretical and empirical connections between attachment, relational spirituality, and forgiveness. Our relational spirituality model uses various relational constructs but focuses on (a) attachment and (b) differentiation of self, both of which have been used in studies on forgiveness and spirituality. Secure attachment and differentiation of self overlap. Each references healthy developmental capacities for (a) balancing connection and autonomy and (b) emotional regulation.

However, in our reading of the literature on these constructs and in popular clinical use, it seems the concept of attachment more often evokes notions of healthy connection and drawing support from others, whereas differentiation of self often connotes the ability to self-regulate emotions and to be secure in one's own sense of self. Attachment has been shown by research to be important across the life span and yet first emerges as a key development process between infants and caregivers. Differentiation of self is often discussed as a developmental task of late adolescents and adults in life cycle phases of "launching" and identity construction. Thus, we use both constructs with acknowledgement of their similarities and unique emphases.

Attachment

The limbic-based attachment system has two basic functions: safe haven and secure base. Both have to do with attachment but are responsible for different actions.

Safe-Haven Function. Within the general and the psychology of religion literatures on attachment, the *safe-haven* function of attachment has drawn the most research attention (Granqvist, 2005). The safe-haven function consists of a diverse set of "affect regulation strategies [designed] to obtain felt security during states of distress" (Granqvist, 2005, p. 37).

Secure-Base Function. The *secure-base* function of exploration, which occurs during times of nondistress, also involves regulating closeness and distance in one's relating to caregivers. However, rather than moving closer and seeking comfort, the individual distances to explore new territory. Whether in relations with others or the sacred, relating from a secure base can involve questioning, wondering, and experimenting. High levels of anxiety or distress can inhibit seeking aspects of secure-base behavior altogether or cause exploring to be impulsive, erratic, or even manic. Neurobiologically, the secure-base function of attachment emotionally regulates the brain's *seeking system*, which has evolved to forage or explore (Panksepp, 1998; Panksepp & Biven, 2012). The seeking system works from curiosity. It empowers an energetic desire to find things, whether food or existential meaning.

Emotions of frustration and rage work against the seeking system and exploration by activating the perceived need to defend territory or one's being against threats. One stays home, so to speak. A securely attached organism will usually accurately perceive threats in the environment and draw on relational resources (interpersonal or spiritual) to sustain secure-base exploration in constructive, but not addictive, ways.

Differentiation of Self

Differentiation of self represents a mature, adult configuration of self–other relations characterized by the ability to balance (a) emotional and cognitive functioning and (b) intimacy and autonomy in relationships. People with high differentiation of self are less emotionally reactive to others, more flexible, and more self-aware than those with low self-differentiation.

Schnarch (1997, 2009) described *differentiation of self* as an ability to "hold onto oneself" in close proximity to others, which suggests a mature relational capacity to handle the anxiety of both closeness (intimacy) and difference (alterity) (Sandage, Jensen, & Jass, 2008). Although Bowen (1985) was initially critiqued for sounding too individualistic in his conception of differentiation, it is now more widely understood in the family systems field that differentiation of self includes the ability to both connect with others and be alone.

Many spiritual writers have spoken to this dialectic of living in community and yet having a capacity to handle solitude. In short, high differentiation of self represents a capacity for wholeness. It balances the emotional regulation that leads to well-being and the distress tolerance of suffering that can lead to maturity.

Although spiritual maturity is multidimensional and complex to define, we consider differentiation of self to be an excellent maturity construct. Social science research has shown that measures of differentiation of self are positively correlated with a variety of indices of both personal well-being and relational maturity (Skowron, 2004). Differentiation-based spirituality is growth-oriented without unhealthy grandiosity or dependence on other-validation (Schnarch, 1991). Although ways of relating to the sacred can be driven by anxiety, more differentiated forms of relational spirituality characterize people who are more motivated by the pursuit of love and integrity than the simple reduction of anxiety. In fact, highly differentiated spiritual leaders can tolerate the anxiety that is necessary for personal and corporate growth (Friedman, 1985). At low levels of differentiation, spiritual leaders are susceptible to overuse of rescuing of others or they tend to manage their own anxiety through relational disengagement and avoidance of both intimacy and conflict.

Low levels of differentiation involve too much anxiety and too little capacity for regulating anxiety to handle the rigors of mature intimacy and alterity, so spiritual defenses are used against relational closeness and diversity. This can be seen in some individuals or communities that focus exclusively on spiritual content to bypass relational process or that enforce extremes of homogeneity to control the anxiety related to differences. In very poorly differentiated families or spiritual communities, spiritual maturity might be constructed through legitimate themes of accountability and obedience. But there is a risk that this can result in the ceiling effect of spiritual conformity and dependence on other-validation, both of which limit adult differentiation and the mature internalization of spirituality (Griffith, 2011; Shaw, 2014).

Dialectics of Spiritual Transformation

Intensification of Anxiety

Our relational spirituality model suggests that transformation involves an intensifying anxiety. The risks of change increase arousal and existential anxiety about the unknown. This is true even when moving into changes that seem positive, such as getting out of prison, getting married, or starting college or a new job. Stressful changes (whether positive or negative) require interpretations and coping strategies. Transformation is a developmental process of relating differently to stressors through new interpretations and coping strategies. Spiritual transformation is a reconceptualization of one's spiritual worldview.

Spiritual Transformation as Second-Order Change

First-order change is change in one's current relational strategies. Second-order change involves a more complex systemic transformation that changes ways of relating to the sacred altogether. Spiritual transformation suggests that profound, qualitative, or second-order changes in the ways in which a person relates to the sacred occur. This does not necessarily mean changing one's spiritual tradition. Rather, an example would be to change one's relational spirituality from primarily fear-based attachment to a more secure attachment. Systems theorists suggest that transformation is an ongoing process across the life cycle as human systems (i.e., persons, families, or communities) are continually challenged to adapt to their changing ecological contexts (Maddock & Larson, 1995).

Spiritual Transformations Can Seem Discomfiting

Finding oneself in the midst of a spiritual transformation can be confusing to those from some spiritual or religious communities that emphasize either a single spiritual transformation (e.g., conversion, initiation) or the lifelong practice of the same religious actions. However, most spiritual and religious traditions offer multiple practices, many threads of spiritual understanding, and an overall complexity that enables adherents to continue to discover new ways of relating to the sacred that can serve the developmental needs of new challenges or stressors or a given phase of the life cycle.

Spiritual Transformations Are Similar to Pargament's Transformative Coping or Might Be Triggered by Spiritual Struggles

Several other psychologists of religion have offered somewhat similar models of spiritual transformation. Pargament's (2007) stress-and-coping model of religion suggests spirituality involves both conserving and transforming forms of spiritual coping within a sociocultural context, with forgiveness often serving as a transformational type of coping. People often attempt to hold onto or conserve sacred meaning through various coping mechanisms, such as positive reappraisals of negative events or engaging in spiritual purification. However, spiritual struggles can lead to new forms of coping that represent a spiritual transformation. For example, a person may move from a focus on anger over a relational injury to practicing forgiveness based on a spiritual transformation.

Spiritual Transformations Are Like Discontinuous, Quantum Changes

Miller and C'de Baca (2001) studied individuals reporting a transformative "quantum change," which they defined as "vivid, surprising, benevolent, and enduring" (p. 4), altering the individual's actions, feelings, thoughts, and experience of meaning in his or her life. They used the term *quantum change* to represent second-order transformation in a person's overall approach to meaning in life. They also suggested that an urge toward transformation can arise from spiritual or existential conflicts that prompt a transition toward new ways of relating with the sacred. The majority of participants in Miller and C'de Baca's study described a greater valuing of forgiveness after their transformative experience.

Spiritual Transformations Are Ruptures in Personal Epistemology

Rambo's (1993) dialectical and process-oriented stage model gives significant attention to contextual, relational, emotional, and meaning-oriented dimensions of spiritual change as part of the "matrix of transformation" (p. 107). Rambo's nonlinear stages include a crisis, or what Loder (1989) called a "rupture in the knowing context" (p. 37), which leads to questing (seeking) for meaning and eventually commitment (dwelling) to a group or community as aspects of the overall process of change. Interpersonal conflicts or an individual's own struggle with guilt could be crises that activate the process of spiritual transformation, and Loder suggested forgiveness is one type of transformation that can give spiritual meaning to an entire sequence of existential struggle.

Jones's Integrative Model

Jones's (2002) model draws on relational psychoanalysis and religious scholarship to view spiritual transformation as a developmental and relational process with inevitable moments of disappointment and the loss of certain spiritual ideals. Jones suggested transformation is generated both by relational desires and by the need for reconstructed meaning following disappointment and spiritual deidealization. Relating to the sacred involves a growth-enhancing search for "a transformational object that can facilitate the integration of new experience" (p. 87). In Jones's view, spiritual transformation is shaped by prior relational experiences but is oriented toward creativity and new integrative forms of meaning-making. He seeks to integrate psychological theorists and Eastern and Western spiritual traditions to suggest a view of transformation as nonlinear and inclusive of "dark nights of the soul"—a usually stressful period, sometimes lasting years, of perceived emotional darkness characterized by an inability to connect with God or periods of spiritual ambiguity and struggle. Again, we suggest that interpersonal disappointments and conflicts often represent unforgiving forms of deidealization that can challenge the need to develop new, authentic forms of forgiveness. However, some clinical situations involve not only disappointments in other humans but disappointment in divine beings or the sacred for allowing tragic circumstances. For Jones, spiritual transformation involves moving through ambiguity, spiritual ambivalence, and dark nights of the soul toward more mature, postcritical forms of relational spirituality, which integrate rather than deny disappointing experiences.

CRUCIBLE METAPHORS OF SPIRITUAL TRANSFORMATION

Crucible Metaphors to Describe Intense Emotional Transformations

The crucible is a metaphor of intensification that is useful for integrating our relational model of spiritual transformation. Schnarch (1991) defined a crucible as a "resilient vessel in which metamorphic processes occur" (p. xv). A crucible is a container for holding the process of intense heat and pressure that can transform raw materials and catalytic agents into new forms.

St. John of the Cross

Spiritual writers have often used the crucible or similar metaphors to depict the intensification of stressors and challenges that can set the context for spiritual transformation. St. John of the Cross (1990) portrayed the dark night of the soul as a purifying "furnace, like gold in a crucible" (p. 107).

Recent Theologians

Theologians concerned with liberation and reconciliation have decried injustice while also giving voice to the ways some oppressed communities have undergone spiritual transformations amidst crucibles of suffering, including Latin American poverty (Gutierrez, 2003), South African apartheid (Tutu, 2013), and the United States' legacies of slavery and racism (D. Hayes, 2012).

Clinical Theorists

Several clinical theorists, most notably Schnarch (1991), have applied the crucible metaphor to the dynamics of relational transformation in couples, families, and communities by emphasizing the roles of stress and conflict in generating opportunities for relational growth. Napier and Whitaker (1978) described family therapy as a crucible-like process. Jung (1944/1953) described the cruciblelike sealed vessel, or sacred *vas*, as symbolic of the individuating the fires of the therapeutic relationship. Wallin (2007) suggested transforming attachment templates in therapy involves a developmental crucible. Cooper (2000) described tensions within the therapy relationship as forming a crucible. Each of these theorists has helped shape our understanding.

The Aptness of the Crucible Metaphor

The crucible metaphor suggests resiliency and nonreactivity of the container. Crucibles or containers with melting points lower than the chemical reaction inside will crack under pressure and spill out the potential transformative process (Schnarch, 1991), which is why the differentiation or anxiety tolerance of a therapist or spiritual leader is so central to their capacity to contain and steward the process of transformation (Moore, 2001).

Schnarch (1991) has developed a crucible model of therapy with couples and theorized that intimate relationships involve a systemic balancing of cycles of stability and growth. Relational systems maintain states of balance or stability through familiar forms of relating. The relationship may or may not be particularly satisfying. Feelings of safety and security can come from familiar relational patterns. At a certain point of systemic destabilization, which Schnarch (1997) called "critical mass," one or both partners become willing to risk the anxiety that is a necessary part of crucibles of change in a transforming growth cycle.

This relational crucible can involve a parallel to what the contemplatives called "dark nights of the soul." Anxiety intensifies. Persons are challenged to stretch toward increased differentiation of self and a capacity for the risks of mature intimacy. Often, the crucible process intensifies conflicts as difficult issues or differences are faced. Spiritual well-being may temporarily decline during the early phases of a growth cycle, but growth in differentiation of self can ultimately increase a person's ability to integrate well-being and relational maturity. Schnarch's differentiation-based theory of relational transformation in couples fits with our interest in (a) transformation in a variety of relationship contexts (e.g., family, friendships, community) and (b) mature, mindful forms of relational spirituality, which move beyond outward conformity to facilitate increased capacities for spiritual intimacy and alterity. The challenges of intimacy and alterity can shape crucibles for spiritual transformation that require a willingness to risk the possibilities of feeling disappointment, rejection, engulfment, confusion, incompetence or other anxiety-provoking emotions. Even positive relational experiences, such as feeling known, understood, or loved, can provoke crucibles of anxiety as the existential shadow of possible loss looms in the unconscious. Differentiation is necessary to mature through both pain and pleasure.

BALANCING SPIRITUAL DWELLING AND SEEKING

Shults and Sandage (2006; Sandage & Shults, 2007) drew upon Schnarch's (1991) differentiation-based theory of transformation in couples' relationships, along with work by other developmental theorists, to depict a relational model of spiritual transformation. In this relational model, spirituality involves a systemic, dialectical balancing of dwelling and seeking (see Figure 2.1), which we describe next.

Unfolding Wuthnow's (1998) Model of Spiritual Dwelling and Seeking

Sociologist of religion Robert Wuthnow (1998) described the changing spiritual landscape in North America since the 1950s as a movement from spiritualities of dwelling toward spiritualities of seeking. *Spiritual dwelling* involves attaching to a particular sacred community and tradition, typically provided by a religious group. *Spiritual seeking* involves questing and journeying toward new spiritual experiences and understandings, which can unfold both within and beyond the boundaries of religious institutions.

In terms of the neurobiology of attachment, dwelling roughly maps onto the safe-haven function and seeking onto the secure-base function. This dialectic of spiritual dwelling and seeking is also similar to Pargament's (1997) coping model mentioned above, which considers both the conserving and transforming functions of spirituality, thereby acknowledging the dialectical needs for stability (dwelling) and growth (seeking).

Although some people habitually gravitate toward either spiritual dwelling or seeking, we believe the dynamic and dialectical tension between spiritual dwelling and seeking is an essential part of the overall process of spiritual transformation. The healthy integration of spiritual dwelling and seeking is an expression of mature differentiation of self.

Walking You Through the Process of Spiritual Dwelling and Seeking

Spiritual Dwelling

The inner ring on the left side of Figure 2.1 represents the cycle of spiritual dwelling, which involves relating to the sacred in familiar ways (including avoiding the sacred). Spiritual dwelling can ultimately involve holding an internalized commitment to an understanding of the sacred, along with practices that facilitate connection with sacred, centeredness, and stabilizing

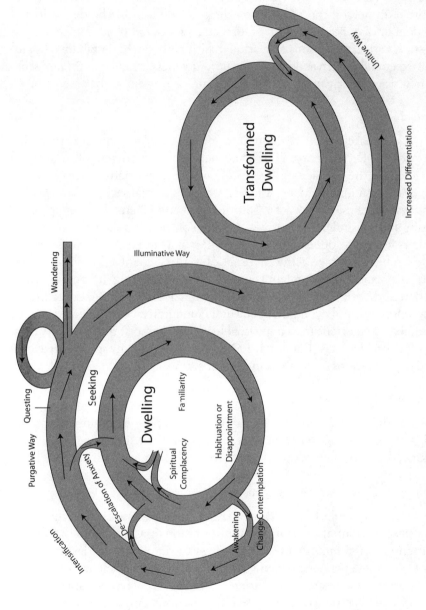

Figure 2.1. Spiritual transformation: balancing spiritual dwelling and seeking.

emotional regulation. But extrinsic or less mature forms of spiritual dwelling can lead to habituation and spiritual disappointment. Spiritual practices and experiences become habituated over time, and this can result in spiritual complacency, a lack of spiritual vitality, or even disappointment with the sacred. Spiritual distancing can result as dwellers defend against the discomfort of boredom or disappointment or avoid facing emotional pain or awareness of injustice. Periodically, forms of relational spirituality can be destabilized by crucible experiences, such as dealing with unforgiveness, which may prompt seeking new ways of relating to the sacred and processing emotional experience.

Spiritual Seeking

A spiritual change can occur if a person contemplates change (Prochaska, Norcross, & DiClemente, 2007) and accepts the pathway of awakening (depicted on the left side of Figure 2.1), which potentially moves a person into intensification of anxiety and the cycle of spiritual seeking. Many traditions describe these features of a "spiritual awakening," and this is often destabilizing and stressful but intensifies attention on certain existential issues and prompts searching, questing (Rambo, 1993), or a kind of "spiritual foraging." A person begins to take action in terms of spiritual change (Prochaska et al., 2007). For example, they might start praying or meditating in a new way, asking new authentic spiritual questions about evil and suffering, or seeking to build relationships beyond one's cultural community. Seeking could also be prompted by questions from a spiritual leader or therapist that intensify deep questions or dilemmas (Rambo, 1993), similar to how many spiritual teachers have used questions or parables instead of giving answers.

Frightened Flight Back to Dwelling

Seeking can be both exciting and scary. If a person's desire for stability and safety exceeds his or her motivation to tolerate the intensified anxiety of seeking, the person might opt to return to familiar forms of spiritual dwelling.

Drawing on Contemplative Tradition

The contemplatives used the term *purgative way* for this dynamic of intensified existential and spiritual confrontation that can include a focusing of attention or commitment, a willingness to simplify priorities and make sacrifices, or an openness to facing painful realities about self and other.

Secure attachments with caring but nonrescuing relational figures can offer a secure relational container, holding environment, or crucible for tolerating the anxiety of seeking with some measure of spiritual comfort or at least controlled discomfort, which might lead to spiritual transformation (depicted in the right side of Figure 2.1). Thus, differentiated and securely attached leaders and therapists who have been through their own crucibles of trans-formation (Hardy, 2000) are necessary. Healthy spiritual practices and coping strategies that can help one self-soothe anxiety and regulate emotions are also central to tolerating the crucible distress.

The questing of the purgative way can lead to transforming moments of illumination involving more differentiated understandings of self and other in relation to the sacred. Contemplatives referred to this as the *illuminative way*. Developing this new, more differentiated sense of self in relation to others in lived experience might be considered to parallel the *unitive way*, from contemplatives. The "seeking cycle" ring in Figure 2.1 of the purgative, illuminative, and unitive ways is symbolically represented by a winding path toward the right half of Figure 2.1 to depict transformative movement into the stability and comfort of a new form of spiritual dwelling. Transformed spiritual dwelling after a cycle of seeking involves new levels of spiritual maturity, if successful, with less use of rigid defenses against anxiety, diversity, and conflict. The person has grown in differentiation of self.

When Spiritual Seeking Does Not Lead to Deepened Spiritual Maturity

Spiritual seeking does not always lead to illumination and spiritual trans-formation. We illustrate this in Figure 2.1 by several paths that lead from seeking directly back to dwelling on the left half of the figure. In fact, seek-ing may, at least initially, intensify relational conflicts. In one study with Christian graduate students, we found a negative correlation between quest religiosity and forgiving others, which suggests that certain forms of spiri-tual questioning and doubting might be at odds with forgiveness (Sandage & Williamson, 2010). This could represent individuals who are in distress over "leaving home" (perhaps spiritually and interpersonally) as they ques-tion some family-of-origin experiences. However, it also could include stu-dents who are authentically angry over injustices because graduate school raised their critical consciousness about those issues. In such cases, important aspects of spiritual development could be unfolding even though the person is not exhibiting forgiveness.

In other cases, the seeking cycle can result in spiritual development becoming arrested. In those instances, struggles with forgiveness may take more chronic forms. On the top part of Figure 2.1, to try to symbolically depict some of the risks of the seeking and questing process, we have a path-way toward spiritual wandering—more of an avoidance of key integrity dilemmas or spiritual identity development than characterizes spiritual seek-ing. Several dynamics might lead a person out of an intensified crucible of seeking and into a path of spiritual wandering. Some have been deeply hurt, abused, and traumatized by past spiritual communities and feel a strong need for autonomy as opposed to using a relational holding environment. Highly narcissistic seekers might feel a limited ability to attach to others or to tolerate feedback. Therefore, they gravitate to spiritual experiences that do not create relational discomfort. Others have experienced oppression (e.g., racism, sexism, stigmatization) or simply communities unable to relate to their spiritual questions. They might not have found trustworthy relationships in which they can invest themselves and experience growth.

Re-entering a Spiritual Crucible After a Period of Wandering

Re-entering a spiritual crucible process of spiritual transformation after wandering can require great courage. It may involve processing and grieving disappointments and taking risks with attachment to key people. Differentiated therapists can potentially facilitate the trust and containment that is necessary for clients to move from wandering into the challenging spiritual crucible process through patient and resilient relationship building that tolerates the ambivalence and the initial mistrust of the wanderer.

What Is Required to Grow?

The relational spirituality model of Shults and Sandage (2006) suggests that the developmental movement from spiritual dwelling to spiritual seeking toward an integration of the two (i.e., the new dwelling cycle on the right of Figure 3.1 in the next chapter) is a nonlinear transformative process that requires the tolerance of anxiety, ambiguity, and conflict. This model is consistent with a growing body of psychotherapy process research suggesting transformative processes of change are often nonlinear, including trajectories that fit a curvilinear pattern (A. M. Hayes, Laurenceau, Feldman, Strauss, & Cardaciotto, 2007). As with psychotherapeutic change, processes of spiritual transformation may also often be nonlinear and discontinuous (i.e., relatively dramatic) as a person seeks a more complex balance of order and chaos (Albright, 2006). This is systemic reorganization. We show this as a new psychological and spiritual dwelling space by depicting it on the right half of the figure.

A Hint of Supportive Research

In their research program involving numerous studies, Sandage and colleagues have empirically tested the relational model of spiritual transformation in several empirical studies of graduate students in the helping professions in a Christian university context. Although we summarize the findings in more detail in Chapter 5, we wanted to whet your appetite with just a couple of studies here. A 2-year longitudinal study found linear trends toward both increased spiritual dwelling and seeking among graduate students. Although the patterns of change were variable across students, a significant percentage of students increased in both spiritual dwelling and seeking. Two cross-sectional studies used a dichotomous measure of spiritual transformation adapted from Miller and C'de Baca's (2001) quantum change research to assess whether participants reported a dramatic spiritual change during the previous year. In support of the relational spirituality model, participants in both studies who reported a recent spiritual transformation differed from those who did not with respect to the dialectical relationship between spiritual dwelling and seeking. For example, the curvilinear relationship between spiritual questing and a dwelling-oriented measure of spiritual maturity was moderated or altered by a report of a recent spiritual transformation (R. Beck & Jessup, 2004; Sandage, Link, & Jankowski, 2010).

A second study found spiritual questing to be negatively related with generativity among those not reporting a recent spiritual transformation but showed a curvilinear pattern with generativity for those who did (Sandage, Hill, & Vaubel, 2011). That is, moderate levels of spiritual questing were associated with the highest levels of generativity for those reporting a recent spiritual transformation, and this effect held after controlling for impression management. Although the cross-sectional design of these two studies limited interpretations of causality, the results showed that those reporting a recent spiritual transformation tended to display a greater integration of spiritual dwelling and seeking than those who did not. Although measures of spiritual dwelling and seeking (or commitment and questing) are sometimes inversely related, these two studies show a different, nonlinear pattern for those reporting dramatic spiritual changes.

SUMMARY

In this chapter, we discussed relational spirituality. We saw its dialectical tension between (for most people) longer periods of spiritual dwelling and more abbreviated and irregularly experienced periods of spiritual seeking.

Spirituality is fundamentally about relationships—both in the sense of two objects having some relationship between them and in the sense of people personalizing the connections into humanlike relations. The key to understanding patients who have spiritually loaded transgressions in their past or present with which they need to cope is to understand the relationships between our stress-and-coping model and the relational spirituality model. This is described by the forgiveness and relational spirituality model's intersection within the stress-and-coping model. In both cases, relationships are vital. In both, coping with interpersonal stressors is essential. In both, people can struggle. And in both, people must cope with their struggles. How that coping emerges, what form it takes, how it progresses, and how and why it does or does not lead to forgiveness must be explained. Those are the tasks we attempt in the following chapter.

3

HOW ATTACHMENT AFFECTS SPIRITUALITY AND WHY SPIRITUAL TRANSFORMATION MAY BE NEEDED TO FORGIVE

Our primary theoretical objective is to improve your understanding of forgiveness by using a nuanced set of predictors that are related to religion and spirituality. We believe this will be useful whether your clients are religious in a traditional way or see themselves more as spiritual. In particular, we view religion and spirituality from a point of view we call relational spirituality (see Figure 2.1), as we described in the previous chapter. We adjusted the original stress-and-coping model of forgiveness (see Figure 1.1) by adding considerations of both attachment relational templates and religion and spirituality, which we described in Chapter 1. The adjusted stress-and-coping model intersects the relational spirituality model, which we described in Chapter 2.

In the present chapter, we first describe the third portion of our theory—the *forgiveness and relational spirituality structural model* (see Figure 3.1). It lays out the relationships among the major participants in resolving a transgression.

Second, we describe a model that unites the three component models: stress-and-coping, relational spirituality, and the relational and spirituality

http://dx.doi.org/10.1037/14712-004
Forgiveness and Spirituality in Psychotherapy: A Relational Approach, by E. L. Worthington, Jr. and S. J. Sandage

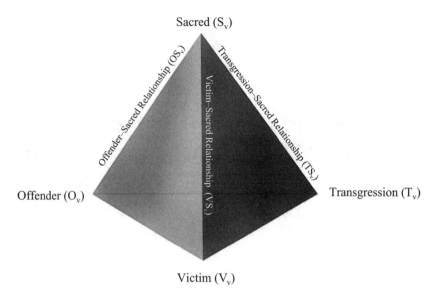

Figure 3.1. The relational spirituality and forgiveness structural model. OS = victim's appraisal of the relationship between the offender and the Sacred; VS = victim's appraisal of his or her own relationship with the Sacred; TS = victim's appraisal of the relationship between the transgression and the sacred. From "Relational Spirituality and Forgiveness: The Roles of Attachment to God, Religious Coping, and Viewing the Transgression as a Desecration," by D. E. Davis, J. N. Hook, and E. L. Worthington, Jr., 2008, *Journal of Psychology and Christianity, 27*, p. 294. Copyright 2008 by the Christian Association for Psychological Studies, Inc. Reprinted with permission.

structural model. We call the three-component combined model the *forgiveness and relational spirituality process model*. It describes how relational spirituality—which is about how people relate to sacred objects—can influence one's response to the offender, one's experience of the transgression, one's experience of stress and coping through forgiveness (adjusted to consider attachment templates and religion and spirituality), and how the entire model fits together to produce changes over time (see Figure 3.2).

THE FORGIVENESS AND RELATIONAL SPIRITUALITY STRUCTURAL MODEL

D. E. Davis, Hook, and Worthington (2008) initially described the forgiveness structural and relational spirituality model. We depict it in Figure 3.1. The figure describes a victim (V), offender (O), transgression (T), and some sacred object (S). There are relationships between each combination of two variables: VO, VT, OT, and also relationships of each (V, O, and T) with the sacred, VS, OS, and TS.

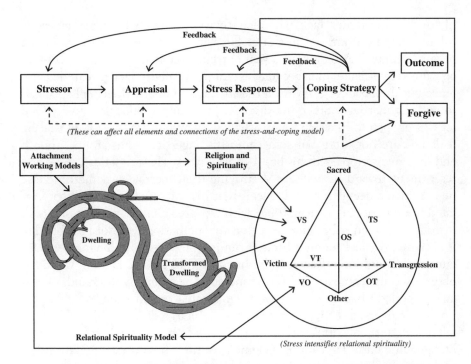

Figure 3.2. The full forgiveness and relational spirituality process model, which combines (a) the stress-and-coping model (top boxes) with (b) the relational spirituality model (circular figure in bottom left), which is in turn affected by (c) the attachment working models (shown as a box with arrow pointed at the relational spirituality model) and connected with (d) the forgiveness and relational spirituality structural model (lower right). From "Relational Spirituality and Forgiveness: The Roles of Attachment to God, Religious Coping, and Viewing the Transgression as a Desecration," by D. E. Davis, J. N. Hook, and E. L. Worthington, Jr., 2008, *Journal of Psychology and Christianity, 27*, p. 294. Copyright 2008 by the Christian Association for Psychological Studies, Inc. Adapted with permission.

Assessment

We have found or developed a number of psychometrically sound measures to aid its investigation, and we review those in detail in Chapter 4. In many cases, measures to assess constructs of the model were not available when we began this project. Our aim was to create measures that were strong psychometrically for use in research and also that were relatively brief to enable their use in clinical practice.

The Forgiveness and Relational Spirituality Structural Model Illustrated

The most central part of relational spirituality is someone's experience of relational dynamics with the sacred (Shults & Sandage, 2006). Consider a highly religious father, Jack, who recently went through a divorce. His wife, Julia, cheated on him not just once but with several men as the marriage began to unravel. After almost a year of trying to repair the damage, conflict continued to escalate, Julia became blatant in her affairs, Jack threatened violence but then backed away from the threat, and finally the couple decided to end the marriage. Since the divorce, Jack cannot understand why God let this happen to him. He frequently feels complaints against God that he feels he dare not utter, but sometimes his anger leaks out around church and in conversations with his best buddy at work. He feels a deep anger and resentment toward his wife for destroying their marriage—something else he considered deeply sacred. He feels that his wife first desecrated—or violated the sanctity of—the marriage with repeated affairs, and then she took it from him when it became clear that reconciliation was not possible. He is bothered because he finds himself ruminating often and having vengeful fantasies toward Julia. Recently, he has gotten in trouble at work when his obsession caused an expensive error and cost the company thousands of dollars in spoiled lab analyses that lost them a valuable customer.

Moreover, after the divorce, he sees Julia in a different light. He once felt a deep spiritual connection with her. Now he questions whether she ever had genuine faith. He cannot imagine how he will continue a relationship with Julia, as they attempt to parent their two children.

To study experiences such as Jack's, we can examine how the victim's interpretation of the relational context of a transgression affects his or her emotional response to that transgression. That response in turn affects whether he forgives the transgressor. Following theorizing by Exline, Worthington, Hill, and McCullough (2003), emotional forgiveness occurs when the victim replaces negative emotions with positive, other-oriented emotions.

Victim (V)

People appraise the components of a forgiveness experience. These include aspects of themselves as victim—their own beliefs and values about religion, about forgiveness, about other people, and about interactions. They also include their own self-construals as being fundamentally an independent entity, a relational interactant, or part of a larger collectivistic group. The V component also includes people's own sense of self-control and likelihood of using various potential coping strategies.

Let us briefly consider the victim's self-construal because this is crucial to the person's openness to relational intervention. People tend to construe themselves in one of three ways that describe their relationship with others (Kashima et al., 1995)—as *independent* of others, as *relational* (e.g., "I'm Julia's husband, my kids' father, my grandkids' grandfather, and a member of the nanotech design team at work"), or as *collectivistic* (e.g., "I'm an American and a Democrat"). Collectivistic self-construal is characteristic of many people within Eastern, Middle Eastern, and African cultures. How one construes oneself—independent, relational, or collectivistic—has been found to be related to various emotions, many types of cognition, and various behaviors (R. E. Johnson & Chang, 2006). Self-construal has also been related to perception of conflict (Gelfand et al., 2001).

Victim self-appraisals affect whether people forgive, both directly and indirectly through how those personality characteristics interact with the offender's personality characteristics and behavior. For example, people might believe they have traits that make them agreeable, forgiving, or grateful. They could see themselves as willing to let minor transgressions slide or as nonjudgmental. Or, less positively, they might simply not want to call attention to their own wrongs. Self-perceptions can push people toward forgiving. On the other hand, they can perceive themselves as being highly justice-oriented, fair, having a moral duty to punish wrongdoers, conscientious, and rational. Those characteristics might influence their unwillingness to forgive.

Internal conflicts are common. For example, people appraise their own behavior against their perceived self-construal regarding their beliefs, values, and commitments. Perhaps a woman sees herself as independent, but she is a member of a Buddhist organization whose norm is to call for deep compassion for others. She must arrive at some sense of self that enables her to deal with the conflict between her independence-oriented sense of the necessity of dispassionate justice and fairness and the deep compassion her Buddhist beliefs prescribe toward the offender.

Offender (O)

The person-as-victim, Jack in our example, also perceives the offender (Julia). Jack sees what his wife is doing, and he interprets the meaning of her behavior, too. Jack is aware of her beliefs and values. Jack is cognizant of Julia's years of love of him and their children, but he might believe that she no longer cares and has put her own needs above those of him and their family. It is important to note that Jack does not really know what Julia is thinking. He is using his theory of mind, empathy, and his experience of many years' interactions with Julia and is imagining what she might be thinking and experiencing. But that perception, not any kind of objective reality, is governing his behavior. Jack probably has a sense of self-doubt about his ability to perceive Julia correctly. It is likely that he did not predict that Julia would have multiple affairs and abandon the family. That experience of unpredictability undoubtedly undermined some of Jack's confidence. So, the victim's perception of the offender is going to figure in to whether he can forgive and under what conditions.

Transgression (T)

Jack perceives the transgression. It might seem more or less hurtful, more or less permanent, and more or less serious. The transgression might seem mostly a physical transgression or as having mostly psychological impact. It might be seen as stable or changeable. It might be seen as internally or externally caused.

Relationships Among Victim, Offender, and Transgression

It is important to note that victims also appraise the relationships between the victim, offender, and transgression. Those relationships are, from the standpoint of the forgiveness and relational spirituality structural model, at least as (if not more) important as the characteristics of the actors.

Victim–Other (VO) Relationship. Relationships are multifaceted and complex. In most psychology departments, there is a course on interpersonal relationships. The nature of the relationships is thus so complicated that whatever we say here is a drop in the bucket.

From the point of view of transgressions, however, one distinction is vital. How valuable is the relationship (McCullough, 2008)? Nonvaluable relationships can be between strangers (i.e., someone mugs you) or between estranged people who do not intend to continue to interact (i.e., ex-partners who have moved apart), or people who do not care what each other thinks (i.e., an ex-partner whom one disdains). A valuable relationship is one that has some direct or indirect value to the person. Kin relationships are usually among the most valuable (all other things being equal), and these include romantic partners who have stated some decision to be monogamously related to each other. Friends and coworkers can be valuable for different reasons. People higher up on the social ladder, such as work supervisors or people with monetary resources people might covet, are valuable materially. Valuable relationships can provide emotional or self-esteem-enhancing support, instrumental support (i.e., tangible aid), directive guidance, and positive social interaction (e.g., friendship, companionship). Those with secure attachment templates tend to value relationships with people capable of reciprocity and health dynamics, whereas those with insecure attachment templates and severe unresolved trauma tend to have more chronic struggles with relational estrangement. We discuss these attachment struggles in greater depth in Chapter 8.

Valuable relationships have been shown to be important in promoting forgiveness (McCullough, 2008; McCullough, Luna, Berry, Tabak, & Bono, 2010). McCullough et al. (2010) found that a self-report measure of the value of relationships predicted change in people's forgiveness over a period of 21 days. Burnette, McCullough, Van Tongeren, and Davis (2012) found that the value of a relationship and the likelihood of being exploited were both considered by the cognitive systems that people use in making forgiveness decisions. That is, people are most likely to forgive people who are valuable to them and who are unlikely to exploit them.

Victim–Transgression (VT) Relationship. Jack perceives that he has a relationship to the transgression. Perhaps he feels that this particular transgression is particularly personally directed at him. Julia's betrayal is not just a betrayal because she could not control her lust; rather, it is a betrayal she perpetrated mostly to hurt him (personally) because she knew of the personal devastation that came from the infidelity of his mother during his school years, which tore his family of origin apart. He might also feel that the transgression is repairable, personally, by him. He might believe that he can put his relationship back in order by dealing with it. In fact, he might hold the (probably irrational) belief that if he is willing to forgive and forget, the relationship will return to its early status.

Offender–Transgression (OT) Relationship. Jack probably has a number of ways he evaluates the relationship between offender and transgression. He might think of it in the classic sense of attribution theory. That is, he might think that the offender more or less intentionally offended. The transgression could be seen as arising from the offender's personality and thus inevitably a part of the offender, or as something that the offender put on due to circumstances and could just as well take off. In the movie *You've Got Mail* (Ephron, Donner, & Ephron, 1998), Tom Hanks plays Joe Fox, head of the huge discount book store, Fox Books. He drives Meg Ryan's character, Kathleen Kelly, out of business. She had owned a neighborhood book specialty shop, "The Little Shop Around the Corner." Kathleen was devastated. Joe was philosophical: "It's not personal," he says. "It's just business." Kathleen responds, "It's very personal to me."

The relationship each sees between the self and the transgression is different. Whether Kathleen will forgive Joe, how easily, and under what circumstances depends both on how she perceives the victim–transgression relationship and how she perceives Joe's offender–transgression relationship.

Displaying the Model Graphically

This model (thus far) might be displayed graphically (see Figure 3.1) as a triangular base of the pyramid, with corners representing V, O, and T. The sides of the triangular base are represented by the relationships between each—VO, VT, and OT.

To simplify, we describe the model from only the victim's perspective. The model helps us predict how the victim does or does not decide to forgive. We can better understand the various internal and external forces that push the victim toward or away from forgiveness, therefore providing more and more profitable entry points into psychotherapy.

Thus, VO describes that victim's perception of the relationship between himself or herself and the offender. The offender might have a different understanding of the relationship (and if we wanted to be complete, we would draw another pyramid with a triangular base from the point of view of the offender). Also, VT describes the victim's perspective of his or her relationship with the transgression (i.e., "Do I really perceive that this is 'just business' and doesn't affect the woman I put out of business?"). Finally, the victim also perceives the offender's relationship to the transgression ("Until Kathleen said what she did, I didn't give it much thought beyond my adage, 'It's just business,' but now, I see that she thinks of the transgression very personally").

Relationships Among Victim, Offender, Transgression, and the Sacred

For individuals for whom spirituality is central to their way of interpreting experience, the relational appraisals among the three elements and the sacred—victim (V), offender (O), and transgression (T) plus the sacred (S)—will be important. (Graphically, this adds the sacred, S, at the top of the model, resulting in the pyramid in Figure 3.1.) Spiritual appraisals that lead to positive emotions and to intentions to behave prosocially toward the offender can promote emotional forgiveness (D. E. Davis, Worthington, Hook, Van Tongeren, Green, & Jennings, 2009). Spiritual appraisals that lead to negative emotions and motives to seek vengeance or avoidance can make emotional forgiveness more difficult.

Sacred (S). People have a sense of what they consider sacred. (Remember, this is from V's perspective.) They might have an ultimate sacred source, such as God or humanity or nature or simply the aspects of life that are beyond comprehension and seen as "higher" or "transcendent." We have called these types of spirituality religious spirituality, human spirituality, nature spirituality, and transcendent spirituality, respectively. People might hold many things to be sacred—the marriage or family, the country, the right to privacy or self-determination, the right to life, or the right to freedom from coercion. People might hold a scattered array of objects to be sacred—God and holy scriptures, but at the same time, humans, nature, and transcendent goals, as well as political, social, or economic objects. There might be some relative hierarchy, or not.

Spiritual Relationships and Relational Spirituality. Thus, people who have been offended (V) may appraise three spiritual relationships (see Figure 3.1) in making decisions about whether to forgive: relationships, as they see them, between (a) themselves and the Sacred (VS); (b) the offender and the sacred (OS); and (c) the transgression and the sacred (TS). We have described the VS relationship as a good example of relational spirituality because it involves a human connection with the sacred, not merely as a correlation between variables but as a relationship between a person and a sacred object.

Victim–Sacred (VS) Relationship. The relationships between the victim and the sacred can be operationalized many ways. Sandage and his colleagues (Williamson & Sandage, 2009) have used *intrinsic religious motivation* (i.e., religion for its own sake) as one way to think of the relationship of someone dwelling in their religious position. High intrinsic motivation could indicate a strong positive connection between a person and the religious sacred. *Extrinsic religious motivation* could also be a measure of religious dwelling, but the dwelling might be occurring for instrumental reasons other than religion for its own sake—such as for business contacts, romantic relationships, social connections, and the like. As Shults and Sandage (2006) observed, times of religious seeking might be either a stable position or part of the fluctuating dialectic of balancing dwelling and seeking with regard to religion. *Quest motivation* (Batson, Schoenrade, & Ventis, 1993) is a measure of such seeking.

Other Measures of Religious and Spiritual Dwelling

Among the many other potential measures of religious or spiritual dwelling within the spiritual relationship between victim and the sacred are the following. The degree of contemplative prayer, in which the praying person contemplates God and spiritual experiences (usually with serene and positive affect) can indicate a desire to strengthen the relationship with the sacred. (Notably, other types of prayer, such as prayers of petition might indicate a period of unsettledness and quest in which the praying person asks or demands that God meets demands or desires.) D. E. Davis, Hook, Worthington, Van Tongeren, Gartner, and Jennings (2010) created a nine-item measure of spiritual humility to indicate satisfied dwelling with the sacred (i.e., the Spiritual Humility Scale). Rowatt and Kirkpatrick (2002) created a measure of attachment to God. The Experiences in Close Relationships has been used to measure not just attachment relationships with other adults but also attachment relationship with God. In that measure, people receive scores on attachment anxiety and avoidance. Low scores on each indicate a secure attachment to the sacred.

Other Measures of Religious and Spiritual Seeking

Among the many other potential measures of religious or spiritual seeking are several that suggest a time of searching. These could include spiritual openness (Williamson & Sandage, 2009), spiritual disappoint with God or anger at God (Exline & Martin, 2005; Exline, Park, Smyth, & Carey, 2011; Exline, Yali, & Lobel, 1999; Wood et al., 2010), or evidence or self-report of a recent spiritual transformation (Miller & C'de Baca, 2001).

Offender–Sacred (OS) Relationships. How the victim perceives the relationship of the offender with the sacred can affect forgiveness. The absolute relationship with the sacred might matter. For example, D. E. Davis, Hook,

Worthington, Van Tongeren, Gartner, Jennings, and Norton (2010) created the four-item Relational Engagement of the Sacred in a Transgression scale. It uses the following items to assess the other's spiritual relationship: "I tried to view him/her as a child of God," "I asked God to help me see his/her good points," "I tried to pray for him/her," and "I believe God wants us to mend our relationship." Also, the similarity or difference of the offender's relationship with the sacred relative to the victim's own relationship could also matter (see the Similarity of the Offender's Spirituality scale; D. E. Davis, Worthington, Hook, Van Tongeren, Green, & Jennings, 2009). Assessment of the spiritual similarity of the two is important to discerning whether the victim believes the offender a spiritual outgroup member.

Transgression and Sacred (TS). The victim's perception of the offender–transgression relationship is concerned with whether the offender offended in such a way to provoke a spiritual loss or a desecration of something that the victim considers sacred. Pargament, Magyar, Benore, and Mahoney (2005) showed that such judgments are highly related to reluctance to forgive.

Jack's Relationships With the Sacred and Their Impact on the VO, VT, and OT Relationships

For example, Jack might exhibit decidedly varied reactions based on various spiritual factors. He may experience strong anger at God (VS). Anger at God promotes powerful, negative emotions that can make forgiveness more difficult (Exline et al., 1999; Wood et al., 2010). He might also view Julia as dissimilar at spiritual (OS) and human (O) levels. His experience of her as spiritually alien could affect his relationship with her (VO), making it difficult to empathize with her. He might also experience the divorce (T) as a destruction or desecration of something sacred (TS)—his marriage or family—as well as a slap at him personally (VT) by a person who would intentionally hurt those she loves (OT). This would affect his view of her as a person (O). Appraising a transgression to be a desecration—such as when people reported that the 9/11 attack on the United States was a violation of sacred national identity or such as when an estranged wife feels that her husband's rejection of marriage is a violation of the sacred marriage vows—has been found to make forgiveness difficult (D. E. Davis et al., 2008).

FORGIVENESS AND RELATIONAL SPIRITUALITY PROCESS MODEL

We depict the full forgiveness and relational spirituality process model in Figure 3.2. This provides a suggestion of how the model might describe, over time, the unfolding of forgiveness (or not) in transgressions that involve religious and spiritual involvement.

How the Stress-and-Coping Model Connects to Relational Spirituality

In Shults and Sandage's (2006) model of relational spirituality, stress is increased by religious and spiritual uncertainty associated with usual religious and spiritual anchors becoming unmoored. In addition, increased stress in turn is a characteristic of the crucible of walking through religious and spiritual uncertainty. Self-differentiation can affect a person's ability to hold the stress. Effective helping can provide a holding relationship that can, in itself, permit the person to have enough sense of safety and containment to maintain the religious or spiritual uncertainty of seeking without needing to escape or triangle others into the system to provide a potential rescuer.

Thus, stress is the major pathway to relational spirituality. In Figure 3.2, we did not draw the two-way arrow of influence from relational spirituality back to increased stress, but it is certainly a major factor in whether a person appraises his or her ability to cope, experiences a higher level of stress, and narrows attention to a limited number of coping mechanisms.

As the relational spirituality processes unfold, the person might experience the paradoxes of seeking and dwelling. The person relates to the sacred differently, depending on where in the process he or she is. Thus, the relational spirituality model affects the forgiveness and relational spirituality structural model by affecting the VS relationship and quite possibly aspects of the self (V), such as beliefs and values. In terms of the VS relationship, it might affect the emotions toward the sacred (i.e., anger, disappointment, deep faith, trust, uncertainty, anxiety), motivations toward the sacred (does one continue to pursue a close relationship or does the nature of the relationship change to become more standoffish), beliefs (one's theological or philosophical beliefs might change or one might either abandon an existing faith in the sacred or embrace a faith not formerly held), and/or practices (perhaps usual patterns of behavior, e.g., regular prayer, are changed by either less or more frequent prayer).

How Relational Spirituality Connects to the Structural Model

As the person (V) moves through dwelling and seeking, the VS relationship is modified dynamically as experiences unfold. The nature and quality of the relationship can change, and both nature and quality might swing dramatically—even from belief in a sacred object to rejection of the object, or from love to anger or to indifference (or vice versa).

Thus, the stress-and-coping model not only is affected by the forgiveness and relational spirituality model directly by feeding into appraisals, stress reaction, and coping but also directly affects the model through attachment-based relational appraisals, which can affect most elements and relationships in the structural model. Also, as stress intensifies, the structural model (particularly the VS relationship) is affected indirectly through the relational spirituality model. Stress intensifies the tension between the dwelling and seeking and creates a cauldron in which the spiritual processes interact. That drives the person to seek relief by resolving the tension, fleeing from it, or seeking to triangle in a rescuer.

How the Structural Model and the Stress-and-Coping Models Connect

Most of the forgiveness and relational spirituality structural model involves the relation-laden ways that a victim perceives or interprets the situation—incorporating appraising the sacred, the self, the offender and the transgression and their interrelationships—and the way he or she decides to act (i.e., whether to forgive or to respond with self-protective freezing, fleeing, or attacking). This calculus is almost never rational logic because it involves the neocortex, limbic system, and brain stem (Cozolino, 2006). Instead, it is quick, intuitive, automatic, and uses shortcuts based primarily on relational images and emotions (System 1 cognition; see Kahneman, 2011). Fast and intuitive as it is, System 1 is surprisingly adaptive most of the time. But sometimes it is just wrong. We might note, though, that logical and rational reasoning (System 2) does not necessarily lead to better solutions. First, the quality of conclusion from System 2 reasoning depends on assumptions, perceptions, and other input—all of which are heavily saturated by System 1 judgments. Thus, thinking logically through something might make us more confident of the conclusions, but ironically, the conclusions are faulty just as often, and (what can be worse), we are more confident and less humble about our certainty of conclusion.

The major connections to the stress-and-coping model are thus at the level of appraisals, the effect on stress reaction, and choice of coping. In Chapter 1, we described the appraisal of the degree of injustice experienced through a transgression, which we called the injustice gap (Exline et al., 2003). That also led to a primary appraisal (i.e., Is this likely to be harmful to me or my relationships?). If it is likely to be harmful, then the person makes a secondary appraisal (i.e., Can I cope to control or minimize the negative effects?). If the person appraises the event as likely to be harmful and coping is not likely, the person will conclude with a threat appraisal. Threat appraisals are more common when someone has an insecure attachment template. When one concludes either that the event is not likely to be harmful or, even if it is, one can probably cope successfully, the person concludes that this is a challenge, not a threat. The sympathetic nervous system is engaged to deal with challenges. Coping that is usually associated with threat—freezing, fleeing, or fighting, or denial, deliberation, and decision to act (Worthington, 2006)—and focusing on survival are not triggered (Sapolsky, 1994).

The elements of the forgiveness and relational spirituality model are engaged in the appraisals. For example, Jack appraises his physical and psychological, moral, and spiritual resources in being able to cope (secondary appraisal). But in addition, the likelihood of harm depends on many of the relationships he is experiencing. For example, whether he forgives or not Julia's infidelities can affect not only his relationship with Julia (VO) but also his relationship with his children, especially if hostility with Julia trickles into his parenting relationships. He might also evaluate an inability to forgive as affecting his own relationship with the sacred (VS). As we observed in the previous section, his ability to forgive is affected literally by every element in the model of forgiveness and relational spirituality—the nodes (V, O, T, and S)—and also the relationships (VO, VT, OT, VS, OS, and TS).

The other major connector of the two models is in coping. People engage in religious coping. Thus, methods of religious coping, as with praying for God's intercession or petitionary prayer, are associated with higher spiritual dwelling. Negative religious coping, such as flight from God or prayers of cursing of the enemy or defensive distraction, can be related to spiritual seeking or to holding onto a tenuous belief system.

Graphically Depicting the Forgiveness and Relational Spirituality Process Model

In Figure 3.2, we depict the synthetic three-component model. Across the top is the stress-and-coping model of forgiveness (see Worthington, 2006) with the resultant arrows leading to forgiveness and to other outcomes (e.g., improved physical and mental health, relationships, and spiritual life). Stress intensifies processes in relational spirituality. Thus, a solid arrow points directly to the dwelling and seeking cycles of the relational spirituality model (Shults & Sandage, 2006). The structural model (shaped as a pyramid; see D. E. Davis et al., 2008) is beneath the stress-and-coping model of forgiveness. It has a (dark) causal arrow from the pyramid to forgiveness as the outcome in the stress-and-coping model. It has (lighter, dotted) arrows to all elements of the stress-and-coping model of forgiveness. Finally, the relational spirituality model, depicted as the dwelling and seeking cycles of Shults and Sandage (2006) is located to the left of the forgiveness and relational spirituality model, with an arrow pointing to the VS connection. We have add two other considerations—attachment working models and religion and spirituality, which point to the dwelling and seeking cycle and (especially religion and spirituality) connect to the VS portion of the forgiveness and relational spirituality model.

In line with stress-and-coping models by Lazarus and Folkman (1984) and Lazarus (1999) and the stress-and-religious-coping model by Pargament

(1997) within spiritual coping, we note that the model is recursive. That is, virtually any box can feed back to affect other boxes and virtually any path operates in two directions (despite the simple linear depiction in the figure). Because the processes are not necessarily linear, it is a mistake to take the model as if it were a causative, time-driven model. Rather, scientists and clinicians must observe the ways the variables change and redirect emphases the person deals with transgressions.

PUTTING SOME FLESH AND BLOOD INTO THE MODEL

I (Everett Worthington) met Father Elias Chacour at the State of the World Forum in 2000, and I had the privilege of sitting by him at a banquet one night. Although I heard him speak and was inspired by his stories, I did not know what a powerful person I had met until I returned home and read his book (with Hazard), *Blood Brothers: A Palestinian Struggles for Reconciliation in the Middle East* (1984). Chacour's story can help us understand the powerful forces of religion that push people toward and away from forgiveness, reconciliation, and peace.

Father Chacour was born in a small Palestinian village of Biram in 1939 into a Melkite Christian family. As a child, he suffered a public beating that took years to forgive. He also was witness to the destruction of Biram. The village residents were told that they were in danger and Israeli soldiers could protect them if they left the village. Villagers did leave, but while they were away, the village was destroyed and the land taken over to become part of the new state of Israel.

Yet Father Chacour was not bitter. As an adult and Melkite Christian, Father Chacour became President of a university with about one third Christian students, one third Jewish, and one third Muslim students. He also served as a humble parish priest at a local village, yet he became a leader for reconciliation among Palestinian Christians, Jews, Muslims, and Druze.

At the 2000 State of the World Forum, he described an incident in which a disturbed Israeli man entered a Muslim worship service and shot praying worshippers. "I wrote a letter to the Israeli government protesting," said Father Chacour (2000). In retaliation for the shooting, a Muslim terrorist exploded himself and injured over 80 people in a market suicide bombing; "To be fair, I wrote a letter also protesting that violence."

This interreligious violence is religion at its worst. It is ingroup and outgroup boundaries marked with blood of innocent victims. It is connection with the sacred but twisted by the desecration of religious life, caused by violent provocation, and empowered by group identity. That power and provocation, for a few people, can incite blood lust. For most people, it leads to horror, fear, and shame that someone from their religious group had behaved so badly.

Father Chacour said, "My students asked, 'Have you become an American? When Americans are upset, they write a letter to their congressman. They think they have solved the problem. That is not enough.'"

"What should we do?" he asked them.

"We want to give our blood to help the injured Jews."

He told the Forum, "So, I asked the Israeli government whether they would send a bus that could take blood. They sent 15 buses with 15 nurses. I was terrified that would be too many, but the 15 nurses pumped my queued-up students' blood from morning to early afternoon."

"We became blood brothers. The blood of my Jewish, Christian, and Muslim students flows in those 80 injured Jewish victims of that bombing. We were not born Jew, Christian, or Muslim. We were born *babies*." (Note his invocation of "babies" that could implicitly activate the attachment system.)

This is religion and spirituality at its best. Redemptive religion and sincere spirituality are about people's relationships with the sacred that empowers them to give their own blood to help babies who grow up and become people of different religions. Their own personal relationships are also involved. The students obviously had talked to and encouraged each other to go to the university President and confront him. Father Chacour revealed his relationship with his students by his willingness to listen to their confrontation and not react to the challenge to his authority but to respond in humility and love to the spirituality of his students.

This was only one of many times that Father Chacour's spirituality led him to act in personally costly and risky ways to promote peace. On August 13, 1972, Father Chacour and Bishop Joseph Raya led a march of Christians, Muslims, Jews, and Druze to the Israel Knesset to advocate for a peaceful settlement of hostilities between Palestinians and Jews. The desired meeting requested between Bishop Raya and Premier Golda Meir did not take place, and Father Chacour was discouraged. Father Chacour had, for years, seen peace as a slender and fragile thread, easily snipped. But he had, in the end, seen that it was more like a chain with every link vital. That bond with the sacred also can be a fragile thread or a steel chain. It is helped to become that chain as people engage in mutually encouraging and edifying relationships and those relationships spread out from the spiritual into the world of the secular.

At one point in 1967, Father Chacour was priest at a parish church in the village of Ibillin. The congregation was strained because four brothers were feuding in the small village. The eldest, Abu Mouhib, the village police officer, was filled with hate for his brothers, and he—and the brothers—had threatened violence if they met. Worship services were tense, with Abu Mouhib and his family sitting in the front of the church, and his three brothers in three other quadrants of the church as far apart as possible. Father Chacour was discouraged that four Christian brothers in his congregation might come to vengeful violence. But God convinced him that their hatred of brothers was a sign of his own and others' hatred of others born babies but embracing different beliefs as adults. He asked forgiveness of God, and then confronted the four brothers one Sunday. At the end of a service, he apologized that he, as a limited man, could not help the brothers forgive and reconcile. In response, Abu Mouhib rose and confessed his hatred and vengefulness and walked deliberately toward the back where his brothers were. "Before he was halfway down the aisle, his three brothers had rushed to him. They held each other in a long embrace, each one asking for forgiveness of the others" (pp. 170–171).

The characters in Father Chacour's anecdotes practiced relational spirituality and they reappraised their hurts and prejudices, found a sense of new meaning, and found the courage to act to promote reconciliation. In the process, they forgave. In Father Chacour's stories, it was not just Christian forgiveness that was practiced. Rather, Muslims, Jews, and Druze people of faith and also Christians practiced sincere relational spirituality. And forgave.

Religion and spirituality can either promote or inhibit forgiveness. For example, most people adopt a practical context for interactions by judging a person's religious or spiritual similarity to themselves. For people high in religious commitment or spiritual identification, that is a major evaluative criterion. For people less involved in a religion or spiritual framework, they pay little attention to religion or spirituality of the offender with a few exceptions, outlined below.

First, if the offender is blatantly religious in some offensive or highly salient way, that draws the potential forgiver's attention to the religious context. If the offender highlights similarity or difference, that too can draw the potential forgiver's attention to the religious context. If a religious issue or spiritual issue is at the root of the offense, that will certainly highlight religious or spiritual similarities or differences. We have developed a rating scale for measuring perceived religious or spiritual similarity and difference with an offender (D. E. Davis et al., 2008; D. E. Davis, Worthington, Hook, Van Tongeren, Green, & Jennings, 2009; see the Appendix of this book). Religious or spiritual similarity can make the same offense more hurtful when inflicted by a person considered to be spiritually similar to the victim relative to one who is perceived to be spiritually different. However, most people are more eager to forgive transgressions by in-group members than by out-group members. It makes more differentiation to forgive out-group members.

Second, anger at God on behalf of the potential forgiver can certainly affect responses of forgiveness, which the Wood et al. (2010) scale measures. In our work, we blend some of the understandings of Worthington's (2006) stress-and-coping theory of forgiveness with the forgiveness and relational spirituality model. These provide a good framework for practitioners to understand forgiveness and the contexts in which it is considered and either granted or not, communicated or not.

SUMMARY

In this chapter, we laid out the forgiveness and relational spirituality structural model and described its components. We then drew together into a large synthetic model the interconnections among the stress-and-coping model, the dwelling-and-seeking relational spirituality model, and the structural model. Finally, we illustrated some of the concepts with the life of a person in a highly stressful boiling pot—Palestine. One might ask whether all of this is mere theorizing or whether it works; in the next chapter, we summarize briefly the research supporting these models.

4

EVIDENCE SUPPORTING THE MODELS

How much would it matter to have specific knowledge about the nature of this problem? Is the improvement in outcome that might occur if I use this new treatment with this client worth the cost I will incur in breaking out of my normal treatment protocol to learn to use it effectively? Those are the types of questions that busy psychotherapists ask themselves every day. Are the benefits worth the costs—for this client? But hidden beneath the surface are other questions: Will the benefits extend to other clients? Will my self-satisfaction at understanding the worlds of clients that I didn't really understand previously add enough to the benefits to make learning new things rewarding?

And underneath all, is this theory true at the basic level? Or does it simply "work" as a treatment—even one that is based on a wrong theory?

Each portion of our approach has evidence supporting it—the stress-and-coping model of forgiveness, the model of relational spirituality involving

http://dx.doi.org/10.1037/14712-005
Forgiveness and Spirituality in Psychotherapy: A Relational Approach, by E. L. Worthington, Jr. and S. J. Sandage

dwelling and seeking, the forgiveness and relational spirituality structural model, and connections among the models represented in the process model. But the type and amount of evidence differs in each case. In this chapter, we give a bird's eye view of the evidence—exploring the following questions: What do we really know about this forgiveness and relational spirituality process model and its components? Is there enough evidence to convince you that you are better off knowing the model than not? We have summarized the results of many studies in tables, in written summaries of studies, and in a final overall summary. If you want to delve in, we hope you'll benefit by the reading and not feel that you are drinking from a research fire hose. If this is still too tedious for you, read about the measures we developed for research and clinical use (pp. 94–98), then skip to the last major heading in the chapter and read the 13 summary findings (pp. 109–111).

ESTABLISHING WHETHER A TREATMENT IS EVIDENCE BASED

Luisa and Carlos, from the Introduction chapter, have a 14-year relationship on the skids, and their son, Jamie, was busted at school for sending naked pictures to girls—something he had learned from other youth who attended his church. Luisa was engaged with psychotherapy, though Carlos was withdrawn. Luisa had found cognitive behavior therapy (CBT) and Gottman's couples therapy on the Internet, and she wondered whether those would help. When treating people such as Luisa, does it really matter that we have a theoretical understanding of her problems, or can we simply find a manual of an empirically supported treatment, such as Gottman's (1999) integrative behavior therapy, or CBT for her anxiety, and apply it to her? After all, Luisa herself referred to those treatments and is presumably open to trying them.

THE EVIDENCE WE ADDRESS IN THIS CHAPTER

In this chapter, we examine the evidence for the theory of change we have proposed in Chapters 1, 2, and 3. First, we summarize research on the forgiveness and relational spirituality model in three steps. We examine the scales that we and others have developed to assess the victim–sacred (VS), offender–sacred (OS), and transgression–sacred (TS) relationships (D. E. Davis, Hook, Van Tongeren, & Worthington, 2012; D. E. Davis, Hook, Worthington, Van Tongeren, Gartner, & Jennings, 2010; D. E. Davis, Hook, Worthington, Van Tongeren, Gartner, Jennings, & Emmons, 2011; D. E. Davis, Hook, Worthington, Van Tongeren, Gartner, Jennings, & Norton, 2010; D. E. Davis, Worthington, Hook, & Van Tongeren, 2009). To begin, in the first step, we point you to summaries of the stress-and-coping model of forgiveness (Worthington, 2006). That research is voluminous, so we just touch on it.

Second, we present evidence for the relational spirituality model of spiritual dwelling and seeking (Shults & Sandage, 2006; described in Chapter 2, this volume). That research on relational spirituality also specifically examined what religious and spiritual traits are interconnected around relational spirituality and connected to trait forgivingness. In doing this, we summarized results from Sandage and his colleagues, who examined the idea of relational spirituality (and sometimes its relationship to trait forgivingness) in more detail. As we saw earlier, Sandage has written theoretically about relational spirituality in collaboration with theologian LeRon Shults (Shults & Sandage, 2006) and others (Sandage, Jensen, & Jass, 2008; Sandage & Moe, 2011). We review some of the series of empirical studies on relational spirituality by Sandage and colleagues (e.g., Jankowski & Sandage, 2011, 2012, 2014b; Jankowski & Vaughn, 2009; Majerus, & Sandage, 2010; Sandage, Crabtree, & Schweer, 2014; Sandage & Harden, 2011; Sandage, Hill, & Vang, 2003; Sandage, Hill, & Vaubel, 2011; Sandage & Jankowski, 2010, 2013; Sandage, Link, & Jankowski, 2010; Sandage & Williamson, 2010; Williamson, Sandage, & Lee, 2007).

Third, we summarize the evidence supporting the forgiveness and relational spirituality structural model from Chapter 3 of the present book (D. E. Davis, Hook, & Worthington, 2008; D. E. Davis, Hook, Van Tongeren, Gartner, & Worthington, 2012; D. E. Davis, Hook, Van Tongeren, & Worthington, 2012; D. E. Davis, Hook, Worthington, Van Tongeren, Gartner, & Jennings, 2010; D. E. Davis et al., 2011; D. E. Davis, Worthington, & Hook, 2010; D. E. Davis, Worthington, Hook, Emmons, Hill, & Burnette, 2013; Greer, Worthington, Van Tongeren, et al., 2014; Van Tongeren, Green, Davis, Worthington, & Reid, 2013; Wood et al., 2010; Worthington, 2009; Worthington, Davis, Hook, Gartner, & Jennings, 2009; Worthington, Greer, et al., 2010). Research on the structural model has concentrated on the ways variables assessing the VS, OS, and TS relationships are related to forgiveness of a single hurt and, occasionally, to trait variables.

We did not summarize the evidence for the stress-and-coping theory of forgiveness (Chapter 1) because that model has been investigated and evidence adduced in Worthington (2006). Strelan and Covic (2006) also studied the stress-and-coping model of forgiveness. Sections of one chapter in Worthington (2006; Chapter 2) and other separate chapters (Chapters 3, 4, and 5) summarize extensive evidence supporting the following: (a) Hurt feelings activate the sociometer (i.e., fear of social rejection), which can lead to unforgiveness (Worthington, 2006; Chapter 2); (b) injustice gaps show that multiple injustices are additive and offender attempts to make amends are subtractive (Worthington, 2006; Chapter 2); (c) rumination turns injustices into unforgiveness, and the type of rumination (i.e., angry, fearful, or depressive) shapes the emotional tone of the unforgiveness (Berry, Worthington, O'Connor, Parrott, & Wade, 2005; Worthington, 2006; Chapter 2); (d) unforgiveness is a stress reaction (Worthington, 2006; Chapter 3); (e) forgiveness is one type of coping with injustices (Worthington, 2006; Chapter 2); (f) decisional and emotional forgiveness differ (Worthington, 2006; Chapter 2); (g) emotional experience and transformation is the key to the stress-and-coping model of forgiveness (Worthington, 2006; Chapter 4); and (h) emotional forgiveness happens by the emotional replacement hypothesis—replacing negative unforgiving emotions with positive other-oriented emotions (Worthington, 2006; Chapter 5).

INVESTIGATIONS OF RELATIONAL SPIRITUALITY WITH GRADUATE STUDENTS

As we see in subsequent sections, studies from Worthington's lab have aimed to find predictors of states of unforgiveness (avoidance and revenge) and forgiveness (benevolence and forgiveness). Sandage has been more interested in the model of relational spirituality as it applied to interrelationships among personality or dispositional traits.

Why Graduate Students?

Sandage's research has tested both undergraduate and graduate students who were moving through their professional degree programs in the helping professions in a religiously affiliated university (i.e., counseling, therapy, ministry, leadership, missions). Graduate students are a prime population to study changes in relational spirituality and the ways those changes might affect the development of the students over the course of a protracted education (Loder, 1998). A graduate school context can potentiate both spiritual dwelling and seeking in a highly religious context. Below are some reasons for this.

- Graduate-level students in seminaries, for example, are typically preparing for vocations that involve spiritual leadership, and they are nodes of socialization in a theological tradition. Upon entering their graduate education, most students expect to emerge from their training more theologically grounded and stronger in faith. However, curricula typically expose students to a variety of religious doctrines, spiritual practices, and faculty and students from other religious traditions, thus often instigated ambiguity, dissonance, and spiritual seeking.
- Seminaries and religious graduate schools have not been frequently studied, even though they are numerous and provide seminal training for those who tend to shape spiritual develop-

ment in the United States and throughout much of the world. There are currently more graduates trainees in seminaries in North America than in psychology graduate programs. There are also approximately 80 "faith-based" professional counseling training programs in North America, suggesting spiritually integrative counselor training is an important, understudied segment of the helping professions.

- Clergy (not psychologists) are the most commonly used helping profession in the United States for mental health problems (Weaver, Flannelly, Flannelly, & Oppenheimer, 2003).
- Religious institutions tend to value forgiveness even more than people who are not practicing a faith perspective, yet individual differences still emerge among the highly religious.
- Seminaries and religious graduate schools have increasingly emphasized spiritual formation recently (Shults & Sandage, 2006), although there has been limited empirical research on processes of spiritual formation and transformations among seminary students (Sandage & Jensen, 2013).
- The complexity of graduate education can thus affect how seminary students develop and change spiritually. Finke and Dougherty (2002) used national survey data of clergy across 45 denominations and found that the professionalization of seminary training might reduce students' emotional attachment to their prior spiritual practices unless spiritual formation is an intentional part of the seminary curriculum.

Summaries of Some Findings

Sandage and his colleagues (e.g., Williamson & Sandage, 2009) have collected longitudinal data from students at Bethel University in St. Paul, Minnesota, to address question of how students might change over their graduate education. They have published numerous studies from that rich, longitudinal data set (Sandage & Jankowski, 2010, 2013). We summarized many of the bivariate correlations in Table 4.1. We chose to highlight some particularly important variables across the top, and we looked study by study at the variables each study assessed down the x-axis. The multiple meditational relationships among the variables uncovered by Sandage and his colleagues' mining of this rich data set cannot be easily displayed in the table.

Trait Forgivingness

Some of the main conclusions in examining Table 4.1 are consistent (strong) relationships predicting measures of dispositional forgiveness by

TABLE 4.1
Studies Investigating the Forgiveness and Relational Spirituality Model
(Including Those That Relate Trait Forgivingness
to Relational Spirituality Variables)

Author (date)	Int rel (D)	Ext rel (D)	Med pray (D)	God att inse (D)	SWB (D)	Pos Aff (D)	Hope (D)	Grat (D)	Hum (D)	DoS (D)
Williamson & Sandage (2009) SWB	.30									
Sprt open	.11†									
Sprt act	.32†									
Realist accept	.28									
Sandage & Williamson (2010) Sprt disapt			−.10†							
Trait forgive			.20					.27		
Grat			.44							
Sandage & Jankowski (2010) Trait forgive						.38				.49
Psych sym										−.55
Pos Aff										.58
Sandage & Harden (2011) DoS	.34							.36		
Grat	.22									.36
Trait forgive	.28							.36		.56
Sandage, Hill, & Vaubel (2011) Grat	.34	−.08†								
Psych sym	−.30	.13†						−.27		
Jankowski & Sandage (2011) Trait forgive			.21				.34			
Hope–P			.13†							
Hope–A			.20							
Anx A			−.22							
Av A			−.24							
Neg Aff										−.38
Pos Aff										
Sprt dwell						.65				.53

Quest (S)	AnxA (S)	AvA (S)	Rcnt sprt transf (S)	Sprt grnd (S)	Pos rel cop	Neg rel cop	ICC	Soc sst cmt	Sprt disapt (S)	Sprt instb (S)	Psych sym (S)
−.11†											
.85											
.08†											
−.04†											
.25											
−.22										−.31	
−.13†										−.11†	
										−.34	−.33
										.33	
											−.48
.04†				.03†							
.02†				−.01†							
.05†				.11†							
−.13†			.02†								
.30			.06†								
	−.41	−.27									
	−.31	−.19									
	−.37	−.27									
							.76	.86			

(*continues*)

TABLE 4.1
Studies Investigating the Forgiveness and Relational Spirituality Model
(Including Those That Relate Trait Forgivingness
to Relational Spirituality Variables)   *(Continued)*

Author (date)	Int rel (D)	Ext rel (D)	Med pray (D)	God att inse (D)	SWB (D)	Pos Aff (D)	Hope (D)	Grat (D)	Hum (D)	DoS (D)
Sandage & Crabtree (2012), Study 1										
Trait forgive (Study 1)										
Trait forgive (Study 2)										
Sprt instb										
Sandage & Jankowski (2013)										
SWB (D)										.47
										.44
DoS (EC,FO)				.47						
				.44						
ICC										.23
										.26
Soc jus cmt										.10†
										.19
Sprt disapt										−.32
										−.35
Jankowski, Sandage, & Hill (2013)										
DoS									.66	
Psych sym									−.44	−.52
Soc jus cmt									.33	.22
Hum										.66
Trait forgive									.56	.59
Jankowski & Sandage (2014a)										
Hum				−.53						.64
DoS				−.51					.64	
God att inse										−.51
Realist accept				−.39					.27	.21
Realist explor				.21					−.05†	.11†

Quest (S)	AnxA (S)	AvA (S)	Rcnt sprt transf (S)	Sprt grnd (S)	Pos rel cop	Neg rel cop	ICC	Soc sst cmt	Sprt disapt (S)	Sprt instb (S)	Psych sym (S)
				.02†	.22	−.06†				−.24	
				−.22	.24	−.18†				−.31	
				−.20	−.24	.33					
							.23	.10†		−.32	
							.26	.19		−.35	
								.22			−.52
								−.15			
											−.15
								.33			−.44
								.31			−.32
										−.41	
										−.60	
										.47	
										−.21	
										.17	

(*continues*)

TABLE 4.1
Studies Investigating the Forgiveness and Relational Spirituality Model (Including Those That Relate Trait Forgivingness to Relational Spirituality Variables) *(Continued)*

Author (date)	Int rel (D)	Ext rel (D)	Med pray (D)	God att inse (D)	SWB (D)	Pos Aff (D)	Hope (D)	Grat (D)	Hum (D)	DoS (D)
Sandage, Crabtree, & Schweer (2014)										
Hope										
DoS							.40			
Soc jus cmt							.24			
Sandage & Morgan (2014)										
Pos rel cop							.18			
Hope										
Soc jus cmt							.19			
Sprt impres mgmt							.29			

Note. D = dwelling; S = seeking; Int rel = intrinsic religious motivation; Ext rel = extrinsic religious motivation; Med pray = meditative prayer; SWB = spiritual well-being; Pos Aff = Positive Affect; Trait forgive = trait forgivingness; Hope-P = Hope-Pathways (Snyder et al., 1991); Hope-A = Hope-Agency (Snyder et al., 1991); Grat = trait gratitude; Hum = humility; DoS = differentiation of self; Quest = Questing; AnxA = anxious attachment; AvA = avoidant attachment; Rcnt sprt transf = recent spiritual transformation; Sprt grnd = spiritual grandiosity; Pos rel cop = positive religious coping; Neg rel cop = negative religious coping; Soc jst cmt = social justice commitment; ICC = intercultural competence; Sprt disapt = spiritual disappointment; Sprt instb = spiritual instability; Psych sym = psychological symptoms; Sprt open = spiritual openness; Sprt act = spiritual activities; Sprt dwell = spiritual dwelling; EC = emotional cutoff; FO = differentiation of self (fusion with others); God att inse = insecure attachment to god; Realist accept = realistic acceptance; Realist explor = realistic exploration; Sprt impres mgmt = spiritual impression management.
[†]$p > .05$ (*ns*) in the particular study.

(a) positive measures of religiousness, (b) differentiation of self, (c) humility, (d) gratitude, (e) commitment to social justice, and (f) positive affect. Low trait forgivingness (i.e., trait unforgivingness) was related to negative measures of religiousness, spiritual seeking—that is, spiritual disappointment, questing, spiritual grandiosity—low relational attachment, unhappiness (as shown by more psychological symptoms). Forgivingness was not related to negative religious coping. By way of a simple generalization, we can say that people who are more forgiving by disposition and usually happier, more mature, more virtuous, and more positive than are people who are less forgiving.

Quest (S)	AnxA (S)	AvA (S)	Rcnt sprt transf (S)	Sprt grnd (S)	Pos rel cop	Neg rel cop	ICC	Soc sst cmt	Sprt disapt (S)	Sprt instb (S)	Psych sym (S)
								.24			
								.28			
								.20			
			.18					.19			
			.20								
			.41					.17			

Differentiation of Self

Differentiation of self was related positively to religious experiences (i.e., intrinsic religious motivation, which indicates pursuing religion for its own sake, instead of extrinsic religious motivation, which indicates pursuing religion to gain external benefits, such as social contacts or prestige) and negatively to insecure God attachment. It was completely unrelated to negative religious experiences. Differentiation of self was correlated with spiritual well-being and was negatively associated with psychological symptoms. It was consistently related to virtues such as humility, gratitude, and hope and prosocial virtues (i.e., intercultural competence, social justice commitment).

In short, both trait forgivingness and differentiation of self, two signs of maturity, are consistently related to religiously positive characteristics and their opposites are related to religiously negative experiences.

Spiritual Seeking

Questing (in which the person is in a stable seeking mode to settle on a set of religious or spiritual beliefs and practices) showed surprisingly few correlations to any variables—not trait forgivingness, gratitude, or differentiation of self. Questing was related to spiritual disruption (i.e., inability to dwell peacefully), spiritual openness (i.e., being open to new spiritual experiences), and psychological symptoms. Questing and spiritual seeking are often noisy and unpleasant, attended by discomfort and psychological pain. Although growth might have been triggered, usually people are not happy when they are actively seeking, questing, or wandering.

Spiritual Instability

Spiritual instability (i.e., flip-flopping among various religious or spiritual beliefs and practices and questing) was negatively related to trait forgivingness and differentiation of self and was positively related to more psychological symptoms. These correlations suggest that forgivingness is related to positive religiousness. Also, when religiousness becomes unstable and negative, and disappointment with the sacred occurs, experiences turn more negative and psychological symptoms become likely. Many relationships exist beyond these, as we see from the narrative summaries below.

Longitudinal Development of Spiritual Dwelling and Seeking

Williamson and Sandage (2009) conducted a longitudinal study of spiritual development among 119 graduate-level seminary students. Williamson and Sandage expected and found that, over time, seminary education would facilitate increases in students' religious dwelling (i.e., intrinsic religiosity) and spiritual seeking (i.e., questing and spiritual openness) and would increase their spiritual engagement (i.e., spiritual well-being and spiritual activity). They also found that higher intrinsic religiosity was related to higher spiritual well-being, spiritual openness, and spiritual activity. Finally, Williamson and Sandage found that increases in spiritual questing would lead to greater spiritual openness and spiritual activity and decreased spiritual well-being. The essence of the Shults and Sandage (2006) model of spiritual transformation is not that spiritual dwelling is "good" and spiritual questing is "bad." Rather, likening it to Schnarch's (1997) model of relationship development, they see spiritual dwelling and questing as an intertwined dialectic (see Figure 2.1), yet they have different correlations during each phase of spiritual change.

Williamson and Sandage (2009) suggested that the dialectic of a healthy spirituality may strike a balance between spiritual dwelling and spiritual seeking. Spiritual dwelling deepens intrinsic religiosity and provides a secure psychological and motivational base for exploring religious faith. Spiritual dwelling also activates prosocial work in the community. Spiritual seeking exacts a temporary cost to spiritual well-being. However, it might open up new, more complex ways of conceiving of the sacred, which might enhance spiritual maturity.

Let us look at an application for these findings. When the client learns new spiritual information, it can create disquiet, worsen symptoms, and kick the person from seeking to questing or even wandering. That may look "bad" to the psychotherapist and often feels "bad" to the client. But the psychotherapist might need to bind his or her anxiety and let the process play out rather than try to "fix" the client's complaints of disrupted spirituality. Fixing the uncertainty-inspired questing might be countertherapeutic. It might drive conflicts underground and deprive the client of working through the questing and gaining a sense of ego strength. The client might not be allowed to discover that difficult problems can be faced and solved.

The Relationship of Spiritual Dwelling and Seeking and Dispositional Forgiveness

Sandage and Williamson (2010) tested the associations between relational spirituality and dispositional forgiveness in 203 seminary graduate students. Many of the findings from Williamson and Sandage (2009) were supported in the expanded sample. In addition, Sandage and Williamson found that if a client presents a problem of unrelenting unforgiveness, then questing coupled with disappointment with God will make that problem very hard to solve. Thus, the spiritual issue might be worth dealing with first. Another application of their findings was that people who are having difficulty forgiving also might be low in spiritual dwelling and also struggle with feeling gratitude. Perhaps intervening by increasing gratitude (Emmons & McCullough, 2003, 2004) or benefit finding (McCullough, Root, & Cohen, 2006) might dislodge a move toward forgiveness, and increased gratitude might be a natural by-product of moving toward more secure attachment (Karen, 2001; Mikulincer & Shaver, 2007).

Adult Attachment, Meditative Prayer, Hope, and Forgiveness

Besides spiritual dwelling and seeking, other qualities are related to forgiveness. Jankowski and Sandage (2011) found in 211 seminary students that meditative prayer (i.e., prayer in which the praying person thinks about God or spiritual truths) depended on both hope and adult attachment to produce forgiveness. The results suggest that a cascade of internal processes might be occurring when seminary students face the need and desire to forgive.

They pray, which can soothe them. The self-soothing, in turn, helps them draw on their sense of a safe haven of good adult attachment relationships. Feeling calm, peaceful, and safe (at least to a higher degree than those who score lower in self-soothing) can lead to hope. Higher levels of hope were related to being willing to forgive more transgressions (hence trait forgivingness).

Some Implications for Psychotherapy

If this, indeed, is a naturally occurring causal cascade—and one would need to carefully assess it with each client—then psychotherapy could seek to use those connections. That is, forgiveness could be taught as a coping mechanism that helps one quiet rumination and negative emotions. As clients gain the sense of being able to self-soothe through emotional forgiveness, they can draw on existing secure attachments. To the extent that few secure attachment relationships exist, the clients can explore past, present (with the psychotherapist), present (with the people in the life of the clients), and future relationships and seek to forgive transgressions in many of those. An important question, however, is whether clients' spiritual practices (e.g., prayer, meditation, chanting) actually foster self-soothing or contribute to further dysregulation.

We note the happy concordance between the psychodynamic "theory of the hour" that proclaims, first in last out, and some exercises in the REACH forgiveness psychoeducational or psychotherapeutic treatments (which, you will recall, we introduced in the Introduction). In the theory of the hour (Soldz & McCullough, 2000), clients typically initiate the hour with complaints, usually against someone. As explorations are made, clients might express emotion toward the psychotherapist in a transference interaction (the emotion presumably arising from relational templates), which is processed and interpreted (i.e., the impulse–anxiety–defense patterns are recognized and named). Clients might spontaneously observe or be prompted to reflect on whether such interactions have occurred in the past in other contexts of the clients' lives (notably, with parents, but often with others; i.e., to notice and name the relational templates). As those interactions are described, processed, and interpreted (again presumably finding the same impulse–anxiety–defense connections as in the transference neurosis), the client might see connections among the transference and interaction with an attachment figure and the events that clients began the session with. Such insights promote ego control (Soldz & McCullough, 2000).

Another interpretation of their findings was provided by Jankowski and Sandage (2011). They suggested that secure attachment and forgivingness were related by positive emotion and acts that regulated negative affect—like hope and meditative prayer, which were both interpreted as acts of affective self-regulation. This suggests that helping people regulate negative affect through building differentiation of self, self-regulation, and self-responsibility (three lynchpins of Bowen's [1985] family systems theory) might help cope with unforgiveness through forgiving and also make longer term and more profound adjustments in their personality.

To forgive, the client must willfully open up space in his or her self to allow the other in and intentionally reorganize the self in response to the other (Volf, 1996). For Volf (1996), the individual's imaginative capacities for differentiation and renegotiating himself or herself must be renewed or transformed by the experience of entering into loving spiritual communion with the divine. Religious activities, such as meditative prayer, worship, and confession, can prompt religious spirituality, and the closeness to the sacred object can provide stability with which to reconnect internally with an offender in a more differentiated manner. More general and less explicitly theological spiritual experiences of gratitude, humility, mercy, and inspiration can prompt humanistic spirituality, and the closeness to humans as a sacred object can also help the person reconnect with a transgressor. Perceiving the sacred in nature, such as experiencing the majesty and beauty of the natural world, called *nature spirituality*, can do the same thing. Activities that promote a sense of transcendence (i.e., awe at something is bigger and grander than mere humans) can promote transcendent spirituality, which can likewise promote forgiveness. Mindfulness and other meditative practices might also foster self-regulation and may also fit well for some clients who hold Buddhist or nontheistic spiritual worldviews.

Religious and Spiritual Pathology and Forgiveness

Forgiveness is not just related to positive spiritual experiences. It can be negatively affected by spiritual experiences as well. Sandage and Crabtree (2012) examined what happens when spirituality is not well functioning. They studied spiritual pathology (i.e., uses of spirituality that indicate underlying psychological problems or severe emotional disequilibrium for which spiritual language, experiences, and behavior are symptomatic), negative (and positive) religious coping, and dispositional forgiveness in two studies. In Study 1, spiritual instability correlated with numerous negative religious coping items (and negatively with positive religious coping), whereas spiritual grandiosity did not. Dispositional forgiveness correlated with more positive than negative religious coping items. In Study 2, they found a curvilinear relationship between spiritual grandiosity and dispositional forgiveness; at both high and low levels of dispositional forgiveness, spiritual grandiosity was high but was lower at more moderate levels. Positive religious coping, spiritual instability (see also Sandage & Jankowski, 2010), and a similar curvilinear effect for spiritual grandiosity, each predicted dispositional forgiveness after controlling for spiritual impression management. Negative religious coping was not related to dispositional forgiveness when included with these variables.

Relational Spirituality, Generativity, Gratitude, and Mental Health

Generativity strivings are motives to establish and guide the next generation. Sandage, Hill, and Vaubel (2011) found that generativity is related positively to age. Even after removing the effects of age, intrinsic religiosity was positively related to generativity strivings, and quest was negatively related to generativity strivings, overall (however, see the moderator effect, described below). Spiritual dwelling frees mental and emotional energy and relational resources to enable people to focus on benefiting others. Spiritual seeking, however, occupies mental and emotional energy and binds relational resources, often making personal and social contributions more problematic.

Spiritual transformations, that is, moves between dramatic qualitatively different spiritual states, often result in people holding generosity and self-giving in higher priority. McAdams and colleagues have found that transformation is a common theme in the life stories of generative adults (McAdams, 2006; McAdams, & de St. Aubin, 1992). Those who score high on measures of generativity tend to tell their life stories by highlighting *redemption sequences*, which are scenes in which bad events turn out to be beneficial at producing growth, meaning, renewal, and insight. The bad event is redeemed through a personal transformation, and that is seen as producing good outcomes for self and others. Thus, McAdams's (2006) research suggests that individuals who have had dramatic spiritual transformations might experience higher levels of generativity than those who have not had such experiences. Sandage et al. (2011) found that those reporting a recent spiritual transformation showed the highest generativity at moderate levels of spiritual seeking, suggesting spiritual seeking might be conducive to caring for others if a transformation has recently served to integrate spiritual dwelling and seeking.

Relational Spirituality, Differentiation of Self, and Virtue in Predicting Intercultural Development

Sometimes, during counseling, the client discovers that he or she holds a grudge against people who belong to a different group than he or she does. For example, a woman might discover that her unforgiveness of a coworker is attributable in part to the woman's different ethnicity or race. How might forgiveness interact with level of intercultural spiritual sensitivity and type of relational spirituality? Intercultural development of sensitivity can be described using a developmental model of increasingly coming to appreciate differences of out-groups and take the perspective of out-group members. Sandage and Harden (2011) found that there were complex predictive patterns for increased intercultural development. Neither intrinsic religiosity nor forgiveness was related to intercultural development, overall, although forgiveness was negatively associated with intercultural defensiveness (i.e., feeling culturally superior to other cultures). Quest religiosity, differentiation of self, and gratitude were positively associated with intercultural development. On the other hand, spiritual grandiosity was negatively associated with intercultural development. Differentiation of self mediated the relationship between gratitude and intercultural development.

Differentiation of Self as a Mediator Between Spiritual Well-Being and Both Intercultural Competence and Commitment to Social Justice

Sandage and Jankowski (2013) found that differentiation of self mediated between intercultural competence and spiritual well-being and between a commitment to social justice and spiritual well-being. Differentiation of self also mediated the relationship between spiritual instability and intercultural competence, but it did not mediate the connections between spiritual instability and commitment to social justice.

Summary

We see from this systematic research program that relational spirituality—in the forms of dwelling, positive religious coping, intrinsic religiosity, and spiritual well-being, and in more pernicious forms, such as spiritual instability, questing, and spiritual grandiosity—has been consistently related to forgiveness, as well as to intercultural competence and a commitment to social justice. Intercultural competence is of particular interest because, for highly religious and spiritual people, many if not most transgressions are interpreted as being from an out-group member (and attributed to the person's religious or spiritual group identity) or to an in-group member. In-group transgressions can be especially troublesome. The person might think, He (or she) is like me! He (or she) isn't supposed to hurt a brother (or sister). One's differentiation of self, however, plays a frequently causal mediating role in these connections.

For the practitioner, several lessons may be tentatively drawn. First, it matters what spiritual state—dwelling or seeking—the person is in. Second, negative religious experiences are rarely associated with good outcomes, which suggests that psychotherapists need to prioritize working with the client to resolve those experiences. And third, whether the client can do so is largely dependent on the person's differentiation of self, which suggests that the psychotherapist needs to strongly assist the movement toward higher levels of differentiation of self.

STUDIES OF THE FORGIVENESS AND RELATIONAL SPIRITUALITY STRUCTURAL MODEL

Measure Development

If you turn back to Figure 3.1, you will see a schematic of the forgiveness and relational spirituality process model. When we created this model in 2007, few measures existing at that time could be used to test the model. Thus, we developed several measures, and we provide those for your use in the Appendix.

Assessing the VS Relationship

For the VS relationships, several measures already existed and have been cited above. For example, Intrinsic and Extrinsic Religious Orientation and Quest Religious Orientation already existed. Sandage and his colleagues used those measures extensively in their studies. Attachment to God (Rowatt & Kirkpatrick, 2002) measured anxious and avoidant attachment to God. Other measures that could have operationalized the VS relationship included Spiritual Grandiosity (Moore, 2003), Spiritual Well-Being Scale (Ellison, 1994), Spiritual Openness (Williamson & Sandage, 2009), other measures of attachment to God (R. Beck, 2006), and individual questions that assess whether recent spiritual transformations have been experienced.

We created some additional measures. For example, D. E. Davis, Worthington, Hook, and Van Tongeren (2009) created a measure called Dedication to the Sacred (DS). In three studies, they found a good fitting five-item scale. It predicted other different measures of VS, such as religious commitment, religious motivation, or attachment to God. It provided incremental predictive validity for forgiveness over religious commitment alone, suggesting that both religious commitment and dedication to the sacred should be used.

D. E. Davis, Hook, Worthington, Van Tongeren, Gartner, and Jennings (2010) created a four-item measure of spiritual humility (the Spiritual Humility Scale), also to measure an aspect of the VS relationship. They showed that having a sense of humility before God was related to positive character qualities.

Wood et al. (2010) created a nine-item measure of one's relationship with God, called the Attitudes Toward God Scale—9 (ATGS–9). People's relationship with God is not always close and comforting. Sometimes it is stormy. Wood et al. created a measure with two subscales—Disappointment and Anger with God and Religious Comfort. Both were related to spiritual struggles, religious seeking, and spiritual upheaval.

Summary of Measures of the VS Relationship

Given the already often used and psychometrically sound measures of VS that existed at the outset of our project and the measures that have been developed during the past eight years, we are now confident that researchers can–capture some of the richness of the relationship between a victim and what he or she holds to be sacred. This set of measures goes far beyond merely describing how close one's relationship is to the sacred; it enables discussing a variety of different dimensions of one's experience.

Assessing the OS Relationship

The forgiveness and relational spirituality structural and process models are not direct measures of interpersonal relationships. Rather, they are measures of one person's experience within such a relationship. From the potential forgiver's viewpoint (i.e., the victim's viewpoint), the OS relationship is a measure of how similar the victim perceives the offender's relationship to the sacred to be relative to his or her own. Similarity of spiritual status is important because it determines whether a victim sees the offender as an in-group or out-group member. That perception has been shown through meta-analyses to strongly affect both forgiveness and reconciliation in many real-life domestic and political situations (Van Tongeren, Burnette, O'Boyle, Worthington, & Forsyth, 2014).

D. E. Davis, Worthington, Hook, Van Tongeren, Green, and Jennings (2009) created the Similarity of the Offender's Spirituality (SOS) Scale. There were two subscales. Five items comprised the Spiritual Similarity subscale, which measures the degree to which people believe that the offender's spiritual beliefs and values and overall spirituality were similar to their own. A typical item is, "I believe that he/she is a similar spiritual person to me." Four items comprised the Human Similarity subscale, which measures the degree to which the person believes an offender is similar and not devalued with respect to the other person as a human. A typical item is, "I reminded myself that I was no better as a person than the one who hurt me." The scale can be used as a whole, but each subscale also predicts some different things. The spiritual similarity scale not surprisingly predicted religious and spiritual variables better.

As a complement to the victim's perception of similarity of the offender's and his or her own relationship with the sacred, it is important to know how spiritually engaged one is with the offender. D. E. Davis, Hook, Worthington, Van Tongeren, Gartner, Jennings, and Norton (2010) created the Relational Engagement of the Spiritual for a Transgression (REST) scale. The REST has only four items, which assessed the degree to which the victim sees the person as a child of God, prays to God for the person, asks God to show the offender's good points, or thinks that God wants the two to reconcile. The more spiritually engaged a victim is, the more the victim is likely to forgive the offender.

Assessing the TS Relationship

A strong measure of TS already existed—the Sacred Loss and Desecration Scale (SLDS; Pargament, Magyar, Benore, & Mahoney, 2005). The SLDS is a 23-item, two-subscale scale. It measures the extent to which participants see the target offense as a loss of something sacred. Participants respond to items (e.g., "This event involved losing a gift from God"). It also measures a perceived desecration of something held to be sacred (e.g., "A sacred part of my life was violated.") Sacred loss differs from desecration in that a desecration involves someone's perceived willful act of defiling something sacred—such as a partner having an affair and defiling a marriage considered by the spouse to be sacred, which also usually results in a sacred loss. Sacred losses, however, could occur without a sense of desecration, if for example, a tornado occurred and a person felt that he or she had subsequently lost faith in God.

Clinical and Research Uses of the Battery of Assessments

These measures help us assess the VS, OS, and TS relationships. We strove to create short and psychometrically sound measures with good construct validity. Most could be used in clinical situations. For example, a client could complete the DS (five items), SHS (four items), and ATGS–9 (nine items), the SOS (nine items), and REST (four items)—only 31 total items—in less than five minutes. The entire battery (except for the 23-item SLDS) could be completed in the waiting room before psychotherapy, and because it consists of self-report items, it could be scored by a technician and graphed for immediate use in psychotherapy. In less than 10 minutes, you could have a picture of the client's relational spirituality. We have provided the scales, with permission to use them clinically, scoring instructions, and brief norms in the Appendix. If a sacred loss or desecration were involved, the 23-item SLDS might take another five minutes to complete.

HOW WE HAVE INVESTIGATED THE MODEL—METHODS

Whereas Sandage and his colleagues (e.g., Sandage & Jankowski, 2013) have examined mostly connections among traits or dispositions, Worthington and his colleagues (e.g., D. E. Davis, Hook, & Worthington, 2008; D. E. Davis, Worthington, Hook, Van Tongeren, Green, & Jennings, 2009) have studied how people's personal characteristics are related to forgiveness of a particular transgression. Although trait or dispositional predictors are studied, on occasion, the major outcome measures have involved unforgiveness (i.e., avoidance or revenge) or forgiveness of a transgression (or benevolent motives toward the offender).

As with the previous table (Table 4.1), we summarize many of the bivariate correlations in Table 4.2 for nine studies using secular samples, usually of college students. In Table 4.3, we summarize five studies of Christians. Some of the main conclusions in examining Tables 4.2 and 4.3 are presented below.

Measures Related to Forgiving Particular Transgressions

Our main interest was in how well variables in the model predicted for-giveness of a particular identified transgression. Thus, we used two measures to assess forgiveness. The Transgression-Related Inventory of Motivations Scale (TRIM; McCullough et al., 1998) has three distinct subscales of seven, five, and six items, respectively: Avoidance of the transgressor, Revenge or vengeful motives regarding the transgressor, and Benevolence motives toward the transgressor. We also used the Rye Forgiveness Scale (Rye et al., 2001).

TRIM Avoidance and TRIM Revenge motivations measure unforgive-ness toward the perpetrator regarding a wrong or offense. TRIM Benevolence and the Rye Forgiveness Scale measure forgiveness, which we defined as the reduction of unforgiving emotions (and motivations) by emotionally replac-ing negative unforgiving motives (e.g., avoidance and revenge) by positive other-oriented emotions (and benevolent motivations).

We asked people to recall a hurt or transgression that they are still hav-ing trouble forgiving. We then had them complete questionnaires about their current experiences, and we correlated characteristics intended to measure each aspect of the model of forgiveness and relational spirituality with some or all of the outcomes (i.e., avoidance, revenge, benevolence, or forgive-ness). Some studies had people select a transgressor from among their entire repertoire of relationships. However, others had people choose a transgressor from the congregation that the victim attended. Thus, for the secular stud-ies, in many cases, it would be possible to cut off the transgressor from future interactions, and many people apparently did just that. For a few, they named a romantic partner, spouse, family member, or work colleague as the offender. Typically, in most of the secular studies, the average offender was more eas-ily avoidable than in the studies involving continued interaction within a limited congregation.

Model-Relevant Predictors of Unforgiveness (Avoidance and Revenge), Benevolence, and Forgiveness in Secular and In-Group Samples

To get an overview of the model, let us look at Table 4.2 and Table 4.3. We take the model one step at a time. For each component, we summarize secular studies and then the studies of ingroup Christian congregation transgressions.

The Human Base of the Model—V, O, T, VO, VT, and OT

The only victim variable measured was trait forgivingness. People who scored high in trait forgivingness consistently were likely to forgive. This was true in both secular and Christian studies. No offender variables were tested. As for the transgression, neither the amount of hurt initially felt nor the time

TABLE 4.2
Comparison of the Nine Studies Investigating the Forgiveness
and Relational Spirituality Structural Model With University Students
of Mixed Religious Identification

Step of the model/ variable	D.E. Davis, Hook, & Worthington (2008) Forgiveness (r)	D.E. Davis, Worthington, Hook, Van Tongeren, Green, & Jennings (2009, Study 1) Forgiveness (r)	D.E. Davis, Worthington, Hook, Van Tongeren, Green, & Jennings (2009, Study 2) Av, Rev, Ben (β)	D.E. Davis, Worthington, Hook, & Van Tongeren (2009) Av & Rev[a] (r)
Victim variable (V)				
Trait forgivingness				
Offender variable (O)				
(None)				
Transgression (T)				
Hurtfulness at time of offense				
Time since the transgression				
Relationship to offender (VO)				
Closeness at the time of offense				
Empathy				
Relationship to trans- gression (VT) (None)				
Relationship O to T (OT) (None)				
Victim relationship with sacred (VS)				
Church attendance				
Religious commitment				−.08
DS				−.21*
Anxious attachment to God	−.31**	−.06		
Avoidant attachment to god	−.25**	−.18		
Positive religious cop- ing (Brief RCOPE)	.15			
Negative religious cop- ing (Brief RCOPE)	−.30**			
Group identification as an identified reli- gious group				

D.E. Davis, Hook, Worthington, Van Tongeren, Gartner, Jennings, & Norton (2010)	D.E. Davis, Hook, Worthington, Van Tongeren, Gartner, & Jennings (2010)	D.E. Davis et al. (2011, Studies 4 and 5)	D.E. Davis, Hook, Van Tongeren, & Worthington (2012)	Greer et al. (2014, Study 2)
Av, Rev (β)	Av, Rev (β)	Av, Rev (β)	Av, Rev (β)	Av, Rev, Ben (β)
				−.32***, −.33***, .39***
				.22***, .11, −.07 −.03, −.05, .01
−.58**, −.47**				−.30***, −.03, .38***
−.06, −.20**	−.08, −.13			−.11, −.20***, .21*** −.12, −.12, .38*** −.16, −.23***, .30***
				−.21***, −.30***, .20***

(*continues*)

Step of the model/variable	D.E. Davis, Hook, & Worthington (2008) Forgiveness (r)	D.E. Davis, Worthington, Hook, Van Tongeren, Green, & Jennings (2009, Study 1) Forgiveness (r)	D.E. Davis, Worthington, Hook, Van Tongeren, Green, & Jennings (2009, Study 2) Av, Rev, Ben (β)	D.E. Davis, Worthington, Hook, & Van Tongeren (2009) Av & Rev[a] (r)
Relationship of offender's similarity to the sacred (OS)				
SOS (SS/HS subscales)		.28*/.29*	−.45**/−.47** −.28**/−.24** .37**/.44**	
SOS				
REST				
Humility (SH, SS, HS, Hum)				
Relational humility rate O (RHS) Study 4 (GH; S; AVS; RHS-Tot); Study 5 (GH; S; AVS)				
Honesty–humility (rate O)				
Relationship of trans-gression to the sacred (TS)				
Sacred loss and desecration	−.31**	−.33**, −.19*		.41**
SFS Will of God to Forgive				
SFS Hurts Relation-ship With God Not to Forgive				
SFS Spiritual Commit-ment to Forgive				

Note. Participants were students in all studies. The forgiveness measure is from Rye et al. (2001). Avoidance (Av), Revenge (Rev), and Benevolence (Ben) subscales are from the Transgression-Related Inventory of Motivations (McCullough et al., 1998). DS = Dedication to the Sacred (D.E. Davis, Worthington, Hook, & Van Tongeren, 2009); RHS = Relational Humility Scale (D.E. Davis et al., 2011); RCOPE = Religious and Coping Scale (Pargament, Koenig, & Perez, 2000); SH = Spiritual Humility judgments; SOS = Similarity of the Offender's Spirituality (D.E. Davis, Worthington, Hook, Van Tongeren, Green, & Jennings, 2009); REST = Relational Engagement of the Spiritual for a Transgression (D.E. Davis, Worthington, Van Tongeren, Gartner, Jennings, & Norton, 2010); SS = Spiritual Similarity of offender; HS = Human Similarity of offender; Hum = Humility judgments; SOS = Similarity of the Offender's Spirituality Scale (D.E. Davis, Worthington, Hook, Van Tongeren, Green, & Jennings, 2009); GH = Global Humility subscale; S = Superiority subscale; AVS = Accurate View of Self; RHS-Tot = Relational Humility Scale–Total; SFS = Sanctification of Forgiveness (D.E. Davis, Hook, Van Tongeren, & Worthington, 2012). [a]The Avoidance and Revenge subscales were added together (in others, Avoidance was analyzed separately from Revenge). *p < .05. **p < .01. ***p < .001.

D.E. Davis, Hook, Worthington, Van Tongeren, Gartner, Jennings, & Norton (2010)	D.E. Davis, Hook, Worthington, Van Tongeren, Gartner, & Jennings (2010)	D.E. Davis et al. (2011, Studies 4 and 5)	D.E. Davis, Hook, Van Tongeren, & Worthington (2012)	Greer et al. (2014, Study 2)
Av, Rev (β)	Av, Rev (β)	Av, Rev (β)	Av, Rev (β)	Av, Rev, Ben (β)
				−.29***, −.22***, .49***
−.25**, −.30**				
	Av = −.25*, −.31*, −.31*, −.41*; rev = −.22*, −.16, −.31*,.−.41*			
		Study 4: Av = −.43*, −.32*, −.40*; −.50*; Rev = −.35*, −.25*, −.22*, −.35*; Study 5: Av = −.31*, −.21*, −.25* Rev = −.29*, −.35*, −.22* Study 5: Av = −.40* Rev = −.32*		
.15*, .16**				.33***, .43***, −.28***
			.02, −.14*	
			.07, .07	
			−.18*, −.27*	

FORGIVENESS AND SPIRITUALITY IN PSYCHOTHERAPY

TABLE 4.3

Comparison of the Four Studies Investigating the Relational Spirituality and Forgiveness Structural Model in Specifically Christian Samples

Step of the model/variable	Greer et al. (2012); students	Toussaint and Zoelzer (2011; 1st number, community) & Greer et al. (2012; 2nd and 3rd numbers, students)			Greer et al. (2012, Study 1); students and community
	Av, Rev, Ben (β)	Av(r)	Rev(r)	Ben(r)	Av, Rev, Ben (r)
Victim variable (V)					
Trait forgivingness	−.33***, −.33***, .39***	−.10, −.32***, −.03	−.22**, −.33***, −.34***	.00, .42***, .22***	
Offender variable (O) (None)					
Transgression (T)					
Hurtfulness	.16**, .01, −.05	.15*, .17**, .36***	.19*, .05, .01	−.24, .04, −.12	
Time since offense	−.06, −.07, .09	−.12, .07, .03	−.17, −.09, .05	.02, −.06, .03	
Relationship to offender (VO)					
Closeness to offender	−.22***, −.03, .31***				
Relationship to transgression (VT) (none)					
Relationship O to T (OT) (none)					

Victim relationship with sacred (VS)				
Church attendance	-.01, -.10, -.02	-.35**, -.16**, -.36***	-.10, .04, .01	.49***, .29***, .21**
Religious commitment	-.03, .10, .25***	.05, -.01, .06	-.12, .02, -.15	.20**, .15*, .27***
DS	.01, -.18**, .07			
Positive religious coping (Brief RCOPE)		-.07, -.08, -.11	-.02, -.05, -.20**	.23**, .25***, .25***
Negative religious coping (Brief RCOPE)		.23***, .23***, .14	.44***, .39***, .24**	-.16*, -.21***, -.13
Past group identification	-.04, -.14*, .15**	-.28***, -.21***, -.09	-.40***, -.22*, -.34***	.42***, .38***, .15* -.31*, -.23, .41**
Relationship of offender's similarity to the sacred (OS)				
SOS	-.18**, -.09, .26***			
Relationship of transgression to the sacred (TS)				
SLDS	.23***, .32***, -.21***			

Note. For all studies, the transgressions were restricted to those in one's congregation. Avoidance (Av), Revenge (Rev), and Benevolence (Ben) subscales are from the Transgression-Related Inventory of Motivations (McCullough et al., 1998). DS = Dedication to the Sacred (D.E. Davis, Worthington, Hook, & Von Tongeren, 2009); RCOPE = Religious and Coping Scale (Pargament, Koenig, & Perez, 2000); SOS = Similarity of the Offender's Spirituality Scale (D.E. Davis, Worthington, Hook, Van Tongeren, Green, & Jennings, 2009); Sacred Loss and Desecration Scale (SLDS; Pargament, Magyar, Benore, & Mahoney, 2005).
*p < .05. **p < .01. ***p < .001.

since the offense was related to forgiveness. McCullough and his colleagues (McCullough, Bono, & Root, 2007; McCullough, Fincham, & Tsang, 2003) have found that unforgiveness declines over about the first three weeks after an offense. However, when people can select an offense to recount from their past, they tend to select one that has not been fully forgiven—eliminating the effect of time at decreasing unforgiveness.

Closeness to the victim was consistently, for both secular and Christian samples, related to forgiveness. Empathy was related to forgiveness in secular samples. No offender-transgression variables were tested.

Relationships With the Sacred—S, VS, OS, and TS

Enter the sacred. Each part of the relational base will also be in relationship with the object the person considers sacred.

Sacred (S). No victim-perceived qualities of the sacred—loving God, vengeful God, hostile God, god image, god concept—were investigated. These provide a rich source of hypotheses, but we have not yet studied them. For example, Tsang, McCullough, and Hoyt (2005) found that people who saw God as loving described themselves as forgiving and were less likely to practice avoidance of offenders after transgressions. Similarly, Webb, Chickering, Colburn, Heisler, and Call (2005) found that people who described God as loving were more forgiving than those who described God as controlling.

Victim's Relationship With the Sacred (VS). Church attendance was inconsistently related to forgiveness, about equally in secular and Christian samples. In secular samples, religious commitment virtually never predicted forgiveness and in Christian samples only about one quarter of the time did it predict forgiveness. For more direct assessment of the victim's relationship with the sacred, we used the DS scale, which was a good predictor in secular but not Christian samples.

For attachment to God—a crucial variable in our theorizing—we used only one secular sample. For anxious attachment, our research is too meager to draw any firm conclusions about. Other researchers have shed some light on this. Strelan, Acton, and Patrick (2009) found, with an Australian sample of church attendees, that disappointment with God was negatively related to dispositional forgiveness, spiritual well-being, and spiritual maturity and was positively related to depression and stress. Byrd and Boe (2001) conceptualized prayer as attempted attachment to God—seeking closeness and connection. Anxious attachment was related to more petitionary help-seeking prayer. Avoidant attachment was related to less colloquial conversational prayer and to less meditational contemplative prayer. McMinn et al. (2008) showed that college students were more likely to forgive when they used inward-directed prayer. Hall, Fujikawa, Halcrow, Hill, and Delaney (2009) found that unforgiveness was positively correlated with both avoidant God attachment and anxious God attachment, suggesting a link between forgiveness, attachment, and relational spirituality. Attachment theorists suggest that forgiveness requires an empathic response rather than a self-protective or aggressive response to internal representations of the other (Burnette, Taylor, Worthington, & Forsyth, 2007). Attachment security has been empirically associated with both empathy and forgiveness following relational betrayals and conflicts (for review, see Mikulincer & Shaver, 2007). Makinen and Johnson (2006) showed that persons experiencing insecure attachment can also forgive significant attachment injuries with intervention that generates more empathic working models of self and other. However, this may be particularly true for attachment avoidance. Burnette, Davis, Green, Worthington, and Bradfield (2009) found that empathy fully mediated the relationship between avoidance and forgivingness. In contrast, rumination partially mediated the link between anxious attachment and forgivingness. The common thread linking attachment, emotional rumination, empathy, and the capacity to forgive others is generally thought to be affect regulation (Burnette et al., 2007). Although our research alone is insufficient to draw conclusions, other research does allow conclusions to be drawn.

Positive religious coping predicted forgiveness in about half of the samples, mostly Christian ones. Positive religious coping seems an important but inconsistent predictor of forgiveness. Negative religious coping is a stronger predictor, almost always predicting unforgiveness. Group religious identification, likewise, is a potential strong predictor of forgiveness.

Victim's Perception of the Offender's Relationship to the Sacred (OS). Using the SOS Scale, we can say that the victim's perception of the offender's similarity as a like-faith individual is important to whether the victim will forgive. In secular and Christian samples, similarity was virtually always a predictor of forgiveness. This is consistent and strong evidence that the victim is evaluating the offender as to spiritual similarity and making decisions on the basis of that evaluation. Using the REST scale in secular samples, REST predicted forgiveness. Perceptions of the offender's humility were important in predicting forgiveness, but it mattered the type of humility. The offender's humility in the face of the sacred was a strong predictor of forgiveness as was relational humility. Honesty/humility was also supported. Perceptions that the offender is humble is vital in whether a victim will forgive.

The Relationship of the Transgression to the Sacred (TS). The perception that a transgression is a sacred loss or a desecration strongly biases the victim against forgiving. The degree to which a victim sanctifies forgiveness can also matter. If the victim believes that it is a spiritual commitment to forgive, forgiveness is likely, but if the person thinks he or she should forgive because not doing so will hurt his or her relationships with God, the likelihood is that forgiveness will not happen.

THE FORGIVENESS AND RELATIONAL SPIRITUALITY
PROCESS MODEL

In general, the three components of our theory-of-change model—the stress-and-coping model of forgiveness, the relational spirituality model, and the structural model—have generated cautiously optimistic evidence that supports the models. But how do the three component models work together?

McCullough et al. (2003) argued persuasively that multiple time points are needed to interpret actual forgiveness and, therefore, forgiveness can be understood accurately only within the context of changes over time. For example, imagine three victims offended at the same time and assessed for forgiveness immediately after the offense and at two weeks postoffense. At two weeks, both score the same on the forgiveness measure. But one started at a moderate level of forgiveness, yet as the person ruminated about the offense, the forgiveness evaporated. The second person started at a moderate level and maintained that level. The third person started at a low level of forgiveness and forgiveness built over time. Although all three had the same score at Time 2, they did not forgive equally. That difference is revealed only if people are observed over time.

Forgiveness equally depends on the context. People in close, valued relationships, when transgressions are raw, tend often to avoid the person to maintaining a sense of safety, given that ongoing interactions are likely and they expect time to lessen the hurtfulness. They might try to stifle revenge motives lest they "leak out" into the relationship and lead to increasingly hostile interactions punctuated by more hurtfulness. However, when people are offended by (a) strangers, (b) those who refuse interaction (e.g., an ex-romantic partner or former friend who moved away), or (c) enemies who feel open antagonism (e.g., enemy soldiers in combat or protracted struggle with a hostile coworker), they might channel resentment into desires for vengeance because avoidance is either assured or impossible. People in valued personal relationships and in-groups with potential for mutual aid are predisposed to restore feelings of benevolence after a transgression. Benevolent motives potentially help restore relationships.

Experimentally testing the models in their full complexity is virtually impossible. They involve too many interrelationships among variables, and the effects from variable to variable often operate on different timetables. For example, a client might have relational templates built from transgressions throughout a lifetime of development. Different templates might be triggered by different events in the life of the client, including events within the psychotherapy hour.

Operating on a different time dimension altogether, some events in a client's recent life might have activated their early attachment templates that have led to a burgeoning of spiritual questioning and seeking. Take George, an avowed lifelong atheist. Yet, he was recently offended by Miguel, an outspoken Christian on George's softball team. George's anguish was deep at the hurt. But Miguel's apologetic and genuinely humble and self-sacrificial response of not only making reparation but also going beyond anything George could imagine has disoriented George. He expected self-righteous defensiveness. Miguel could not have been more different from George's anticipation. Not only that, but other members of Miguel's church provided help for George in a difficult at-home situation. All of these acts, triggered by the transgression, have thrown George into a period of questioning stereotypes he held for many years against Christians. George's period of spiritual seeking has far exceeded in time his coping with his unforgiveness. His spiritual relationships with the sacred—his VS relationships—and the way he perceives his relationship with Miguel (VO) and Miguel's friends (VO) and his perception of Miguel's relationship with the sacred (OS) are all being shuffled during his time of spiritual seeking.

Although we cannot imagine any kind of experiment or even longitudinal study being able to adequately capture and test the sequential nesting of these relationships, we can easily imagine that psychotherapists see such transformations all of the time. The evidence for the process model of forgiveness and relational spirituality is likely to come only piecemeal through science but to accumulate in clinical experience across practitioners who use the method.

SUMMARY OF THE SYNTHETIC MODEL

Overall, we believe that we have good empirical support for the following baker's dozen (13) propositions (some have more support than do others). These propositions outline the stress-and-coping model of forgiveness and relational spirituality.

1. People's relational spirituality can be described in terms of its development, structure, dynamics of operation, and triggers that might set off changes.
2. Relational spirituality can change as people pass through periods of spiritual dwelling and seeking.
3. Particularly important aspects of relational spirituality are (a) whether people are in spiritual dwelling, in spiritual seeking, or in the process of transforming from one to another of those; (b) the degree of differentiation of self; (c) possession of the ability to self-soothe and regulate negative emotional experience; and (d) coping repertoire that includes decisional and emotional forgiveness.

4. Those four aspects of relational spirituality affect interpersonal relationships.

5. Chronic or severe unforgiveness is stressful and unpleasant. People thus seek relief from chronic or severe unforgiveness by seeking input from other relationships—which can include affectively loaded existing relationships and also psychotherapeutic relationships.

6. People are not passive with respect to their spiritual lives either. They try to approach the sacred more closely or distance from the sacred. They do so as a response to unforgiveness or as a coping mechanism that aims to reduce unforgiveness.

7. When they do change their relationship with the sacred, that might lead them to be more or less likely to forgive an offender.

8. The likelihood of forgiving the offender depends on the variables in the forgiveness and relational spirituality model—the people and transgression, their relationships with each other, and the relationship of each with the sacred.

9. In addition, forgiveness will depend on the variables within the stress-and-coping model of forgiveness—(a) nature of the transgression; (b) appraisals of threat or challenge; (c) appraisals of injustice and size and nature of the injustice gap; (d) stress reactions in cognitive, emotional, motivational, physiological, and spiritual realms; and (e) coping responses involving alternatives to forgiveness or forgiving responses.

10. Each element in the forgiveness and relational spirituality model can affect each aspect of the stress-and-coping model. Relational spirituality most directly affects (a) appraisals, (b) stress responses, and (c) coping responses.

11. Personality structures and dynamics, changes in interpersonal structures and processes, and environments changes are proximal causes of change. Most proximal causes are influenced by interpersonal relationships.

12. The experiences of forgiving occur through (a) making a decision to forgive and (b) experiencing emotional replacement of negative with positive emotions.

13. Personality change to a more forgiving personality occurs through three major avenues: (a) generalization of many individual forgiveness decisions and experiences of emotional forgiveness; (b) spiritual empowerment from holding a spiritual belief that forgiveness is virtuous and knowing when to apply and when not to apply that belief; and (c) becoming more self-differentiated and self-aware because of more thor-

ough emotional processing, more self-regulated through better affect regulation, more self-controlled through managing one's behavior, the stimulus situations one is exposed to, or rewards and punishments, and more self-responsible for one's own part in transgressions. Namely, personality change is toward maturity when one increases the ability to hold tension among opposites in intense transgression-hot situations. These opposites include one's own and the other's roles and responsibilities in the transgression, the need to fix it versus the need to sit with the tension, humility versus self-defense, justice versus mercy, and empathy for the offender versus empathy for the self.

II
PROMOTING FORGIVENESS

When people are ready to, they change. They never do it before then, and sometimes they die before they get around to it. You can't make them change if they don't want to, just like when they do want to, you can't stop them.

—Andy Warhol, *Andy Warhol in His Own Words*

Stepping onto a brand new path is difficult, but not more difficult than remaining in a situation, which is not nurturing to the whole woman.

—Maya Angelou

Change does not roll in on the wheels of inevitability, but comes through continuous struggle.

—Martin Luther King, Jr., "I See the Promised Land"

And so, it is not astonishing that, though the patient enters therapy insisting that he wants to change, more often than not, what he really wants is to remain the same and to get the therapist to make him feel better.

—Sheldon Kopp, *If You Meet the Buddha on the Road, Kill Him: The Pilgrimage Of Psychotherapy Patients*

Change, like healing, takes time.

—Veronica Roth, *Allegiant*

5

HELPING PEOPLE FORGIVE

In Victor Hugo's novel *Les Misérables*, Jean Valjean, a good man, was transformed into a bitter, resentful, and unforgiving man because he had been unjustly treated by the system. But after receiving forgiveness by a kind bishop, Valjean was transformed into a thoroughly forgiving person. For the rest of his life, he was an exemplar of forgiveness.

Do such changes happen only in fiction? Or is it possible for people to change unforgiving personalities into more forgiving personalities? Personality theories and psychotherapies for personality disorders show that personalities can change. Reflection on normal living supports that notion. Most people do not have exactly the same personality at 80 as at 50, at 30, or at 15. Genetics are strong in the beginning, but the environment of parents, then school peers, then work settings mold us. The longer we live, the more we select environments that are consistent with many of those early genetic proclivities. But sometimes big life events transform us. Diseases sometimes

http://dx.doi.org/10.1037/14712-006
Forgiveness and Spirituality in Psychotherapy: A Relational Approach, by E. L. Worthington, Jr. and S. J. Sandage

wipe out families. Poor decisions can send a husband to jail and change the entire family. Loss of a spouse to a murder can embitter. If personalities can be strongly affected by tragedy, then can't psychotherapy provide healing events of similar magnitude? Whether negative or positive change agents, usually the change is slow, but not always. We hope to help you see ways that you, as a psychotherapist, can help your patients make faster, more wide-reaching, and more lasting transformations to promote forgiving.

In this chapter, we examine why it is hard to change personality. Then, we lay out a general strategy for personality change and apply it in a case to a patient, Ying. We identify four keys to personality change, which correspond to the following six tensions introduced at the beginning of this volume: (a) tension between conflict, which tears relationships apart, and restoring relationships; (b) tension between attachment and differentiation of self; (c) tension between emotional processing and emotional regulation; (d) tension between hope and humility; (e) tension between times of stable spiritual dwelling and other times of spiritual seeking; and (f) tension between justice (which may require things beyond one's control, such as the offender's willingness to atone) and the emotional and physical benefits of releasing resentment. Finally, we describe a general model of psychotherapy and illustrate it with a case.

WHAT DOES IT TAKE TO CHANGE PERSONALITY?

Some Challenges in Treating People Who Want to Become More Forgiving

Most people who wish to become more forgiving will find themselves somewhere in the middle of the normal distribution of trait forgivingness. Let's face it: As much as people like to believe the best about others, some are habitually hateful, revenge-filled grudge holders. They may come to psychotherapy, especially if they are involved in a religion that values forgiveness, and they feel disappointed in themselves for being chronically unforgiving. Such people are challenging for any psychotherapist. They usually have trouble sticking with psychotherapy because the therapist will inevitably disappoint them, provoking resentment that builds into a grudge, and driving them to disengage from psychotherapy. If the psychotherapist can keep them from disengaging from psychotherapy, there are plenty of transference events to process, so that they can actually move the relationship forward. On the other side of the spectrum, sometimes a person who expresses forgiveness too readily might feel like a doormat and might want to become less often walked on.

In all but the extreme cases, most people can become more forgiving without two-plus years of psychotherapy. In our research, we have seen shifts in trait forgivingness in psychoeducational groups within 6 to 8 hours of intervention, although those are probably rare cases for reliable, lasting, and transformative personality change. For most people, meaningful change in a forgiving character might occur within an intensive effort to change of 6 to 8 hours, but only if they continue to use the skills they developed.

Skill change is typically a first-order change. To change personality is a second-order change. Second-order change rearranges the relational schemes, and that often requires more than selecting forgiving coping strategies more often. Nevertheless, changing coping strategies through methods such as the REACH forgiveness method (Worthington, 2006) is vital to sustained and deeper change.

How Can Psychotherapists Help Trigger Second-Order Change?

Changed Coping Skills

Sometimes that sustained and deeper change emerges from a simple change in coping skills. Thus, we as therapists should never shy away from helping people develop simple behavioral and relationship skills.

Changed Structures Through Religion or Psychotherapy

Changed coping skills can lead to deep personality change. At other times, psychotherapy or religious or spiritual transformation is needed in addition to the skill changes. Sometimes a personality change stimulates people to develop better forgiveness coping skills.

Why It Is Difficult to Change Personality

People experience their own personality characteristics as being stable, cross-situational, enduring organizations of thoughts, images, feelings, attitudes, values, beliefs, and motivations that give rise to relatively consistent behaviors. Personality is an accumulated set of experiences. It is united by a common narrative and empowered by a need to be internally consistent. Personality provides an understanding of self and the world, draws selectively on memories to support its consistency, and motivates behaviors consistent with it. Personality seems consistent and hard to change. If a person sees himself or herself as particularly forgiving or vengeful, either self-perception can be hard to dislodge.

Yet, when we think our personalities must be consistent, little things bother us. We all realize that we have nagging little (and sometimes not so little) inconsistencies. We are at times struck by how differently we act in different situations. We do not act the same way with our children as we do on the volleyball court in a league match or with our work supervisor in her office. This is simple good sense. If we acted as formally with our children as with the company president, our kids would be saying, "Who are you and what have you done with my parent?"

The Situation Side of Personality

So, we realize that the situations in which we live profoundly shape our thoughts, feelings, and behaviors. Yet we usually do not admit that to ourselves, as the discipline of social psychology has shown repeatedly. That is a doorway into the life of a person who says, "I'm a vengeful person." Look for inconsistencies in which he or she forgave and acted mercifully. They might be buried, but often just in a veneer of dusty (selective) memories.

The Personal, Subjective, Narrative Side of Personality

We are exposed to and expose ourselves to many situations in which norms guide our behavior. But there is a lot of subjectivity in deciding which situations we put ourselves in. For example, we choose our mate. That choice structures millions of future situations. We choose our careers—millions more situations. We choose our avocations—millions more. These subjective choices lend consistency to experience. Because we need a sense of consistency, we use a narrative thread to tie together the experiences. Consistency helps us predict others' responses and plan our own responses. It is adaptive to be able to predict what will occur. Thus, we spin a story about our consistent behavior. That story describes our Self and its relationship to others and to events we are likely to encounter.

The stories we use to frame our lives are relational—organized from womb to tomb by a series of relationships, usually with people, but also with things such as jobs, hobbies, or living spaces. The sacred symbols in past relationships are particularly strong glue.

The Personality × Situation Interaction

Sometimes people stumble into more or less unusual situations. Those unusual situations cause us to do the unexpected. We do not have rehearsed moves in unusual situations. When we find ourselves in a strange situation, we draw on our familiar personality characteristics. Or we look around to decide what we should do by seeing how others react.

Strong situations do not engender vengeful (or forgiving) behavior. Rather, those situations focus our attention and experience on salient role-defined virtues within our hierarchy of virtues. Strong situations make other virtues recede in the background. Relational systems have powerful effects by shaping patterns that come to seem normative. These patterns pull for certain behaviors that we find virtuous. Early relational templates often are at the root of the patterns that become our hierarchy of virtues.

GENERAL STRATEGY FOR CHANGING PERSONALITY

So, how is personality changed? Changes must be made in both the external and internal worlds of the client.

External and Internal Transformations

Externally, at the most general level, one must change (a) the situations one is exposing oneself to, (b) the relationships within which one is embedded, or (c) the narrative thread that ties together experiences. Because the situations to which we usually expose ourselves are relatively stable, as are our relationships, and because the stability and consistency of the narrative thread that we call the self is tenaciously defended, it is difficult to make much headway at personality transformation.

Internally, changing personality usually requires either intentional and dramatic changes of the physical, relational, or mental structures in one's world or one (or an accumulation of many) powerful emotional experiences to create a noticeable personality change. Engaging seriously in psychotherapy can set off changes. It can succeed at changing personality to the extent that it provides a strong, emotionally important relationship; helps the person change other relationships and structures in his or her life; and enables emotionally near experiences that can help reprogram the person's relational and cognitive schemes.

Application to Forgiveness

Let us apply this understanding of changing personality to helping someone become a more forgiving person. Generally, one will have a great challenge in psychotherapy trying to help clients change the Big Five traits thought to underlie most of personality: Openness to Experience, Conscientiousness, Extraversion–Introversion, Agreeableness, and Neuroticism (Costa & McCrae, 1992). Much time is spent with many clients in trying to help them change the emotional reactivity of neuroticism. Those personality traits are deeply ingrained by nature and nurture and usually give way only to long-term psychotherapy, spiritual transformation, and major life circumstances.

One will have more success even in focused brief psychotherapy of 12 to 20 sessions helping clients modify the dispositions specifically related to decreasing unforgiveness or promoting forgiveness. The person presumably became either a grudge-holding or vengeful personality through having experienced many transgressions and eventually responding to them consistently. Rumination almost certainly played a large part. The entire stress-and-coping process becomes scripted. Acts are often interpreted as transgressions and appraised to be threats. The emotional reactions of anger and fear trigger rumination, which breeds grudges or plans for vengeance. Coping includes reacting hostilely, which leads to new transgressions.

An Example

Imagine that as a child, Ying was offended by her middle school friends rejecting her because she was not "cool." Ying reacted emotionally, and she responded by fixating on the offense and the impact of the rejections and exclusions. Perhaps Ying replayed the incidents mentally, seeking to understand and shape future emotional responses and behavior. Other transgressions occurred in rapid succession. After all, life is full of transgressions. Ying blamed the original rejection, but of course she had changed her own behavior and tended to provoke others by her belligerence. As Ying began to develop a relatively consistent set of responses, her thoughts, feelings, and attitudes began to generalize.

Perhaps she developed a grudge against a teacher for calling her out publicly; the teacher was responsible for some kids rejecting her. She developed both a grudge and a tendency to seek vengeance toward Lori, a schoolmate who bullied her. Ying nursed a small grudge against her mother for not protecting her and a large grudge against her father for being authoritarian and judgmental of her for her pugnacious demeanor—"so not Chinese," he would often say.

Generalization continued to occur. After being bullied by Lori several times, Ying concluded, "I resent Lori." Perhaps later she concluded that she resented her teacher. Other grudges built up over time. Generalization extended to Ying's personality. She became a person with a grudge-holding personality.

In high school, discussions in some classes stimulated talk of God. Ying had been raised by parents who had immigrated from the People's Republic of China. They were not religious, although they held onto some Confucian beliefs about orderliness and the importance of family. Still, Ying was American born and had been raised her entire life in two worlds—the world of her parents and the world of her schoolmates, most of whom had been raised within Christian or Jewish families. Ying's concept of God was not sophisticated or theological. It was experiential, and powered mostly because of her judgmental and authoritarian stance that she perceived her father to hold.

Although that could happen to any child, the likelihood is high that Ying was temperamentally set up to respond with anger, resentment, and grudge holding by attachment interactions with her primary caregivers. Whether her mother initiated resentment-provoking interactions, or Ying provoked her mother, who then angered Ying, or both did so together in a reciprocal cycle is impossible to determine. However, the patterns were usually present even before the rejection incidents in middle school started her on the road to resentment as a way of life. And as talk in her peer group circulated around God, Ying declared herself by firmly rejecting God as a concept and becoming angry and combative if she thought someone was trying to "convert" her. Usually, the mere mention of God in any context was enough to provoke her to anger, which reflected underlying ambivalence she felt about her relational spirituality. Ying's parents were concerned about her but were also struggling with many acculturation stressors and were unclear on how to support her in dealing with rejecting peers who were acting in ethnocentric or even racist ways toward her. This lack of secure attachment between Ying and her parents, as well as the absence of supporting figures in the school or in the family's social network, added to the growing symptoms of unforgiveness in Ying.

ANALYZING SIX KEYS TO PERSONALITY TRANSFORMATION IN PSYCHOTHERAPY

We mentioned in the Introduction and also earlier in this chapter the six tensions within personality transformation—tensions between (a) conflict that tears apart relationships and interactions that draw together relationships; (b) attachment templates that bind people to families in and differentiation of self, which separates; (c) emotional processing and emotional regulation; (d) hope and humility, one looking fervently for change and the other leery that it can happen; (e) spiritual dwelling and spiritual seeking; and (f) justice and forgiveness. In this chapter, we turn toward trying to promote change in personality. Personality transformation involves changing the enduring structures of the self and one's coping repertoire. In this section, we describe how to change the enduring structures of relationships, spiritual connections, and inner attitudes about forgiveness through the therapeutic relationship. In the following section, we describe changing the coping repertoire of forgiveness skills, which can occur through psychotherapy, psychoeducational groups, self-help manuals, small-group discussions, or reading self-help books or Internet material about how to forgive better.

The forgiveness and relational spirituality psychotherapy model builds off six sets of complementary psychotherapy themes for personality transformation: (a) healing conflict that tears apart relationships and promoting interactions that draw together relationships; (b) uncovering and using attachment templates and promoting differentiation of self; (c) facilitating emotional processing of template-related emotions as triggered by current events and emotional regulation of intrusive emotions; (d) inspiring hope and humility in the client to move to a more mature spiritually formed place; (e) seeking to be present in either spiritual dwelling or spiritual seeking to manage a fulfilling spiritual life; and (f) promoting justice and forgiveness.

Key No. 1: Centrifugal Conflict in Tension With Centripetal Forgiveness

First, there is the tension between conflict, which tears relationships apart, and acts that restore relationships. This tension has to do with defending (psychological, physical, and social) boundaries against assault and violating others' boundaries. Ying had developed early conflicts that she blamed on her nonprotective mother and her authoritarian and judgmental father, but mostly she attributed much of her subsequent bitterness to Lori. Ying had many relationships in her life that pointed her toward conflict and centrifugal, outward slinging tendencies. Her parents tried to support her (i.e., a centripetal, cohesive move), but they were not well equipped to do so, and their own cultural adjustments kept them more focused on themselves than on the needs of Ying.

Key No. 2: Attachment Templates That Bind in Tension With Differentiation of Self

We have to maintain a balance between two systems that pull us in different directions. Attachment pulls us back to relational templates that reflect early learning patterns regarding how to be in relationships. Differentiation of self, on the other hand, pulls us toward individually responsible behavior within valued relationships as they exist today. A patient's emotionally charged relational templates usually cannot be changed in a relationship that has no emotional significance to her or him. The psychotherapist–patient working alliance (Horvath, Del Re, Flückiger, & Symonds, 2011) is essential to change in psychotherapy.

Ying might go to one psychotherapist and learn coping strategies for dealing with unforgiveness. Through those coping strategies, she might learn to function better. After that brief psychotherapy, she might be able to deal with seething resentment, and she can avoid provocative behaviors that could elicit more reactivity from peers. Overall, she might be able to live a happier and less conflicted life. Yet, Ying might still feel like a bubbling cauldron of anger waiting to spew out. She still has a set of relational templates that prescribe old patterns of behavior. They are emotionally and relationally empowered, even though after brief coping-oriented psychotherapy they are better defended. She is struggling against those relational templates using coping strategies that are more about managing her emotions and impulses as they pop into her consciousness than about changing deep-seated structures and processes at levels of her life where she might not, at first, even be aware. The first-order changes are valuable and—especially for those who have limited time, money, and capability of using psychological insight—are good enough to set most people back to the levels of functioning before developing the problems that drove them to psychotherapy. On the other hand, Ying will no doubt continue to encounter intercultural and attachment challenges. She may still lack the intercultural understanding and relational security to navigate difficult dynamics. As a psychotherapist, though, you must assess what is best for her and offer that choice to her noncoercively.

How to Increase Attachment Security

You can increase attachment security several ways (Cozolino, 2006). First, promote the open, authentic expression of primary emotion related to the interpersonal injury within a safe relationship (Greenberg, Warwar, & Malcolm, 2010). Unacknowledged and unexpressed primary emotions might be preventing the person from regulating his or her emotions. Prosocial relating is thus inhibited. Unforgiveness of early caregivers may be having a deleterious effect on preventing the person from positive attachment experiences today. Increase the victim's awareness of his or her inner experience to begin to alleviate unforgiveness.

Second, directly intervene into the victim's significant attachment relationships. This might include the relationships of offender and victim and of victim and a significant other who was not directly involved in the wrongdoing.

Third, explore the attachment relationship that the client—Ying for example—has with God. Or, coach a romantic partner to respond attentively and empathically to the victim's hurt (Greenberg et al., 2010; S. M. Johnson, 2002). Examples occur in the evidence-based practice emotion-focused therapy (see S. M. Johnson, 1996, 2002). Some relational partners or perpetrators would not be suitable for empathic relational work; individual work may be the only option (Greenberg, Warwar, & Malcolm, 2008).

Promoting Differentiation of Self

Differentiation of self is managing anxiety without emotional reactivity that catapults people into reactive interpersonal behavior. In short-term psychotherapy or group psychotherapy, we (as therapists) seek to help people control their emotional reactivity, but we cannot always promote differentiation of self as deeply as we might like. Sometimes we must work with people for a limited time, and our goals have to be focused on short-term coping solutions to unforgiveness and spiritual unrest. In spite of settling for less-than-optimal change, we still think strategically in terms of helping clients move toward more spiritual, emotional, and relational maturity through self-differentiation.

Differentiation of self requires five resolutions to polarities created by anxiety. The self-differentiated person (a) has a clear sense of being an individual in relationship (as opposed to either just an individual or just a relationship); (b) has an accurate sense of his or her individual worth, a sense of his or her own strengths and weaknesses; (c) can distinguish between what he or she is thinking and feeling; (d) fears neither abandonment nor engulfment into the other; and (e) can tolerate pain to permit personal growth. In each case, self-differentiation requires living with anxiety and discomfort instead of trying to shunt it away from the self or avoid it. Differentiation of self requires the ability to soothe oneself. Self-soothing is a skill learned under fire that enables a person to live with anxiety without being overcome by it.

Within the Bowen family systems theory (Bowen, 1985; Kerr & Bowen, 1988), many ways of promoting differentiation of self have been developed and tested for numerous families. Traditional Bowenian methods include the following, which can be worked into your therapeutic repertoire if you are not already using them: (a) Increase a client's awareness of dysfunctional intergenerational relational patterns, particularly as the patterns operate in the present; (b) to help make the client aware of his or her role in contributing to those patterns, get the client to pay attention to and try to regulate the emotion that may be fueling those patterns; and (c) teach the client directly about differentiation of self (Kerr & Bowen, 1988; Skowron & Dendy, 2004).

One way to accomplish each of these three objectives is to help the client to construct a genogram (Kerr & Bowen, 1988). A *genogram* is a family tree that focuses on family dynamics and the way the emotional system of the extended family works. Cultural and spiritual dynamics and changes in those dynamics over time can also be considered in the genogram. Once a client has begun to understand the intergenerational emotional system and his or her role within the system, work together at constructing concrete ways in which the client might develop one-to-one relationships with each system member. Understanding one's individual self and interactions within such one-to-one relationships are the essence of self-differentiation. The psychotherapist and client construct practical, situation-specific ways that the client might relate nonreactively and more intentionally within those relationships. This genogram process is not a purely cognitive or an information-focused exercise. However, it can be engaged in a relational style in which the therapist's attunement and empathy help the client work through shame or reactivity in response to understanding family patterns.

Schnarch's (1997, 2009) adaptation of Bowen's family systems theory involves using the therapeutic relationship and a couple's relationship to intensify anxiety related to developmental dilemmas of growth in differentiation of self. Forgiveness is an important part of that. Again, we see potential reciprocity among forgiveness, differentiation of self, and developing greater spiritual maturity and differentiation (see Sandage & Jankowski, 2010). Those who are growing in differentiation are also developing more flexible capacities for emotional processing and regulation. That makes unforgiveness less necessary as a coping strategy. To promote forgiveness, counselors might encourage religious or spiritual experiences to promote attachment security and hope. Both will likely create a larger chance that a person will forgive an offender. Clinical interventions focused on forgiveness typically involve two emotional processes (Greenberg et al., 2010). Greenberg et al. (2010) suggested that forgiveness can be promoted when the client (a) begins to resolve the negative emotions associated with a relational or attachment injury and (b) promotes positive affect and prosocial relating to the injurer. Empathy-based interventions have been investigated—with empty-chair dialogue holding a prominent place—and empathy for the offender has been consistently a mediator between the intervention and increased forgiveness (McCullough, Worthington, & Rachal, 1997; Sandage & Worthington, 2010).

The clinical utility of forgiveness may be enhanced by a focus on differentiation of self and on self-regulation. Many models of psychotherapy have sought to help clients regulate their affect (e.g., Linehan, 1993). But something has been missing: An approach to working with those struggling with forgiveness that draws on clinical approaches to affect regulation and integrates theoretical and empirical research on forgiveness, differentiation of self, and spirituality. Forgiveness is tied to issues of spirituality for many persons (D. E. Davis, Worthington, Hook, & Hill, 2013; Holeman, 1999, 2004; Shults & Sandage, 2006), so spiritual considerations need to be integrated with emotional regulation and forgiveness to foster differentiation of self. Forgiveness also requires that people face hurt and injustice and not get lost in self-pity or angry vengeance (Shults & Sandage, 2003; Volf, 1996). Forgiveness is simply one habitat of differentiation of self—adaptive working out of one's own identity within complicated, emotion-laden relationships. By helping a client forgive, we might help the client toward a more differentiated life.

Key No. 3: Emotional Processing and Emotional Regulation

Emotional Processing

Emotion marks experiences as important. We do not get emotional about successfully arriving at work each morning or fixing a cup of coffee. We get emotional about important experiences. If Ying is to forgive Lori, she will need to forgive two or three emotionally important transgressions. If she chose unimportant transgressions, she might forgive seven or eight transgressions but still hold a grudge.

Some have difficulty accessing or understanding their emotions. A psychotherapist must help the client first understand the emotional impact of offenses. This can heighten attachment to a therapist who can connect with a client in his or her emotional vulnerability. Some clients hold a belief-centered theology. They might even view emotional processing as foreign to their experiences of relational spirituality. In contrast, others may be familiar with spiritual forms of lament or are open to integrating emotional processing within their relational spirituality.

Emotional Self-Regulation

Focusing on self-regulation is required so that one can forgive without becoming a doormat or without becoming fused into an offender's dominant personality. Self-soothing requires emotional self-control. It must break the client from dictatorial control by emotional processes, often those set down early in life. Being able to disengage, especially when that is a characteristic of differentiation of self (and not primitive dissociation) is necessary to process one's emotions productively. Such emotional processing can increase the client's level of differentiation of self, which might (as a collateral effect) facilitate growth toward spiritual maturity. This maturation might possibly spread to the client's religious or spiritual networks (Christakis & Fowler, 2009).

Becoming a more forgiving person involves a generalization across relationships, too. That generalization can occur even if Ying grants decisional forgiveness but does not yet experience emotional forgiveness. For example, if Ying declares decisional forgiveness for Lori accompanied by an emotional insight into Lori's background and motivations, that is a start. Ying might see the same pattern in her teacher, her minister, or even her parents.

Successful psychotherapy that produces lasting effects, though, usually does not seek merely to produce an insight. Successful psychotherapy usually requires many repetitions before it makes its way into the enduring thoughts, attitudes, and behaviors of the client. Furthermore, typically, the cognitive–affective systems are the ones that are tied up in long-standing personality problems and even acute unforgiveness. Emotional experience is needed to transform those systems (Fosha, Siegel, & Solomon, 2009). Securely attached relationships—such as the one that the psychotherapist tries to form with the client—will provide a key holding environment for emotional transformation. A person with a grudge-holding personality usually is beset by anxious, depressed, resentful, and bitter unforgiveness. If a grudge-holding person is to change his or her personality, the person must change the pattern of emotional experience, with which the psychotherapist can help. Changing emotional experience in one or two important relationships is a start, but those changes must be done repeatedly for the experience to be powerful enough to allow generalization. This is the key to changing a vengeful personality.

Key No. 4: Hope and Humility

Hope

Hope is an essential element in effective psychotherapy (Snyder, 1994). Facilitating hope in counseling involves constructing goals and providing concrete direction about how to achieve those therapeutic goals in the context of a collaborative therapeutic relationship. Yet, goal setting and directing therapeutic processes to achieve those goals is not disconnected from attachment processes. When the psychotherapist provides direction to goal attainment, he or she facilitates the experience of security for the client. He or she reassures the client that change is possible and that the psychotherapist is invested in helping realize that possibility. Reassurance and psychotherapist investment convey a sense of valuing, worth, and care for the client. They thereby strengthen the therapeutic relationship.

Humility

People need to perceive that they have some personal control over their life. Yet, experience has shown that chance, luck, powerful others, fate, and divine intervention make us at times doubt how much, if any, control we really have. That is, we must all come to the conclusion that we are not the measure of all things. The psychotherapist cannot simply pop the client's bubble. That will bring despair. Rather, humility can be subtly taught through setting the eyes of the client on humility as a virtue, helping the client habituate the heart to a habit of humility, helping the client place the virtue under mild strain to practice humility and to deal with failures when they arrive.

Key No. 5: Spiritual Dwelling and Seeking

Spiritual Dwelling

Spiritual dwelling usually feels like a safe and stable place to be. As we have seen, though, it can also be a place of stagnation, inertia, and decay. Ying was not raised in a heavily spiritual tradition within the home, but she certainly encountered it with her schoolmates. Some residual spiritual concepts of honor, family ancestors, and order remained in her family. Those ideas were at times also at odds with the more traditionally individualistic culture within which her peers operated. In middle school, experimentation with new religious ideas—such as Eastern religion–based mindfulness, meditation, or yoga—had not yet blossomed. Human spirituality was promoted through patriotic messages about troops serving in Iraq and Afghanistan. Nature spirituality was nascent in the environmental conservation movement but had not captured the minds of the youth in their middle school years.

Spiritual Seeking

For Ying, concerns about spirituality were on the horizon. She was cutting herself off emotionally from her parents. Her emotional cutoff was leading her to avoid her parents, especially her traditional father. She also was pulling back from friends as more friends distanced themselves from her increasing acrimony and complaints. Ying was building up a deficit of connections. She was becoming unmoored from virtually every relationship in her life, family, peer, and spiritual. This inevitably would set her off into some period of instability. As we discussed in the previous chapter, most people who come to psychotherapy—like Ying—have entered into a seeking phase of the dwelling–seeking cycle. Typically, that involves what we called "noisiness." The noise includes sadness, reduced focus on others, an orientation to solve the problem and return to a more comfortable place, less performance of virtues, and the presence of psychological symptoms. The tendency is to run from seeking back into the safety of dwelling. There are certainly times when this is necessary to allow the client to maintain integrity of personality. But, often, the more therapeutic move is to provide a safe crucible that can stand the heat and emotion, allow intensification to build, enable the client to investigate new solutions, and allow the client to find a new dwelling place. Ying was moving from a period of relative stability, youthful spiritual dwelling, to a period of unsettledness, or spiritual seeking. Her interpersonal, emotional, and spiritual cutoff initiated a seeking of stable dwelling, from which she was increasingly alienated. One of the causal problems at the center of her alienation was unforgiveness. The rejections she had experienced had swept her up in emotional unforgiveness. The unraveling of her social world became a template for unraveling her family life and unraveling of a settled sense of spiritual disengagement. Her relational spirituality of moving from dwelling to seeking was a core issue for Ying.

Key No. 6: Justice in Tension With Forgiveness

And sixth, there is tension between justice (which may require things beyond one's control, such as the offender's willingness to atone) and the emotional and physical benefits of releasing resentment. Ying felt a keen sense of injustice across many relationships. With her parents, she mostly felt that she deserved more support than she got, so her belief that she was being deprived of love heightened her belief that her parents, and God, were failing her in distributive justice. However, Lori's bullying provided a sense of injustice that was being perpetrated against her. She held resentment and desires for payback for that bullying. There was a sense that she might forgive her parents, her friends, or even Lori, but the weight was clearly on the side of the teeter-totter that measured injustices. What would Ying need if she were to balance the justice–forgiveness tension more in favor of forgiveness?

What Will Trigger a Personal Opening That Could Permit Forgiveness?

To forgive, the person must willingly engage or reengage the offender internally. Something must trigger an opening to the offender that will allow the other to be taken in. Something must intentionally reorganize the self in response to the other (Volf, 1996).

An Encounter With the Sacred Could Be a Trigger

One way this might happen is through an encounter with the sacred. Whether the person is already religious or spiritual, or is virtually unspiritual (like Ying), an encounter with the spiritual, whether through an experience with nature, with human solidarity, with God, or an experience of transcendence can rock the person's world and create cracks in the boundaries, permitting forgiveness to be considered when it might not have been previously. Encounters with the sacred can open new horizons of meaning and purpose that can facilitate reworking the meaning of past experiences and unforgiveness.

Sometimes a spiritual or religious experience can draw a drifting person close to some sacred object. The person might feel strength and love perceived to reside in the sacred and use it to buoy the self. Although unmoored spiritually, the person at least is attached to a floating buoy. With a hint of stability, the victim can perhaps reach out to the offender and reencounter him or her. Thus, forgiveness might become possible or might, at least, be considered.

The psychotherapist who notes that a person is adrift from family, peer, and sacred objects can help the person consider potential connections to sacred objects. Thus, the psychotherapist might have a number of suggestions that might appeal to different clients: worship, spiritual intimacy, meditative prayer, communing with nature, feeling a sense of solidarity with others at a large rock concert, or just gazing at the night sky and experiencing that there is transcendence beyond the meager human existence. Each can make forgiveness more possible. The sacred serves as a safe haven for emotional regulation. Connective spiritual experiences are essentially a means of moving emotionally closer to the sacred so that the person might experience spiritual closeness. This engages positive spiritual emotions, which Fredrickson

(1998) has shown broaden one's receptivity and build one's resources psychologically. To the extent people anthropomorphize the sacred or treat it as personal—as with God or human spirituality—the sacred can serve as an ideal substitute attachment figure.

Creation of a Content-Focused Conversation Could Be a Trigger

The psychotherapist can help clients explore reconnective experiences with the family members from whom the clients are estranged. Creating genograms, which often require clients to interview family members to find out about connections that they recall, can provide opportunities for cutoff relationships to be reopened.

Forgiveness Could Trigger a Reconnection With an Offender

Clients can consider whether they wish to forgive people who have hurt and offended them. Forgiveness occurs within the forgiver. Thus, forgiveness does not risk new rejection from requested reconciliation. Forgiveness is a safe first step into possibly reconnecting with estranged offenders.

Each Can Create Renewed Attachments, Contributing to a More Secure Attachment Base

By pursuing an approach to the sacred, to the family, or to forgiving an unforgiven former friend, clients can be strengthened through a more secure attachment to the sacred, through a conversational interview with a cutoff family member, or through forgiving an offender (even though not telling the offender of what is being attempted). Thus, clients are more capable of accepting the wrongdoing without fusing with it. That is, to the degree that the person is more differentiated, he or she is able to accept that the wrongdoing was wrong, harmful, angering, and anxiety producing. Yet, he or she can treat the sacred as a viable option for connecting the family member as at least a source of information and the offender as a valuable person, without fusing his or her identity with the wrong the person did. The person does not hold on to unforgiveness but is free to regulate his or her emotions and relate prosocially to the other.

A number of spiritual experiences might accomplish or facilitate these changes. Such spiritual experiences include prayer for the wrongdoer, mindfulness and other meditative practices, acceptance, self-compassion, other-directed emotions (e.g., empathy, sympathy, compassion, love), and non–self-focused emotions (e.g., hope, gratitude, humility). Practices such as mindfulness meditation (i.e., focusing completely on one's momentary experiences), lovingkindness meditation (i.e., focusing on loving experiences), Zen meditation (i.e., emptying the mind, and usually focusing on breathing), or yoga might also foster self-regulation of emotion, especially if the person is already high in self-differentiation. Those practices may be useful for some clients who hold Buddhist or nontheistic spiritual worldviews.

HOW TO INTERVENE IN A RELATIONALLY ORIENTED PSYCHOTHERAPY OR TREATMENT

Personality change involves initiating change attempts, sustaining effort at change, and maintaining gains. To do so requires that a person modify the strong situations that govern unwanted behavior, replacing them by strong situations that will foster desired behavior. Personality change also involves modifying the narrative threads that unify many of the person's experiences into reasonably consistent narratives.

Psychotherapy must help the person accomplish those tasks. Psychotherapy can do so because it is, itself, a strong situation. Psychotherapy is an unusual event for most people. It occurs in times of emotional upheaval and arousal and when a person is trying to solve his or her problems. True, often the person is almost unconsciously saying, "Fix my problem, but don't change me." Master psychotherapist Sheldon Kopp (1970) once likened change in psychotherapy to Dorothy in *The Wizard of Oz* (LeRoy & Fleming, 1939). Dorothy wanted to get back to Kansas. She appealed to the ostensibly powerful Wizard for help. Yet, in wisdom, the Wizard sent her not to Kansas but on a quest in which she had to intentionally defeat the source of pain and evil in the kingdom— the Wicked Witch of the East. By the end of her successful quest, in which Dorothy discovered her clear-thinking brain, heart of compassion for others, and a sense of courage in the face of uncertainty and danger, she returned to the Wizard only to discover that he was a mere human, rather than a super change agent. She found that she had always had the power within her to return home, if she but used it.

Psychotherapists hope that psychotherapy will be a powerfully strong situation. In fact, we, as therapists, personally (irrationally) hope that we can help every client. That is, we hope to create a psychotherapeutic situation that is so strong that every client responds in the same way—changing so that he or she achieves his or her beneficial goals. Of course, the goals, life circumstances, and challenges differ. Each client requires the psychotherapist to adjust the general plan many times, so that each counseling interaction— indeed, each moment of counseling—is in some ways unique, even if the strategy is universal.

Psychotherapy is like building a trail from the foot of a mountain to its peak. Hikers follow the same trail, and yet each hiker has a different experience on the hike. Occasionally, one goes off-trail and still fights his or her way to the top. But most psychotherapists seek to lead all clients up the mountain along the same basic trail.

In the same way, the psychotherapist knows in general how to help every person before seeing the person. That is, psychotherapists have a general strategy for psychotherapy. That strategy has little variability from person to person. Psychodynamic psychotherapists find unconscious dynamics, cognitive therapists find distorted cognition, and family therapists find faulty family dynamics. All psychotherapists have their general strategy. They hope their general strategies are flexible enough to accommodate most clients, and most of the time—says the research—they are correct.

PSYCHOTHERAPY FOR CHANGING PERSONALITY—GENERAL APPROACH

We have described a model of personality and principles for a general approach to psychotherapy in working with people who wish to forgive troublesome transgressions. People who seek psychotherapy and struggle with unforgiveness often have a sense of disruption in their lives and families. Their spirituality is often involved in potential treatment because their unrest has moved them from a sense of spiritual dwelling to spiritual seeking. The problems and personal issues they face arose in relationships and—because unforgiveness is a focal part of psychotherapy—relationships are intimately involved with the treatment. Some treatment is inevitably aimed at improving coping. But other treatment seeks not just to shore up coping but also to work transformation in the structures, processes, and triggers of the person's life—inner and outer. Thus, the targets of psychotherapy will involve changes in relationships and relational spirituality. They will aim to help the person better mature through differentiation of self.

Seven General "Rules" of Psychotherapy

From our collective experience as psychotherapists, we might tentatively suggest that there are some generally understood "rules" of psychotherapy, outlined below.

- Helping occurs within a relationship.
- Trust is required. Clients must reveal personal information, including personal failures and (often shameful) aspects of their lives, which make them even more vulnerable than the inability to solve his or her problems has left them.
- The interaction is focused solely on the client's life, not the psychotherapist's life, so the relationship is asymmetrical.

- The interaction is primarily for the client's welfare, although what is in the client's welfare must be seen in light of the way that others are affected and might affect the client. (Thus, as you know, a psychotherapist has a duty to warn someone that a client might be plotting violence against him or her.)
- The interaction is aimed at helping the person deal more effectively with the mental health, behavioral, and relational challenges to return to normal functioning and in some cases to move beyond business-as-normal to flourishing.
- The psychotherapist has a general understanding of people, problems, and likely solutions—generically, a theory. But the psychotherapist is committed to applying the theory only to the degree that the client's life corresponds to the theory. To the degree that there is a discrepancy between the client's life and the psychotherapist's theory, the psychotherapist is committed to tailoring his or her theory to fit the client's life, not imposing the theory on the client.
- The psychotherapist's theory should be supported by evidence (or if it is not, it should be in line with accepted practice), and the psychotherapist is duty-bound to use the treatment thought to be most likely to produce client-sought (and prosocial) outcomes.

Use Evidence-Based Practices in Psychology

Increasingly, the treatments most likely to produce the best outcomes are those that have been supported by clinical science research both on the treatment packages and on the theory of change behind them. That is, increasingly, evidence-based practices in psychology are preferred (American Psychological Association Presidential Task Force on Evidence-Based Practice, 2006). (However, there is still room to innovate as long as a panel of one's peers would evaluate the therapeutic innovation as likely to produce results in the client's best interest.)

Fit Triggers, Structures, and Processes to the Interpersonal Relational Templates

People behave as they do because triggers stimulate or call attention to environmental, behavioral, emotive, or cognitive structures, which relate to certain environmental, behavioral, emotive, or cognitive processes, which in their turn trigger progressive experiences. A large majority of these triggers, structures, and processes were formed and are maintained with a relational context. Psychotherapy is finding triggers in ways that fit and reinforce prior relational templates and then guiding the client to modify those toward more mature living.

CASE STUDY—ANALYZING JACK AND JULIA

Treatment

Recall Jack (see Chapter 4), who came to psychotherapy because he was having difficulty forgiving Julia, his repeatedly wayward spouse. The unforgiveness was getting in his way. He was obsessing about her when he was at work as a laboratory technician. He had made several errors in delicate (and expensive) analytic procedures, which resulted in one big error that not only had been a costly oversight but also lost the company a valued customer. The supervisor was very angry with Jack and reprimanded him strongly. Jack reported that the supervisor had urged Jack to "get his stuff together before I have to let you go." That got Jack into treatment.

Treating Jack's Unforgiveness of Julia

The psychotherapist that Jack went to after Julia and he divorced was a middle-aged woman, about 10 years older than Jack, whose name was Paula. Jack was hesitant about attending psychotherapy, and slow to engage with Paula. Jack had lots of questions about Paula's success rate and whether she had encountered (and successfully helped) people who had been victimized by a spouse who had multiple affairs.

Connecting in Session 1

In the first session, Paula tried to get a good sense of the extent and severity of the problem. Jack was not depressed, but he complained of anxiety and intrusive rumination that he could not seem to control. It was interfering with his work, social life, and family interactions. Jack not only was concerned that he might lose his job but also had lost his temper explosively at his children on several occasions—"something I don't think I ever did before the problems with Julia."

"I think something is wrong with me," he told Paula. He said,

> I'd like to believe it is just a quick-fix kind of thing, but I think something more basic is wrong. I've never been really happy at any time in my life. As a Unitarian, I've always had my issues with God. I have trust problems all over the place—the church, unloving acts within my own religious community, and sometimes feeling that God wasn't available,

just obscured in social interaction. Yet, at other times, feeling a closeness from inspirational meetings at services. I wasn't drawn to Unitarianism because of authority conflicts—though heaven knows I've had enough of those. But our loose structure certainly is preferable to my strict Baptist background. So, I've thought about coming to therapy for years, but never could justify the time and cost. This has scared me enough that I think I'm ready to do something to get some of my issues taken care of, once and for all time.

Paula suggested weekly meetings, but Jack wanted to "make some progress" quickly. He pushed for twice-a-week meetings. Paula suggested that such a schedule might not make that much difference if what Jack desired was really deep-seated personality change. Jack said that he was concerned that he would lose his job if something was not done quickly. They agreed to meet twice weekly for the first month and then reevaluate.

In Retrospect

In later sessions, Jack said that a critical moment in psychotherapy was when Paula was willing to compromise about the frequency of sessions. As he said,

> At that point, I really needed some sense of control in my life. Looking back at it now, I see that you were right. It didn't make any difference coming once or twice a week. But if you had insisted on once weekly, I think I would have gone looking for someone else—or actually, probably just not bothered with therapy. I was a product of my past, and running away from any conflict I could get away from was where I was at during that point in my life.

Conflicts

Jack soon brought in a series of conflicts that he wanted to discuss. In the second session, he began the session with a resentment of his boss for "scapegoating me for losing the . . . account." This reveals a common pattern in which struggles with unforgiveness seem to multiply. He began the second session with a discussion of a conflictual interaction with Julia that had occurred over visitation of the kids. She had failed to show up on her regular Saturday visit, and Jack could not reach her by phone. He had to put off plans he had made to go fishing with his buddy. When he finally got Julia on the phone, she said that she had phoned and left a message on the home answering machine on Thursday that she had to go out of town on an "opportunity." She said that she had offered to take the kids the next weekend on Saturday and Sunday. When Jack had checked the messages, though, there was no message, he said. "The conversation deteriorated into our usual shouting match about her irresponsibility and my unreasonable rigidity," he told the psychotherapist. "She has just absolutely not been there for me. I can't believe I would pick a spouse like her. It was the story of my life."

Renegotiating the Frequency of Meeting

By the end of a month, Jack said he saw that therapy was going to be a long-term thing. He and Paula discussed it, and Jack agreed to meet weekly.

What They Were Learning

They had begun to uncover some of the roots of Jack's unforgiveness in what was beginning to look to Paula like an insecure parental attachment to Jack's father. Jack's father had often let him down. Those repeated betrayals and disappointments created relational templates, and as Jack got old enough to think about God, Jack was able to connect with God but only tenuously. He always felt like God might not be there for him. Throughout life, he had numerous times of disappointment with God, the church, and priests. And he had times of alternately doubting God's goodness or faithfulness and feeling that God was always "lurking just out of sight."

His marriage to Julia had been rocky, especially in the early years. Jack explained, "Julia always considered me to be 'holding something back, unable to be fully able to connect with me,' she used to say." Jack mimicked her voice in a whiny, unflattering tone. "She always accused me of defending myself rigidly and being afraid to risk a personal relationship."

"Hmm," said Paula. "What do you think about her accusations?"

"Damn unfair! As if she had no responsibility! Makes me furious."

As treatment proceeded, Paula developed her hypothesis. In a staffing at the agency, Paula presented her work with Jack for collegial consultation:

> Jack was acting out his relational schemes of insecure attachment that had generalized to insecure adult attachments. Jack was high on both anxious and avoidant attachment. He avoided full engagement with Julia, just as he did with God, and yet when things did not go well for him, he became anxious, clingy and fearful of abandonment. And he always seemed to expect that abandonment was just around the corner.

Jack's relationship with Julia was a fused relationship—one tied together in emotional pushes and pulls in which the partners seem to react to each other without even conscious thought—rather than a well-differentiated one. That is, he was very emotionally reactive to Julia's actions, and their relationship was characterized by a push–pull dynamic that never seemed to be entirely comfortable. They always seemed to be in the midst of a power struggle.

They were uncovering important dynamics about Jack's background and some of the ways it was driving his relationships with his work supervisor and Julia. Paula was cautiously optimistic about their progress. Jack seemed to have the capacity to use what he was slowly discovering about himself and was beginning to make some small inroads into changing. But, to Paula, it looked as if Jack's goal of becoming a more forgiving person and one with a better relationship with God was quite far in the future.

It is worth noting that Paula processed both her relational hypothesis and some of her own countertransference about the case in the context of consulting relationships with colleagues. A relational theory needs to be practiced relationally with both clients and colleagues, as the latter can provide supportive professional attachments that are crucial to long-term effectiveness and clinician resilience.

SUMMARY

In the first part of the book, we described our stress-and-coping model of forgiveness, spiritual transformation within relational spirituality, and the forgiveness and relational spirituality structural and process models. In the second part of the book, beginning with the present chapter, we describe a general approach to changing personality. We get more specific in the following chapter on brief psychotherapy to help people forgive.

6

FORGIVENESS IN BRIEF PSYCHOTHERAPY

It is important to make a distinction between brief psychotherapy and either long-term or open-ended psychotherapy. Brief psychotherapy tends to be for a negotiated maximum number of sessions. The number of sessions agreed to might not be the actual number of sessions in counseling. The client might drop out earlier than the maximum, might get better more quickly and decide to terminate early, or might agree with the psychotherapist (and insurance company) to extend the number of sessions.

Open-ended or long-term psychotherapy will typically last many more sessions. Of course, open-ended psychotherapy may end after only a few sessions for various reasons (e.g., dropout, getting better more quickly than anticipated, moving away).

We could make a case that there is not a lot of justification for treating brief and open-ended counseling differently, even if one usually takes longer

http://dx.doi.org/10.1037/14712-007
Forgiveness and Spirituality in Psychotherapy: A Relational Approach, by E. L. Worthington, Jr. and S. J. Sandage

than the other. In business agreements, people tend not to look at the end date. They just proceed as if the relationship will be interminable. In marriages, people do not assume the relationship may end, even though the fact is about 50% will end, many within the first year. People do not think about it much, but they know even before the birth of a child that children grow up and the relationships change with each new stage of development. And people rarely think about how the parent–child relationship will transform, and then the child leaves home.

But as psychotherapists, we know that the relationships with negotiated end dates are different from those that are open ended. We perceive of them differently, even if the clients do not always do so or even if in practice, they each end after only one or a few sessions. So, we characterize the two ideals as *brief* or *long-term* psychotherapy. In this chapter, we first look at some of the similarities across brief and long-term psychotherapy. Then, we examine salient differences. By examining similarities and differences, we describe a six-stage model of brief psychotherapy. We then discuss what different theoretical approaches to psychotherapy say about forgiveness and about involving religion and spirituality in psychotherapy. Finally, we examine how to produce first-order changes, which are what we see most often in brief psychotherapy. This readies us to see a case study of brief psychotherapy in the following chapter.

SIMILARITIES BETWEEN BRIEF AND LONG-TERM PSYCHOTHERAPIES

Relationships Are Still Central

Whether psychotherapy is brief or long-term, the working alliance has been found to be a consistently important factor in whether people change (Horvath, Del Re, Flückiger, & Symonds, 2011; Norcross, 2011). In brief psychotherapy, the psychotherapist is more a source of information, suggestion, and encouragement. In long-term psychotherapy, simply because there is more time to get to know each other, the client–psychotherapist relationship is more complex. Client interactions with the psychotherapist provide ways for clients to see how they use the same dynamics in their relationships with parents, the psychotherapist, and supporters as they do with the people with whom they are having trouble. This is particularly important in dealing with forgiveness. When trust in an important relationship might have been shattered, the psychotherapist–patient relationship must be central and must be characterized by trust.

The Change Processes Are the Same

Worthington (2006) suggested that there are six stages to helping relationships, and he applied them to cases involving forgiveness within a stress-and-coping model of psychotherapy. In a nutshell, the six stages—describing each of six processes—he outlines (with an accompanying transcript) are more suited to promoting forgiveness in brief (semistructured) psychotherapy. Although the six processes are the same in brief and long-term psychotherapy, the model is less of a stage model with long-term psychotherapy. There is recycling through the stages. In fact, the idea of stages, per se, loses its meaning. In latter portions of this chapter, we look at how brief psychotherapy to help people forgive can be used to at least get the client thinking about personality transformation.

Briefly, the six stages (or processes) of psychotherapy are connect (Step 1), rethink the problem (Step 2), make action plans based on the new conceptualization (Step 3), follow up on action plans and support change attempts (Step 4), plan for maintenance (Step 5), and terminate psychotherapy (Step 6). We discuss them further as the present chapter unfolds.

The Theory of Change Is the Same

In both the short-term and longer term psychotherapies, the general theory of change that we have laid out in the first part of the book will remain the same. The client is driven to psychotherapy usually because of stressors that will not abate. In addition, often clients have exhausted their social networks in seeking advice about how to solve their problems.

On a psychological level, stressors can lead to challenge or threat. Loss, stress, or threatening events can activate our templates of relational spirituality (attachment theory). With appraisals and stress reactions, coping efforts have been instituted. Because coping efforts to resolve the stress have not produced the desired relief, anxiety has built to the place where the client believes a professional psychotherapist can provide the needed help. Loder (1989) hypothesized a cyclical set of processes of trying to deal with this disequilibrium the client experiences. Conflict leads to an interlude for scanning ways to deal with, solve, or reconfigure the situation. Those considerations lead to constructive acts of the imagination that suggest potential solutions. When the client attempts new potential solutions, those attempts release energy that was bound up previously in tension around the conflict. Depending on the outcomes of the attempted solutions, the client thinks (more or less rationally) about the outcome and derives an interpretation of the experience through reflecting on what occurred.

Especially in short-term psychotherapy, clients usually just want to solve their problems, and quickly. They want what family therapists have called first-order changes. If religion is involved, they want conservative religious coping that makes only minor changes (Pargament, 1997), not transformative religious coping that might make them rethink their entire religious framework. They want a quick return to dwelling. Clients seek new understanding and new emotional experiences—but within a relatively familiar cognitive meaning framework. True, the psychotherapist probably will have to provide a different conception of cause and effect that will force changes in the client's meaning system, but those are seen as relatively superficial changes. So, an unforgiving, vengeful patient who sees her boss as a horrid abuser might be helped to see that she had substantially provoked her boss and brought some of the criticism (no longer "abuse") on herself. That reframing might help her forgive and have a more productive working relationship with her boss.

If problems can be solved in brief psychotherapy, then anxiety is bound and clients can return to a homeostatic state either near or not too distant psychologically from where they were. They might have had new insights, developed new ways of coping, and experienced personal and spiritual growth. But the change is usually incremental rather than transformational.

When problems do not abate with repeated efforts at first-order changes, the client's anxiety intensifies. Intensification drives people either to more defensiveness, denial, projection, and other defensive behaviors or to seeking more franticly new solutions. In the religious realm, this can move clients from spiritual dwelling to spiritual seeking.

The resolution of this anxiety depends on the client's attachment working models and on their religious beliefs, values, and practices, and their religious processes. The resolution can be (a) stable spiritual seeking, questing and an unsettled life; (b) denial and burying the problem with refusal to face it (which can be adaptive in the short term but might lead to problems in the long term); (c) solving the problem within the existing worldview and operating framework with only first-order changes, insights, and modifications of life and relationships; or (d) spiritual and personal transformations (in normal situations, processes, and structures). Relational templates regarding forgiveness can become dominating or can be at least acknowledged if not controlled.

Even in brief psychotherapy, a good working alliance is necessary for psychotherapeutic progress (Horvath et al., 2011). Schnarch's (1997) model of the crucible still applies to short-term psychotherapy. Although transformation of the client's spirituality does not occur as often as in longer term psychotherapy, it can occur, and even if it does not occur, the seeds can be laid for postpsychotherapy adaptation to transformative spirituality. Often, for transformation to occur, differentiation of self, as opposed to fusion to the psychotherapist, can be an aid. (It can also hinder change.)

Transformation can be evolutionary or revolutionary in its development. The end point of transformation will be a revolution (a dramatic and substantial second-order change), but it can come about either gradually or suddenly. Although spiritual seeking is emotionally hot, the dynamic tension between dwelling and seeking might build. There is pressure to keep seeking to find a new spiritual state, but there is also a pressure to return to a comfortable state of dwelling—the conservative state. So, the patient and psychotherapist are always fighting a tendency to return to the unforgiving state, even after the person has worked through a forgiveness program. Revolutionary changes are those that make sudden or more insightful changes second-order systems (e.g., rearranging the client's worldview or significant aspects of it). Although these revolutions do occur, most changes evolve.

Thus, we see an overlap in the psychology of change within our model of forgiveness and relational spirituality for short- and long-term psychotherapies. Let's try to zero in on the differences.

DIFFERENCES BETWEEN BRIEF AND LONG-TERM PSYCHOTHERAPIES

Assumptions May Differ

Often, different assumptions are made about the relationships. In long-term psychotherapy, people often assume that the patient has inflexible behavioral strategies (in fact, this is sometimes seen as being the problem) and by changing the interactions with an important person (the psychotherapist), the patient will (a) be forced to interact differently, (b) increase the flexibility of responding, (c) stop being so inflexible, and (d) apply the new interpersonal strategies in the real life. This is not our assumption. We do not assume that the person cannot forgive or that the person is necessarily rigid in relational spiritual responding. Rather, we assume that the person has gone from dwelling to seeking or is stuck in dwelling, which is not working so the client needs to change into seeking to get to the place where a new type of dwelling is needed.

Relationships May Differ

In brief psychotherapy, contacts will be bounded, with agreed upon time limits. That usually feels somewhat contractual. Long-term psychotherapy feels more like an ongoing friendship (although ongoing professional-yet-personal relationship is a more apt but more cumbersome description)—at least while the psychotherapy is in progress. Of course, psychotherapy inevitably ends. That eventual boundary will make the psychotherapy relationship recede into memory, leaving the changes and transformation within the client life as the permanent monument to the psychotherapy experience. Because of the protracted and convoluted movement of patients through psychotherapy, it will usually be necessary to highlight the gains in forgiveness and the role of patients' spirituality in bringing forgiveness about.

Goals Must Be More Limited

Goals Might Not Be as Different as You Might Think

Not all psychodynamic psychotherapy takes a long time. Brief psychoanalytic approaches suggest that people can learn in months to exert more ego control in their lives and rid themselves of negative symptoms (Soldz & McCullough, 2000). Also, although cognitive therapies are also effective at helping people change relatively quickly, cognitive therapies may aim at changing worldviews, assumptions, expectations, attributions of cause, and even self-talk, which require complex planning and execution. In most brief psychotherapies, profound changes can come out of making seeming small modifications that have huge ramifications. Thus, that leads us to minimal change therapy.

Minimal Change Therapy

Leona Tyler (1973) suggested that psychotherapies attempt what she called *minimal change therapy*. Psychotherapies do not have to transform an entire personality, she argues, to transform a client's life. If a man were standing in New York looking at San Diego, and the person made just a 3-degree shift north in direction, then by the time he arrived at the West Coast, he would be North of Los Angeles. Thus, Tyler suggested that if a person makes a small but significant change in life direction and maintains that change over time, then the person can eventually effect a huge change in personality.

Solution-focused therapies (de Shazer, 1985, 1988) also suggest that a person, couple, or family make a small but significant change in their actions and build on that change. They assume that the person already knows the solution but has been wrapped up in the problem and has not been able successfully to do what needs to be done.

One might imagine, for instance, that a person is often criticized by his new boss. The person has become angry, resentful, bitter, and grudge holding. He often complains and whines to his wife and friends. That negative affect poisons relationships resulting in (you guessed it) a vicious cycle: criticisms from his friends, new rejection, whining, anger, spread to new relationships, new rejections, new whining, and so on. If the person can change his or her personality such that resentment and hostility cease and the person practices more forgiveness and agreeableness and less emotional reactivity, then less criticism will likely be provoked. This might transform the person's life because of the ripple effect of making a significant change.

Dose–Response Relationship

In the same way that researchers establish a graph of the dose of a medication plotted against the effect it has, it is possible to discern dose–response curves for three types of brief forgiveness interventions. If we simply exhort people to forgive because forgiveness is demonstrably good for them in aiding their physical and mental health, relationships, and spirituality, then that exhortation yields about 0.2 standard deviations of lasting change. That is true regardless of whether it is made in only a few minutes or is buttressed with data for up to eight hours. The dose–response curve is flat. If one seeks to promote a decision to forgive, the dose–response curve is gently sloping upward (Baskin & Enright, 2004) from virtually no effect in just a few minutes of appeal to a maximum of about 0.3 to 0.4 standard deviations of change at 3 hours and no gain for spending more time on it.

For promoting emotional forgiveness, most programs start with exhorting people to change for their own self-benefit, then appeal to make a decision to forgive and then put effort into (a) helping the forgiver understand the offender, (b) motivating an unselfish gift of forgiveness, and (c) seeking to promote maintenance of change after the program ends. That dose-response curve is a straight line moving steadily upwards from 0 in a few minutes (or an immediate bump if the appeal to self-benefit occurs early) at a rate of about 0.1 standard deviations of change per hour of treatment (for a meta-analysis, i.e., a quantitative analysis of the efficacy of virtually all studies on any topic, see Wade, Hoyt, Kidwell, & Worthington, 2014). This covers a vast range of interventions—including 23 using the Enright (2012) process model, 22 using the REACH forgiveness model (Worthington, 2006), and 22 by all other models.

The practical implications are these:

- If you have less than two hours to work with a person on forgiving, appeal first to self-beneficial motives. That gets an immediate benefit within ten minutes.
- Emotional forgiveness and decisions to forgive both take time to yield positive effects. Decisional forgiveness yields slow and steady gains, but do not spend more than three hours on it (DiBlasio, 1998).
- Our suspicion is that it takes at least two to four hours to build any emotional forgiveness. In the first few hours of most interventions to promote forgiveness, only the foundation for emotional forgiveness can be laid.

- In treatments such as the REACH forgiveness model, expect about 0.1 standard deviations of change in forgiveness per hour of treatment (Wade et al., 2014).

The Sense of Time Is Different

Psychotherapy has more or less time pressure associated with it. Sometimes, brief psychotherapy feels time-pressured because a third-party payer allots a specified amount of time. At other times, the clients allocate a fixed amount of money for treatment, or the psychotherapist, after assessment, suggests a time frame for counseling. In long-term psychotherapy, we do not have the sense that "we must accomplish a lot in a little time." Because of the sense of urgency that can arise in brief psychotherapy, patience is more important for the psychotherapist in brief than in unlimited psychotherapy. In an ironic turn-around, this requires differentiation of self and self-regulation for the brief psychotherapist. Brief psychotherapy can feel like a crucible in which clients expect that something (good) will happen and anxiety builds until the client can see progress. The psychotherapist quickly feels that anxiety. The psychotherapist must self-soothe. Finally, the psychotherapist must take responsibility for what he or she can and cannot change in a limited time.

Attack Points for Stimulating Change Are Likely to Be Different

Psychotherapy moves through a predictable process. Psychotherapists first make a personal connection with (i.e., join) the client. Second, together psychotherapist and patient move toward the client's goal. Third, psychotherapists pull the client along. Fourth, psychotherapists separate from the patient, leaving the patient capable of sustaining the new direction.

Even though the process of psychotherapy is the same and the coping theory of forgiveness and relational spirituality is the same, the pressure points for change might be different between brief and long-term psychotherapy. Psychotherapy is like war aimed at defeating a stubborn foe—the client's problem. Strategic warfare first determines one's strengths and weaknesses and those of the enemy, and then strategically seeks to pit one's strengths forcefully against the weak point of the enemy. The idea is to maintain flexibility in the face of an enemy's attack. When the enemy attacks (as has happened with the manifestations of the client's symptoms that brought him or her to psychotherapy), it limits the focus to the point of attack. The clever strategic psychotherapist is patient, lets the enemy expend its energy in attacking a well dug-in defensive force, and then as frustration of the unsuccessful attacker increases, the psychotherapist can sense that there are many options to route the enemy. A massive counterattack can be launched against a disorganized and frustrated enemy. Having kept one's options open, the counterattacking force can know exactly how to apply the psychotherapeutic resources intensely in a concentrated point. Tyler's (1973) minimal change psychotherapy can thus make the crucial direction-altering change that is able to set people on a new course.

If psychotherapy is like a war, then brief psychotherapy is like a battle, and tactics—how the psychotherapist deals with the immediate presentation of the client—will rule how the battle is played out. The battle, though, is potentially decisive, and it must be treated as if the war hinged on it. Long-term psychotherapy is more like a campaign than a mere battle, and it thus demands a grand strategy (as well as tactical plans for sessions or portions of the psychotherapy).

How We Deal With Differentiation of Self Will Be Different

The pressure of the brief psychotherapy situation can be a teachable moment for the client on the need to self-soothe and to differentiate and to take responsibility. This can occur after the initial burst of progress, when the downer time of doldrums of progress comes. It also can come after psychotherapy has gotten back on track. It can also come as the person realizes, through trying to bring about the first-order change of short-term psychotherapy, that there are personality issues at work and that much more is at stake psychologically than short-term symptom reduction. The client might at that point decide to switch to a longer term or open-ended psychotherapy or at least recognize that he or she has some serious soul searching to do before continuing with or asking for a different type of longer term psychotherapy.

Other Methods Might Be Different

In a time-limited contact, it becomes more important to get the client to engage extra time and effort, beyond the scheduled psychotherapy hour, in his or her change. Brief psychotherapy is not set up to be compatible with forgiveness therapy. That is, few people with a limited number of sessions approved by an insurance company can devote six hours to dealing with one particular offense. Although it is possible on (rare) occasions in longer term psychotherapy, it simply will not occur in brief psychotherapy. Thus, some intervention to promote forgiveness must be made outside of the psychotherapy hour if substantial forgiveness is to be experienced. Fortunately, there are options. One might try to persuade clients to attend REACH forgiveness groups; watch DVDs on forgiveness (e.g., *The Power of Forgiveness*; Doblmeier, 2008); read books on it, such as trade books that rely on scientific evidence by Enright (2012), Luskin (2001), and Worthington (2003); and work through workbooks on forgiveness (Greer, Worthington, Lin, Lavelock, & Griffin, 2014; Harper et al., 2014). For other free resources, see http://www. EvWorthington-forgiveness.com and http://www.forgiveself.com.

Closer Adherence to Treatment Manuals

Brief treatments tend to rely more on treatment manuals than does long-term treatment. For evidence-based psychotherapy, following the treatment manual becomes increasingly important. This is not something that is true merely for highly controlled clinical trials; following manuals is just as important for field studies, effectiveness trials, and dissemination efforts (McHugh & Barlow, 2010). Not all disorders have a single evidence-based treatment that has been shown to be the most effective. For most disorders, psychotherapists have a choice among evidence-based treatments that have not been shown to be differentially efficacious.

Some misconceptions exist about treatment manuals. One misconception is that all treatment manuals tend to be aimed more at tactics than at strategy. Even treatment manuals for conducting long-term psychotherapies tend to have a flavor of "what do I do next?" Yet most treatment manuals spend significant time discussing the strategy of the intervention, not just the tactics. Second, some people think that following a treatment manual is like following a cookbook: sterile and mechanical. However, psychotherapists who use treatment manuals are encouraged to use their psychotherapeutic sensitivity, acumen, skills, and judgment to depart from the nuts and bolts of tactics and pursue other ways of achieving the strategic objectives of the treatment if their clinical judgment warrants.

In brief psychotherapy, we therapists must be sure that we keep in mind the strategy—personality change so that the person is psychologically (and perhaps spiritually) more mature. That goal should guide our conduct of brief psychotherapy, with and without a manual.

WHAT DO PSYCHOTHERAPIES HAVE TO SAY ABOUT PROMOTING MORE FORGIVENESS?

Occasionally, theorists will apply theories of psychotherapy specifically to forgiveness, such as Vitz and Mango (1997a, 1997b), who wrote from a psychodynamic perspective; Malcolm and Greenberg (2000; Malcolm, Warwar, & Greenberg, 2005), from an emotion-focused therapy perspective; and others, from a blended cognitive, cognitive behavior, and psychodynamic psychotherapy perspective (Baucom, Snyder, & Gordon, 2011).

In recent years, several psychotherapists have written specifically about promoting forgiveness. Enright (Enright & Fitzgibbons, 2000, 2014; Freedman & Enright, 1996) has described a forgiveness therapy that focuses specifically on the psychotherapeutic goal of promoting forgiveness. Enright and Fitzgibbons have conceptualized many psychological disorders as being due to unforgiveness, or at least as having it as a major component.

Bona fide forgiveness therapy, in which the full focus of psychotherapy is solely on forgiveness, is actually unlikely. It undoubtedly happens, and it is certainly needed by many clients. However, few people come to psychotherapy to learn forgiveness or because forgiveness is seen as the major solution to their struggles with unforgiveness. Instead, they come to psychotherapy to get over unhappiness or to deal with worrisome and limiting psychological symptoms. When it arises, unforgiveness occurs within the ongoing psychotherapy as one source of unhappiness and as one cause contributing to psychological symptoms. Issues regarding forgiveness can occur more easily during psychotherapy than under normal circumstances because (a) the person is under other stress due to the psychological disorders with which he or she is dealing and (b) the psychotherapist might ask the client to reflect on relationships that the client might ordinarily avoid thinking about.

Religious issues can also come up also during those stressful times—even for people who are spiritual and not religious. Again, the stress triggers relationship templates, that is, working models of relationships. When those involve god images or conflictual past interactions around spiritual or religious objects, those issues can be opened up again.

What typically happens when issues of forgiveness come up, even if they are mixed with religion and spirituality, is that the client and psychotherapist agree to spend a bit of time focusing on it. Usually they agree to no more than a session or two in brief psychotherapy. Spending more time is possible but unlikely. Returning to forgiveness issues at later times after the first pass at them is much more likely in long-term psychotherapy than in brief psychotherapy. Forgiveness and religious or spiritual issues—although seemingly central to the client—tend to be seen as complicating factors or roadblocks when evidence-based treatments are being used to treat symptoms.

WHAT DO PSYCHOTHERAPIES SAY ABOUT INVOLVING RELIGION OR SPIRITUALITY IN TREATMENT?

Most theories of psychotherapy do not address religious or spiritual issues or forgiveness directly. Usually, standardized treatments have been religiously or spiritually accommodated to make the treatments more palatable to religious or spiritual people with particular beliefs. Worthington and his colleagues have reviewed these efforts on a variety of occasions (Hook, Worthington, & Davis, 2012; Worthington, Hook, Davis, & McDaniel, 2011).

On one hand, several empirically supported religiously accommodated treatments have been shown to be available (Hook et al., 2010; Worthington, Johnson, Hook, & Aten, 2013). Overall, a consistent effect size has been shown in meta-analytic research to be comparable on psychological symptoms in evidence-based treatments that have and have not been religiously accommodated. The ones that have been religiously accommodated have been found to have superior spiritual outcomes in promoting better spiritual well-being by treatment's end and at follow-up.

On the other hand, in Pargament's (2013b) *Handbook of Religion and Spirituality*, Worthington, Hook, Davis, Gartner, and Jennings (2013) suggested that a problem with the research is that the amount or type of religious or spiritual accommodation has not been specified. In some ways, comparing (for instance) cognitive behavior therapy (CBT), in which some material has been removed to make way for religious or spiritual interventions with the full CBT treatment, is unfair to the spiritual accommodation. Some material can be simply integrated in by changing the context from secular to religious—for example, giving religious or spiritual examples instead of a secular example, having people pray instead of meditate. But some instances of religious accommodation are not so comparable. For example, a religiously accommodated treatment might direct people to read scripture instead of reading a secular CBT self-help text; that might deprive clients of a strong reinforcing CBT intervention in place of a more diffuse and religiously oriented one in which the client's attention is shared between the religious content and the CBT content. Even with such substitutions, however, religiously or spiritually accommodated treatments have been equally efficacious as their secular counterparts.

The criticism of the literature remains. The exact amount and content of accommodation is different across studies in religiously or spiritually accommodated treatment studies.

BRINGING ABOUT FIRST-ORDER CHANGES

First, as we offer support to the client, we assess potential points of change. Is the person in a period of spiritual seeking or spiritual dwelling? Either of those will indicate that spiritual experience is likely to play a role but is also likely not to change quickly. For brief psychotherapy, this indicates that spiritual intervention might not be the point of counterattack. Is the person in a confusing state of spiritual transformation or is the person upset due to the unsettledness of spiritual seeking? That might indicate that spirituality is the window to change.

Second, we must assess the person's working model of relationships. This will strongly influence the ability of the person to engage in the challenge of the crucible of psychotherapy. Even brief psychotherapy will often heat up the internal anxiety. In couples therapy, for example, there is a well-known third- or fourth-session slump. The couple is optimistic at the outset, and change occurs quickly. But setbacks are inevitable. By about the third or fourth week (sometimes much earlier—the third or fourth minute, it seems), the couple becomes discouraged with couples therapy. The couple begins to challenge the idea of couples therapy, and breeches in the working relationship with the couples therapist might occur. This happens in individual psychotherapy (see Norcross, 2011), and good outcomes depend on the psychotherapist's ability and success in repairing ruptures in the psychotherapeutic relationship.

Third, we must deal with intensification of anxiety when it occurs. In our relational spirituality model, intensification is occurring because of the ramping up of stress. Coping efforts are failing. The stress reaction—in general and often involving unforgiveness—is increasing. As it intensifies, the client is simultaneously seeking to solve the problem, losing hope and confidence in psychotherapy to be able to yield a solution, and feeling increased anxiety. Defenses become more rudimentary. Some clients freeze and seek to make progress. Others flee, terminating psychotherapy. Others become angry, belligerent, hostile, and they attack the psychotherapist. The psychotherapist experiences a great challenge when this disappointment is sensed. He or she must be a good crucible. He or she must be flexible and yet able to contain the heat of the intensified anxiety. Although not rescuing the client from the anxiety and thus short-circuiting the process of transformation, the psychotherapist must repair the ruptured working alliance and help the client move forward instead of getting stuck in freezing, fleeing, or fighting.

Fourth, we must anticipate likely issues so we can prepare. Although being careful to attend to each client individually and deal with what the client brings forth, it is wise to anticipate some issues that are simply statistically more likely to occur. Because intensity is increased in this third- or fourth-session slump, issues that have the potential to be transformative tend to emerge more often than in other parts of psychotherapy. For instance, the psychodynamic concept of transference, in which the client acts out his or her conflict with the psychotherapist, might occur. The intensified stress and failed coping mechanisms—which for religious people often include religious coping mechanisms—are likely to result in frustration or anger at God. If the person holds to a nondeistic spirituality, a disruption from the person's connection with the spiritual might occur. The person experiences and expresses alienation. If the person is involved in interpersonal conflict, which is common for psychotherapy patients, unforgiveness with its bitterness, resentment, hostility, hate, anger, and fear might erupt and spew forth in session.

Fifth, we must deal with the predictable psychotherapeutic dilemmas that we are likely to face. The psychotherapist is pulled in several directions at the same time. To begin with, progress depends on repair of the working relationship if it has been damaged (Horvath et al., 2011), so there is a strong pull to make things better on that front. The second pull is that the psychotherapist often feels challenged when the working relationship is not working. The ego is threatened. The psychotherapist might defend the self. D. E. Davis and his colleagues have written much about the necessity of a psychotherapist having humility (D. E. Davis, Hook, Worthington, Van Tongeren, Gartner, Jennings, & Emmons, 2011; D. E. Davis, Worthington, & Hook, 2010). Humility has two characteristics: an accurate assessment of one's self (and modest self-presentation) and a value of placing others' agendas at least on equal footing as one's own, not becoming engaged in self-protective defensiveness (D. E. Davis et al., 2011). Challenges can come (a) when the ego is threatened (through conflicts, power struggles, attacks against a valued in-group, or through winning recognition of awards), (b) when people experience negative moral emotions (e.g., anger or concern that a client is making a poor choice), and (c) when a client challenges the psychotherapist's competence directly or indirectly. Thus, a competent psychotherapist feels the pull to react in humility. Third, the psychotherapist feels the need—especially in brief psychotherapy—to get the treatment back on track rapidly. This third pull is a necessity of short-term psychotherapy when treatment sessions are limited (often because of restrictions from third-party payers). But it plays into the way that psychotherapists can deal with threats to the ego and challenges to the competence. It is easy to retreat to adherence to the treatment manual or the treatment plan. That can be the right decision. But it can also be the wrong decision if the client needs something else besides symptom reduction. The fourth pull is to let the crucible of psychotherapy contain the conflict and expand with it to let motivations toward spiritual and psychological transformations intensify further. The right choice is a matter of psychotherapeutic discernment.

Sixth, use the forgiveness and relational spirituality model to conceptualize and look for issues that are likely to come up. Sometimes aspects of the forgiveness and relational spirituality model seem to be very important in dealing with the client's problems with forgiving. The person might be angry or disappointed with God (the victim–sacred [VS] relationship). That can be due to spiritual seeking or spiritual dwelling coupled with, perhaps, disrupting spiritual transformation on the near horizon. Sometimes the group identity of the client seems to be a key to the unforgiveness, especially because the offender (as a member of the same group) was the offender. The offender–sacred (OS) relationship is challenging. Thus, the psychotherapist must sort out the similarity of group identities from the personality of the offender and client. Sometimes, clients believe that some in-group member should not have offended (again, the offender's similarity to the client in the OS relationship). "Fellow Christians shouldn't act that cruelly," they say (OS). As another example, "other ex-pats should be more understanding" (the victim–offender [VO] relationship). And, as a final example, Shiites may believe that they should understand what other Shiites are going through (the OS relationship). When group identity seems pivotal, clients can take an inventory between the way things should be and the way that imperfect humans actually act.

The transgression can sometimes be construed as a desecration of something sacred. If that is the case, forgiveness is usually very difficult, and the psychotherapist must address ways to deal with such desecrations or sacred losses.

By asking these theory-driven questions, we determine which battles to fight. We cannot fight every battle, and the ones clients want to fight are not always the ones that are in the clients' best interest to fight. Use the theory to ask strategic questions.

SUMMARY

We have described an approach to brief psychotherapy that takes seriously the limits of treatment imposed by client, third-party payer, or other circumstances. However, it still considers the structures and triggers that make up the complex personalities of clients. But how does our brief psychotherapy work in practice?

7

CASE STUDY OF FORGIVENESS IN BRIEF PSYCHOTHERAPY

In this chapter, we describe a composite case in which the client, Claude, has issues in relational spirituality. He has begun to doubt God's goodness and on bad days, God's existence, because of a series of evil events in his life and family. Claude immigrated to the United States after marrying Monique, whom he met in France, where she spent a semester abroad during her college years. They are in their middle to late 40s and have been married 22 years, and have spent all of them in the United States. They have two daughters: Robbie (20 years old) and Martinique (18 years old).

Claude is on the cusp of what could be a spiritual transformation. But at present, it feels like chaos. He has begun to experiment with alternatives to the Roman Catholic orthodoxy with which he was raised (e.g., finding peace in nature, attending a Unitarian Universalist weekly meeting, and seeking a transcendent experience through some Americanized methods, e.g., meditation and yoga, derived from Buddhist or other Eastern religious traditions).

http://dx.doi.org/10.1037/14712-008
Forgiveness and Spirituality in Psychotherapy: A Relational Approach, by E. L. Worthington, Jr. and S. J. Sandage

Claude also is struggling to forgive two people who grievously wronged his children. One is a drunk driver who crossed the median and hit his daughter Martinique's car head-on, which resulted in a traumatic brain injury. The other was a young man who raped Robbie when she went on a date with him, leading to a pregnancy (due within 3 months). In (relatively) brief psychotherapy (given the magnitude of the events he has been dealing with and the subsequent emotional and spiritual turmoil he is in the midst of), Claude wishes to explore ways that he might forgive the drunk driver and the rapist and get over his "seething internal rage," which bubbles up inconveniently in his personal relationships with his boss and his wife at times. He also wants to "get my center back. Get some stability back in my life so I can get on with living."

He attributes some of his frustration to his upbringing. He sees his Roman Catholic roots as demanding that he forgive—which "I sometimes want to and at other times absolutely do not want to"—but not providing any practical help at forgiving. "My faith isn't working. It's just another source of guilt and another sin!" he said.

He has been having conversations with his wife (who retains a solid Roman Catholic faith) about forgiveness and the role of faith in forgiving. Those conversations have become negative, filled with conflict and Claude's explosive shouting ("the first time in my marriage I've raised my voice"). These "discussions—arguments, really" have brought up new questions and doubts about his Roman Catholic faith tradition.

Claude's work has suffered since the two tragedies occurred back to back. He has an employee assistance program referral for a maximum of 20 sessions. We give particular attention to how to intervene in a brief psychotherapy modality and still be mindful of stimulating personal maturity.

In the present chapter, we begin by discussing a few considerations about seeing Claude as a client in brief psychotherapy. We look toward some point of leverage for change and then examine Claude's fit for our brief psychotherapy that includes forgiveness and relational spirituality. Then, we walk through the six stages of counseling, giving dialogues with the psychotherapist so you can experience, at least vicariously, what the psychotherapy feels like.

WHAT IS THE POINT OF LEVERAGE?

Change agents seek a leverage point to shift clients from negative to positive living. Clients—at least in Claude's case—must change cognition to be more positive; expectations to be more hopeful; emotional experiences to be more positive; rumination to be less angry, vengeful, and bitter; and actions to be more reconciliatory. By changing people's experiences, the hope is that people in the client's social world will eventually respond more positively. It is unlikely that social changes will happen rapidly. Many people will not even notice new patterns of behavior, and even if they do, they may not trust that the changes will last, or they might even perceive the changes negatively. Eventually, people begin to treat the forgiving person differently than they did when he or she was vengeful or grudge-holding.

Claude's point of leverage is the stress he is under. The stress has brought him to psychotherapy. The stress has intensified the process of relational spirituality, moving Claude from stable dwelling to unsettled seeking. The stress has unsettled his normal family and work relationships. He wants the stress to end. Although Claude might say that he knows he is in for the long haul and that he understands that work is needed if he is going to put his life satisfactorily back together, that is not what he desires. He is in pain, and he wants the pain to stop. He wants the psychotherapist to magically use some "intervention" that will make all of the problems go away—preferably, yesterday. Claude has a rational understanding that psychotherapy will take work and courage. However, he also has a fantasy that an "intervention" will end his stress; Claude is at once motivated to work and ambivalent about having to work. "It's not fair," Claude thinks, as do most people experiencing such multiple severe stressors: "I don't deserve this. I deserve for someone to take away my pain."

They are correct. It is not fair. And on some level, they also usually know that someone is not going to simply take away the pain. But the unrealistic fantasy—while making it more difficult to enter into the hard work needed in psychotherapy—also means that they are primed to cooperate with the psychotherapist, at least at the beginning until the psychotherapist fails to magically remove the pain. After that, things become dicey.

CLAUDE AS A CANDIDATE FOR PSYCHOTHERAPY FOCUSED ON FORGIVENESS AND RELATIONAL SPIRITUALITY

As we have discussed before, Claude is dealing with many elements that make our theory of change particularly cogent. Let us look at each.

Severe Stress

With multiple, unrelenting stressors, he is in a particularly intense period. Those stressors have activated his processes of relational spirituality, moving him from dwelling comfortably in his Roman Catholic religious spirituality to seeking from a variety of more diverse sources. That process affects his ability to respond to transgressions, which in turn affects his coping with the stressors and spills over into his relationships.

Causal Processes Beneath the Surface

There are deep levels of causal forces at work within Claude, we assume, although the psychotherapist has not gotten to know him yet to know precisely how the relational templates are pushing and pulling Claude. Of similar importance to Claude, he has religious and spiritual forces at work. Based on what he shared in his intake session, those have also been part of his life since being born. Those are in flux because of the intensity of the stress and are on the surface. So, it is likely that they will be addressed at some length in psychotherapy. Claude's personality characteristics and family dynamics will be addressed as they surface in psychotherapy. However, in brief psychotherapy, the psychotherapist might not be able to help Claude resolve them by the end of psychotherapy.

Content of the Sessions

The content of the sessions will center on the direct issues Claude has come to psychotherapy to address: (a) solving the problems that are causing him stress, (b) regulating his emotions, and (c) finding meaning in the problems. Those correspond to problem-focused coping, emotion-focused coping, and meaning-focused coping, respectively. Dealing with his unforgiveness and his shaky ground of faith will also occupy psychotherapy time and attention. As he moves through the tension between spiritual dwelling and seeking of the relational spirituality model, psychotherapy time will consider the adjustments and possible transformations he is likely to experience.

The Role of the Psychotherapy Theory of the Psychotherapist

Although the psychotherapist conceptualizes strategically in terms of (a) structural changes in attachment working models; (b) the stability and transformation of religious and spiritual beliefs, values, practices; and (c) the process of relational spirituality, the content of the sessions will center on stress and coping. The conduct of psychotherapy—the tactics—will likely be governed mostly by the psychotherapist's theory. Many different psychotherapy theories could be accommodated.

A Six-Stage Process Through Which Psychotherapy Usually Passes

As we discussed in Chapter 6, one might describe the process of psychotherapy broadly (see Worthington, 2006) as passing through the set of loose stages—connecting with the client, helping the client reconceptualize the problems, making action plans and bringing them about through the theory of the hour and homework, following up on the clients efforts to use changes and supporting those attempts, planning for maintenance, and terminating. It might be easiest to see how this works, even in relatively brief psychotherapy, if we focus on the way psychotherapy proceeds with Claude.

PSYCHOTHERAPY WITH CLAUDE

Connect (Step 1)

Establish a Good Working Alliance

The psychotherapist connects with Claude through listening, understanding, and communicating his or her understanding to the client. The method of accomplishing this—through concern, active listening, empathy, genuineness, acceptance, and respect for the client—is common knowledge among psychotherapists and is woven into training from Day One. For relational psychotherapies, the establishment of a good working alliance is particularly important (Horvath, Del Re, Flückiger, & Symonds, 2011).

Differences Between Claude and the Psychotherapist Must Be Considered

Psychotherapy inevitably involves differences between the client and psychotherapist. Those differences can be troublesome for some clients and not bother other clients. Much depends on the client's working model of relationships and his or her ability to make secure adult attachments. It is best to assume that stress has unleashed childhood-formulated working models or working models of relationships from other important or traumatic times in Claude's life. So psychotherapists are likely to see some sort of recapitulation of earlier working models. Nevertheless, with cultural, ethnic, socioeconomic, and religious differences, the psychotherapist must cultivate a sense of cultural humility writ large.

Hook, Davis, Owen, Worthington, and Utsey (2013) and D. E. Davis, Worthington, Hook, Emmons, Hill, and Burnette (2013) have described *cultural humility* as understanding one's cultural competencies and limitations, and even if one thinks one understands the culture of a client, one is to remain humble about assuming one understands the client as an individual. The concept of cultural humility is a subset of *relational humility*, which D. E. Davis et al. (2011) described as having two attributes. The relationally humble person must (a) have an accurate perception of the self and (b) remain other-oriented especially when the ego is strained, which it is at times of recognition for achievement; at times of violations of a sense of justice; or when engaged in conflict, power struggles, or stress. Cultural humility (including ethnicity, religion, etc.) occurs when the psychotherapist knows

his or her competencies and limitations in the area of concern and also operates in the best interest of the client by seeking knowledge of the particular
client, which might (or might not) be accurately informed by the psychotherapist's understanding of the culture of the client. Cultural humility is less
a set of cultural competencies (although those are presumed) than it is a way
of relating to the client.

What the Psychotherapist Draws Attention to Is Probably What Claude Will Come to See as Causal

As Meichenbaum (1977) showed in his cognitive behavior modification, a psychotherapist has many choices in what to express curiosity about,
reflect back, and what to ask the client to talk more about. Whatever the
psychotherapist pays attention to, the client will talk about. The client will
soon adduce evidence from his or her own life that the problem (and solution)
lies in the topics that are receiving the most attention from the psychotherapist
and the client. If the psychotherapist attends to client thoughts, the client will
soon see how thoughts play a pivotal role in the problem; if the psychotherapist
attends to client emotions, the client will see how important emotions are; if
the psychotherapist attends to early experiences with parents, the client will
assume those are significant.

Role of Treatment Manuals and Other Treatment Plans

The counseling template of the psychotherapist includes the tenets of
the particular theory that is being used, attention to any existing treatment
manual in spirit (not necessarily to the letter of the manual), the understanding of relational spirituality, the understanding of the stress-and-coping
model of forgiveness, and the understanding of the forgiveness and relational
spirituality model.

Using Our Model to Focus Claude's Attention

So, when a client begins to identify unforgiveness as a focal problem,
the psychotherapist should listen, reflect, and inquire curiously about several
things. The psychotherapist will be curious about current stressors, appraisals, stress responses, and coping mechanisms and the ways that both working
models of relationships from past relationships and religion might influence
each. These are the elements of the stress-and-coping model of forgiveness.
Stress is not merely something to be coped with. It also (a) intensifies the
process of relational spirituality and (b) can push the client toward transformation rather than problem solving if the stress is intense and unabated.

The psychotherapist will also be curious about the current relationships, early relationships, working models of relationship brought out from

exploring early and later relationships—including current relationships—and the perceived degree of differentiation of self. Along with those, the psychotherapist will try to ascertain the degree of anxiety and intensification over potential spiritual turmoil, the degree to which the client is experiencing chaos between dwelling and seeking, and the trajectory of spiritual movement. These are all elements of the relational spirituality model. Finally, the psychotherapist will be curious about the way the client relates with a transgressor, the transgression, and the sacred. The psychotherapist will assess the degree of perceived similarity between the person's own and the offender's relationship to the sacred and also whether the transgression might be considered to be a desecration of the sacred or a sacred loss.

Focusing on the Essence of the Model for Short-Term Psychotherapy

Whereas a psychotherapist in long-term psychotherapy might actually be able to pay attention to all of these elements over the course of extended counseling, this is impossible in short-term psychotherapy. So, she or he generally prioritizes the relationship first and the treatment manual (if one exists) second. The other elements serve as a background for the psychotherapist's sensitivity. Experienced psychotherapists can often tell quickly when attachment issues are likely to intrude in psychotherapy. Involvement of religion and spirituality is also often obvious, especially when they are a source of confusion, and when spirituality is chaotic or intensified.

Let us listen to a digested version of this conversation between the psychotherapist and Claude. The psychotherapist is an eclectic psychotherapist, leaning more toward cognitive behavior therapy than psychodynamic psychotherapy for short-term counseling, although his emphasis shifts as psychotherapy becomes longer term. The 20-session limit places him in the midrange, but the time limit that was imposed by the third-party payer yields an urgency that might not be there in open-ended psychotherapy.

When Claude arrived, the receptionist had him (a) sign the Health Insurance Portability and Accountability Act form, (b) read and sign an informed consent form, and (c) complete a short questionnaire about the nature of his current problems. He checked *depressed*, *unforgiving*, and *religious/spiritual*. Then, the receptionist gave him three brief questionnaires that corresponded to the areas Claude had checked. These were, for depression, the Beck Depression Inventory (BDI; A. T. Beck & Steer, 1993); for unforgiveness, the Transgression-Related Inventory of Motivations (TRIM; McCullough et al., 1998); and for religion/spirituality, the Religious Commitment Inventory—10 (RCI–10; Worthington et al., 2003). The receptionist scored the questionnaires and plotted the scores on a summary sheet and sent the folder into the appointment with the psychotherapist. This took only about 10 minutes.

At the beginning of the session, the psychotherapist went over the informed consent form to make sure Claude understood what he was agreeing to. The psychotherapist noted that Claude fell into the level of substantial depression on the basis of his score on the BDI. Claude completed the TRIM in reference to the wreck and brain injury of his daughter Martinique. On the form describing his problems, Claude had also mentioned another incident, but the receptionist had not noticed that Claude could have been asked to complete a separate TRIM for the rape of his other daughter. The psychotherapist asked whether Claude would be willing to complete that brief, 5-minute (12-item) rating form after the end of the session. The psychotherapist noted also that Claude had completed only about half of the RCI–10, and then wrote "not applicable" at the top of the page. When asked, Claude said, "I was raised Catholic and kind of practiced for years, but now I don't feel settled enough about my faith to give meaningful responses."

Claude began the narrative part of the session by talking about the stress he has been under, but he quickly began to rant about the driver who killed Martinique and the young man who raped Robbie. When the psychotherapist heard this theme so early in psychotherapy and with such passion, he immediately began to think about forgiveness and relational spirituality as a model that might govern his psychotherapy with Claude. That was bolstered by recalling that Claude had checked unforgiveness as one of his major concerns.

> *Claude:* I hate myself because I can't forgive these people. Rationally, I know that I ought to forgive. It isn't hurting either of these people that I can't get over the harms they did to my girls. I think it's one of the hardest things anyone can try to forgive—hurt done to the people you love. I think I could forgive a harm done to me a lot more than to my girls. I know my inability to forgive isn't rational. It's emotional. I feel unforgiving. It bothers me to no end. I want to forgive. But can't. It's wrecking my faith.

> *Psychotherapist:* You say you are having trouble forgiving and you want to be more forgiving. What kinds of emotions do you experience when you're feeling unforgiving? [Comment: The psychotherapist began with Claude's emotional experience of unforgiveness. The psychotherapist believes that is the best way into the issue.]

> *Claude:* I don't think about it all the time, but when I do, if I dwell on it, I get in an absolute rage. I want to hit and scream, and at times I feel like if I had either one in front of me, I might do violence to them. I want to hurt them and get back at them.

Psychotherapist:	You sound furious. But you said you didn't think about it much. Yet you do think about it?
Claude:	Yes, many times a day. Anytime I'm sad, or feel like I can't act in a *normal* way.
Psychotherapist:	Normal?
Claude:	You know. If I can't get over a slight. If I get to feeling sorry for myself. That isn't *normal*. I don't want to be that way. My mind goes back to how it just isn't fair.
Psychotherapist:	But you feel upset, angry, and full of rage at these men several times a day. That must be hard to keep experiencing. Do the men run together for you, or do you feel differently about each?
Claude:	It seems to intrude on whatever I do. If I'm at work, those thoughts come. If I'm driving, the thoughts are there. I crank up the radio, but it doesn't help. When I'm at home, especially if it's a time when things aren't very active—like watching television or getting ready for bed. As for whether I separate the men, well, of course I do. I picture each one. Well, actually, it's the driver I can picture. I attended his trial, so I know what he looks like. I've been afraid to let myself find out about the rapist. Pretty much, though, my reaction is the same. Rage and an urge to hurt. I wouldn't really hurt them, of course. I'm a nonviolent guy. But the feelings and images are there.
Psychotherapist:	That must be scary for you.
Claude:	I don't like not having control over my feelings. It makes me feel like a failure. It makes me ashamed of myself. [Comment: The psychotherapist and Claude have been talking around the experience broadly, but the essence of good psychotherapy is not in general description but in powerful immediate experience. The psychotherapist needs to get him to talk more immediately about his experience.]
Psychotherapist:	I know it's embarrassing, but would you just pretend that you are alone. You are driving and thinking about one of the guys. Pick one. Would you narrate your thoughts aloud?
Claude:	Well, that's different—with you here and all. And I don't think organized, really. I just think things, you know. But I'll try. Okay, so, like yesterday, I was driving

and came to a section of road that had a little median. It was like the one crossed by the drunk driver who hit Martinique, so it got me thinking about that accident.

Psychotherapist: So, just pretend you are talking to yourself.

Claude: Okay, I'll try. I would say something like, "What a waste! I am so glad that the guy got jail time. What an irresponsible person. He already had a DUI and he couldn't stop himself from drinking and driving. Now we have to live with the consequences! And poor Martinique. She knows things aren't right, but she can't do anything about it. She gets so frustrated and that gets me frustrated, and it's so wasted and worthless. I need to get past this. I get all worked up, but it doesn't do any good to rant and rave. It's just getting my stomach all upset and it's going to give me an ulcer. I know God doesn't like this. I hate this part of me!" Then I get home, and I'm all wound up, and Monique says something, and, bam, off I go, venting my anger on her and hurting her feelings and ruining a long marriage, and . . . [Claude stops.] See, this is what happens. I get wound up and it's just a nonproductive rant. It's killing me—body and spirit.

Psychotherapist: It seems terribly stressful and painful for you. I can see that you got more animated and more emotional as you got into it. I could really feel your frustration. And you berated yourself for not being able to control your feelings of anger. That just seemed to make it worse.

Claude: It is stressful. And it is very painful. It's painful because I hate the guy. And I hate myself so much that he still gets to me—even after seeing him go to jail. Surely that ought to be enough justice. Knowing that I get wound up like this is a constant source of stress—one more of many. I can't get away from it. It's depressing.

Psychotherapist: I feel the powerlessness and sadness. You seem to have a tender heart toward your daughters. You are stressed and pained, and you try to cope with it by stopping yourself from thinking about it. But you can't seem to get away from reminders. [Claude (talking over): Yeah, seeing Robbie pregnant gets me going there, too. The psychotherapist continues.] So, the reminders keep coming. As you get triggered and lose control of your emotions, you feel bad about yourself. Disappointed in yourself. Worried about what it's doing to your body and spirit.

Claude: It's not just anger. It's frustration, resentment, rage, and, well, like you said, stress. I hear bitterness just pouring out of me. I hate what he did to us—what both of these guys did to my daughters and our whole family. We'll never be the same. I hate that it's still bothering me. Sometimes I think it has even gotten worse lately. More seems to set me off. It affects my whole life. The worse I get, too, the more it worries me about my spiritual intactness.

Psychotherapist: It sounds as if you feel a lot of unforgiveness, and you can't control it at all. And besides being stressful, you wonder what it's doing to your spiritual life as well.

Claude: Yeah, I feel pure hate. I'm Catholic. But that isn't working for me anymore. I can't just go to Mass and confess and get it off my chest. I've been trying to get a sense of peace by meditating using mindfulness mediation. Then I try to practice mindfulness. But it just seems that my mind is full of all the things it shouldn't be full of—like hate. And I can't seem to make myself just attend to the moment. I heard recently about a different kind of meditation—lovingkindness meditation. Maybe that's what I ought to be doing. I need to do something that can nip my ranting and raving in the bud. [Comment: At this point, Claude tries to take the conversation toward coping. This is an attempt to escape from the distress of contemplating an anxious situation that he cannot see a way out of. The psychotherapist must not get pulled into trying to provide solutions this early in psychotherapy.] You know, I feel like if I can keep trying to find some way to successfully distract myself and if I respond better to the cues that seem to trigger me, then maybe I can control it some.

Psychotherapist: So, you see the solution to this as finding the right sort of spiritual distraction—one that will help you not to feel such turmoil. [*Claude:* Yeah.] But so far, nothing has been able to calm the spiritual fires within.

Claude: I'd like to extinguish them. But I'd settle at this point for just getting them burning less out of control.

The first step, connecting, and the second, helping the client rethink the situation, go hand-in-glove. By directing reflections or questions, even when following the client, the psychotherapist helps the client begin to rethink the problem.

Rethink the Problem (Step 2)

People are meaning-making creatures. They try to understand how the pieces of their life fit together. When they enter psychotherapy, they have a conceptualization of their problems. But it is not helping them solve the problems. So, psychotherapists must guide the client toward some different understanding of the problem. Furthermore, the understanding leads the person to change the situations of his or her life or the personal narrative connecting the strands of experiences. This, of course, is where the personal theory of psychotherapy of the psychotherapist enters the equation. A psychodynamic psychotherapist will help the client see (and later change) the psychodynamics dominating behavior. The behavior therapist will help the client see (and later change) the roles of thoughts, situations, rewards, and punishments. The emotion-focused psychotherapist will help the person process the relevant emotional conflicts that disturb adult attachment relationships and integrate emotional experience and later adjust differently to those.

If the psychotherapist wants to help Claude rethink his unforgiveness in a way that helps him change, then she must get across the main points derived from the stress-and-coping theory of forgiveness, the model of relational spirituality, and the forgiveness and relational spirituality structural model. Forgiveness is one way of coping with the stress of unforgiveness, as the psychotherapist acknowledges and reflects when Claude says "It's killing me—body and spirit." However, it is not just a coping mechanism that Claude seems to need ("It affects my whole life. The worse I get, too, the more it worries me about my spiritual intactness"). That might just turn out to be a beginning.

The psychotherapist has also observed and suggested to Claude that the spiritual connection is important ("you wonder what it's doing to your spiritual life, as well"), and Claude agrees wholeheartedly. He even expands the discussion to talk about ways that he has begun to seek spiritually. She needs to get Claude to talk more about this and consider how it might affect his possibility of forgiving.

> *Psychotherapist:* It must feel unsettling to see your previously stable Catholic faith become unmoored. [Comment: The psychotherapist makes a good response to divert Claude from premature problem-solving efforts and also to let the experience of anxiety build intensity.]

> *Claude:* Yes, I feel as if I'm on some kind of a platform and I'm poised to jump at anything. But, so far, nothing is able to make me feel like I have a firm footing. I'm up in the air spiritually, emotionally, and every other way.

Psychotherapist:	And besides being really, really hard—to not feel you have a firm footing—that doesn't make you feel like you can forgive these crimes and harms against your daughters.
Claude:	That's exactly what they are: crimes! Literally! While I'm wandering around, trying to figure out how to get out of this wilderness, I can't forgive. I used to be able to count on my stable relationship with the Church, my relationship with Jesus, and even the support of our small group at church. Now, I feel alienated from all of those. It's unsettling. I don't have a foothold. It's like being in a tug-o-war and having the other side dug in but I'm on sand.

According to the stress-and-coping theory of forgiveness, the magnitude of the injustice gap is generally proportional to the amount of unforgiveness felt and to the difficulty of forgiving. So, Claude can make forgiveness easier if he can reduce the injustice gap. That will permit forgiveness. Claude can decide to forgive. But he must deliberately try to experience emotional forgiveness. That will not magically occur even if he decides to forgive. Emotional forgiveness occurs through emotional replacement of unforgiveness with positive other-oriented emotions toward the two men who hurt his daughters. This is a tall order—and one that takes time. Claude must work through an approach to forgiveness slowly. Any immediate attempt to promote forgiveness on the part of the psychotherapist will likely drive Claude away. Eventually, Claude will have to come to view the two men differently—with empathy or compassion—if he is to forgive them. At this point, Claude is not capable of empathy and compassion.

The psychotherapist is facing several psychotherapeutic directions. First, more information is needed about the events. The psychotherapist knows almost nothing about the date rape and knows little about the accident except that the driver was drunk and was convicted of some crime that sent him to jail. The psychotherapist must evaluate what to seek more information about first.

The psychotherapist opts for pursuing more about the relational spirituality because that will feed into forgiveness. Also, if Claude were more settled about his spirituality, that could help him consider forgiveness. As stress continues, spiritual seeking will become even more likely, making forgiveness even less likely. That could affect Claude's spiritual identity. But in terms of his psychotherapy, if the psychotherapist deals with the two big offenses, it will affect the victim–sacred (VS) relationship (i.e., the way Claude relates to the sacred), the offender–sacred (OS) relationship (i.e., the similarity that Claude perceives between the way he relates to the sacred and the ways his two offenders relate to the sacred). So, the psychotherapist pursues finding more about Claude's spiritual relationship with the sacred.

The psychotherapist is helping Claude explore the problem not to find out the key information and then spring a solution on Claude, which is what Claude wants to happen; rather, the psychotherapist is helping Claude explore his experience with the eye to helping Claude become his own psychotherapist. This requires additional rethinking of the problem. Obviously, helping a client rethink a problem is not a matter of direct instruction, as it can be in portions of psychoeducational interventions. Rather, helping rethink the problem blends intimately with understanding the client and communicating that understanding to the client (Connecting, Step 1).

> *Psychotherapist:* So, you've given me a lot here. Let me just see if I'm tracking with you. You are stressed for a lot of reasons, including the brain injury of Martinique and the rape and pregnancy of Robbie, and you are struggling to forgive the guys who caused those tragedies. But you've so far been unsuccessful at forgiving. That stress plus the added stress of feeling spiritually unable to do what you feel you need to do are unsettling you and making you feel like you are in a tug-of-war on a slippery surface. You'd like to get a sense of stability back into your life, but you don't see how you can. And, what's worse, without feeling some sense of spiritual stability, you aren't sure you can forgive either or both of the two men. Am I tracking with you?

> *Claude:* Yes. My relationship with the Church is screwed up. My faith is all over the place. I like Pope Francis. He keeps me somewhat attracted to the Church. It's hard to admit, but I'm a little pissed at God. [Pauses.] Actually, I'm probably a lot pissed at God, but just saying that makes me feel even more sinful and worse. I'm basically screwed up.

> *Psychotherapist:* And you feel like, "If I can just get my spiritual life together, I could maybe find forgiveness, and that would help my spiritual life even more."

> *Claude:* Yeah, it's the chicken-and-egg thing. Like you say. I can't forgive because my spiritual life is messed up and I can't get my spiritual life straightened out unless I forgive. Forgiveness and my spiritual life are all balled up together.

> *Psychotherapist:* And that feels like a pretty hopeless place to be.

> *Claude:* You said it!

At that point, the psychotherapist looped back and had Claude talk about the two events he could not forgive. Each was taken in turn, and he described the events and their aftermath. Here is how the session concluded.

Claude: Well, I can't say I feel much better. Maybe I feel like it's more hopeless than when I came in. I just think that somehow forgiveness is the key to all this mess, and yet my spiritual life is so confused that I don't even know how to start.

Psychotherapist: You have definitely been under a lot of stress with the two problems piled on top of each other. Earlier in the session, you said that your forgiveness was tied up with your spiritual life, and you were angry with both God and the Church. You said you couldn't get your faith straightened out unless you had forgiven and you couldn't forgive unless you got your faith together. That didn't leave you feeling you had a place to start. But you have to start somewhere.

Claude: Well, I guess I see the religious and spiritual problem as more basic.

Psychotherapist: So, you want to work on that first.

Claude: It's scary, but yeah.

Psychotherapist: So this week, what do you want to do to prepare for next week's session?

Claude: Well, I'm confused about things I still believe and things I don't believe anymore. And I don't know what to do about my anger at God. Until we started talking, I didn't really recognize that I felt so *much* anger at God. So, I'll try to think of how we can talk about some of these things next week.

The second session was dominated by complaining. Claude traced his journey from being a stable attendee of Mass at the time of the accident to being a "slacker." The psychotherapist did not feel that much psychotherapeutic progress was made other than telling Claude's story. In the third session, though, the psychotherapist felt that Claude made a lot of progress.

Claude: I guess my faith really started to fade after Martinique got injured. After the accident, there were a lot of things to do. Visits to the hospital, getting Martinique settled in. Feeling like the family needed to stay home and keep her company instead of going anywhere, including to Mass. I finally volunteered to be the one to sit with her because Monique didn't want to miss Mass.

She felt like her prayers were important. I felt like mine didn't matter. God's going to do what God's going to do. It doesn't matter if I'm praying, or attending Mass, or praying the rosary, or anything. Once I started pulling back and got out of the routine of going to Mass, it was harder and harder to resume a routine. And to tell the truth, I started to feel like there was less reason to. But, damn, I am Catholic. Guilt is my middle name. So I was glad not to be having to think about all the inconsistencies in my faith and mortified that I was not doing so. Typical Catholic guilt that I was raised with.

Psychotherapist: Tell me a bit more about that.

Claude: Mum was a stickler. She made us toe the line. Whenever we got out of line, it was always, "Just wait until your Dad gets home." He didn't want to take Mum on, and so he'd take us in the bathroom and wallop us with the belt. He was, as they would say these days, "conflict avoidant," at least with Mum. Dad was the "man of the house," but it was kind of like the line from *My Big Fat Greek Wedding* where the mother says, "He's the head of the house but I'm the neck, and I can turn the head however I want." That was the way it was.

Psychotherapist: So, how did that work with you as a child?

Claude: There were three of us, and I was the middle. My older brother was about six years older than me. I never really knew him. But my brother, Charles, and I were only a year apart. We were much closer, and we went through things together. We respected Dad and Mum, but we didn't feel close to either. In fact, if Mum and Dad were at odds with each other, we pretty much knew Mum was going to win, and if we were around, it was likely to end up with a hidin', as Dad used to call it.

Psychotherapist: I can feel the caught-in-the-middle feeling. So, you were wary of your Mum and a little standoffish.

Claude: That describes my early relationship with her. As I got older, I found that I didn't have much in common with either Mum or Dad, and I sort of edited them out of my life.

Psychotherapist: How so?

Claude: Talked the minimum. When I did, I tried not to let her get very close. She felt basically, uh, I don't know, dangerous, I guess.

Psychotherapist:	And did that type of relationship continue?
Claude:	Well, Mum died of cancer about 30-plus years ago. [*Psychotherapist:* Humm. I'm sorry.] [Talks over.] I was 15. Dad got killed that same year in an accident at work. A machine just pitched off the side of a building and landed on him. He was in a coma for weeks, but in the end didn't have any brain functioning, and we brothers decided that we would have to pull the plug. It was hard, but he was gone already.
Psychotherapist:	Oh, my gosh. Lots of things piled up there! That must have been difficult for you as a teen. [*Claude:* Yeah. Well, anyway.] [*Claude:* Pauses, looks as if waiting for the psychotherapist to say something.] I kinda hate to ask this on the heels of you talking about those deaths, but some people say that people's relationship with God is like a mirror of their relationship with one or more parents. Others say that people's relationship with God makes up for deficits in relationships with parents. What do you see, if anything, in your relationships with your parents and your relationship with God?
Claude:	I've not really thought much about it, but, hum [silence]. Well, in a way, I didn't have much relationship with the Church or with God until a few years back, you know, after Martinique's accident. Monique was always a churchgoer. I went with her enough to keep her happy. But one of the Fathers at the Church got me involved in some singing, and we got a little men's singing group together. That gave me a sense of closeness with that group. That connected me with the Church.
Psychotherapist:	That must have been good for you—to feel connected, at least somewhat. And is that when things changed for you? At Martinique's accident. What then?
Claude:	Well, I pulled out. It didn't seem that important anymore. I guess, thinking about what you said about my relationship with God and the Church and with my parents. At first, I'd say I was very attracted to the whole God thing. It was exciting. I'd say it was like the parents I never had.
Psychotherapist:	You said, "At first . . ."
Claude:	Yeah. Since things have been going bad—as they have for quite a while now—it's more like waiting until Dad

gets home and getting a hidin'. [Claude pauses and sits silent for about a minute.] And I guess, it kind of feels, like I said, "dangerous" to be around God. Even though I was a Catholic, that didn't seem to matter. Bad stuff happened. What's the use of holding onto faith? The Catholicism didn't work, at least not for me. It seemed to help Monique. For me, it just took up time and didn't give me the comfort I had once known. I missed the comfort. I would like to recapture that.

That interchange triggered 2 weeks of discussion about what it means to be spiritual (for Claude, mostly an experience of peace and freedom from turmoil) and how Claude was trying to recapture those feelings. Much of Claude's quest had been to "run from one spiritual new experience to another." In the fourth session, he seemed to get discouraged about the seeming hopelessness "of chasing after a sense of peace."

By the fifth session, however, Claude was back on track emotionally, and continued his self-exploration. About midway through Session 5, Claude reported that when he did get a sense of peace, the "highs are fleeting. They seem like something that can give me peace for a moment, and then will simply disappear. I can't seem to sustain any feeling that I'm connecting with something bigger and grander than myself."

The psychotherapist noted that the feelings of closeness sounded similar to things Claude had expressed in earlier sessions regarding feelings with his parents, especially his mother.

After a moment of seeming to stare off into space, Claude agreed.

> *Claude:* Yes, I had those same feelings often with Mum. I could never really connect with her other than very briefly.
>
> *Psychotherapist:* So, how did you respond?
>
> *Claude:* My gosh! I just cut her out of my life. I disengaged. I'm kind of doing the same thing with God and the Church—and maybe spirituality in general. It isn't safe to count on. If I try briefly, and if it can't satisfy me pretty much immediately, I run away from the experience.

The psychotherapist let Claude sit with that insight. By the following session, Claude came in with an announcement:

I'm going to try to give spiritual experiences more of a chance. It might be I am simply incapable of experiencing a stable spiritual life, but if I try something out and then almost immediately cut it off, I certainly will just keep reinforcing the experiences I've been having. I'm going to try to be a bit different.

After Claude and the psychotherapist processed the meaning of Claude's decision, Claude said that he felt as if he was willing to consider what it might take if "I am ever going to have the remote chance of forgiving the two guys who messed up my daughters' and our lives."

Make Action Plans Based on the New Conceptualization (Step 3)

Rethinking alone will rarely help a person experience emotional forgiveness. The person must carry out action plans, in or out of session, to change his or her experience.

The psychotherapist said he thought that Claude's suggestion to begin to consider forgiveness might be productive. However, before considering forgiveness, it might be good to decide exactly what Claude was going to do differently as a result of his earlier decision to give spiritual experiences more of a chance.

Good action plans must make change seem possible, make it count, make it sensible, make an emotional impact, make change last, and make changes generalizable.

Make Change Seem Possible

By the time people get to psychotherapy, they are usually discouraged about the possibility of change (e.g., "I'm up in the air spiritually, emotionally, and every other way"). They lack hope. They lack the willpower to change and the waypower to change (Snyder, 1994). That is, they might have lost the motivation to try to change, or they might believe that they have exhausted all the ways possible to bring about change. The psychotherapist's task is to restore both willpower and waypower to change. Willpower can be restored by calling the person to a high challenge. The psychotherapist can attribute positive motives or personal ("I feel the powerlessness and sadness. You seem to have a tender heart toward your daughters. You are stressed and pained, and you try to cope with it by stopping yourself from thinking about it") to the person when the psychotherapist detects those motives. (Insincerely or falsely attributing positive motives to a person will boomerang.) The psychotherapist can also attribute the desire to change to the client, when appropriate. The psychotherapist can share the past successes to promote hope for success. This includes mentioning empirical support for treatments.

Make Change Count

All changes are not created equal. When clients make some changes, those changes redirect the course of their life. Forgiveness is difficult. When a client works hard to forgive someone who is hard to forgive, the event makes a big impression. The struggle, when it works, can change the course of psychotherapy. A psychotherapist and client can work on only a limited number of issues over the course of brief psychotherapy. So, it is important to choose targets wisely. In Claude's case, discussion in the early part of psychotherapy revealed to Claude an order that he wanted to pursue to try to untangle what seemed to be confounded issues—relational spirituality before forgiveness.

That is not necessarily always going to be true for clients. Claude was able to decide. Given the amount of stress he was encountering, this is quite remarkable. Once psychotherapy moves to forgiveness, it is often wise to start with a transgression that is not the most difficult to forgive. There is a learning curve. The forgiver must learn about the REACH Forgiveness method (see the summary in the Introduction to this book) and how to apply it. That is often easiest to learn while applying it to a transgression of moderate difficulty. That should prepare the person to try to forgive a difficult, personally meaningful transgression. Both of Claude's problems were severe transgressions. Neither was an obvious starting point. With the time-limited nature of Claude's counseling, also, it was not possible to seek an easier transgression to begin with. Given the struggle with relational spirituality during the first seven sessions, it is ambitious to think that the psychotherapy might be able to deal adequately with a major spiritual transformation and two severe transgressions—one of which (the rape) seemed to desecrate one daughter's sexual purity and the other of which (the wreck) seemed to desecrate the other daughter's right to live a healthy life. Both transgressions also seemed to be a major abandonment by God and a withdrawal of any sense of God's protection, care, and love, which likely recapitulated the experience of Claude in abandonment by his mother and perhaps his father.

Make Change Sensible

People often learn better when they manipulate concrete objects rather than mere words or when they turn concepts into something tangible. Worthington (2006) argued that in couples and family counseling, effective psychotherapy needs to use tangible objects and activities rather than mere talk. Activities should, as often as possible, be sensed—hence "sensible." In individual psychotherapy, many of the exercises that form the basis of the action plans involve manipulating physical objects. People (a) complete written assessments rather than merely report how they feel, (b) build empathy through an empty-chair experience, (c) make up a written certificate to signify that they have forgiven, and (d) complete a take-home workbook.

Make Change Emotional

Emotion marks important events. Thus, emotion is at the core of almost every psychotherapy. It is thought to play a different role in each. In psychoanalytically informed therapy, emotion-near experiences are the grist for the psychotherapeutic mill. Abreaction involves an emotional working through of conflicts. In emotion-focused therapy, emotions reveal and conceal inner values. Thus, displayed anger may conceal fear. Displayed anxiety might conceal anger. People learn to identify the opposite pole of their emotional experience to get in touch with the full range of their emotional experience. In rational emotive therapy (RET), cognition connects situations and emotion rather than situations directly affecting emotions. In traditional behavior therapy, rewards arouse positive emotions, which often form the basis for change.

In promoting forgiveness, the heart of emotional forgiveness is emotional replacement of negative unforgiving emotions with positive other-oriented emotions. The psychotherapeutic route by which it occurs is not prescribed. Psychotherapies tend to be either emotionally evocative or emotionally calming.

Emotion-evocative psychotherapies depend on stimulating emotional reactions in clients. Emotion-focused therapy is emotionally evocative, as are psychodynamic approaches. They arouse emotion, and if they do not do so, success is thought to be hard to come by. For example, if a client in psychodynamic psychotherapy does not resist, the resistance cannot be interpreted. RET is emotionally evocative. If RET does not arouse emotions, the rational refutation of the maladaptive cognition is obscured. Other psychotherapies are emotionally calming. Behavior therapy does not seek to promote resistance, but to promote cooperation. Thus, emotion is calmed. Cognitive behavior therapy is typically emotionally calming. It seeks to promote cooperation and keep the emotions low.

In our forgiveness therapy, the psychotherapist will not stifle emotional expression. However, psychotherapeutic progress in emotional replacement is most likely when the unforgiving emotions are experienced at a low level, rather than when the client is highly aroused. It is then—when they are "as-if" emotional experiences—that they are most susceptible to replacement. If a person is highly aroused in expressing unforgiveness, a large amount of positive emotional experience is needed to neutralize the negative emotion.

Make Changes Last

To make changes last, it is necessary to make the psychotherapeutic events memorable, use ceremonies and symbols, and repeat the basic forgiveness activities often. Memorable events are punctuated. They stand apart from the normal flow of conversation. In psychotherapy, the psychotherapist can punctuate events by making them unusual or by designating them as important. For example, in the dialogue earlier in the session, when the psychotherapist asked Claude to narrate his thoughts, doing so was an unusual event for Claude. It triggered deep involvement, which the client punctuated by emotion. For example, as Claude narrated his thoughts, he became increasingly "wound up": "That gets me frustrated, and it's so wasted and worthless. I need to get past this. I get all worked up. . . . It's just getting my stomach all upset and it's going to give me an ulcer." Another way to set a psychotherapeutic event apart is to ask the client to do an exercise.

Ceremonies and symbolic activities also will make the effects of an intervention last. When a person works through the five steps of the REACH Forgiveness model (see the summary at the outset of this book, in the Introduction), then the person can make a certificate attesting to himself or herself that forgiveness has been granted and experienced. One of the exercises used to help people signify successfully forgiving is to have them write a short version of the transgression on their hand using permanent black ink—the original shorthand. Then, the person washes the transgression from their hand. Usually, though, the ink will not come completely off, which allows the psychotherapist to note that repetition is often needed before forgiveness is complete.

Make Forgiveness Spread

To help a client forgive a person or become a more forgiving person, forgiveness must generalize. Generalization will happen mostly through repeating interventions. A person can move through the REACH Forgiveness acrostic with a moderate transgression, then repeat the REACH Forgiveness acrostic with a severe transgression, and repeat it again with another important transgression. The repetitions continue as long as the client has not fully forgiven the person. A second person can be forgiven in a similar way—using multiple transgressions. Additional people are added, with each helping the client to generalize and become a more forgiving person.

The Client Must Carry Out the Plans

Action plans are formulated piecemeal, perhaps one or two exercises or spontaneous enactments during a session and another as homework. The essential part of change, though, is creating experiences for the client. Homework is essential. Psychotherapy is usually limited to one of the 168 hours in the week. If change is to occur and to last, it must extend into the other 167 nonpsychotherapy hours. It is essential, then, that the psychotherapist seeks to ensure that the client is carrying out attempts to become more forgiving in his or her nonpsychotherapy hours.

Follow Up on Action Plans and Support Change Attempts (Step 4)

Clients often stop doing homework because psychotherapists fail to ask whether the client actually did the homework as it was assigned and what the client got out of it. Client compliance is essential. If the psychotherapist does not take the homework seriously enough to spend time talking about it, then the client also will not.

And We Have Not Even Begun to Talk About Forgiving With Claude

Once Claude and the psychotherapist have brought some order to Claude's spiritual relationship—not "solved it" or even "stabilized it"—they need to connect what he learned about relational spirituality with forgiveness as a coping mechanism (within the stress-and-coping model of forgiveness) and the elements of the forgiveness and relational spirituality model.

That requires going back to listening and helping rethink the problem (Steps 1 and 2). There are several likely points of connection. First, the stress is an obvious point of connection. Stress intensifies relational spirituality and also provides a drive to cope. Unforgiveness adds to the stressfulness from other stressors. Second, if we are to connect the stress-and-coping model of forgiveness with the forgiveness and relational spirituality pyramid, there are other points of contact. For example, the relational spirituality model, which the psychotherapist just worked through with Claude, yielding Claude's insight (from Session 5, about both transgressions seeming a major abandonment by God and a withdrawal of any sense of God's protection, care, and love, likely recapitulating parental abandonment) that his emotional cutoff with his mother was like he is doing currently with religion, is a way that the client is relating to the sacred (victim–sacred [VS]). Third, the client is also making judgments about the offender. For example, the most basic judgment is whether the person is spiritually similar or different from the client (offender–sacred [OS]). In recent studies, we (Greer, Worthington, Lin, Lavelock, & Griffin, 2014) have found that when clients appraise the offender as spiritually different from themselves, they tend to feel a bit less hurtfulness than they might have experienced if the person was spiritually similar to themselves. People find it a particularly bitter pill to swallow if they are hurt, betrayed, or offended by someone who is spiritually similar to them. On the other hand, the ingroup connection plays its hand when it comes time to consider forgiving. People are much more able to forgive someone who is spiritually similar to them than to forgive someone who is spiritually different (Greer, Worthington, Van Tongeren, et al., 2014). Fourth, another important point of connection between the models occurs when the offense seems like a sacred loss or a desecration of something sacred (Mahoney, Rye, & Pargament, 2005). These points help us make conceptual connections across the three models. Let us just look at a little of that conversation.

> *Psychotherapist:* So, you have a few ways to cope with this stress of your unforgiveness and desire to get even. But you think that they aren't fully effective.

Claude:	Not at all.
Psychotherapist:	So, once your "moods" get started, how do they end? How do you get out of one of your moods? [Comment: The psychotherapist is asking about coping within the stress-and-coping model]
Claude:	Sometimes, like just a few minutes ago, I just get so upset that I wind up angry, depressed, and wounded. I hate that.
Psychotherapist:	I could see how wounded you were.
Claude:	Sometimes, I just grumble around and then my mind moves to something else. Not very often, I recognize that I'm about to flame out, and I stop myself.
Psychotherapist:	How do you do that?
Claude:	I think something like, "Don't go there." Or, "You know where this'll lead."
Psychotherapist:	And that helps?
Claude:	Sometimes. Mostly, though, I don't recognize until I'm too far into raging.
Psychotherapist:	Let me ask you to estimate about how many times out of 10 you can either stop or head off your thoughts before they get you into a rage or a brooding mood?
Claude:	I don't know. Maybe one out of 20, I suppose.
Psychotherapist:	I wonder. You seem resourceful. Is there anything that you might do to increase this to two out of 20? [Comment: The psychotherapist uses a solution-focused therapy technique; de Shazer, 1985.]
Claude:	Sure. I think just paying attention to it could probably up it to five out of 20.
Psychotherapist:	Yes, but paying attention to our thinking is something we get used to quickly. Then we don't pay attention, and we slide back. Is there anything you could change to remind you "don't go there," or could take you to a different emotional place? Not big—just change from one in 20 to two in 20. Can you come up with something that would make it likely that the small improvement lasts? [Comment: The psychotherapist is trying to get Claude to make change sensible.]

Claude: Maybe physically moving. Like if I am at home, I'll go out maybe and get some exercise or work around the house. That might work.

Later, we pick up the conversation at a different topic.

Claude: So, I want to forgive that driver. But I've wanted to forgive for years, and I can't make myself. Every time I try to forgive, I get angry all over again.

Psychotherapist: What would it mean if you forgave him? What would be different?

Claude: I would be less bitter. And I would not get into so many negative moods. I guess, if I forgave, I'd be free from the hate I've felt for years.

Psychotherapist: So, you'd feel differently? You'd feel less negative emotion?

Claude: Yes. I'd be free of the hate and anger.

Psychotherapist: You said that you have tried to forgive many times. How?

Claude: You know, I just said I forgave him.

Psychotherapist: Hummm.

Claude: What's with the "Hummm?"

Psychotherapist: Just putting together what you were saying. You expect to simply say, "I forgive him" and then "poof," you'd be completely free of hate and anger.

Claude: [Laughs.] Yeah, I guess that sounds a bit like magic. It sounds unrealistic that I ought to feel so free of the hate just because I said I forgave him. I mean I've said, "I forgive him" a thousand times and somehow it hasn't freed me from my hate yet.

Psychotherapist: I think it is important to decide you want to forgive. So you are on the right track. I also think it is important that you get rid of your hatred and anger toward that drunk driver. That is a part of forgiving, too. But maybe those two parts of forgiving are not joined at the hip. [Comment: The psychotherapist is separating decisional and emotional forgiveness for Claude.]

Claude: So, I don't get it. So, you mean, do each separately. How can I feel less hate and anger if I haven't decided to forgive?

Psychotherapist:	I'm not sure you can. You have to decide to forgive. But just because you decided to forgive doesn't mean you'll automatically feel emotional forgiveness.
Claude:	So, I need to do something special to experience less hate and anger?
Psychotherapist:	Yes. What do you think you could do to change your feelings from negative to more positive?
Claude:	Maybe if I went to prison and he got down on his knees and groveled in front of me and begged me to forgive him, I might—just might—feel a little more positively toward him. Maybe that would make it easier to forgive him. If I thought he meant it. Oh, yeah, and if he gave me about a million dollars—not that any money could make up for a person. But it'd help.
Psychotherapist:	So you feel that he did such injustices that there is this huge amount of injustice that has to be taken care of before you could feel forgiveness for him? [Comment: The psychotherapist is getting across the idea that there is a big injustice gap here.] And this was such a big injustice because it really was the sacred loss of your full relationship with your daughter and it seems like a desecration of the public trust—that he already had a DUI and yet he betrayed the public trust that didn't lock him up on the previous DUI.
Claude:	Right! He needs to pay big time. It was a violation of something precious—a human life, justice. And, well, personally, it set me off on my spiritual confusion and I'm still struggling with that, although they are a bit better than they were a month ago.
Psychotherapist:	So you said, if he gave you a million dollars, you'd forgive him? [He nods.] What if he gave you $999,999? Could you forgive him then?
Claude:	Well, yes. [Laughs a snort] Yeah, I see where you're going with this. You'll say one less dollar each time. Well, I don't think there is anything special about a million dollars. I don't know where to draw the line. I just want to see him get what he deserves.
Psychotherapist:	That makes a lot of sense. The more justice that you see done (and with his prison or jail time, you are getting to see some of it) and the more he might make some kind of apology and restitution (which he probably isn't going to do, it seems), then the less the amount

of injustice you have to forgive. So, even though he violated something precious, it would be easier to feel more emotionally forgiving. But if you are to forgive, you must, in the end, forgive something that justice couldn't pay for.

Claude: Right. If I could really pay him back completely, there wouldn't be anything to forgive. But how can I change my feelings? I've tried. How can I forgive?

Psychotherapist: You tell me. How could you somehow replace those negative unforgiving emotions you feel?

Claude: [Long pause] Well, his apology would make me feel better toward him, so I guess anything that made me feel better toward him might work the same way.

Psychotherapist: Great thinking! But you seem very down on him. So, there might not be any way to think differently of him.

Claude: Well, he's not all bad, I guess. He's somebody's kid and somebody's parent, and he's in jail. In fact, he's really more pitiful than evil. I mean, really, I hate what he did, and I will always hate what he did. It was totally irresponsible. But I guess if I were being philosophical about it, no one is really defined by any single act. I've certainly screwed up my share of other people's lives. I would hope no single screw-up defines me. As I think about it, I know he didn't want to ruin his life and Martinique's. And mine. And Monique's. And Robbie's. It hurt him, too. He couldn't stop himself from drinking, I guess [Comment: Claude has worked with the psychotherapist to develop an idea of forgiveness, but the idea developed during the ebb and flow of conversation. So the psychotherapist thinks he needs to put it all together for Claude.]

Psychotherapist: Okay. Hummm, okay. Let's pause a minute and see if I understand what you're telling me. You've moved a long way. Let's see if I have it all. You said that this is a kind of violation of something sacred that set you off on spiritual confusion.

Claude: [Speaking over P.] More like hunting, I think.

Psychotherapist: Then [continues] you said that simply making a decision to forgive isn't enough by itself to make you feel more forgiving.

Claude: I've tried that a lot. It doesn't work.

Psychotherapist:	You need to do something in addition to deciding to forgive, or he does, that would make you feel more positive and therefore would neutralize your feelings of negativity and of unforgiveness. You could wait around for him to come grovel at your feet.
Claude:	Not in this lifetime.
Psychotherapist:	And you obviously don't want to stake the family ranch on that. Or you could try to understand his weakness, rather than just treat it as if he had set out with single-minded purpose to destroy Martinique, and in the process you and your family.
Claude:	Whether that was his purpose or not, I feel that he did a pretty good job at that. But yes, that wasn't what he wanted to do. I guess I see him now as weak more than evil.
Psychotherapist:	So, if I understand you correctly, if you put your mind to understanding, empathizing, pitying him, maybe someday feeling compassion toward him and for his weaknesses, then that might combat your negative unforgiving feelings. That might help you *feel* forgiveness, not just decide to forgive. Did I get it right?
Claude:	Right. Yeah. I hear you. But, I've hated him for so long. How can I change?
Psychotherapist:	Well, if you're right in your "theory"—that you need to empathize more or pity him more, and that will help you forgive—then I think I can work with you to develop some practical plans to try and see whether it works.

The psychotherapist and Claude kept working on forgiveness. They used the ideas developed by working with Claude, which were consonant with the stress-and-coping theory of forgiveness, but they also kept relating them back to the loss of something "precious," which later in psychotherapy was renamed *sacred*. That connection helped unite the forgiveness sought through decisional and emotional forgiveness with an awareness of the sacred losses and desecrations (i.e., the transgression–sacred [TS] connection in the model) and the similarities and differences (including spiritual differences) between Claude and the driver responsible for the accident and Martinique's brain injury (i.e., the OS connection). Also, near the end of the working part of psychotherapy, in Session 17, they looked at the ways that the forgiveness Claude had been able to experience for both the driver and the man who raped Robbie had helped bring some direction back into his own spiritual wanderings. Although he would undoubtedly percolate for much longer with the new spiritual directions he was heading, Claude reported being "more settled" in his questing.

Plan for Maintenance (Step 5)

Gains will be maintained if the client has changed structures in his or her life. The structures could be cognitive or behavioral—the narrative threads linking meaningful experiences, memories, and associations and associated behavioral habits—or other structures, such as relationships, situations to which people expose themselves, or people with whom they interact. So, during the last three sessions, Claude and the psychotherapist explored concrete changes he had made already and those he wanted to make—changes such as organizing a reading program aimed at exploring different types of spirituality, involvement in environmental groups to reinforce his nature spirituality, reconnection with the group of men who had organized the singing group at the Catholic church, and a recommitment to "at least putting my butt in the seat at Mass each week. That'll make Monique happy. And I need to do it for me, too."

Terminate Psychotherapy (Step 6)

Rarely is forgiveness the total focus of psychotherapy. Other issues must be dealt with before termination. In this instance, though, the issues that were dealt with in the 24 weeks of psychotherapy (20 sessions plus a few weeks because of missed or rescheduled sessions) were focused on forgiveness and relational spirituality.

SUMMARY

We have shown how the general approach to psychotherapy developed in the first part of the book could be applied by an eclectic psychotherapist to a person struggling directly with both forgiveness and spiritual disruption. We do not presume whether any psychotherapist's theory is psychodynamic, cognitive, or behavioral, or is identified with any established school of psychotherapy. Any could be used in this brief psychotherapeutic approach. We have applied a process approach with brief, time-limited psychotherapy.

However, the model we have been working toward is more about long-term personality change. That is most likely to occur in long-term, time-unlimited psychotherapy. That is what we address in Chapter 8, and we illustrate it with cases in Chapter 9.

8

FORGIVENESS IN LONG-TERM PSYCHOTHERAPY

Brief psychotherapy is effective for many clients. However, for a significant percentage of clients, long-term psychotherapy is a better fit. We find that even when we are conducting brief psychotherapy, it is helpful for us to think about what we might want to accomplish if the client were actually going through long-term psychotherapy. That helps us visualize a goal that might not be approximated in brief psychotherapy but is still a guide to our thinking.

In the present chapter, we define *long-term psychotherapy* as either a minimum of 40 sessions or 1 year in duration (Smit et al., 2012). Long-term psychotherapy enables a more substantial relational process to unfold over time. This is particularly important for clients who experience insecure attachment templates (about 36.5% of the population; Ravitz, Maunder, Hunter, Sthankiya, & Lancee, 2010). Such clients sometimes demonstrate first-order changes of symptom relief in brief therapy, but if relational templates do not undergo second-order changes (i.e., transformation), interpersonal wounds

http://dx.doi.org/10.1037/14712-009
Forgiveness and Spirituality in Psychotherapy: A Relational Approach, by E. L. Worthington, Jr. and S. J. Sandage

and conflicts will likely recur and reactivate past attachment injuries. In fact, some evidence suggests that empirically supported brief psychotherapies do not work for some clients with higher levels of impairment and problematic attachment histories (Castonguay, 2013; Newman, Crits-Cristoph, Connolly Gibbons, & Erickson, 2005).

Interpersonal struggle is one of the most frequent reasons people seek out psychotherapy. Client positive ratings of psychotherapy outcomes have been associated with help in resolving interpersonal problems (Boswell, Castonguay, & Wasserman, 2010). Clients who continue to experience interpersonal problems at the end of brief cognitive behavior therapy have also been found to be at an increased risk of relapse (Borkovec, Newman, Pincus, & Lytle, 2002). This is likely because insecurely attached individuals tend to reenact certain patterns of relationship, which can contribute to further struggles with unforgiveness and can compound the impact of past injuries and emotional difficulties.

Implicit memory and the way it stirs reactions in the limbic system propel people toward familiar relational responses (Lewis, Amini, & Lannon, 2000). Benjamin (2003) argued that "nonresponders" to brief psychotherapies may have insecure attachment histories and maladaptive internal representations of relational figures. These attachment-based representations promote internalized "copy processes." Nonresponders may seek approval from these pathogenic relational figures, imitate their patterns, or treat the self similarly. Particularly relevant for our considerations, Benjamin suggested that these implicit relational patterns often involve unconscious motivations to seek forgiveness or restitution with internalized relational figures. A "limbic revision" is needed through a new, more secure attachment experience that can transform internal working models and foster more effective relational patterns and coping responses. Considering several relational dynamics helps one to understand the need for long-term psychotherapy and the change processes in long-term psychotherapy.

In many ways, the present chapter is the focal point of this book. In it, we lay out the relational development that fuels the psychodynamics of clients. We discuss transference and countertransference in psychotherapy. Then we discuss relational objects of hope, who are people who provide relational experiences that nurture and sustain hope. We describe the crucial role of *mentalization*, which is the ability to attend to the mental states of self. These both lead to humility in the ideal case. So, the psychotherapist is trying to help clients use relational objects of hope, develop skills in mentalization, and develop a sense of humility as part of the curative process.

With an idea of what we are aiming at, we then discuss many personality factors that can inhibit healthy personality development—factors we often see to interfere with both forgiveness and the experience of forgiveness within relational spirituality model. These organize around three types of insecure attachment experiences that yield different attachment templates, and often they lead to different diagnoses when they become personality problems.

Finally, we discuss trauma. We examine its relationship to forgiveness of others and also its relationship to self-forgiveness. That readies us to see the psychotherapy applied in cases in Chapter 9 and to adapt it to couples (Chapter 10) and groups (Chapter 11).

RELATIONAL DEVELOPMENT DYNAMICS AND LONG-TERM PSYCHOTHERAPY

Attachment Dynamics

First, those with insecure attachment templates often struggle with two key developmental tasks that are crucial for forgiveness and healthy relational spirituality: (a) self-regulation of emotions and (b) forming new secure attachment relationships. The lack of an ability to self-regulate emotions results in frequent distress, which is managed by either hyperactivation or deactivation of the attachment system, neither of which fosters authentic forgiveness. Insecure ways of relating with the sacred mean that spiritual resources may be used in attempts to cope with interpersonal injuries and conflicts, but they will be largely ineffectual. Over time, this can be discouraging to such individuals and imply God or the sacred is unhelpful to them in their struggles. This is particularly the case if the person has not reflected upon psychological dynamics that can influence spiritual experience. Alternatively, some insecurely attached individuals may not personally experience their relational spirituality as ineffectual. However, they basically use their spirituality to sustain hostile or other self-protective stances toward others.

Insecure Attachment Templates

Insecure attachment templates can also foster disappointment, mistrust, and hostility toward current or new relational figures (including psychotherapists). This makes it difficult to attach or connect with others as a source of relational regulation and support for processing new or old injuries. The cost of this pattern is that it is difficult to construct new meanings of painful experiences without the limbic connection provided by secure attachment figures. This can also leave in place insecure relational images of the sacred, which reinforce various forms of unforgiveness. Moreover, as we have suggested, healthy forms of relational spirituality can motivate work toward forgiveness. But insecure forms of relational spirituality are unlikely to foster motivational resilience.

One Important Task for Long-Term Psychotherapy

Long-term psychotherapy—if the psychotherapist is successful in engaging the person—can provide a relational context for reworking sources of motivation, or what Benjamin (2003) called the "will to change" (pp. 436–438). By providing an attachment that offers relational attunement and limbic resonance, psychotherapists can establish a "somatic state of relatedness" with clients. That relatedness enhances relational regulation and motivates effortful behavior to discover new stable frames of meaning (Lewis et al., 2000, p. 168).

Transference and Countertransference

Transference and countertransference dynamics—the neurobiological realities that clients transfer expectations onto their relationship with a psychotherapist and tend to respond to emotional patterns familiar to their past and that psychotherapists can similarly transfer their own expectations onto clients, in countertransference—are more complicated with clients with insecure attachment templates. Lewis et al. (2000) explained: "Transference exists because the brain remembers with neurons . . . we are disposed to see more of what we have already seen, hear anew what we have heard most often, think just what we have always thought" (p. 141). Securely attached clients have more flexible relational templates. They are typically capable of greater openness to new interpersonal experiences compared with insecurely attached clients. Thus, psychotherapists working with insecurely attached clients need more time to allow transference to develop. Although transference typically is not a healthy way by which clients relate, psychotherapists have found it useful to allow it to flourish and then to interpret it. This enables working with emotion-near experiences in the psychotherapy relationship. That is thought to be a better way to promote lasting healing than supplying information about how dynamics influence clients' behaviors. However, the insecure attachments will also mean that it typically also takes longer to work through the limbic revision process than with more securely attached clients. Frequently, this will require a rupture-and-repair process as frustrations, conflicts, or perceived empathic failures emerge for clients in their experience of the psychotherapeutic relationship (Castonguay, 2013). These can potentially serve as useful enactments of unforgiveness and forgiveness dynamics directly in the psychotherapeutic relationship.

However, the relational style of insecurely attached clients may help coconstruct experiences of countertransference in the psychotherapist. Those experiences can make it difficult to maintain a healthy psychotherapeutic alliance. It is also important to note that contemporary intersubjective approaches to transference–countertransference also highlight the ways in which clients do not always distort and may accurately perceive certain emotional responses in psychotherapists (Wallin, 2007). When worked intentionally and effectively, transference and countertransference processes can be immensely valuable to long-term psychotherapy, and we describe this in more detail below.

Relational Objects of Hope

Cooper (2000) described psychotherapists as relational "objects of hope" who can help clients to "bear experience, to learn from experience, and to learn how to have new experiences" (p. 20). He suggested that transference is essentially a process of a client reenacting both their hoped-for relational experiences and their resistances to hope. We pointed out in Chapters 4 and 5 that forgiveness and hope have been positively correlated in empirical research. However, that finding was from research with people who typically were not in long-term psychotherapy. Long-term psychotherapy involves clients who often have little hope about reworking the past and even defend against hopefulness that their emotional wounds and attachment injuries can be healed (Wallin, 2007). Implicit despair is attached to some forms of unforgiveness, which involves unconsciously holding onto negative experiences of self and other. It is kind of like pressing one's tongue on a sore tooth to feel a measure of control over inescapable pain.

Clients can express dilemmas of hope in psychotherapy in many ways. They can wonder about the relevance of processing emotions, question whether change is possible, or even express fear that their psyche has been ruined permanently by past injuries.

Of course, hope has long been identified as a common factor of effective psychotherapy (Frank & Frank, 1993). Many relational theories of human development and psychotherapy also implicitly or explicitly suggest that relational experiences of hope are central motivators of healthy adaptation and change, and we identified it as a key to psychotherapy (see Chapter 5). The psychotherapeutic contract, whether stated explicitly or not, involves a psychotherapist who can envision change for a client and who explores both present and prior experiences in the implied hope of revision, healing, and growth. At times, psychotherapists need to "hold hope" for clients who might at that time be incapable or unwilling to hold hope for themselves. This holding of hope involves a kind of secure-base attachment dynamic that suggests it is possible to move through pain toward some kind of positive future. This kind of relational hope in individual psychotherapy can be counterintuitive for some clients because (a) it does not involve the assumption of reconciliation, (b) it does not assume or admit that others (e.g., offenders) will change, and (c) it suggests a form of "complex hope" that invites moving deeper into processing emotional conflicts and grieving losses and disappointments (Cooper, 2000).

We further discuss this latter part, complex hope, below. Grieving is a form of emotional processing that can unfreeze certain forms of unforgiveness, facilitate new meaning construction, and shift underlying attachment-based self–other configurations in more hopeful directions.

Humility Through Mentalization

What Is Mentalization?

Clients who need long-term psychotherapy typically have relational struggles with *mentalization*, which is the ability to attend to the mental states of self and others. Healthy and accurate capacities for mentalization are formed through well-attuned, securely attached relationships. Mentalization contributes to the ability to construct coherent narratives of personal experience, requires tolerating ambiguity and feeling secure enough to be curious and to explore meaning, and counters anxiety-driven and repetitive rumination. Deficits in mentalization are found in autism spectrum disorders and also personality disorders. These deficits lead to misinterpreting the thoughts, emotions, and intentions of both self and other. Mentalization-based therapy approaches can be effective with clients with personality disorder diagnoses (Bateman & Fonagy, 2004, 2006), so capacities for mentalization can be improved. Mentalization has been proposed as the most common factor across diverse approaches to psychotherapy, although some approaches major on increasing self-awareness rather than more complex self and other awareness (Allen, Fonagy, & Bateman, 2008).

Humility

As mentioned in Chapter 5, humility is a multidimensional construct consisting of (a) accurate self-appraisal (i.e., accurate assessment of self and recognition of limits), (b) an open and receptive orientation toward others, and (c) the capacity for emotional self-regulation (D. E. Davis et al., 2011; D. E. Davis, Worthington, & Hook, 2010; Exline & Hill, 2012; Jankowski, Sandage, & Hill, 2013). Humility is considered a virtue in many spiritual, religious, and cultural traditions. It correlates with numerous measures of relational well-being, including secure attachment (Jankowski & Sandage, 2014a), differentiation of self (Jankowski et al., 2013), and forgiveness (D. E. Davis, Worthington, & Hook, 2010). Humility is also consistent with well-developed capacities for mentalization, which involves "an implicit sense that the world is not necessarily as we experience it to be" (Allen et al., 2008, p. 37).

How Humility Helps Mentalization and Vice Versa

Egocentrism is a human default mode, and differentiation of self and mentalization represent nuanced intersubjective capacities to recognize both that one's internal emotional state may not match that of the other person and that one might misunderstand the other's intentions and experience. It is often necessary to try to take the perspective of the other. That involves a kind of interpretive projection. Humility helps quarantine one's own subjective experience from overdetermining interpretations of the other in the mentalization process (Allen et al., 2008, p. 47). Long-term psychotherapy based on our model centers on a relational process that reworks the dynamics of attachment, differentiation, and mentalization to foster hope, humility, and forgiveness.

PERSONALITY FACTORS THAT INHIBIT FORGIVENESS AND HEALTHY RELATIONAL SPIRITUALITY

Many personality factors can inhibit capacities for forgiveness and healthy relational spirituality. For the sake of parsimony, we use Bartholomew and Horowitz's (1991) model of categories of attachment (see Figure 8.1) to summarize some key individual differences in struggles with forgiveness and spirituality. We also highlight implications for long-term psychotherapy based on these differing attachment profiles.

MODEL OF SELF
(Dependence)

	Positive (Low)	Negative (High)
MODEL OF OTHER (Avoidance) Positive (Low)	Secure	Preoccupied
Negative (High)	Dismissing	Fearful

Figure 8.1. Categories of adult attachment. From "Attachment Styles Among Young Adults: A Test of a Four-Category Model," by K. Bartholomew and L. M. Horowitz, 1991, *Journal of Personality and Social Psychology, 61*, p. 227. Copyright 1991 by the American Psychological Association.

Bartholomew and Horowitz's (1991) model is based on internal working models of self and other and levels of dependence and avoidance. Securely attached individuals tend to view both self and other positively and are typically comfortable with both intimacy and autonomy.

We reviewed empirical evidence in Chapter 1 showing attachment security has been positively associated with forgiveness and indices of healthy relational spirituality, and people with a secure style of attachment do not usually need long-term psychotherapy. Therefore, we consider the other three categories of insecure attachment.

Dismissing/Avoidant Attachment

Personality Dynamics of Dismissing/Avoidant Attachment

Those with a dismissing or avoidant style of attachment tend to deactivate the attachment system under stress and seek to maintain hyperindependence rather than trying to connect with another amid vulnerability. This includes narcissistic and obsessive–compulsive (OC) personality styles, which organize around negative views of others and more positive views of self. Both styles generate difficulties forgiving others and inhibit awareness of a need to seek forgiveness from others.

The two styles differ. A narcissistic personality style involves an excessively positive view of self (albeit often vulnerable to ego threats and invalidation). An OC personality style involves perfectionism, cognitive and moral rigidity, and a controlling interpersonal stance. Another hypothesized difference (although it has yet to be tested) is that a narcissistic personality style is not usually overtly self-condemning for his or her own failings (which are often explained away, minimized or overlooked). However, shame and guilt might lurk beneath that exterior. But an OC personality style often experiences falling short of perfection and, thus, feels self-condemning (see Worthington, 2013), unloved, and rejected by God for perceived moral failures (Griffin, Worthington, Wade, Hoyt, & Davis, in press; Worthington & Langberg, 2012), unforgiven by God (Toussaint, Williams, Musick, & Everson, 2001), or anger toward God or the sacred (Exline, Yali, & Lobel, 1999; Strelan, Acton, & Patrick, 2009).

Narcissistic Personality

Narcissism is a personality trait of self-involvement and includes grandiose and vulnerable forms (Pincus et al., 2009). The *Diagnostic and Statistical Manual of Mental Disorders* (5th ed.; American Psychiatric Association, 2013) description of narcissistic personality disorder fits the grandiose form with a focus on symptoms such as arrogance, entitlement, exploitiveness, lack of empathy, envy, and excessive need for validation. The vulnerable form of narcissism is considered below because it involves underlying shame and negativity about the self and has been associated with preoccupied or ambivalent attachment (Banai, Mikulincer, & Shaver, 2005). As Bowlby (1988) originally noted, those with a narcissistic personality structure typically have a dismissing or avoidant style of attachment and have learned to focus on emotional self-reliance because seeking support from caregivers was likely to be rebuffed. Empirical studies have supported the connection between grandiose forms of narcissism and dismissive attachment. Also, there is evidence that parental patterns of overindulgence or cold rejection can each lead to grandiose narcissism (Meyer & Pilkonis, 2011).

Narcissistic Entitlement and Forgiveness. Narcissistic entitlement has been negatively associated with forgiveness in numerous studies (Eaton, Struthers, & Santelli, 2006; Exline, Baumeister, Bushman, Campbell, & Finkel, 2004; Konrath & Cheung, 2013). Grandiose narcissists' struggles with forgiveness often involve resentment or anger when others are not adequately validating, admiring, or responsive to their self-perceived needs. Angry devaluing of others can serve the function of maintaining emotional distance and shameful feelings of dependency. Entitled narcissists often prefer the dominant position in a relationship and are susceptible to what Kohut (1977) called *narcissistic rage*, which is an anxiety-driven response to an experience of self-fragmentation. The colloquial term "coming unglued" fits this sense: the lack of a cohesive self being revealed because of the stress of a lack of mirroring or validation from others. Grandiose narcissists have very limited capacities to consider the perspective of others, so an episode of narcissistic rage is rarely followed by an apology or concern to repair the interpersonal impact. Empathy and the humility of seeing oneself as capable of similar offenses are key factors that can help with forgiving others. These are deficits for those high in grandiose narcissism.

Narcissism and Relational Spirituality. In terms of relational spirituality, narcissism has been associated with extrinsic or expedient religious motives, which means that people use their religion as a means to other ends (Sandage & Moe, 2011). Welwood (2000) used the term "spiritual bypassing" to describe forms of relating to the sacred that involve narcissistic defense as a way of appearing spiritually healthy while avoiding underlying psychological problems and insecurity. High levels of spiritual grandiosity have also been negatively associated with interpersonal forgiveness, which fits with Welwood's conception of spiritual bypassing (Sandage & Crabtree, 2012).

Obsessive–Compulsive Personality Disorder

Obsessive–compulsive personality disorder (OCPD) is the most prevalent of the personality disorder and is more common among males than females (de Reus & Emmelkamp, 2012). The obsessive need for interpersonal control can reflect a desire to avoid feelings and intimacy, as well as an attachment history centered around power and control struggles with parents (Wallin, 2007). Although those with OC traits can often be overcontrolled in their affective expression, there is also evidence of an increased risk of domestic violence among those with OCPD (Fernández-Montalvo & Echeburúa, 2008). The theme of control is important for this personality style. Rigid expectations, blame, and relational distance may be used to manage an underlying fear of being controlled by others or looking "faulty" or shamefully defective. A heavy emphasis on "shoulds" creates an orderly system of rules for maintaining control and avoiding shame. When those strategies are challenged, anger or acting out (i.e., a lack of self-control) may occur.

Lynch and Cheavens (2007) suggested that those with OC traits or OCPD struggle with an overly "fixed mind" and need to move toward "fluid mind" through forgiveness and mindfulness practices fostering radical acceptance (pp. 274–281). Rigid avoidance of certain emotional conflicts or relational struggles functions to distract these individuals from underlying bitterness but prevents the emotional openness that can lead to more flexible relational patterns.

Obsessive–Compulsive Personality Disorder and Relational Spirituality

In terms of our relational spirituality model, people with OCPD engage in very little spiritual seeking because of a lack of a spiritual secure base and an extreme difficulty tolerating ambiguity and uncertainty. Their spiritual motivations can often be perfectionistic, dutiful, and extrinsic or overly concerned about how their behavior appears to those around them as a way to try to avoid underlying shame proneness (Schoenleber & Berenbaum, 2010; Sorotzkin, 1998). They typically do not understand spiritual or relational growth as a process. They are usually not experienced with internally reflecting on their subjective viewpoint. If you were to ask them directly if they are having trouble forgiving someone, they would usually say no. This is because they avoid feelings such as anger. They are concerned not to appear to lack in virtue.

Also they habitually hold people accountable to high standards of behavior, almost as if they carry an interpersonal police badge. Those around them will often feel unforgiven or "always in the wrong." They may also become frustrated that the OCPD person is so miserly about apologizing for their own mistakes.

It is also easy to get pulled into the power and control struggle and too readily submit to the demands of the OCPD person or become critical and controlling in response (Wallin, 2007). But one must understand that they are not invested in validation or being better than others (as with narcissism). They simply fear the helplessness they associate with imperfection and are threatened when others do not conform to their rules or organizational structure.

Preoccupied/Ambivalent Attachment

Personality Dynamics of Preoccupied/Ambivalent Attachment

Those with a preoccupied or ambivalent style of attachment experience hyperactivation of the attachment system under stress and vacillate between anxiously soliciting help and, sometimes, getting angry and complaining about a lack of support from others. This style involves ambivalence about attachment—that is, the person desperately longs for supportive connection while simultaneously feeling anxiety and agitation about the risk of further abandonment or disappointment. People with dependent personalities and people who are vulnerable narcissists each tend to have a preoccupied attachment style. They can have difficulty with differentiation and detachment from sources of interpersonal pain. Both styles often involve quick, but surface-level almost pseudoforgiveness in the early parts of psychotherapy, but as psychotherapy unfolds, they experience increased levels of anger and unforgiveness (but for somewhat different reasons).

Dependent Personality Traits

Those with dependent traits tend to feel helpless when alone. They are anxious about abandonment and hesitate to disagree, which they fear might lead to abandonment (Gore, Presnall, Miller, Lynam, & Widiger, 2012).

Dependent Personality Traits and Forgiveness. People with dependent traits combine insecure attachment with a high level of submissive agreeableness. They thus often express "premature forgiveness" (Akhtar, 2002, p. 190) or a kind of prereflective "forgiveness-in-theory" (Shaw, 2014, p. 93) that avoids or dissociates awareness of offenses and injuries rather than working through the emotions involved (Vitz & Mango, 1997b).

Dependent Personality Traits and Relational Spirituality. Those with dependent personalities resist the differentiation of spiritual seeking because of high levels of separation anxiety and shame about their own agency or competence. They lack an emotional or spiritual secure base to help them (a) to cope with the anxiety of interpersonal conflict and the potential need to set boundaries with others or (b) to manage situations autonomously. Dependent personalities may often use passive or "deferring" approaches in their religious coping, which could fit with an assumption that one is powerless or ineffective in coping. That in turn might lead to yielding all power or control to God or spiritual forces. This deferring style of coping may function effectively in situations in which there is little that one can do to change matters. However, responding to interpersonal conflict and unforgiveness is typically not one of those situations. Fabricatore, Handal, Rubio, and Gilner, (2004) found that greater use of deferring forms of religious coping under stress predicted low senses of power, positive affect, and life satisfaction. Those findings suggest that overuse of passive styles of spirituality may not be helpful.

Personality Dynamics of Vulnerable Narcissism

Those high in vulnerable or "covert" narcissism tend to also have a preoccupied attachment style. They tend to idealize others as a way of trying to avoid underlying shame, depression, and emptiness (Banai et al., 2005; Meyer & Pilkonis, 2011). They project perfection or omnipotence onto idealized persons and then seek to "bask in the glow" through mirroring forms of connection with those persons to soothe shame and anxiety about their own sense of defectiveness (Masterson, 1993).

Their attachment histories likely involved a role of mirroring the grandiosity of one or both parents. They tend to be particularly sensitive to criticism, invalidation, and perceived rejection. Thus, they often avoid direct confrontation of others related to conflicts and may express anger passively aggressively.

Vulnerable Narcissism and Forgiveness. Nauta and Derckx (2007) found vulnerable narcissism was positively associated with resentment, depression, and envy in a sample of Dutch spiritual leaders and negatively associated with meaning and satisfaction in life. Vulnerable narcissism has been negatively associated with forgiveness, and this effect was mediated by "conflict-promoting attributions" of causality and responsibility for offenses as intentional, selfishly motivated, and blameworthy (Ra, Cha, Hyun, & Bae, 2013, pp. 883–884). Whereas grandiose narcissists find negative public events harder to forgive than private ones, probably because of the risked loss of social face, the opposite pattern holds for vulnerable narcissism (Besser & Zeigler-Hill, 2010). Private interpersonal conflicts likely involve closer relationships, thus intensifying fears of rejection that characterize vulnerable narcissism.

Vulnerable Narcissism and Relational Spirituality. Unlike grandiose narcissists, vulnerable narcissists are not skilled in defensive self-enhancement (e.g., downgrading the source of negative feedback) to buffer the shame of conflict and invalidation. Their unforgiveness typically increases when their idealization of others begins to dissolve, and they feel disappointed. Disappointment and de-idealization cause a destabilization of the self, emotional dysregulation, and spiritual turbulence or disillusionment (Jones, 2002; Sandage & Moe, 2011). A lack of feeling understood can also increase agitation and anger in psychotherapy. They may initially feel shame at realizing that their idealization of their psychotherapist recapitulates a family-of-origin pattern.

Fearful/Disorganized Attachment

Personality Dynamics of Fearful/Avoidant Attachment

Those with a fearful or disorganized style of attachment struggle with negative views of others and themselves. They have typically suffered trauma, abuse, or severe neglect in their past. As Wallin (2007) put it, they tend to be deeply "embedded" or immersed in their interpersonal experiences with feelings that are so powerful it is hard to step back and reflect at all (p. 135). The internal world consistently trumps external reality, particularly when it comes to interpersonal interactions, with limited differentiation of perception and self–other awareness. "Danger" is the consistent message about relationships. It is hard for those with a fearful attachment style to form any consistent attachment strategy. They probably have experience as scapegoats in their family of origin or other relational systems. This can lead to vacillating between relational distancing (dismissive strategy) and pursuit (preoccupied strategy). Those with traits of borderline personality disorder clearly fit this style. Some paranoid personalities also demonstrate fearful attachment.

The fearful attachment style of paranoid personalities reflects their difficulties trusting others or tolerating closeness combined with a preoccupation with others and their "hidden motives" (Sherry, Lyddon, & Henson, 2007, p. 343). They tend to test the loyalty of people around them, are provocative or ornery, and typically show a restricted range of affect that can mask their chronic anxiety and tension (Benjamin, 1996).

Personality Dynamics of Paranoid Personality Disorder

Paranoid personality disorder, one of the most common personality disorders, has been conceptualized as a combination of high neuroticism (i.e., emotional reactivity) and low agreeableness (Brieger, Sommer, Blöink, & Marneros, 2000). They experience the world and people as dangerous and unsafe. This likely contributes to the negative empirical correlation between forgiveness and paranoid traits (Muñoz Sastre, Vinsonneau, Chabol, & Mullet, 2005). Fearful attachment has also been associated with paranoid traits of interpersonal coldness and vindictiveness (Haggerty, Hilsenroth, & Vala-Stewart, 2009).

Paranoid Personality Disorder and Forgiveness. Unforgiveness protects against dangerous, "demonized" others. It is maintained by the unconscious projection of anger and hostility from the paranoid person onto other persons or the world in general (Karen, 2001). This reflects the splitting of good and bad objects in the psyche. The bad is projected out, and intense, chronic hatred is used as a defense mechanism. That makes it nearly impossible to achieve much self-awareness (Kernberg, 1991; Vitz & Mango, 1997a). Klein (1975) offered another way of thinking about the persecutory anxiety behind this paranoid process. Paranoid people are unconsciously anxious that their anger and envy will provoke others into persecuting them. Those who are paranoid typically maintain that their fears are realistic. Their interpersonal style makes it likely they will indeed be rejected or at least encounter relational problems.

Paranoid Personality Disorder and Relational Spirituality. The relational spirituality of paranoid personalities typically organizes around a prominent moral rigidity. The self is viewed as righteous but under constant threat of attack and victimization (Terman, 2010). The person usually believes strongly in the importance of spiritual power. In contrast to pure narcissism, a highly paranoid person actually feels vulnerable to malevolent power from outside and that power can desecrate what is considered most holy. Thus, it is often easy to learn what he or she is against spiritually or religiously, but it is hard to get to know what it is about the sacred that he or she might have any warm or tender feelings toward. These people deeply fear the shame and humiliation of being revealed as helpless, weak, or controlled by others. They hold a moral perception that injustices need to be spiritually rectified to vindicate the self (Strozier, 2010). This vindication of the righteous is an element of apocalyptic vision in many fundamentalist religious groups, although paranoia is not limited to religious fundamentalism. Also, actual experiences of discrimination, particularly religious discrimination, may have contributed to a paranoid worldview. In some contexts, there is an adaptive function to a certain level of mistrust, particularly among nondominant groups. However, there are psychological costs to maintaining a chronic paranoid mindset, and anger and mistrust can sometimes be overgeneralized. If they belong to a spiritual or religious community, their style of relational spirituality will be characterized by ingroup loyalty with rigid boundaries against "outsiders." However, others with paranoid personalities pursue spirituality in an autonomous or separatist fashion.

Personality Dynamics of Borderline Personality Disorder

Those with borderline personality profiles have negative views of self and other with high levels of abandonment and engulfment anxiety. Although the paranoid personality often manages splitting by focusing on threats outside the self, those with borderline traits more often turn hostility and harm toward themselves. They have immense amounts of shame, which promotes swinging between emotional dysregulation and dissociation. They are often highly sensitive to interpersonal dynamics involving injustice or invalidation, and although often accurate in perceiving that a problem exists, they have trouble managing their emotions about the problem. Once angry or disappointed, they can become glued to a conflict and feel a need to grind out their complaint with others in ways that can be either intimidating or fatiguing to the others. They engage in a conflict-centered form of attachment while fearing further abandonment. In other cases, their emotional dysregulation about a conflict or injustice is so high that their capacity to communicate is compromised or they seem only to be able to communicate abusively.

Borderline Personality Disorder and Forgiveness. Borderline personality symptomatology has been negatively associated with forgiveness (Sansone, Kelley, & Forbis, 2013). Searles (1986) suggested that for clients who have been diagnosed with borderline personality disorder, their vengefulness and difficulties forgiving involve defenses against grief and separation anxiety. They attempt to consolidate personal identity around anger at others. Benjamin (1996) viewed borderline anger as an attempt to coerce availability and nurturance from a rescuer. Clients with borderline traits who start to forgive others may rapidly experience shame and dangerous levels of self-recrimination or suicidality unless they can actualize self-compassion or self-forgiveness. Unlike people with personality profiles that more readily accept relational distance, those with borderline profiles long for relational reconciliation while also fearing it (Holm, Berg, & Severinsson, 2009).

Borderline Personality Disorder and Relational Spirituality. The relational spirituality of those with borderline traits tends to be consistent with underlying problems in emotion regulation and a lack of spiritual attachment security. Spiritual practices may be used to temporarily dissociate from shame-laden pain, but the recurrence of shame will usually activate feelings of spiritual deprivation and depravity (i.e., "sinfulness") or anger at God or the sacred. Others, whether human or divine, are often initially idealized by those with borderline personalities. But they rapidly fall from grace as unavailable or disappointing. This profile does not promote healthy spiritual seeking or dwelling, although often, the borderline person might cycle through spiritual programs, communities, or teachers. Empirical studies with Christian samples have found a negative association between a borderline style of relational spirituality and forgiving others (Sandage & Crabtree, 2012; Sandage & Jankowski, 2010).

Trauma, Forgiveness, and Spirituality

Many clients who need long-term psychotherapy or who meet criteria for a personality or other chronic mental disorder will have experienced psychological and spiritual effects of trauma. Trauma involves threats to survival or other extreme danger, which can be roughly expressed by metaphors such as "black hole" (van der Kolk et al., 1996) or an emotional "tsunami"

(Bromberg, 2011). Psychologically, trauma can activate overwhelming levels of attachment anxiety, which leads to contrasting response patterns of hyperarousal and dissociation, intrusive reexperiencing and emotional numbing (Schore, 2012).

At a spiritual or existential level, trauma can sometimes shift a person's basic trust in benevolence or justice in the universe (Bryant-Davis & Wong, 2013). Wiesel (2006) described his own spiritual trauma during the Holocaust upon getting off the train at the death camp and squeezing his father's hand as he realized what was happening there. Wiesel recounted, "Never shall I forget those moments that murdered my God and my soul and turned my dreams into ashes" (p. 34). The traumatic horror destroyed his attachment with God and the sacred at a moment when his human attachments were being destroyed. In less extreme ways, Pargament (2007) described the constructs of negative religious coping and spiritual struggles as rooted in a template of fear, doubt, or mistrust of the sacred. Combing the attachment-based interpersonal impact of trauma with the effects on relational spirituality, one can see that a trauma template forms, which shapes neurobiological patterns of expectation and response. The personality differences described above reflect differing trauma templates. It is typically more difficult to recover from trauma involving family attachments (e.g., domestic violence) than impersonal forces (e.g., natural disasters) because of the importance of interpersonal attachment dynamics and safe forms of relational dwelling for adaptive functioning.

Trauma and Relational Spirituality

Doehring (1993) described ways the trauma of abuse can sometimes lead to "internal desecration" (p. 2). Intrapsychic connections to God or the sacred are shamed or contaminated in a way that prevents the person from experiencing a safe form of relational spirituality. This is a particular risk when spiritual or religious concepts or language are used either abusively or to justify abuse. But even when spirituality and religion are not explicitly invoked by an abuser, it is possible for victims of trauma or abuse to experience their own internal spiritual and existential struggle with maintaining a connection with the sacred in the context of their pain, injustice, and feelings of abandonment.

Trauma and Forgiveness

Not everyone who experiences potentially traumatic events experiences trauma (Bonanno, 2005). Traumatic events can be followed by posttraumatic growth, which can include forgiveness (Bonanno, 2005; Bonanno, Brewin, Kaniasty, & La Greca, 2010). But many trauma survivors encounter at least a temporary period of spiritual and existential "moratorium" or "diffusion." In Marcia's model of identity development, moratorium involves a period of active seeking of identity by trying different experiences, values, and relationships before making commitments that stabilize identity (Marcia, Waterman, Matteson, Archer, & Orlofsky, 2011). *Diffusion* refers to a lack of identity combined with a lack of active searching. Trauma can promote spiritual and existential seeking of meaning and questing to try to find healing or understanding. But trauma can also generate a kind of spiritual and existential diffusion in which a person is frozen in capacity to make new meaning or connect with the sacred in constructive ways. Spiritual diffusion can inhibit the differentiated process of working toward forgiveness.

In fact, symptoms of posttraumatic stress disorder have been negatively associated with various aspects of forgiveness in empirical studies (Dekel, 2010; Orcutt, Pickett, & Pope, 2008; Reed & Enright, 2006; Solomon, Dekel, & Zerach, 2009; Weinberg, 2013; Witvliet, Phipps, Feldman, & Beckham, 2004). The traumatized brain is "poised for battle" (Cozolino, 2006), but fear-based arousal can promote fight, flight, or freeze responses. In trauma survivors, unforgiveness can often be understood as anxiety-based, self-protective responses to perceptions that danger is ongoing. In some cases, danger may actually be ongoing, but in other cases the chronic mobilization of defenses reflects a reexperiencing of trauma and activation of the autonomic nervous system. Trauma survivors also can experience revenge fantasies and a longing for other forms of justice or restitution (Herman, 1992). It is particularly tragic when trauma templates formed in relation to past perpetrators activate symptoms of "generalized unforgiveness," which rupture or erode new relationships. Those with fearful/disorganized styles of attachment are particularly at risk to eventually live in a kind of angry, defensive fortress with a shrinking set of attachments due to conflicts and cutoffs.

Trauma and Self-Forgiveness

A prominent and often-underrated consequence of trauma is shame or internal feelings of worthlessness, self-contempt, or even self-hatred combined an experience of external humiliation or exclusion (Budden, 2009). Traumatic shame has the psychological power over time to infiltrate or even "regulate" other emotions (Schore, 1994). Shame often promotes disconnection or withdrawal from relationship. However, shame has also been associated with anger, hostility, and unforgiveness (Sandage & Worthington, 2010). As Wilson, Drozdek, and Turkovic (2006) put it, "shame damages the soul of a person" (p. 139) as an assault on identity and a sense of shared humanity. In traumatic shame, the self reflexively turns against itself as an unconscious attempt at a shred of existential control or blame for uncontrollable circumstances.

Self-compassion and self-forgiveness feel completely elusive to many trauma survivors whose trauma experience is encased in a capsule of shame, which protects against explicit memory. However, self-compassion and self-forgiveness become important goals in psychotherapy for many trauma survivors in the overall psychotherapy process outlined below (see Worthington & Langberg, 2012).

SUMMARY

In the present chapter, we reached the focal point of this book. We provided a conceptualization in terms of attachment schemas for some major personality profiles of clients that we often see in long-term psychotherapy in which forgiveness and relational spirituality come together in complicated ways. We also discussed the potential impact of trauma in terms of struggles with forgiveness and relational spirituality. There are, of course, other ways of conceptualizing these clinical issues, but we attempted to offer a coherent relational framework that incorporates empirical research on human development; psychopathology; and the psychology of religion, spirituality, and forgiveness. Our intention is to help clinicians nuance their relational approach to psychotherapy based on clients' attachment templates and relational spirituality profiles. In Chapter 9, we outline our approach to long-term psychotherapy based on this relational model.

9

CASE STUDY OF FORGIVENESS IN LONG-TERM PSYCHOTHERAPY

In this chapter, we build on the conceptual model described in Chapter 8 to outline a four-phase overall process of long-term relational psychotherapy, which can facilitate forgiveness. We use this process in individual, couples, and family therapies. It is easy to think of such a process as linear. However, we roughly describe some general sequencing in an iterative, nonlinear process that can involve cycling through these differing dynamics and interventions (A. M. Hayes, Laurenceau, Feldman, Strauss, & Cardaciotto, 2007). We consider the overall process as one of relational transformation through differentiation. We start by forming an attachment with the client (Phase 1). Then, we attempt to cocreate a crucible-like process in which insecure attachment templates can be experienced and processed in emotion-near interactions (Phase 2). As change happens, loss will be experienced and we (and outcomes) will inevitably disappoint the client. We must help the client process grief and disappointment that attend change (Phase 3). To the extent the

http://dx.doi.org/10.1037/14712-010
Forgiveness and Spirituality in Psychotherapy: A Relational Approach, by E. L. Worthington, Jr. and S. J. Sandage

client, and we, working with the client, succeed, the client should move toward a more differentiated self (Phase 4) so that a healthy termination can occur. This organization is the way the chapter unfolds.

We find it convenient to use different terminology to describe the walk through long-term psychotherapy than we did through brief psychotherapy, but you can no doubt see the resemblance between these four phases and the six steps we named in Chapter 6 and described and illustrated in Chapter 7. Connect (Step 1) is similar (but feels less intense) than Phase 1, forming an attachment with the client. Rethink the problem (Step 2) and make action plans based on the new conceptualization (Step 3) together are like Phase 2, cocreating a crucible-like process in which insecure attachment templates can be experienced and processed in emotion-near interactions. Following up on action plans and supporting change attempts (Step 4) is similar to Phase 3, helping the client process grief and disappointment that attend change. Planning for maintenance (Step 5) is similar also to Phase 4, in which the client should move toward a more differentiated self. Then, in both sets of terminology, we are able to successfully terminate psychotherapy (Step 6; not labeled a "phase").

THE FOUR PHASES OF LONG-TERM RELATIONAL PSYCHOTHERAPY

Phase 1: Forming an Attachment

In our relational model, change starts with forming an attachment and developing a psychotherapeutic alliance. This is done, throughout psychotherapy, by pacing and leading.

Pacing

A key part of this involves *pacing*, which is a term Maddock and Larson (1995) borrowed from Eriksonian hypnotherapy. Pacing means attuning one's behavior and concerns with those of the client. Empathy is a form of pacing, but pacing can also include matching the emotional intensity, posture, topical interest, and other facets of the client's presentation.

Leading

Leading occurs when the psychotherapist attempts new inputs into the client system. For example, leading can include introducing a new idea or a reframe, challenging or confronting existing perspectives, or suggesting some change in behavior or goals. Typically, lead moves in psychotherapy do not work unless a client feels well-paced. Clients sometimes say they do not feel understood by the psychotherapist. That can mean that the client felt the psychotherapist's intervention (lead move) was not adequately embedded in an understanding of either the client or his or her particular context (or both). This is intersubjective; clients may sometimes not feel ready for a lead move even if a psychotherapist has worked hard at pacing.

Safe Haven and Secure Base of Attachment

Pacing and leading also map onto the safe-haven and secure-base functions of attachment. Lead moves potentially invite clients into secure-base behavior of exploring a new perspective or taking action toward new behaviors. Secure-base behavior requires trust and security of attachment to the psychotherapist, who is perceived as a safe haven. This raises the paradoxical challenge of long-term therapy: The very clients who need long-term psychotherapy tend to have insecure styles of attachment while also probably needing a sense of safety and security to change. Maddock and Larson (1995) noted that these clients need more than the usual doses of pacing, and yet their relational styles can tempt psychotherapists into premature or reactive lead moves that reinforce attachment insecurity and struggles of power and control.

Several pacing dynamics can foster secure attachment. This extends beyond the obvious importance of empathic attunement and willingness to process vulnerable emotions.

Mirroring

First, note the kinds of language used by clients, particularly as it reflects important values, beliefs, and cultural, spiritual, or religious traditions (Dueck & Reimer, 2009). Note the specific terms or metaphoric phrases clients use. These are often tied to implicit meanings. Metaphors sometimes reveal a client's underlying sense of spiritual, existential, and relational predicament (e.g., "I feel trapped in a room and no one can hear me calling for help"). Engaging clients' language and metaphors can help pace stronger attachment. It is important to clarify meanings rather than to assume understanding. Salient aspects of clients' self-definition and cultural, social, or spiritual identity are important to acknowledge. Attunement to their seeming level of comfort with discussion of those facets of identity is necessary.

Maintaining a Psychotherapeutic Distance

Second, it is important to seek balanced relational positioning over time—not too close and not too distant. This will require repositioning at various points. Consider clients' attachment styles in this regard. In short, anxiety will be increased in dismissive clients by feelings of intimacy, in preoccupied clients by distance, and in fearful clients by inconsistency. Working with these anxieties can involve strategic lead moves as psychotherapy unfolds, especially moving to more intensification of anxiety. However, pacing requires sensitivity to the positioning that is most comfortable to the client so intensity can be ratcheted down if needed. Clients with insecure attachment histories will feel ambivalence about the psychotherapeutic relationship as attachment unfolds. So, psychotherapists can expect periodic relational shifts from clients, toward anger, distancing, pursuit, and other expressions of anxiety. In extreme cases, clients might test the psychotherapist's commitment or somehow destroy the tension of the relationship by cancelling sessions and temporarily dropping out of psychotherapy. Psychotherapists should attempt relational consistency and stability in managing the attachment process.

Understanding What the Client Wants, Believes to Be Important, and Treats as Sacred

Third, pacing also involves trying to understand what clients want and what is most deeply important or even sacred to them. This often moves us toward (a) deeply held hopes and longings and (b) vulnerable emotions (e.g., sadness, anxiety, shame). Understanding these can heighten interpersonal connection. However, for some clients, surfacing and getting close to a clients' desires and sacred values might feel too much. Think in terms of revealing and sealing back up in the relational dynamic, especially early in psychotherapy.

Noticing and Affirming Strengths

Fourth, genuinely notice and affirm clients' strengths. That is valuable for pacing, unless the client's self-contempt about those issues is strong. Trying actively to get a client to feel good about certain strengths can involve underpacing her or his personal feelings of shame or negativity. It also can invite a power struggle. Instead, note the difference in perspective—for instance, "I can see how my comment that I felt you showed impressive courage in confronting that issue missed your own feelings of weakness and feeling alone. I'd like go back to how you felt about it."

Being Sensitive to the Client's Life Context and Important Transitions

Fifth, attention to the client's present life context and past or present transitions can often intensify pacing of attachment. Clients with insecure attachment histories are sometimes surprised when a psychotherapist remembers some attachment-oriented detail of the prior week. For example, the client might be touched if the psychotherapist asked, "How did it go with your parents' visit?" or "You said you were nervous about talking to your friend Luis about your conflicts. How did it go?" Recollection of some specific details communicates that a psychotherapist is tuned in and following the story. Transitions also tend to activate the attachment system. Pay attention to the significance of transitions. That can often increase a sense of relational understanding. For example, the psychotherapist could indicate awareness to an important transition but asking, "So, you relocated here two years ago. How has that transition been going?" Or, "You mentioned you are getting assigned to a new department at work next month. I'm wondering how that's sitting with you." Attachment patterns are often heightened at transitions. So, explore transitions for assessment information but also for conveying that you understand important dynamics. In some cases, clients will have not tuned into how a transition has affected them and be ready to process related emotions. In other cases, particularly with dismissive clients, there may be an initial minimization of the significance, and the psychotherapist will need to be patient.

Phase 2: Coconstructing a Developmental Crucible

As mentioned in Chapter 2, the crucible is a metaphor for the intensification and necessary containment for the transformation process. The concept has been invoked by many psychotherapy and spirituality writers. Schnarch (1991, 1997, 2009) has articulated an approach to couples and sex therapy centered on "constructing the sexual crucible" with clients, by which he means holding out a key developmental challenge for growth in differentiation. Wallin (2007) referred to "constructing the developmental crucible" (p. 193), referring to ways psychotherapists can help shape growth in attachment security during a sometimes turbulent process.

Our engagement of attachment and differentiation builds on the writings of both Schnarch (1991, 1997, 2009) and Wallin (2007). We view long-term psychotherapy as focused on a developmental challenge of inviting transformation of relational templates and growth in relational maturity (i.e., secure attachment and differentiation of self). We prefer the intersubjective language of "coconstructing" a developmental crucible because we believe clients and psychotherapists both contribute to the shaping of a key growth dilemma or crucible. Psychotherapists cannot construct this on their own for clients. Clients need to reveal enough of their own values, concerns, and vulnerability for a crucible to be coconstructed. Coconstruction language highlights the relational process inherent in crucible formation. This language also affirms that most clients desire growth and challenge even if they sometimes resist staying in crucibles.

Spirituality

Clients who are highly committed to a spiritual or religious worldview also tend to believe that divine beings, spiritual forces, or other understandings of the sacred contribute to the coconstruction of crucibles of transformation. Clients hold ideals of integrity and virtue based on their religious or spiritual worldview. That worldview and also presence in a religious or spiritual community can motivate and also confront them with internal and communal discrepancies from their ideals.

The Relationship of the Crucible to Forgiveness and Relational Spirituality

So, what is a *developmental crucible*, and how is that related to forgiveness and relational spirituality? A developmental crucible essentially involves a key relational growth process that the client needs to be able to move beyond maladaptive relational patterns and work toward secure attachment and differentiation of self. As psychotherapist and client collaborate in tracking problematic relational patterns embedded in insecure attachment and personality styles, thematic issues often emerge. Crucibles are formed by big-picture relational theme issues, such as trust, commitment, control, intimacy, fusion, disappointment, shame, difference, superiority, surrender, emotional cutoff, or collaboration. Those are usually embedded in relational patterns.

Facing the Heretofore Avoided Dilemma

Most long-term clients have a dilemma that they have been avoiding. But the dilemma must be faced to enter the crucible and move beyond past relational patterns. For example, Arnold is a 57-year-old European American who lost his job 3 years ago when his company downsized. He had started attending a conservative Protestant church a few years before that point during his recovery from alcoholism and following a difficult divorce. Arnold believes God rescued him from a downward path of destruction and has a "special plan for the righteous" (which includes him now). Arnold is quick to add that God will "clear a path through any unrighteous who gets in the way." He tries to move forward with finding a job and new relationships but has been unsuccessful. He often feels angry and depressed. At those times, he ruminates on the idea that "God punishes wrongdoers." When he thinks of his ex-wife and former boss, he feels better temporarily knowing they are earmarked for divine discipline. However, the anger and despondency quickly return. Arnold eventually faced the dilemma that he wanted to have relationships in which he felt secure and respected but he did not have to trust anyone. Schnarch (1997) called these "two-choice dilemmas," meaning that people often want to somehow have two choices—to have their cake and eat it, too—when really they need to pick one option. It is not realistic to believe one can have secure relationships without risking trust. But we are not really talking about a rational process as much as the deep ambivalence that is part of humanness. Kegan and Lahey (2009) suggested that development moves forward by facing these kinds of two-choice commitment dilemmas.

Forgiveness Can Be Part of the Unfaced Dilemma

Sometimes forgiveness is a central part of the dilemma, such as Arnold's dilemma that if he forgave his ex-wife for divorcing him he would have to (a) face ways his alcoholism and chronic mistrust contributed to their estrangement and (b) stop demonizing his ex-wife as spiritually inferior to himself (Krumrei et al., 2008). Thus, forgiveness would involve Arnold's surrendering superiority and one-upping his ex-wife. It would cause him to grapple with the difference between humility and shame in his own past shortcomings. The same relational patterns and themes were evident for him in the workplace before his dismissal. One important part of coconstructing a crucible is to note those parallel patterns and dynamics (e.g., "Based on your description, it sounds like you had some of the same relational struggles in your marriage and in your job").

Maintaining a Curious and Nonjudgmental Stance During Confrontation

Noting these parallels often feels similar to a confrontation for clients and heats up the crucible. Some clients feel threatened or ashamed if they have not seen the parallels. The therapist's curious and nonjudgmental stance is key to offering a new relational experience at those moments. This can seem like an implicit forgiveness in the relational dynamic of "being seen" by the therapist. Clients who are not used to relationships of nonjudgmental acceptance combined with honest exploration will usually feel anxiety increase initially.

When Forgiveness Is Not an Overt Part of the Unfaced Dilemma

In other cases, forgiveness is not an obvious part of a dilemma. But unforgiveness may defensively or self-protectively avoid a crucible dilemma. Jacinta is a 35-year-old African American woman. She struggles with pain and anger related to her father, who was physically and emotionally abusive. She worries these unresolved issues affect her lack of success in romantic relationships. She holds an eclectic spiritual orientation drawing on Christian, New Age, and Afro-Caribbean beliefs and practices. Most of her beliefs and practices "focus on the positive." She engages in prayer, meditation, and yoga to cultivate spiritual and emotional health. But her performance is cyclical. She is consistent in her practice for a few months at a time, but she inevitably drops off. Her style of relational spirituality is "driven." She aims for perfection and pursues it with (sometimes) desperate aggressiveness. She also flies "solo," rarely connecting with others. Her spirituality is shaped by an insecure attachment and thus is hard to sustain. Recently, after a painful breakup with another in a line of rejecting and uncommitted partners, Jacinta began to question whether God had given up on her. "I don't know whether I'm just not good enough for healthy relationships," she said. Jacinta came to realize that avoiding her feelings of unforgiveness toward her father through attempts at spiritual bypass protected her from the emotional turbulence of disappointment, shame, and rage at her father's treatment of her. More important, unforgiveness also unconsciously protected her from becoming attached to a healthy relational partner. That would risk even greater disappointment and pain if the relationship did not work out. Jacinta held an ideal of a relationship that never came close to the men she dated. All the while she remained stuck in powerful and understandable feelings of resentment toward her father, which periodically broke through her spiritual defenses. Jacinta eventually stated her crucible dilemma quite clearly herself: "Deep down, I believe I need a man to be happy, but I actually hate men." Such globalizing or undifferentiated expansion of resentment is a risk of chronic unforgiveness and insecure attachment.

Increasing Anxiety

As a client's crucible takes shape, anxiety will often increase. As it does, clients with insecure attachment styles often wrestle (at least temporarily) with struggles of power and control with the psychotherapist. Anxiety increases for several reasons: (a) attachment templates are activated; (b) existential and relational dilemmas are surfacing, and choices must be made; (c) clients have not previously internalized a relational secure base for making meaning out of difficult experiences; and (d) clients often come into therapy expecting simpler solutions provided by the therapist than is indicated by a crucible-like process.

Exploring Coping Strategies and Emotional Regulation

This becomes a valuable time to assess and begin to explore coping strategies for emotion regulation, particularly ways of self-soothing anxiety (Schnarch, 1997). However, in long-term psychotherapy (in contrast to brief psychotherapy) emotion regulation coping strategies are not explored as a primary solution to the underlying relational problems. Rather, when the psychotherapist explores client coping strategies, it serves two primary functions. First, it heightens the attachment experience of showing concern and practical helpfulness about the client's emotional experience and well-being. Second, this exploration identifies coping resources to help with tolerating further intensification of the crucible process. The latter is a bit like learning to stretch before and after a workout.

Clients with a fearful attachment style will almost certainly need to develop solid emotional regulation coping strategies before moving into crucible intensification. This is an important strength of dialectical behavior therapy for the treatment of borderline personality disorder. Psychotherapists must be attuned to the proper balance of (a) emotion and crucible processing versus emotion regulation and (b) challenge versus support. These sensitivities are necessary for a healthy psychotherapeutic relationship.

If a client has experienced trauma, the psychotherapist must detect this. Rather than allowing crucible-like processes to intensify, the psychotherapist must shift the focus to treat trauma. There are multiple empirically supported psychotherapies for posttraumatic stress disorder, so psychotherapists have options. Some psychotherapists will be comfortable using specific trauma techniques (e.g., eye movement desensitization and reprocessing) themselves within long-term relational psychotherapy. Others will not. We prefer to closely collaborate with trauma psychotherapy specialists while continuing to hold the place of primary psychotherapist in a long-term relational process. Consistent with our relational theoretical orientation, we consider this an attachment and differentiation process with clients. We seek to maintain a solid working alliance with a few key specialists who have a healthy relational style rather than simply referring a client to an unknown psychotherapist.

Exploring the Client's Relational Spirituality

During this attachment phase of psychotherapy, we often have an opportunity to further assess a client's style of relational spirituality. We seek to discern what spiritual practices or resources may help during the crucible process. If spirituality is important to the client, it may motivate, at least in part, the hard work of changing relational patterns or overcoming chronic resentment, particularly if the person believes his or her relational spirituality is affected by these psychological struggles.

Inviting the Client to Explore Relational Spirituality Coping Resources

As crucible themes clarify and as the psychotherapist becomes resonant with the client's understanding, we can invite consideration of various coping resources, including the explicitly spiritual. For example, the psychotherapist asked Jacinta:

> It seems to make sense to both of us that you have a lot of anxiety about facing your hurt and anger at your dad and the ways that is still affecting you. But it sounds like you agree it is important for your healing and for moving forward. I also know you value spiritual practices. I wonder if

you have a sense of any spiritual practices or ways of connecting spiritually that won't necessarily make all the difficult feelings evaporate but might help you remain grounded and soothe some of the anxiety as you face the hurt and anger.

Dealing With Reactance

For some clients who have very high levels of attachment anxiety, the struggles of power and control as the crucible intensifies may take the form of projecting a coercive stance onto the therapist's intentions. For example, Arnold became angry at one point with his therapist. He said, "Are you saying I *have* to forgive my ex-wife?" The therapist responded,

> I'm not saying you *have* to do anything. Your psyche belongs to you. I'm trying to understand, along with you, how these relationship patterns have taken shape inside you and what you consider your options for how you can work with them. When you think about your feelings about your ex and are honest with yourself about how those feelings have been impacting you, what do you see?

Note the repeated use of "you," which can invite self-reflexivity and return some sense of power to the client to self-confront and self-define his own experience. It is important that the psychotherapist is not detoured from the crucible despite the client's challenge. As the crucible process intensifies, it is vital that the relational stance of the psychotherapist is to remain present, caring, appropriately playful, and flexible without capitulation to the client's fear or reactivity against the challenge. The psychotherapist needs to offer a secure attachment and a differentiated stance even when temptations may arise to try to rescue or run away. The psychotherapist needs to keep working at a crucible formulation and use a treatment plan that the client will endorse and commit to working on.

Providing a Sense of Tempered Hope

As clients begin to accept the coconstructed crucible framing, it is natural for clients with insecure attachment styles to desire some reassurance of hope from the psychotherapist that change is possible—to relate to the psychotherapist as an object of hope. We suggest relating through what has been called *complex hope*—that is, being hopeful about the potential for change integrated with realism about (a) the importance of choices the client needs to make during psychotherapy and (b) the existential realities of suffering that are often part of growth. Unbridled optimism can convey a possibility of rescuing clients from their crucible process. Too much detachment or withholding of hope can communicate a lack of empathy for the importance of hope as a motivator.

Phase 3: Processing Disappointment and Grief

Besides both the attachment phase and the coconstructing a developmental crucible phase of long-term psychotherapy, there is another important consideration—processing disappointment and grief. We have suggested that emotion processing and emotion regulation form an important dialectical relationship in our model of forgiveness. Processing emotion becomes a pathway for new attachment experiences to shift relational templates. Many facets of forgiveness include working with emotions. But we want to highlight that long-term relational psychotherapy often necessitates processing particular emotional dynamics related to disappointment and grief. This can potentiate forgiveness.

Interpersonal injuries can challenge or even fracture certain ideals individuals hold. This can be particularly painful if they are unexpectedly hurt by someone they have idealized, or if another person attacks that idealized person.

Case Example

Eduardo was a 16-year-old biracial boy whose family moved into a new community that was predominantly White. Several White boys started bullying him and making racist comments about his mother, who was Mexican American. After getting in trouble at school for fighting one of the boys, Eduardo finally explained the situation to his mother. Her response was one of shock; defensiveness related to her own earlier, unprocessed traumatic experiences as a victim of racism; and guilt over moving him into that school. His father, a German American, was unprepared to help him cope with racism, and both parents rather coldly told him to "stay out of trouble in the future." This was a double dose of extreme deidealization for Eduardo: his peers' attacks on his race combined with his parents' initial lack of capacity to actively and constructively respond to his developmental and sociocultural needs. Eduardo was initially rage-filled toward his peers, but his anger quickly turned toward his parents in his disappointment over their lack of ability to relate to his struggles by providing some coping resources. This resulted in internalized shame over the racism he experienced. His anger turned inward with various forms of self-harm and self-medication in maladaptive attempts at coping.

Deidealization of Important Adults—During Nontroubled and Traumatic Development

Kohut (1977) argued that humans have developmental needs to idealize caregivers or other relational figures as part of forming a cohesive self.

By admiring parents and other adults, children can feel connected to stable and positive anchors for their own self-development. Those adults who are affirming motivate growth. Disappointments in parents and other relational figures are inevitable and can even lead to differentiation of self and mature integration of a humble realism about imperfections in people, but traumatic disappointments are hard to integrate because they injure or emotionally bruise the developing self.

Responding to Deidealization in Adults With Different Relational Templates

Adults with insecure styles of attachment will tend to have idealization wounds or sensitivity to losses of idealization. This can lead to powerful feelings of anger or shame when interpersonal conflicts touch on deidealization. Even use of the word *disappointment* is often effective with long-term clients ("I am guessing that it might have felt disappointing when . . ."). Preoccupied and fearful clients often feel disappointment, so that language registers as pacing or even accurate empathy. Dismissive clients do not want to acknowledge emotional vulnerability early in therapy, and a word such as *disappointing* does not require them to admit being highly affected by something or in great pain. Put differently, dismissive clients will often reject early probes about powerful feelings of relational impact (e.g., "Wasn't that painful when your boss criticized you in front of your coworkers?"). But it will be hard for them to deny feeling disappointed (e.g., "Was it disappointing when your boss criticized you in front of your coworkers?"). If they acknowledge disappointment, it enables a small dose of relational connection around a tolerable level of vulnerability. This is kind of like inching one's way into a cold pool of water rather than being thrown in all at once. Over time, current disappointments can be connected to parallel themes of disappointments in family-of-origin relationships, which often illuminates the dynamics behind cases of unforgiveness.

Deidealization of the Sacred

Relational patterns of disappointment are also often parallel between interpersonal disappointments and spiritual disappointments or deidealization of the sacred (Jones, 2002). Acknowledging disappointment is a pathway to dealing with loss. Bowlby (1969/1982, 1980) has noted that relational loss is a primal activator of the attachment system. Deep attachment injuries involving losses (e.g., a parent that abandons the family or dies, a spiritual leader who violates ideals with poor behavior, a spouse who betrays trust through an affair) can create the emotional vulnerability to struggle with unforgiveness. In fact, several therapy theorists have connected forgiveness to grieving or mourning (Augsburger, 1996; Karen, 2001). Processing loss with clients becomes a valuable form of corrective attachment experience that can foster the emotion regulation conducive to forgiveness. Experiencing attachment with a caring figure who can tolerate and help contain our protest and pain can generate hope (Karen, 2001). In some cases, particularly ones involving trauma, clients may yearn for a witness who can offer solidarity as they reprocess their emotions without judgment and with a sense of relational presence (Herman, 1992). Heightening awareness of connections between these differing dimensions of disappointment and loss with current interpersonal relations, family-of-origin memories, and relational spirituality connections with the sacred becomes an opportunity for growth in differentiation rather than emotional fusion.

Emotional Processing as a Pathway Toward Forgiving

This emotional processing of loss as a pathway toward forgiveness has been likened to engaging in lament (Shults & Sandage, 2003). *Lament* means complaint and is a spiritual practice, particularly in the Jewish tradition, of expressing grief, pain, and lament in raw authenticity to God. Many spiritual traditions have practices like lament, which rest on a secure attachment with the sacred (i.e., trusting God or the sacred is caring and accepting of pain and struggle). Yet, in our experience, most clients start therapy having never experienced forms of relational spirituality that include lament or other constructive ways of attaching with the sacred for emotional processing. This means they are likely emotionally cut off from the sacred during pain, or their ways of relating to the sacred in those contexts are highly dysregulated (e.g., voicing doubt followed by intense shame). It can be helpful to explore with clients whether their spiritual tradition offers any ways of relating to the sacred amid pain, doubt, disappointment, or grief. This requires sensitivity to a client's openness and interest, but it can gradually result in identifying coping resources and also normalizing grief and disappointment in ways that mitigate shame.

Unprocessed Grieving

Unacknowledged or unprocessed grief can inhibit or even freeze the phenomenological process of making differentiated meaning out of difficult experiences. Ambiguous losses in which a loved one is physically present but psychologically absent (e.g., Alzheimer's) or psychologically present but physically absent (e.g., family member in prison) can be particularly difficult to resolve because the loss and any associated ritual processes are unclear (Boss, 1999). These are often very undifferentiated losses that partially encapsulate intense levels of unconscious anxiety, anger, shame, and sadness. The encapsulation is partial in the sense that the ambiguous losses provoke further reactivity to interpersonal dynamics. The impending or recent death of a family member sometimes instigates conflicts and bitter unforgiveness in some families. Low differentiation or limited capacities to (a) tolerate differences in coping styles and (b) balance connection and self-regulation will put family systems at risk for serious and even chronic unforgiveness related to loss.

Experiencing Disappointment and Loss Within Psychotherapy and Helping Repair Therapeutic Ruptures

Clients can also experience disappointment and loss related to their experience of the psychotherapy relationship, and this often emerges in long-term psychotherapy. In fact, one of the advantages of long-term therapy is that it offers opportunities for these dynamics to develop. That enables psychotherapist to help the client rework relational experiences of idealization and disappointment. For the reasons mentioned above, client disappointment in the psychotherapist is virtually inevitable when clients have insecure attachment histories. There is a body of theory and research now on working with rupture-and-repair dynamics in psychotherapy. That research shows that repairing ruptures in the therapeutic alliance is associated with positive treatment outcomes (Safran, Muran, & Eubanks-Carter, 2011). This requires psychotherapists who are attuned to signs of rupture and are willing to engage in repair processes. Psychotherapists need to be willing to own their contributions to rupture, although simple apologies are less often a key source of gain. Rather, invitations to seek mutually to understand the dynamics that contributed to the rupture are more likely to be helpful. Clients with insecure attachment histories often have little experience with relational partners, particularly authority figures, who are willing empathically to acknowledge the contributions to a rupture and convey active interest in repair. This offers enactments of forgiveness in the therapy relationship. Clients with a fearful attachment style (e.g., paranoid or borderline personality styles) may get stuck at times in grinding out expressions of their disappointment, and the therapist's repeated owning of responsibility may have less impact than inviting collaboration with the client on constructing a new way of approaching that relational dynamic in therapy in the future. This can be interpreted as a situation in which some clients find it exceedingly hard to forgive (i.e., regulate emotions related to the conflict) and feel hopeful until there is an explicit and compelling plan for change in the relational pattern going forward. In spiritual terms, they need to see more concrete repentance from the psychotherapist before their forgiveness of the psychotherapist, and the psychotherapist's humility of collaborating on a plan, may convey sufficient reason to extend trust and hope.

Experiencing Growth in Psychotherapy Can Activate Grieving

It is also easy to miss the ways in which positive relational experiences and growth in psychotherapy can sometimes activate grief. Masterson (1993) noted that as clients take action and move toward growth, a wake of anxiety or sadness sometimes emerges that can be likened to grief-related growth. Sometimes steps of growth or secure-base behavior are scary, thus raising anxiety. It can also feel depressing or sad to work at hard, significant growth steps that do not immediately lead to transformation (e.g., a client who takes the risk of starting community college at midlife and is initially scared and dejected at how hard it feels). Resentment toward self or others can arise at these points, in part because the person is taking risks and moving toward growth. This can be confusing to clients who may not understand why they initially feel worse or even angry despite taking constructive action.

Experiences of Secure Attachment Can Stimulate Grieving

Positive experiences of more secure attachment in long-term therapy can activate grief. This might occur as clients experience a relationship that is healthier than what they experienced in their family of origin. Of course, that kind of comparison is unfair because the psychotherapy relationship is much more limited than was the family of origin. Nevertheless, the security of a healthy psychotherapeutic alliance enables the expression of grief over the limits of other more primary relationships. Growth involves differentiation and typically moves clients beyond their family of origin in certain ways. Boszormenyi-Nagy (1984) argued that unconscious loyalty dynamics run deep, and it can be unsettling to differentiate toward growth because it can distance people from their families of origin. In some cases, it might be preferable to remain in an angry, unforgiving fusion than to actually differentiate and suffer certain necessary losses that come with growth.

Phase 4: Cultivating and Extending Differentiation of Self

Movement toward relational healing and growth starts with forming a secure attachment to provide a secure base for exploring meaning through more differentiated understanding of self and other (i.e., mentalization). This means greater complexity in understanding of the motives and contextual factors that influence interpersonal experiences. Unforgiveness is typically maintained by relatively polarized views of self and other, which are low in differentiation and complexity. Differentiation of self has been found to mediate the relationship between forgiveness and mental and spiritual health and has been positively correlated with both hope and humility (Jankowski et al., 2013; Sandage & Jankowski, 2010; Williamson, Sandage, & Lee, 2007).

Thus, differentiation is a valuable target of relational intervention in promoting healthy forgiveness.

Mentalization Techniques Can Help Promote Differentiation of Self

Several relational strategies can promote differentiation of self in long-term psychotherapy. First, mentalization-based techniques of showing curiosity about clients' perspectives and experiences without making assumptions even as they differ from the psychotherapist's perspectives provide a valuable starting point. This communicates noncontingent interest in the client's mind and emotional experience. An example of this is something along the lines of, "When you described your response to your mom's comment, I was aware that I would probably feel hurt but I noticed you said it didn't bother you. I'm curious to understand your view of that interaction." This introduces a difference in perspective but maintains respect for the client's experience and perspective. This might threaten some clients, but if the psychotherapist maintains a receptive, respectful, and curious stance, many clients will eventually trust this healthy attachment and differentiation (Holmes, 2001). Clients can begin to understand that their relationship with the psychotherapist does not depend on agreement. Of course, this is not a one-time intervention. Rather, it needs to be communicated many times.

Setting Boundaries Can Help Promote Differentiation of Self

Second, the basic strategy in interpersonal psychotherapy (Weissman, Markowitz, & Klerman, 2007) of helping clients consider the use of boundaries is another aspect of differentiation of self that can, paradoxically, promote forgiveness. Setting healthy boundaries enhances differentiation of self, especially when boundaries are allowed to be permeable in non-abusive relationships. This offers a couple of major sources of gain. Clients with insecure attachment styles often lack experience with setting healthy permeable boundaries, and the psychotherapy relationship can model the combination of a caring relationship within the limitations of professional boundaries. Clients will need humility to accept this form of attachment.

Distinguishing Forgiveness and Reconciliation Can Help With Differentiation of Self. Third, learning to set healthy boundaries can mitigate the need for some forms of self-protective unforgiveness. Many clients find the differentiation between forgiveness and reconciliation quite revolutionary. Choosing to set boundaries and not fully reconcile in certain cases opens space for the idea that one can work toward forgiveness without needing to remain a victim of recurring dysfunctional patterns. This can enable a more differentiated placement of boundaries and lower levels of self-protective reactivity or the angry justification of extreme avoidance. Rather than directing clients where exactly to set boundaries, the relational process of psychotherapy can enable collaboration between client and psychotherapist in exploring options for boundary setting and the values and commitments involved in those decisions.

Inviting and Modeling Humility Can Promote Differentiation of Self. Fourth, psychotherapists can invite and model humility about personal limitations. Moore (2003) suggested that humility essentially involves acknowledging limitations and being willing to receive help, which are consistent with secure attachment and differentiation of self. Over time, psychotherapists can often promote candid discussion of client's limitations if there is respect for client strengths and psychotherapists are humble about their own limitations and shared humanity. In spiritual terms, this is a mindful or compassionate stance of nonjudgmental description, which is different from shame or self-contempt. Once a therapeutic alliance has been established, clients often appreciate the psychotherapist's willingness to be respectfully challenging (Holmes, 2001). Tolerating constructive interpersonal challenges leads to humility, which is a pivotal virtue for promoting forgiveness. Most spiritual traditions invite self-confrontation, so clients who are committed to spirituality will likely have resources in their tradition that offer sacred meaning to the process of personal challenge and humility.

Maximizing the Impact of Interpersonal Challenges

Interpersonal challenges in psychotherapy are most effective when interspersed with empathy, and empathy has accounted for changes in forgiveness in intervention studies (Sandage & Worthington, 2010). Empathy and humility both counter narcissistic tendencies that inhibit forgiveness. We resonate with Mitchell's (2000) approach to treating narcissism, which is actually relevant to all insecure attachment styles. Mitchell suggested a dialectical process: mirroring or showing empathy toward client perspectives but challenging client illusions. This is the dialectic of pacing and leading described above. Empathy provides pacing. Leading involves challenging perspective or behavior. Challenges or lead moves are often most effective when framed in terms of attachment support. For example, such a velvet-gloved challenge might be, "I am on your side, and yet I am concerned that your anger may be getting the best of you in this situation."

Inviting Empathy for Others

Inviting empathy for others can be effective in long-term psychotherapy once it has been modeled for and sufficiently experienced by the client. Rather than directly suggesting empathy for others, the psychotherapist might validate a client's experience of anger or disappointment and then eventually ask something like, "What is your sister's story? Is there anything going on in her life that would help us understand her behavior there?" These kinds of questions involve invitations to mentalization and can extend narrative horizons (Sandage, 1999a, 1999b; Shults & Sandage, 2003); that is, empathy enables therapists to see a larger story to conflicts and interpersonal injuries. This does not necessarily mitigate the painful impact of offenses, but it can promote differentiation and the depersonalization of offender's behavior. There are often numerous contextual factors that lead to conflicts or patterns of offense. When hurt or angry, it is natural to psychologically distance from offenders, but this causes people to lose touch with their shared humanity. This form of low differentiation and emotional cutoff reduces compassion or empathy for the offender and adds to the temptation to totalize them as a characterologically "bad" person (Shults & Sandage, 2003). This can even be a form of negative other-validation, where one bolsters his or her shamed sense of self by affirming how he or she is not like that person.

Like all interventions, inviting empathy requires therapist attunement to timing and the overall relational process of therapy. Premature invitations to empathy can frustrate or even shame clients, especially if a psychotherapist seems inflexible and lacking in curiosity or empathy for a client's experience and difficulty in extending empathy. That is one reason that inviting awareness of an offender's "story" is a safer initial intervention because it is not a suggestion of empathy as much as differentiating a broader horizon of contextual awareness. In some cases, this awareness may suggest ways in which an offender lacked the capacities for healthy relations; for example, a parent whose own abuse history compromised his ability to connect or communicate acceptance and validation. In such cases, the client's empathy may circle back to grief over what was missed in their experience of parental attachment. The mindful dimensions of forgiveness and compassion can involve a simultaneous combination of emotional freedom and sorrow (Kabat-Zinn, 2013).

Summary of the Four Phases

We have laid out a four-phase process. It begins with forming an attachment to the client. Then, we as psychotherapists attempt to cocreate a crucible-like process in which insecure attachment templates can be experienced and processed in emotion-near interactions. We must help the client process grief and disappointment that will almost certainly attend change. Finally, we seek to engage the client in building a more differentiated sense of self. These are not necessarily sequential. In fact, they rarely are. Rather, psychotherapy winds back and forth among the processes, although there is movement along the four experiences as we have described them.

In the previous chapters, we laid out six processes by which helping occurs: connect (Step 1), rethink the problem (Step 2), make action plans based on the new conceptualization (Step 3), follow up on action plans and support change attempts (Step 4), plan for maintenance (Step 5), and terminate psychotherapy (Step 6). One can see these processes occurring in the long-term relational psychotherapy we have been describing. However, with the complexity of long-term psychotherapy, we have found it better to think more strategically along the lines of the three processes mentioned above.

SUMMARY

In this chapter, we walked you through conceptualization—especially those cases involving forgiveness and relational spirituality—for long-term treatment based on our relational model. We discussed the essential nature of pacing and leading and of maintaining one's own differentiation of self that can withstand inevitable challenges to you to run away or to rescue clients. We discussed how to remain in the crucible process with the client, provoke intensification of anxiety as long as the clients can benefit by it, and move toward emotional processing and emotion regulation. We also discussed the dialectic between mirroring and challenging the client. As we did this, we sought to provide enough examples that you can see how this might look in actual practice. Finally, we noted that the psychotherapist must cultivate his or her own humility, forgiveness, and differentiation of self, and we recommended establishing a mature, differentiated support group to help.

Clinical research evidence specifically supporting methods and approaches from Bowen (1985) family systems theory is more limited than that supporting our relational theory of change. Moreover, there is empirical support within the common factors literature on couples and family therapy for many of the sources of gain we have used in our approach (e.g., therapeutic alliance and attachment, emotion regulation, making space for the other, encouraging personal responsibility, helping couples stand meta to their relationship; see Sprenkle, Davis, & Lebow, 2009). Correlational evidence also supports promoting higher levels of differentiation of self. We encourage integration of the treatments in working with clinical cases, and we urge further research investigation of the efficacy of the integrated model.

10

FORGIVENESS IN COUPLES AND FAMILY THERAPY

In a mindfulness meditation on pain and forgiveness, Mueller (1992) wrote, "Forgiveness is the enzyme that makes possible our freedom and liberation from family pain and sorrow" (p. 16). He advised being patient and compassionate with oneself, even honoring the resistance to forgiving with recognition that pain and unforgiveness can be woven into people's deepest attachments to family. It can be challenging to let go of such pain and allow those family attachments to change because it can feel like a loss of the relationship altogether.

Our approach to forgiveness and relational spirituality in couples and family therapy builds on the constructs and overall model described in previous chapters. Key therapeutic dialectics that can encourage forgiveness and healthy relational spirituality include

- conflict and interactions promoting intimacy;
- attachment and differentiation;
- emotion processing and emotion regulation;
- hope and humility;

http://dx.doi.org/10.1037/14712-011
Forgiveness and Spirituality in Psychotherapy: A Relational Approach, by E. L. Worthington, Jr. and S. J. Sandage

- spiritual dwelling and spiritual seeking; and
- justice and forgiveness.

In this chapter, we apply our model to both a couples therapy and a family therapy case. First, we identify some key systemic dynamics that are particularly relevant to couples and family therapy (i.e., triangulation, parentification, scapegoating, and power and control). Next, we discuss three other aspects of a systems-oriented approach (i.e., differentiated pacing, attention to strengths and systemic functioning, and transitions in the moment). We then describe a couples therapy case of Ann and Thomas, which illustrated both the conceptualization and treatment process. We then describe a family therapy case, centering at first around a 13-year-old adolescent boy with parents from different ethnic backgrounds.

SYSTEMIC DYNAMICS, FORGIVENESS, AND RELATIONAL SPIRITUALITY

Triangulation

A *triangle* describes relationships when, analogous to a third leg of a stool, a third party serves to temporarily stabilize a dyad. This could be a person who intervenes in a troubled marriage, but more broadly could include impersonal resources (e.g., alcohol) that are used to compensate for something lacking in a relationship between two people. Kerr and Bowen (1988) suggested that relational triangles are ubiquitous. Triangulation is not problematic in and of itself. It depends on the differentiation of the triangulated party and whether that person or resource will nurture dependence and conflict avoidance or help the system further develop greater differentiation. Psychotherapists need to be experts in managing triangulation. This is particularly the case in couples and family therapy. Different members of the system will pull the therapist to take sides or otherwise maintain homeostasis (Guerin, Fogarty, Fay, & Kautto, 2010).

Chronic triangulation typically perpetuates problems of unforgiveness by preventing growth in differentiation. In some cases, triangulation may even intensify problems of unforgiveness, such as when a spouse is discovered in an affair or a person turns to substance abuse to deal with family conflicts. Poorly differentiated triangulation can also impede couples and family therapy. This might occur if a person were in both individual and couples therapy and the individual psychotherapist always sympathized with the client's marital complaints without even meeting the spouse. A person's use of God or the sacred can also be a source of unhealthy triangulation (Heiden Rootes, Jankowski, & Sandage, 2010), as we describe in the cases to follow.

Such cases highlight the importance of psychotherapists being competent to integrate spiritual and religious dynamics into psychotherapy with systemic, differentiated awareness.

Parentification

Children in *parentified* roles in family systems have been recruited into responsibilities or levels of functioning that are beyond their age or competence. This kind of role reversal puts children in an impossible position of trying to compensate for parental limitations. The context is obviously important, and certain sociocultural contexts or situations may make parentification necessary for one or more children. But the risks of parentification include a high probability the parentified child will experience (a) anger over the perceived injustice of the role and (b) shame over their inability to fully succeed in a parentified role (Jankowski et al., 2013). Both risks can contribute to unforgiveness.

In some cases, parentification can include aspects of relational spirituality. For example, a child might be somehow come into the role of the "good kid" or the "spiritually sensitive child" who mirrors one or both parents' spiritual commitments. A sibling might fall into the role of the "problem child" or the "heretic" who challenges the family spirituality. In poorly differentiated family systems, these roles can become rigid and lead to resentment.

Scapegoating

Scapegoating is a form of triangulation in which a system channels all anxiety, blame, and shame toward a particular family member. This can support cohesion and forgiveness in the rest of the system at the expense of the scapegoat. Couples or family systems that use scapegoating are also low in differentiation. Therapists who aggressively challenge the scapegoating system may be surprised to find even the scapegoated person resists their interventions.

Chronic scapegoating relies upon unforgiveness to maintain systemic stability. If the scapegoating system is destabilized, which is eventually necessary for therapeutic progress, other conflicts will emerge in the system. In some cases, religious communities may contribute to scapegoating if moral prohibitions are especially strong against certain behaviors (e.g., substance use, sex outside marriage, divorce) but lax against other problematic behaviors or attitudes (e.g., workaholism, judgmentalism, exclusion). Most spiritual or religious traditions include compassion-oriented contemplative streams that emphasize internal attitudes of the heart as even more important than behaviors, which can limit scapegoating.

Power and Control

All systems need to balance power (i.e., influencing others) with control (i.e., limiting the influence of others; Maddock & Larson, 1995, 2004). Power and control are not good or bad per se. It depends on how they are expressed and balanced. Abusive systems are characterized by certain persons using too much power and allowing too little control to others. Physical or sexual abuse involves, among other things, an overuse of power than crosses boundaries of control. Couples and family therapy clearly requires attention to dynamics of power and control and an assessment of safety risks. The language of "forgiveness" can be exploited by perpetrators who try to manipulate victims into giving up boundaries or legitimate means of social control. There is some empirical evidence that victims of domestic violence may often conflate forgiveness and reconciliation, believing that forgiving means one must reconcile with their batterers (Gordon, Burton, & Porter, 2004). One other tragedy of victim–perpetrator cycles is that victims often become perpetrators by lacking self-control and learning to use the boundary-crossing coping strategy when frustrated in their own relationships.

Spiritual and religious communities differ greatly in how they approach power and control in couples and family relationships. Therapists must seek to understand how their clients' communities may view these issues. A term such as *boundaries* might be extremely foreign in some spiritual or religious communities, whereas other traditions have spiritually integrative books written on the topic of boundaries (Cloud & Townsend, 1992).

COUPLES AND FAMILY THERAPISTS AND SYSTEMIC STANCE

A systemic stance of a therapist includes many dynamics that go beyond this chapter, but it is important to highlight three key issues. These include pacing based on being at once a member of the system and differentiated from it; noting strengths within the system as a whole and individuals and not just pathologies; and considering the transitions clients are moving through and transitional goals clients are moving toward as well, as the realities of the present situation clients are facing. In the following subsections, we describe each one more fully.

Differentiated Pacing

The therapist needs to seek to join the system through effective pacing, yet it is also important to keep one foot outside the system. "One foot in, one foot out" is consistent with a differentiated stance. In terms of our relational spirituality model, the therapist needs to dwell with the system before activating a seeking cycle. This is particularly the case when systems are low in differentiation, which means there is a high level of anxiety about seeking new information or perspectives.

In couples and family therapy, differentiated pacing mean the therapist has the important challenge of not siding with a particular member of the system. Safety issues can trump this, but that also involves a concern for the overall system. In this approach, the therapist seeks to attach with all the persons in therapy, but there is also a concern for the system as a whole. Learning to pace or connect with different members of a couple or family system with their differing personalities and temperaments requires a therapist to be highly flexible and differentiated.

Attention to Strengths and Systemic Functions

A systemic perspective involves noting systemic and individual strengths and not just pathologies. This involves asking questions about the functions of certain patterns and behaviors, even ones that seem destructive or dysfunctional. Such a nonjudgmental stance is consistent with differentiation and intercultural competence. One does not need to agree that certain behavioral choices were adaptive to understand how they fit within the context.

This stance also fits with a systemic prioritization on description and understanding before prescriptive intervention. Some spiritual or religious clients might assume that authority figures will rapidly recommend virtuous solutions to problems. However, our approach is consistent with many spiritual and religious wisdom traditions, which value accurate, dialectical understanding and facing deep dilemmas.

Transitions and the Present Moment

Systemic therapy also invites consideration of the transitions being sought and of the present situation clients are facing. A valuable assessment question is always, "Why are these people seeking help now?" Systems are often most malleable to change during life transitions, when attachment templates are activated and there is the possibility of transformation. The anxiety and ambiguity of transitions can sometimes intensify conflicts and forgiveness struggles, yet transitions also hold promise for reworking attachment templates.

Therapists need to be sufficiently differentiated to sit at the crossroads of transition with clients without needing to solve every problem. Many spiritual traditions have proverbs, teachings, or narratives about these kinds of liminal or between-state situations (Turner, 1969). Transitions provide opportunities for new attachment experiences to foster a more secure base for exploration. But this works only if therapists have worked through their own attachment dynamics.

COUPLES THERAPY CASE STUDY

The following case illustrates the use of our model with a couple. Ann (age 37) and Thomas (age 39) had been married for 15 years and had three children between the ages of 8 and 13. They started couples therapy after feeling "disconnected" for several years and sensing increased conflict in the previous year. Both agreed that they had never really had an extended period of feeling deeply connected in their marriage. During the intake, Ann stated she was "confused about what marriage is for." Thomas admitted, "I'm not sure I really want to be married anymore." This immediately brought a look of anxious despair to Ann's face. She in turn complained that she was "low on his priority list," referring to Thomas's busy career as a successful attorney and master of business administration student. She said, "Suddenly he will press me to 'open up,' which doesn't come easy for me. Actually, it feels like 'emotional assault.' He gets frustrated and then moves on to something else." When asked how she coped with this, Ann said, "I try to rely on God and spend time with Him. This is a part of my life I feel I can't share with Thomas. And honestly, I don't really want to. God is my refuge." Thomas countered, "She's inaccessible. She wants me to be around but treats me like a stranger. She acts 'spiritual' but won't admit she's rejecting me over and over."

Four years earlier, they had a marital crisis when Ann discovered Thomas had been having an affair with a coworker. This came during a time he had been depressed after the death of his uncle, a man who had basically been a father to him after his own father died in a car accident when Thomas was 7. After the affair came to light, Thomas seemed remorseful to Ann and asked to be forgiven. They went to a Christian counselor through their church for 6 months, and things seemed to smooth over. But now both felt that they continued to lack the intimacy they wanted from their marriage.

Recently, Thomas started attending a mindfulness meditation class at a Buddhist center. He said he was "trying to figure out what he really believes about God, religion and everything." Ann experienced this as another betrayal of the beliefs she thought they held in common.

Thomas was African American, and his family moved to Brooklyn from the South when he was 9 to be closer to relatives after his father's death. His mom worked two jobs, and Thomas managed his autonomy by becoming a high achiever in school. Although Thomas's mother idealized him, he always felt a weight of pressure and anxiety that he had to "do right" and to "be perfect" to compensate for losses and chronic stress on his family.

Thomas's mother had the family attending Black Baptist churches throughout his childhood. The first summer they moved to New York after his father died, Thomas asked his uncle if he believed in God and was shocked to hear him reply, "Nah . . . this world is too screwed up for there to be any God on duty." Thomas pushed this memory away, but anxiety, relational dissonance, and doubt had been established in his attachment with the sacred. Thomas described his own relational spirituality as vacillating between trying to "please God" through intense spiritual behaviors and withdrawing from any spiritual practice when starting to feel frustrated, lonely, or "not good enough."

Ann was Irish American and grew up in a small town on the East Coast. She was the oldest of seven kids and said she had been close with her mom "who was always sad but could never admit it." She described her dad as "always busy" and not interested in deep conversation. Both of her parents relied on her as a kind of "special confidante" while growing up. Ann's mother was twice hospitalized for mental illness, but those issues were never discussed in the family, as her mother would simply return as if it had been an extended vacation. Her family had attended a Catholic church. She explained,

> Trusting God was said to be an act of faith, but practically speaking I felt God's presence when I obeyed my parents, went to Mass and prayed, and went to youth group. In practice, I was focused on doing the right thing.

Ann's family prioritized time together, but they avoided conflicts and difficult issues.

Ann and Thomas met right after college while working for the same large corporation. She liked his emotional intensity, goals, and confidence. He liked her calm pace, generosity, and reliability. Although the families on both sides showed signs of accepting their marriage, there were ongoing problems. Ann's parents often made thinly veiled derogatory comments about minorities with no acknowledgment that Thomas was African American. Before couples therapy, these comments had gone unchallenged and even largely unacknowledged between Thomas and Ann. Ann, although initially idealizing of African American culture when they met, had grown defensive about diversity issues and preferred to try to take a "color blind" stance.

Parallel issues emerged for Ann in terms of gender. She was a biology major early in college but her father often joked about her science interests and said she would have a "hard time finding a husband and job" with that major. She switched to accounting, but her heart was not in that field. She quickly conceded to staying home with the kids once she and Thomas had their first child while trying to juggle part-time accounting work. Ann did not mind the accounting work because she was good at it, but vocation was another place she had "given up" on prioritizing her deepest goals and desires. She came to realize that she had never found an authentic voice in her family of origin or her marriage. Thomas did not think of himself as "sexist," but he had implicitly accepted a view of women as either passively subordinate or threatening and adversarial. He viewed his mother as a strong woman with lots of personal agency, but he had an undercurrent of resentment for ways she seemed overly identified with his achievements as a way of distancing from her own pain and disappointments.

Case Conceptualization

Ann and Thomas were both intelligent people who cared about their children, were involved in their religious and social communities, and had managed to overcome many challenges individually and as a couple. Their various ongoing challenges, conflicts, and ruptures were like those of many of the couples we work with. From a differentiation-based systems perspective, they were a highly fused couple, which means they lacked emotional boundaries that enabled genuine connection without the loss of self (Skowron & Schmitt, 2003). This made it difficult to tolerate the anxiety of differences of opinion or conflict and resulted in their felt need to distance and manage life tasks separately. Trying to collaborate was too stressful. So, paradoxically, their underlying fusion led both to use extreme measures of relational control (i.e., limiting the influence of the other; Maddock & Larson, 2004). Each experienced the other's control moves as rejecting and withholding. Thomas felt that Ann withheld her passion, feelings, and authentic self. Ann felt Thomas withheld his commitment to prioritize her and the kids ahead of his career and other interests. This symmetrical pattern of withholding generated mutual resentment and reinforced the walls between them. Why share your deepest passions and feelings with a husband who is uncommitted? Why commit to a wife who locks her heart away? Their relational dynamics of unforgiveness were perpetuated by this interlocking control standoff.

Boundaries of control are a necessary part of life, but an extreme imbalance of control can represent a self-protective stance that severely limits attachment or intimacy. Control temporarily reduces the anxiety of risking the vulnerability of revealing one's real self to the other. But over time, extreme use of control drains vitality, limits growth, and contributes to other problems. Thomas and Ann managed to stay married with so much control and such limited intimacy through, in part, triangulating other sources of connection and coping. Thomas's sexual affair was an obvious example of seeking pseudoconnection. But he also seemed to maintain a chronic affair with career success, which he privileged over his marriage and family connections. One might empathize with the intergenerational and sociocultural reasons Thomas felt such pressure to prioritize his career, and it distracted him from his loneliness and lack of marital satisfaction. One could even admire Thomas's lifelong pattern of achievement as a coping device to try to compensate for attachment injuries, but he was at a point in his life where his well-patterned coping strategy was not working.

Ann's triangulation with her projected relationship with God is a less obvious example of maintaining control and compensating for limited intimacy than is Thomas's affair. At the content level, the language and idea of "God as refuge" was consistent with Ann's spiritual tradition. In couples, it is not uncommon for a spouse who feels lonely or betrayed to turn to the sacred in this way for compensatory coping. But a process-oriented assessment of Ann's relational spirituality reveals several important limitations. First, Ann admitted she had quarantined her relationship with God away from Thomas, thus her marriage was not integrated into her relational spirituality. This reflected her avoidant style of attachment rooted in her family of origin. It meant that she shared little emotional vulnerability and tried to cope with anxiety through distraction and interpersonal distancing. Second, Ann had trouble seeing this at first, but she often used her relational spirituality for a one-up position in her marriage in a way that conveyed judgment of Thomas. The implication Ann conveyed was that Thomas's workaholism was a "selfish" and "secular" interest, whereas her relationship with God was virtuous. And although Thomas had apologized for the past affair, and Ann had told him she forgave him, they had never tried to understand how the affair happened or work through the deeper attachment injuries involved. This created a paradox in power in the relationship. Ann was often disempowered in terms of Thomas's many other commitments and his economic position in the relationship. But Ann had the power of moral superiority. Finally, Ann was quite committed to her relational spirituality. However, she seemed imbalanced toward spiritual dwelling with a low level of differentiation from her family of origin. She had never really engaged in spiritual seeking or sought to make her spirituality "her own." This meant her spiritual development did not include much integration of tolerating and repairing conflicts, sharing authenticity and intimacy, or confronting issues of social justice and valuing differences.

Thomas's relational spirituality reflected his ambivalent style of attachment. He could be passionate and vulnerable spiritually at times, something Ann had initially found attractive. But he was inconsistent. When distressed, he might pray intensely to God for help but then feel discouraged or even angry when he did not feel God's response. He would then typically ignore spiritual practice for months until he felt particularly grateful for an achievement or shamed over a setback. His projected God image was shaped primarily by his mother, so his relational spirituality was laced with performance anxiety. His uncle's doubt was also an important experience of relational spirituality that was "split off" or repressed because had been too dissonant or anxiety-provoking to explore. In light of this, his recent move toward mindfulness meditation and Buddhism indicated the start of a spiritual seeking cycle with potential for a more differentiated form of relational spirituality. But at the start of therapy, Thomas's spiritual difference seemed to Ann more like another example of his dangerous lack of fidelity and a new point for her unforgiveness to coalesce.

Couples Therapy Process

Couples therapy with Ann and Thomas progressed in a nonlinear fashion, winding its way toward growth in differentiation, intimacy, and cooperation. The main relational source of gain in this approach to couples therapy involves trying to develop a securely attached and well-differentiated relationship with the couple through dialectically balancing challenge and support. Action-oriented interventions focused on transformed coping strategies and relational patterns that gain strength from a healthy therapeutic alliance. We summarize the couples therapy process as iterative movement through the same four interrelated phases described in Chapter 9 on long-term psychotherapy.

Phase 1: Forming an Attachment

The early phase of therapy emphasizes pacing. In pacing a couple, the therapist needs to move rather fluidly between the two partners, seeking to understand and validate the concerns, values, and goals of each person. This involves empathy, but a therapist is also engaged in pacing when trying to line up with a client's emotional tempo or body posture. This was a challenge for the psychotherapist working with Ann and Thomas. Thomas tended to be emotionally intense and to speak in bursts before slumping back into the couch with a look of exhausted despair. Ann tended to speak in a slow, methodical manner, with limited affect. The therapist needed the moment-by-moment differentiation to shift the style of interaction in pacing both Ann and Thomas, in turn, while also calming the system with attentive presence.

Couples therapy and family therapy add other levels of complexity with multiple members of the client system in the room, each wondering whether the therapist is "on their side." In addition to basics of pacing, it is particularly important for the therapist to (a) seek to understand each person's perspective on the definitions of problems or conflictual patterns, (b) seek to understand the wants or goals of each person, and (c) begin to explore what is most important or sacred to each person (i.e., his or her relational spiritualities).

This involves relating to the couple or family out of a warm curiosity while exploring these questions with the kinds of pacing that can keep anxiety within tolerable limits. Therapists are wise to use clients' specific language or metaphors to reflect back understanding of their concerns, wants, goals, and values. For example, in the few lines quoted above from Ann and Thomas, the words *assault*, *refuge*, *stranger*, and *rejecting* were each potentially loaded with meaning and metaphorical significance.

Therapists also need to balance emotional processing and emotional regulation. Compared with therapists doing individual therapy, couples and family therapists often need to intervene more actively to keep emotional processing from resulting in severe conflict and dysregulation within the session. For example, the therapist needs to try to stop or redirect a hostile or anxiety-laden interaction that is spiraling downward, even inviting each person to emotionally regulate by taking a moment to "take a deep breath" before trying to understand how the interaction got derailed. Emotionally "soft" or vulnerable "softening" interactions involving sadness can be more effectively processed than hostile or anxiously reactive interactions (S. M. Johnson, 2002). Couples therapists who can effectively orchestrate a balance of emotional processing and regulation are more likely to enhance clients' experience of secure attachment. Couples therapy will start to feel like a safe haven for connection and exploring meaning.

For many couples and families, this early phase of forming an attachment will also involve the dialectical themes of hope and humility we have discussed. This was certainly the case in the early phase of couples therapy with Ann and Thomas. Once the therapist intervened to help each "stay in their own lane" by not interrupting each other or engaging in passive-aggressive gestures (e.g., eye rolling), the interaction slowed down (Sprenkle, Davis, & Lebow, 2009) and they each began to move into a more emotionally vulnerable place where they wondered aloud whether (a) they were simply too defective with too many problems to be capable of a healthy marriage (humility vs. shame dilemma), and (b) it was actually possible to achieve healthy connection and intimacy in marriage or if that is just a sham propagated by psychotherapists and religious communities (hope vs. despair dilemma). Rather than offering superficial reassurance, the therapist offered pacing and empathy related to their questions and a framing of complex hope about moving forward. That is, the couples therapist communicated the developmental frame that couple relationships inevitably reveal people's limitations and needed growth areas (calling for humility rather than shame) and that it is usually possible to move forward if there is a deep commitment to the work (conditional or complex hope). This stance required the couples therapist to practice a humble hopefulness, that is, neither promising miraculous solutions nor giving into judgment or despair.

Phase 2: Coconstructing a Developmental Crucible

Schnarch (1991, 1997, 2009) has used the metaphor of a crucible in reference to a severe test that heats up with the anxiety of a core integrity dilemma, and we are highlighting the relational nature of such dilemmas. During this phase, the couples therapist tries to (a) form an attachment with them as a couple; (b) help each, in turn, coconstruct and face a key relational dilemma; and (c) understand the reality that there are no guarantees about outcome.

The therapist helped Thomas clarify his commitment dilemma by framing it like this: Thomas could give up his primary commitment to achievement and validation from others and fully commit to building the kind of marriage he wanted, even though, at the moment, he could not envision how this could possibly happen with Ann. Or he could "push away from the table" without really trying and yet he would never know how that would have turned out. This raised many deeper questions about self-identity, personal values, emptiness behind his confident façade, and difficulty trusting God or himself to move forward in marriage. The therapist allowed Thomas to wander into other topics during sessions but kept seeking to wrap his commitment dilemma into the conversation several times each session.

The therapist worked with Ann to coconstruct her dilemma: She needed to decide whether to come out of her spiritual refuge and actually put her heart, feelings, and voice into her relationship with her uncommitted husband. Or she could continue to keep her heart behind the fortress walls and see what would happen. The spiritual reflection question became whether she believed God wanted her to keep her heart out of her marriage or put it back into her marriage, which the therapist offered as an honest question. This is a common and understandable dilemma for someone whose partner has enacted infidelity.

Like many couples, Ann and Thomas each had very painful attachment experiences earlier in life that contributed to their marital alienation. The therapist offered some psychoeducation about attachment to help both understand their backgrounds and working models of relationship. In control-based cases such as this, in which each partner is afraid of further attachment injuries, unforgiveness reduces the risk that would come with "going all in." It is important in this phase of therapy to make sure each member of a couple is committed to working on healing and growth in the relationship. The commitment dilemma becomes a valuable existential and spiritual issue involving themes of choice, trust, and integrity. When there has been deep hurt and mistrust in ongoing relationships, such as marriage, the hard work of forgiveness and building a secure attachment will typically require substantial levels of commitment to growth and a willingness to at least attempt possible reconciliation.

Although Ann and Thomas both valued spirituality, their spiritual worldviews were fairly idealistic. That kept them oscillating between a kind of passive hope for spiritual rescue and feeling ashamed of not living up to spiritual ideals. Yet, their spiritual traditions (Christianity for Ann and a Christian–Buddhist combination for Thomas) did offer teachings suggesting that (a) suffering can be normative rather than shameful and (b) spiritual development and virtue can be cultivated through sustained and intentional practice. The therapist initiated discussion of how their spiritual traditions and commitments might be useful to each of them while continuing to hold up the question of whether they each wanted to commit to the working on their relationship. Eventually, each decided to commit to invest putting their hearts into the work.

Phase 3: Processing Disappointment and Grief

Movement into their personal crucibles also increased anxiety and depressive symptoms for both Thomas and Ann, similar to contemplative descriptions of the "dark night of the soul." As with most people, they had been hoping for an easier pathway toward healing and intimacy, and it is hard to surrender those idealistic fantasies. This phase is analogous to the spiritual practice of lament, as the painful realities of life are authentically faced and emotions are processed. The therapist used the word *disappointed* repeatedly with both in pacing their sense of loss and disappointment in their families of origin. Thomas lamented being emotionally neglected and so conditionally loved, which contributed to his intense fear of failure. Ann lamented being expected to deny all unpleasant feelings and discrepant opinions, take care of her parent's insecurity, and pretend she was not an adult, contributing to her condition of psychospiritual exile. Despite their differing family-of-origin experiences, they both felt underparented in certain ways. They actually began to connect around a shared sense of loss.

The chapter of their story involving Thomas's sexual affair was particularly painful to revisit. Yet, it held important pockets of grief and points of learning for both of them. Thomas faced ways his desire for constant validation had led to the affair and also contributed to the invalidation and unforgiveness in his marriage.

At times, they were disappointed in their couples therapist for not coming up with better solutions, and they were surprised when their therapist helped name this. Both found it an unusual relational experience to try to authentically attach to someone (each other and their therapist) while processing emotional challenges and disappointments. They began to develop more secure attachment and differentiation as they learned to sit empathically with one another in their pain without trying to rescue or fix one another.

The therapist eventually prompted exploration of the realities of racism and sexism. This was a biracial couple with both members operating from intercultural minimization (i.e., dealing with cultural differences by ignoring or minimizing their significance; Hammer, Bennett, & Wiseman, 2003). On the one hand, this common strategy represented a successful assimilation into their overwhelmingly White church, neighborhood, set of friends, and people in Thomas's profession. On the other hand, it also represented a relational stance of numbness that helped them cope with implicit and explicit racism and sexism but also limited intimacy with one another.

Both Ann and Thomas had major parts of their selves and social identities in exile, which reflected tragic ways they had internalized discrimination and exclusion. They were once incredibly courageous individuals who came together to do something relatively new in human history and definitely novel in their family histories—construct a biracial marriage. But social oppression and their own vulnerabilities had worn them down into fighting with each other with no collaboration in working together against threats outside their marriage.

Grieving their disappointments, including disappointments with God for allowing such suffering, shifted their God images toward a more secure attachment with God. They felt less repressed anger and fear toward God and the sacred. Ann was particularly helped by the integrative and empowering realization that she could both connect with God amidst pain and also draw on the spiritual value of justice to advocate for herself or others to limit certain forms of suffering. Thomas became fairly consistent in his practice of Buddhist lovingkindness (*metta*) meditation, which helped him become more emotionally regulated and less reactive even during periods when he was also processing pain and disappointment. Both had found it hard to pray or meditate for one another for long time. However, each developed an ability to integrate this into their spiritual practice. This helped cultivate more consistent forgiveness and compassion. These results are consistent with empirical studies showing partner-focused prayer or meditation can foster forgiveness and cooperative motivation (Lambert, Fincham, DeWall, Pond, & Beach, 2013; Lambert, Fincham, Stillman, Graham, & Beach, 2010).

Phase 4: Cultivating and Extending Differentiation

Initial progress on forgiveness in couples therapy involves reductions in motivations toward revenge and internal avoidance and increases in benevolent motivation. This opens the potential for further work on differentiation as expressed in collaboration and deeper intimacy. Differentiation can result from surviving unilateral risk taking and engaging in the humility necessary for collaboration. The couples therapist explored with Thomas and Ann (in the presence of the other) strategic risks they might each take in their marriage for the sake of their personal integrity and spiritual formation. In this model, it is important to not broker deals between the two, as that would nurture the couples' dependence on triangulation and limit secure-base behavior. Their changing forms of relational spirituality were engaged by using the frame that spirituality involves wise and deliberate risk taking.

Ann began to explore risks of passion and voice. She revealed herself at multiple levels. Ann began to speak up for herself in her family of origin, at church, in her workplace, and in her marriage. Thomas also stepped into the risk of setting boundaries with work and career goals, which felt risky to him because he had significant anxiety-driven achievement motivation. They began seeking authentic connection and collaboration in areas such as parenting and finances, even though their exchanges did not always feel great or go the way they each wanted. They started to work together in these areas and initially found it anxiety provoking and frustrating because they were "out of rhythm." However, they continued to engage spiritual and emotional practices for regulating anxiety.

In the past, one of them might initiate something new (e.g., sexually or in managing finances), and if it did not work the first time, they would usually feel shame, lose hope, and slide back to prior patterns. The therapist nurtured hope and humility by normalizing the challenges of trying new patterns of behavior and suggesting that they use sessions to troubleshoot ways of working with new patterns. This increased the recovery rate of forgiveness following conflicts and prevented deep trenches of resentment and internal avoidance from reemerging.

The therapist promoted and moderated healthy, respectful discussion of differences between the two of them, such as differences of personality, race, ethnicity, gender, and spirituality. Differences had been too anxiety provoking in the past for them to engage, with the dark irony that chronically avoiding conflicts over differences had the result of creating severe conflicts and unforgiveness. It was as if they found the differences between them to be so scary at a primal level that the other person was just unforgiveable. The therapist modeled a nonanxious and positive attitude toward exploring and appreciating differences.

Summary

Clearly, not all of the tensions between Thomas and Ann were removed by couples therapy. Yet, within 18 months, each had moved to a more mature and differentiated place, and together, they could relate to each other without having to avoid conflict or be unforgiving to keep conflict quarantined. The couples therapist established a successful working alliance with them as a couple and as individuals through pacing and balancing challenge and support well to enable the partners a safe haven to wrestle with some very emotion-charged personal issues in their crucible. This initial work on forgiveness enabled them to continue to work toward healthier collaboration with enhanced capacities for dealing with subsequent conflicts.

FAMILY CASE STUDY

The following is a family case that enables us to explore family systems dynamics related to forgiveness and relational spirituality. Andy is a 13-year-old boy who was referred to a psychologist by his school counselor. After missing many days of school over the prior months, Andy seemed to be school phobic. He told the school counselor he had fantasies of shooting kids at school, particularly some Latino boys who had been picking on him recently. He did not seem to have access to weapons, nor did he report an active plan, but the school took this very seriously with his parents and ordered a mental health evaluation.

Andy slumped into the first session with the psychologist. His mother, Anita (age 35; Mexican American), slid her chair close to Andy. His father, Bill (age 44; Swedish American), sat on the other side of the room. Andy initially grunted or answered briefly to questions. He had difficulty making eye contact with the psychologist. Anita often rushed in to answer for him. She explained that he had always been shy and had frequently been picked on by other kids. However, this year, his resistance to going to school had gotten much worse.

She had started working full-time managing a dry cleaning business that fall. Andy seemed to struggle with her being gone more. She had been trying to get time off work to be around for him, but the owner of her business was threatening to replace her. Anita was visibly anxious, and her speech was pressured when she talked about Andy and his recent struggles. She often turned to look at him, twisting nervously in her chair. She said many days she brought him treats because she felt guilty about her work, but he was usually angry at her anyway.

Bill was less obviously nervous and even jovial in tone:

> I'm not sure what's going on, but Andy is a great kid! I've been talking with him about getting a paper route or some work in the neighborhood. I was working close to full time when I was his age, and it sure kept me out of trouble.

Andy's biological father, Reid (German American), was someone Anita dated casually, and he moved away shortly after conception with no interest in fatherhood. Bill had entered the picture around that time and offered Anita a more stable partner for starting a family. They had never told Andy of this.

Andy and Bill did not spend much time together and did not have much rapport. Bill was working two jobs to try to help make ends meet. His father had died of a heart attack when he was about Andy's age, and as the oldest of five children he went to work in a grocery store full time. He had spent most of his life working hard.

With his parents out of the room, Andy finally began to offer some information. He said he "hated school and everyone at school." Kids had always picked on him for being "weird," but it had gotten much worse this year with racial slurs directed toward him and also about his mom. This teasing and racism usually came from a group of "White boys," but he also had an incident the month before in the locker room where four Latino boys who had been friendly suddenly pushed him into the shower with his clothes on. Andy slipped in the shower and sprained his ankle severely. The gym teacher (also Latino) had intervened and followed up with Andy in ways that sounded supportive, but Andy said, "Something snapped inside me" at that point. The other kids in class saw him sitting with clothes drenched, and he felt humiliated. His temporary hope of finding solidarity with other boys of color was quashed in this perceived rejection.

Spirituality had become an issue of contention in the family system. Andy had started to look into Satanism and to define himself as a Satanist over the past month. He said he wanted "spiritual power over his enemies" and that "God is weak." This was very upsetting to Anita, who belonged to a United Methodist church in the neighborhood, where she had attended Alcoholics Anonymous meetings when she got sober many years before. She explained,

> God saved me from myself . . . my wild life, getting drunk, running around. I owe everything to God. He's my rock. I know I am failing Him . . . with all these problems we are having. I'm praying harder than I ever have. We need a miracle! But I am so afraid of this Satan stuff Andy is saying. I am scared I will lose his soul and don't know what to do.

The church congregation was mostly older adults, but Anita attended faithfully on Sundays and a weekly Bible study. Andy had resisted attending any youth group activities for the past year. He stopped attending after the previous youth group leader, Iris, abruptly left her position and seminary studies to go back to help relatives in Haiti following a devastating storm. Andy had liked Iris, had confided in her about his struggles, and was despondent at her leaving. When asked if he attended the church, Bill explained, "I work on Sundays. I go with Anita at the holidays. I was raised Lutheran. What's important is doing the right things and helping others. That's my religion."

Case Conceptualization

This family system was dealing with multiple stressors and conflicts, which resulted in serious crisis. From a systems perspective, Andy had become the "identified patient" who was manifesting intense symptoms of anxiety, anger, and unforgiveness reflective of family and relational dynamics beyond his own individual functioning. Andy certainly needed a psychiatric and psychological evaluation and crisis management to stabilize his symptoms. However, a broader relational and systemic perspective was also needed to understand the numerous factors influencing this case. The psychologist recommended family therapy.

We can start by noting attachment and differentiation dynamics. Andy and Anita had historically both experienced an anxious ambivalent style of attachment and considerable fusion with one another. Anita was quite committed to her parenting of Andy and concerned about his well-being, but her own ongoing struggles with anxiety and shame led her to overfunctioning for him. She struggled (not very successfully) to set structure or limits. She was often preoccupied with his wants and mood states and tried to soothe him (and her own anxiety) by excessive accommodation. That worked for a time, but was no longer effective. For many youth, the transition into adolescence or young adulthood is often when permissive parenting runs into problems because of the teen's developmental need for increased autonomy and self-regulation. Attachment dynamics become particularly important during developmental transitions. Andy lacked any secure attachment figures. He was wounded by the loss of Iris, who might have provided some support were it not for her quick departure (perceived as abandonment). Bill displayed characteristics of avoidant attachment, which added to the coalition between Anita and Andy. Bill had seemingly been parentified around Andy's age and had to grow up too quickly, and this contributed to his limited ability to help Andy with his own differentiation.

But Andy's attachment struggles had become more complicated with the recent experiences of bullying and racism, which had reached traumatic levels. He had often been picked on in the past, but now he had reached an age where he was more self-aware of the dynamics of racism and more vulnerable to internalizing shame related to his social and cultural identity. Research literature on both bullying and racism demonstrates the traumatic impact this can have, and the increased stigmatization and exclusion experienced by kids such as Andy can boil over into violent ideation and rage. For anxious, internalizing kids such as Andy, this move toward externalized aggression is obviously dangerous. However, it can also represent intrapsychic defenses of splitting and projection to stave off self-hatred and self-harm.

Andy can be viewed as a spiritual seeker through his recent exploration of Satanism. His spiritual search seemed primarily driven by anxiety and anger. However, the therapist also believed it could be understood as a quest for justice and spiritual protection. Andy found his mother's religious community to be disappointing and to lack resources to help him deal with his recent vulnerabilities. To cap it off, the unexpected and unprocessed loss of Iris was an attachment injury. Thus, benevolent forms of relational spirituality had been desecrated for Andy, and his movement toward dark, powerful, and vengeful spirituality (i.e., this version of Satanism) revealed his skepticism about the agency of most authority figures and his honesty about his antisocial feelings and motivations in a family system that hid significant secrets.

The family system also revealed several forms of triangulation. The most important was a rescuer drama triangle (L'Abate, 2009). Bill had played a rescuer role for Anita and Andy. When extreme forms of rescuing form the basis for starting a relationship, there is a temporary stability, which usually erodes into significant conflict, dysfunction, and unforgiveness. Bill had learned a parentified rescuer role in his family of origin, and becoming the rescuer was his main way of attaching. When there was not a crisis, he was not sure how to relate. He tended to withdraw into work or reading. Because Anita felt negative about herself and emotionally cut off from Bill, she felt a need to continue to relate to God as a rescuer and to focus on Andy. One study has found that extreme family triangulation can either inhibit spiritual questing or add such intense anxiety that spiritual questing may become reactive among adolescents and emerging adults (Heiden Rootes et al., 2010). The latter had become the case for Andy.

Family Therapy Process

Phase 1: Forming an Attachment

This was a complicated case that required multiple modalities of intervention and, therefore, several therapy attachments. Andy first entered a day treatment program to gain some stabilization, learn some anxiety management skills, and try some medication for his anxiety and mood difficulties. Bill was initially concerned that Andy would not fare well around "a bunch of troubled kids," but Andy actually responded positively to the well-structured groups and seemed to find some of the alternative community of fellow outsiders he had been seeking.

Perhaps even more important was Andy's opportunity to work with an individual psychotherapist of color who was highly competent in dealing with sociocultural and spiritual issues. Andy was initially resistant and closed off, but his psychotherapist validated Andy's desire for justice, protection, and power. This surprised Andy. Over several months, he began to share some of the vulnerable experiences of victimization that led to his anger. He had not previously experienced an adult who was sufficiently differentiated to sit with him amid his anxiety and pain. Iris had come close, but he had lost her, and things had turned more traumatic after that. Andy had some important and sophisticated questions about suffering in life, and his experience had been that authority figures (divine, parental, academic) could not be trusted to help. When a young person experiences an unresolved existential crisis, it is not hard to understand how it might feel absurd to sit in an algebra class. Andy needed a secure attachment to someone who could support the meaning-making process.

The psychotherapist also engaged Andy in discussions about cultural and racial issues. He validated the challenges of being biracial and a boy or man of color, and he exposed Andy to literature by Latino authors. The psychotherapist's goals were to help Andy (a) heal from trauma and internalized racism and (b) develop positive cultural identity. Identity work is part of developing differentiation of self. Without this, the self is vulnerable to severe shame and narcissistic injuries resulting in unforgiveness.

Anita and Bill also started meeting with a marriage and family therapist, who validated that they were both responsible people who had shown resilience in dealing with many life challenges. The therapist paced their emotions and concerns, and suggested a marital frame of working together to help Bill and Anita further collaborate as marital partners and parents. They both found the humility to acknowledge they could use some help. This dissipated some of the shame they had felt about Andy's struggles. This involved a kind of self-forgiveness.

Phase 2: Coconstructing a Developmental Crucible

In couples therapy, the coconstruction of the developmental crucible unfolded as the couples therapist probed what Bill and Anita each wanted in their relationship and family life. Schnarch (1991, 1997) has pointed out that revealing one's wants and desires is an act of intimacy and often comes with anxiety that heightens a crucible process. Like many couples in this situation, Anita and Bill each found it easier to talk about (a) their family dynamics over their couple dynamics and (b) what they did not want as opposed to what they did want. The couples therapist continued to pursue their marital wants, and this intensified the emotional process. Eventually, Anita provided the key crucible language construction in blurting out, "I guess we need to decide if we are going to just go on being roommates or have a real marriage." Both seemed initially shocked and scared to have that out on the table but also felt relieved over the next few sessions to be able to discuss that dilemma as adults. Rather than quickly suggesting a remedy to this, the couples therapist stoked the fire under the crucible by exploring how the situation had developed and the possibilities for a different type of attachment.

Important relational spirituality dynamics began to emerge. Bill wanted to spend more time with Anita but did not feel he could compete with her church activities, saying, "That stuff is about her and God . . . and what's more important than God?" Anita started to see the rescuer dynamics in her relational patterns. She felt "undeserving" of the help she had received from both Bill and God. In the case of Bill, she now admitted she was frustrated that he was often closed off emotionally and prioritized other things over their relationship. She had avoided dealing with her internal feelings about this, explaining, "How can I be upset with someone who works so hard and helps people so much?" The couples therapist began to help each to draw on their deepest values in considering how to approach the partner and the overall marital dilemma differently. They started to experience mutual forgiveness as they found hope for new patterns of interaction and a greater commitment to prioritize their marriage relationship.

Once Andy's mental health started to stabilize, they started work with a family therapist who collaborated with the couples therapist and Andy's individual therapist. Anita and Bill had already come to the conclusion they needed to tell Andy the truth—that his biological father was Reid. Privately, they asked the family therapist for help and processed this disclosure during a session. It is not surprising that Andy had a range of reactions, including anger at being deceived for so many years. Anita apologized but had difficulty for several weeks dealing with shame over the issues. However, a major turning point came with Anita finding the differentiated stance to empathize with Andy's feelings and offer validation but also insisting that it was not acceptable to keep calling her derogatory names. When their family therapist noted this change and wondered about it, Anita explained that she had received a picture in her mind from the Holy Spirit during a recent worship service and could see herself being both strong and merciful with Andy. She said she had never had an experience like that before. However, in that moment, her anxiety about working through this particular issue "faded away." The fact that this experience overlapped with the therapist encouraging Anita to deal with parenting dynamics raises interesting possibilities about the unconscious integration of psychology and spirituality.

Andy's identification with Satanism also waned as his mental health and attachments improved. The family therapist was able to help the family work at skills in accepting differences and managing their anxiety in the moment when different views arose. This enabled each to begin to voice some questions or perspectives on various issues, including spirituality, and this improved spiritual differentiation lowered the reactivity and conflict in the system. Anita and Bill came to appreciate that, beneath his flirtations with Satanism, Andy's spiritual anger was largely due to injustice and victim-ization. Both were helped when Anita observed that this anger was like the prophets in the Bible. An important relational spiritual process was Bill and Anita communicating solidarity with Andy in outrage over the racism he had been experiencing. About a year into the family therapy process, they began visiting various churches together with the intention of finding one that could fit for all of them.

Phase 3: Processing Disappointment and Grief

As things started to improve in the nuclear family system, it provided the security to begin to process various points of disappointment and grief. Andy had sadness about Reid not being part of his life, and the family thera-pist helped Bill to connect with Andy about this, rather than take it person-ally. They had both lost their biological fathers. The therapist also teased out their differing defaults on coping with sadness. For Andy, sadness typically morphed into anger and avoidance of everyday life whereas Bill tended to pour himself into work. This differentiation work further softened the reactivity of unforgiveness.

Anita and Bill used couples sessions to process family-of-origin issues. Their increased security of attachment and improved family relations paved the way for the couples therapist to explore what they had missed out on in their families of origin. In this way, forgiveness work turned intergenera-tional as each worked to make narrative sense out of their parents' struggles. With the therapist modeling a caring and calm approach to unpacking dif-ficult events and emotions, Bill and Anita were scaffolded into learning to attach and help relationally regulate emotions as they did this grief work together. Bill eventually realized being fully engaged as a father brought him in touch with unprocessed grief about the tragic loss of his own father, which opened him to deeper spiritual seeking and moving past a foreclosed relational spirituality based on his parentified family role.

Phase 4: Cultivating and Extending Differentiation

It would be hard to summarize all the areas of therapeutic work this family did over a 3-year period. This fourth phase of the therapy process involved further cultivation and extension of differentiated relating in the family sys-tem. Andy transferred to a different school the following year, one that had a strong antibullying program and more therapeutic supports. Anita and Bill were more proactive—an important sign of differentiation—in making efforts to help Andy connect with the school psychologist and several short-term groups for social skills development while also continuing in therapy. Bill stayed engaged with the family. Although finances were tight, Bill was able to pull back from some extra work shifts in order to be more present to Anita and Andy. This allowed Anita space to work on developing herself (including starting college) and not feel as tempted to overfunction in their family life. The family continued to struggle with challenges and bouts of reactivity, but their move to more secure attachments and differentiated functioning shortened their recovery time following setbacks.

This case reveals ways in which chronic avoidance-based unforgiveness contributes to weakened attachments and the risk for a counterbalancing rage crisis. The treatment shows that these could be restored and sometimes averted through relationally informed psychological and spiritual interventions.

SUMMARY

Complexity increases within couples and family therapy. However, the basic processes are the same: forming an alliance, coconstructing a developmental crucible, processing the grief and disappointment that arise from change (and therefore loss), and promoting differentiation. All of these strategic objectives take place using a general relational plan: connect and provide a secure base, help the clients explore the issues and tolerate differences, plan and carry out actions, and then process the results.

11

FORGIVENESS IN GROUP INTERVENTIONS

In the mid-1990s, I (Steve Sandage) was a psychology intern working in a federal prison, and one of my responsibilities was to lead an anger management group for male inmates. We used a standard cognitive behavioral protocol in a structured 8-week format focused on skills in coping with anger. I was working on forgiveness research at the time, and I decided to work some forgiveness material into a group session to see how it would go over. One inmate immediately read aloud with laughter the Yoruban proverb I had quoted at the top of the handout: "The one who forgives gains the victory." I can picture him with his head rolling back and amidst his laughter announcing that was the craziest thing he had ever heard. This had a powerful effect on the group dynamic, and although none of the other inmates laughed, it was the least interactive session of that group cycle. As that inmate was laughing, I could not help but be struck by the irony that he had shared the

http://dx.doi.org/10.1037/14712-012
Forgiveness and Spirituality in Psychotherapy: A Relational Approach, by E. L. Worthington, Jr. and S. J. Sandage

previous session that the scar covering one side of his face was from a bar fight he had started when feeling insulted by a stranger's glance.

Years later, I was invited to meet with a group of nurses who wanted to study the topic of interpersonal forgiveness together as a group after work hours. They had become familiar with some of the health research on forgiveness and were eager to learn more. But I was struck by their observations that many of their patients, particularly ones close to death, voiced struggles and concerns related to forgiveness. This group of nurses decided to work on developing their own capacities for forgiveness using some of the psychoeducational materials described in this chapter, and they went on to organize a community seminar on forgiveness through a local church drawing on psychological research and spiritual practices. Their grass roots initiative focused on forgiveness as a public health issue, but they showed the humility to start by working on themselves.

These were two very different group experiences with contrasting attitudes toward the relevance of forgiveness. They can highlight several valuable questions about the place of forgiveness in group interventions and the fact that individuals enter forgiveness groups with varying levels of motivation. There are now many empirical studies of forgiveness group interventions in nonclinical settings. However, there is comparably less research on forgiveness groups dealing with severe conflicts, challenges, or diagnosable mental health struggles than research on psychoeducational interventions for mild conflicts with college student populations. There is also more research on group interventions focused on forgiveness per se than on efforts to integrate forgiveness as a component of some other kind of group intervention (e.g., anger management). We offer a summary of major research findings in this area with implications for our model, and we try to differentiate applications with clear empirical support from applications that are more speculative and based on clinical inferences.

On a single day, it is impossible to estimate the number of groups in the United States alone that discuss the topic of forgiveness. But we personally know there is wide diversity of groups engaging in explicit efforts to practice forgiveness, including groups in prisons, outpatient and inpatient clinics, 12-step meetings, religious congregations, meditation centers, divorce recovery and support groups, couples enrichment seminars, university counseling centers, law offices, and geriatric facilities. The state of Hawaii even holds an annual public holiday—Hawai'i International Forgiveness Day—to celebrate Hawaiian practices of forgiveness. And it offers year-round public classes to learn forgiveness. With such a variety of groups seeking to promote forgiveness, it is important to consider some of the theoretical and empirical insights that can maximize the effectiveness of forgiveness group interventions.

Thus, in this chapter, we discuss often-used psychoeducational forgiveness group treatments, especially those based on the model by Enright (2012; Enright & Fitzgibbons, 2000, 2014; i.e., 20-step process) and the model by Worthington (2006; i.e., REACH Forgiveness). We emphasize those two because those two varieties of groups are the most researched; however, we spend most of our discussion on REACH Forgiveness groups and refer readers interested in Enright's model to Enright and Fitzgibbons (2014). After describing the conduct of REACH Forgiveness, we examine uses of that model within other treatment formats, including self-administered workbooks, and use with more than one person in the room so that both sides of transgressions are represented (i.e., couples therapy, parent training, and self-forgiveness). We conclude discussion of the REACH Forgiveness groups by providing a case study. Then, we briefly describe two promising areas into which forgiveness interventions can be inserted: (a) mindfulness-based stress reduction (MBSR) and (b) dialectical behavior therapy (DBT). We then tackle forgiveness in process-oriented psychotherapy groups and then in religiously or spiritually accommodated forgiveness groups—especially important, as much of the population, at least in the United States (but also in many other countries outside of Europe), identify as being involved in religion (Berger et al., 1999). We close with three case examples from different religions.

PSYCHOEDUCATIONAL FORGIVENESS GROUPS

The vast majority of empirical studies on forgiveness and group interventions involve psychoeducational interventions. These interventions focus on helping people forgive others. The two most common group forgiveness interventions in this area of research are Enright's 20-step process model (Enright, 2012; Enright & Fitzgibbons, 2000, 2014) and Worthington's (2006) REACH Forgiveness model, although other models have received empirical attention.

Enright's Process Model Groups

Enright and Fitzgibbons's (2014) process model focuses on four phases: (a) uncovering negative feelings and processing emotions and thought patterns; (b) decision to pursue forgiveness based on other coping strategies not working; (c) work toward understanding the offender and giving forgiveness as a moral gift; and (d) discovery of meaning in suffering, finding unexpected positive outcomes, and developing empathy for the offender. The efficacy of the Enright model has been demonstrated with a variety of differing groups and issues (for a meta-analysis, which is discussed in more detail below, see Wade, Hoyt, Kidwell, & Worthington, 2014). These include adult incest survivors (Freedman & Enright, 1996), adult children of alcoholics (Osterndorf, Enright, Holter, & Klatt, 2011), adult inpatients struggling with alcohol and drug addiction (Lin, Mack, Enright, Krahn, & Baskin, 2004), elderly adults (Ingersoll-Dayton, Campbell, & Ha, 2009), and postabortion men (Coyle & Enright, 1997), among others. In fact, it is a reasonable conclusion to say that the clear choice for protracted forgiveness therapy for difficult targeted problems is Enright's model, hands down.

REACH Forgiveness Psychoeducational Groups

Many, if not most, applications of groups for forgiveness are not long-term groups that have been aimed specifically at severe problems. They are short-term (5–9 hours), general forgiveness groups aimed at learning forgiveness skills through applying them to a particular hurt or offense and then building generality by applying them to other hurts or offenses. Anyone with a transgression he or she would like to forgive could attend the groups. Although Enright's groups have also been used effectively for brief psychoeducation, the REACH Forgiveness groups have much more supportive evidence on these briefer, nontargeted forgiveness groups. REACH Forgiveness has also been religiously accommodated to Christians (and investigated empirically with that population on several occasions), as well as having most of the research be with secular populations.

REACH Forgiveness psychoeducational interventions are often useful as adjuncts to therapy—to brief psychotherapy, long-term psychotherapy, couples therapy, family therapy, and group therapy. The elements of the intervention can also be incorporated within the treatments.

Resources

The REACH Forgiveness model (Worthington, 2006) helps people move through a set of experiences in which five are at the center. Resources (i.e., Microsoft Word versions of facilitator and group member manuals for secular and Christian-accommodated psychoeducational groups, how to get a free training DVD on how to run either secular or Christian-accommodated groups, and Microsoft Word versions of secular and Christian-accommodated self-directed workbooks) are available through http://www.EvWorthington-forgiveness.com. On the website, sufficient psychoeducational group exercises are available to conduct a 20-hour group if one desires. The strongest 6-hour version for groups is recommended.

Aims of REACH Forgiveness

REACH Forgiveness is a manual-driven, empirically supported treatment for forgiveness of a particular transgression. As part of the treatment, it helps people generalize their learning to other hurts not dealt with specifically in the treatment to forge a more forgiving character. The immediate aim is to help people forgive a particular offense that is troubling them. The ultimate aim is to help people build more trait forgivingness.

Prompting the Most Effective Motivation to Forgive

We initially motivate clients to forgive for their own sake. That is, holding grudges can lead to problems in physical health, mental health, relationships, and spirituality. We suggest that the offender might not even know he or she has offended, as worse, not care. Yet the person offended is paying the cost. Thus, we encourage the person to forgive for his or her own sake. That self-beneficial motive is easier to accept than forgiving to help a needy offender. We do not broach the altruistic motive until well into psychotherapy. Parametric studies have shown that forgiving for one's own sake is effective and produces about 0.2 to 0.4 standard deviations of lasting change. However, appealing to altruistic forgiveness rarely works well within less than 2 hours of psychotherapy and yet works much better than the self-interested appeal if the client has more than 2 hours of intentional effort to forgive.

Content of the REACH Forgiveness Intervention

Definition. Leaders help group members come to common definitions about decisional forgiveness and emotional forgiveness (Worthington, 2006). Group members select two correct definitions from 14 definitions—with 12 of those being common misconceptions.

Decision to Forgive. Decisional forgiveness is stating (to oneself or others) an intention to act differently toward the offender. Participants in groups are led through an exercise in which they pretend to have their grudge clasped tightly in their hands, outstretched to maximum distance from the participants' bodies. The group leader drones on about the benefits of making a decision to forgive (i.e., on relationships [Riek & Mania, 2012] and on one's spiritual freedom and in facilitating emotional forgiveness). The participants' arms become progressively tired. When the leader senses people are sufficiently tired, he or she invites people to feel what it would be like to release the grudge, having people open the hands and drop their arms to their sides. This is likened to the feeling of release and freedom available when a person makes a decision to forgive. Not everyone makes a decision to forgive during or before that exercise, and the leader says that not being willing to forgive is okay. However, the leader promises to revisit the exercise near the end of the group after participants have worked toward emotional forgiveness. Some make the decision to forgive before experiencing emotional forgiveness. Others make decisions to forgive in the midst of or after emotional forgiveness.

The REACH Acrostic for Emotional Forgiveness. Each step of REACH stands for a step, as we described in the Introduction and briefly summarized here:

R: *Recalling* the hurt differently than as a source of rage or woundedness.

E: *Emotional* reprocessing.

A: Giving an *altruistic* gift of forgiveness—one that is predicated on blessing the offender who is a needy person.

C: *Commitment* to the emotional forgiveness experienced.

H: *Hold* onto the forgiveness when doubts occur.

How Groups Are Conducted

The psychoeducational group method is guided by a leader manual and accompanied by a participant manual. The manuals serve as guides to interpersonal exercises that are meant to help structure a therapeutic process. Interpersonal and mostly dyadic (but some whole-group) discussions are the primary mechanism by which change occurs.

How the Treatment Proceeds

At the outset, participants identify an unforgiven index transgression that they will work to forgive. The group process begins with an icebreaker, in which participants introduce themselves to people in the group. Each person describes to the group as a whole the most difficult transgression that they ever successfully forgave. After forgiveness is defined (as two types, decisional and emotional), participants are invited to make a decision to forgive (described above). The group then focuses most effort on learning the five steps to REACH emotional forgiveness. Most of the time, participants are paired with another person and they work with that person throughout the group to move through the five steps. One key part of the group procedure is when each person, having gone through the first three steps, is asked to state aloud the percent of the hurt that they have forgiven by going through the group to that point (C = Commitment). Stating aloud that they have forgiven "75% of the unforgiven hurt I started with," or 90%, or 50%, and so on, provides a public commitment that helps maintain gains. At the end of the five steps to promote emotional forgiveness, people are given another opportunity to grant decisional forgiveness if they have not already done so. In the final portion of the group, each group members does a writing exercise as the group leader narrates the stimuli. Group members recall 10 hurts from their past that they have not completely forgiven. Then, they work through the five steps to REACH emotional forgiveness on several of those, resulting in overall increases in trait forgiveness.

Nongroup Uses of REACH Forgiveness

The REACH Forgiveness model is aimed at changing people's experiences of several hurts through forgiving. Although that affects the overall likelihood that one will be more forgiving, it is clear that deep-seated personality transformation will not usually occur with this method. REACH Forgiveness has been used as psychoeducation, as a module in psychotherapy, as part of couples and family therapy, in small groups within organizations (e.g., businesses, churches), and as an adjunctive group to individual long-term psychotherapy and brief, time-limited psychotherapy.

The REACH Forgiveness model has also been adapted to be a workbook and has been described in trade books (Worthington, 2003, 2013), training videos (available through http://www.EvWorthington-forgiveness.com), and documentary movies (Doblmeier, 2008). We think of it as being effective as a change agent, but we also think of it as being something that supplements relational psychotherapy and saves time with coping approaches to forgiveness.

Forgiveness and Reconciliation Through Experiencing Empathy Within the Hope-Focused Couple Approach

The hope-focused couple approach (HFCA) is Worthington's (2005; Ripley & Worthington, 2014) approach to brief couple counseling (20 sessions or fewer). See http://www.hopecouples.com for resources. It has been evaluated to have the research support to meet the standard for empirically supported treatment (Jakubowski, Milne, Brunner, & Miller, 2004). Within the HFCA are two major components—one aimed at communication and conflict resolution (handling our problems effectively [HOPE], providing assessment and feedback and teaching communication, conflict resolution, and intimacy) and the other (forgiveness and reconciliation through experiencing empathy; FREE). FREE contains within it the five steps of the REACH Forgiveness, with some exercises to promote reconciliation (see Worthington & Drinkard, 2000). Reconciliation is restoring trust. It requires mutually trustworthy behavior and thus cannot be achieved by couples in which one partner continues to act untrustworthily. FREE has been offered as a couples (Burchard et al., 2003), parenting (Kiefer et al., 2010), and (relevant to this present chapter) group intervention (Ripley & Worthington, 2002).

In the reconciliation portion of FREE, the leader teaches four steps (Worthington & Drinkard, 2000). First, people must make a decision about whether and how to attempt reconciliation. Second, partners are trained to have positive discussions around transgressions. Those hurt or offended learn how to (a) make good reproaches; (b) respond in a differentiated way to offender denials, justifications, excuses, or confessions; and (c) deal with a request for forgiveness when no forgiveness has yet been experienced. Offenders learn to make good confessions (and avoid denials, justifications, and excuses), bind anxiety instead of demanding immediate assurance of forgiveness, and wait patiently for whatever forgiveness (or none) the offended person can muster. Third, in FREE people learn detoxification of the relationship. This requires, for the hurt or offended party, detoxification of unforgiveness and bitterness through forgiving. For the offender, this requires detoxification from shame, regret, remorse, and self-condemnation through responsible self-forgiveness. Fourth, in FREE, partners rebuild devotion through increasing productive and positive interactions, reducing negativity, and promoting intimacy. The four parts are thus decision, discussion, detoxification, and devotion, with the alliteration aimed at aiding memory for clients and psychotherapist.

Resources

These self-forgiveness methods, such as the REACH Forgiveness methods, have been developed for secular use (see Griffin, Worthington, & Lavelock, 2014). They have also been developed for Christian-accommodated use (Worthington, n.d., 2013; see also http://www.EvWorthington-forgiveness.com).

Empirical Basis for REACH Forgiveness

The REACH Forgiveness model has been evaluated as an evidence-based practice in psychology (Hook, et al. 2010). The research generally has followed best practices for conducting psychological group research (Worthington, Sandage, & Berry, 2000). Most of its empirical support has come through secular samples. Several studies in recent years have shown that a Christian-accommodated version is also efficacious with Christian clients. This has been true in published studies with psychoeducational REACH Forgiveness groups in the United States (Lampton, Oliver, Worthington, & Berry, 2005; Stratton, Dean, Nooneman, Bode, & Worthington, 2008), REACH Forgiveness groups accommodated both to Christian beliefs and Filipino culture in the Philippines, and using REACH Forgiveness workbooks in the United States. In a meta-analysis, Wade et al. (2014) found that 22 randomized controlled trials (RCTs) from numerous laboratories have supported its efficacy. Other outcome studies were also available but were not RCTs, generally conceded as the most rigorous comparisons.

Shared Empirical Support for REACH Forgiveness and Enright's Process Model

REACH Forgiveness and Enright's Process Model. Importantly, REACH Forgiveness (Worthington, 2006) and Enright's process model (Enright & Fitzgibbons, 2000, 2014) had 22 and 23 RCTs on each, respectively. All other models together had 22 RCTs. However, wide usage does not translate directly into efficacy. The meta-analysis of 67 studies found that time was the most important variable and washed out any relative effects of different treatments (Wade et al., 2014). So, any evidence-based forgiveness group will produce about 0.10 standard deviations of increase in forgiveness (and hope) per hour of treatment and about 0.05 standard deviations per hour of reduction of depression and anxiety, even though hope, depression, and anxiety were not mentioned specifically in the forgiveness treatments.

Mode of Delivery Might Matter. Mode of delivery might end up making a difference, although it is too early to say with confidence. Individual delivery in psychotherapy was more effective (given treatments of the same duration) than couples or group therapy. Although our three self-administered workbook studies of forgiveness (another type of individual administration) were not included in the meta-analysis, the two that have been published to date (Greer, Worthington, Van Tongeren, et al., 2014; Harper et al., 2014) have been compared with benchmarked group intervention studies of the same duration and far outperformed benchmarked groups.

Empathy Mediates Change. Research on active ingredients or mediators of change in group forgiveness interventions has been limited. Yet two studies have found empathy to mediate changes in forgiveness in 6- and 8-hour formats using both empathy-based and self-enhancement-based forgiveness interventions (McCullough, Worthington, & Rachal, 1997; Sandage & Worthington, 2010). That is, even in forgiveness intervention condition that focused only on forgiving for personal benefits, empathy still mediated changes in forgiveness.

Shame and Guilt Play a Role. Sandage and Worthington (2010) also measured traits of the moral emotions of shame and guilt at pretest in their study and found shame was negatively associated with forgiveness scores at posttest, whereas guilt was positively associated with the same. Shame appeared to be a risk factor limiting the efficacy of the forgiveness interventions.

Reasons for Similar Findings Across Intervention Models

None of these studies specifically tested all elements of our forgiveness and relational spirituality model; however, there are several points of rapprochement. First, both the Enright process model and the REACH Forgiveness model emphasize emotion processing and emotion regulation strategies as part of forgiving. Forgiveness interventions show efficacy in reducing anxiety and depression. Second, forgiveness interventions increase hope, which is important to our model. Third, the relational development factors of attachment and differentiation have not been specifically tested in forgiveness interventions. However, the mediator effects for empathy suggest that forgiveness interventions can generate changes, at least temporarily, in self–other relational templates.

Forgiveness Interventions With Christian-Accommodated Participants

A couple of available studies have compared religiously integrative and secular forgiveness groups with Christian participants (Rye & Pargament, 2002; Rye et al., 2005). Both groups have been equally efficacious. At the end of the study, interviews showed that some participants in the secular condition were drawing on spiritual or religious beliefs and practices to forgive. This fits our overall framework of relational spirituality in revealing ways many people will implicitly relate to the sacred in their coping efforts whether the group therapist encourages that or not.

Six Steps to REACH Self-Forgiveness

In two early research efforts, before the development of the full six steps to self-forgiveness, two clinical trials were conducted. First, Campana (2010) created a brief workbook (about three hours to complete) regarding self-forgiveness among unmarried female students who had experienced failed romantic relationships. Some positive effects were found. Scherer, Worthington, Hook, and Campana (2011) tested a prototypical version in a brief group treatment of adult inpatients for alcohol addiction. As part of treatment, inpatients select 3-hour modules. The patients who selected the self-forgiveness module expressed less self-condemnation at follow-up than did those in the same in-patient program who elected a different 3-hour supplemental module.

Griffin, Worthington, Lavelock, et al. (2015) completed an RCT with almost 200 undergraduates for an online 6-hour workbook to promote self-forgiveness. He used a waiting list design. Both immediate treatment and waiting list participants improved markedly during the time when they were treated. The immediate treatment participants maintained those gains. The waiting list participants were retested at posttest but were not retested at follow-up.

Case Example of a Psychoeducational Forgiveness Group

Neal (age 35) was a Gujarati American student studying at a university in the United States. He decided to attend a 6-hour psychoeducational forgiveness group primarily to gain extra credit for an introduction to psychology course. However, he also knew he had been struggling with resentment and bitterness toward his ex-wife, Amisha, who had divorced him 2 years earlier after 8 years of marriage, and was curious what might be involved in moving toward forgiveness. Their families had introduced the couple because they belonged to the same caste and community. After 5 months of courtship, which included weekly dates and phone calls, they decided to marry. Two years later, they had a daughter. They had tried couples therapy because of Amisha's wish to seek a divorce and Neal's desire to save the marriage, but after 5 months of treatment, Amisha pursued the divorce. She said she had felt no passion in her marriage from the start. She married Neal from obligation. Initially, Neal struggled to let go of trying to make the marriage work and expressed enormous anger at Amisha for what he saw as a "selfish choice" based on "corrupt values." Neal had felt he could never forgive Amisha for her choice, given how much harm it caused him and their daughter, and how much shame it brought upon both of them from their family and community.

During the group, Neal was surprised by several things: (a) learning that forgiveness did not require condoning or excusing what Amisha had done; (b) hearing others describe similar struggles with a confusing combination of anger, sadness, shame, and fear about the future; and (c) coming to realize his resentment was mostly hurting himself and keeping him from opening his heart to the risk of being disappointed again. But amidst the psychological focus of the group content, Neal also had a relational spirituality process unfolding rooted in his Hindu tradition. He asked for a follow-up meeting with the group leader (a doctoral student in psychology) to share some of what helped him forgive, which is paraphrased below:

> I've never been a devout Hindu in the sense of praying to Krishna every day, doing my *mala*, or singing scriptures. But I am Hindu in my core beliefs. I realized this past week that I can only control my own behavior and my own destiny, and I have to let her go. If I choose to hold onto my anger and not forgive, then I am only increasing my bad karma because it is a consuming emotion that keeps me stagnant from fulfilling my dharma. If I decide to forgive and continue to be a good father to my daughter, then I am moving closer to God in my next life, as the cycle of reincarnation dictates. This is what I concluded, and I feel much more at peace with my future. I am likely paying for something from my past life because my wife chose to divorce me in this one. So, I have something to learn. I don't feel any anger when I look at it in this way. It's what I believe in my heart after months of searching for the truth. I hope Amisha also finds what she is looking for and what she could not find in me. I am saddened by our divorce, but I am grateful that our marriage brought me our daughter.

As we have done in earlier chapters, we could describe this using the language of differentiation of self, hope, humility, and emotion regulation. (We trust you are thinking along those lines now.) But focusing on the psychological would have missed the dynamics of relational spirituality revealed when Neal offered a thicker description of his experience.

There is also empirical evidence that those with Neal's particular post-divorce struggle with forgiveness can also be helped through psychoeducational group forgiveness interventions. In two different studies, Rye and his colleagues have shown that group interventions can be effective helping to forgive an ex-romantic partner or spouse (Rye & Pargament, 2002; Rye et al., 2005). In both studies, forgiveness of an ex was associated with better mental health functioning. In a third study, Rye et al. (2012) compared gratitude journaling versus daily events journaling as follow-up interventions to a forgiveness workshop. Participants in the gratitude journaling condition improved more on forgiveness over time, suggesting further evidence of the links between forgiveness and gratitude (recall the correlational evidence from Chapter 5). This area of postdivorce forgiveness intervention research has important implications for coparenting and child development, as well as the personal and relational well-being of the many adults who experience divorce. Divorce often contributes to extended symptoms of depression, anger, unforgiveness, social isolation, and weak attachments to social supporters. Most spiritual and religious communities promote the view of marriage as sacred, which is healthy and can promote relational commitment and working at overcoming conflicts. However, in some spiritual or religious communities, divorce may be so severely stigmatized that those who experience divorce may feel excluded or judged and may create distance from their spiritual or religious community. By offering divorce care support groups, such as the Rye forgiveness program (see Rye et al., 2012), spiritual and religious communities can reduce shaming stigma, promote healing and constructive coparenting, and possibly prevent future divorces.

FORGIVENESS SKILLS WITHIN OTHER PSYCHOEDUCATIONAL GROUP INTERVENTIONS

Failures of forgiveness surface often in many kinds of groups. Most of the empirical research available focuses on forgiveness-specific group interventions, but emerging work is aimed at including forgiveness as a component of a broader psychoeducational group intervention. Two areas of psychoeducational intervention are promising for older adults: (a) MBSR and (b) DBT.

Mindfulness-Based Stress Reduction

In his book *Full Catastrophe Living*, Jon Kabat-Zinn (2013) described elements of his MBSR program, which has now been tested in dozens of empirical studies. Kabat-Zinn spoke to the benefits of including a forgiveness component in meditation training. He wrote,

> We do a lovingkindness meditation . . . to give people a taste of the power a concentrated and calm mind can generate when evoking feelings of kindness, generosity, goodwill, love, and forgiveness. The response is invariably moving; a great many tears are shed, both in joy and in sorrow. (p. 182)

It is interesting to note the emotional dialectic of joy and sorrow, emotion regulation and grief, in his observation.

Two empirical studies have investigated connections between mindfulness and forgiveness. Webb, Phillips, Bumgarner, and Conway-Williams (2013) found mindfulness was positively associated with forgiveness of others, forgiveness of self, and forgiveness of situations in a cross-sectional study of undergraduates in Appalachia. Oman, Shapiro, Thoresen, Plante, and Flinders (2008) published the first empirical test of the effect of MBSR on forgiveness in a 12-week trial with undergraduates. Compared with controls, those in both MBSR and an alternative meditation condition (Eight-Point Program; Easwaran, 1991) showed pre–post benefits in stress reduction and forgiveness.

To date, MBSR has not been compared head-to-head with forgiveness-specific group interventions, so we do not know whether there would be similar efficacy. But these findings suggest the potential benefits of integrating forgiveness into mindfulness training, or possibly integrating mindfulness or other forms of meditation into forgiveness training. Emerging understandings of relational mindfulness, or mindfulness applied to interpersonal dynamics, could be particularly useful for integration with forgiveness processes (Falb & Pargament, 2012).

Dialectical Behavior Therapy for Borderline Personality Disorder

Lynch and Cheavens (2007) integrated forgiveness skills training into standard DBT for the treatment of comorbid depression and personality disorders in older adults. Their focus is on the targeting rigid thinking that is often characteristic of the personality disorders commonly diagnosed in older adults. They contrasted "fixed mind" (closed to new perceptions) with "fluid mind." They described exercises in forgiveness training that are framed as part of practicing fluid mind and letting go of past suffering. The concept of fluid mind resonates with our emphasis on differentiation as a pathway toward forgiveness and growth. Although Lynch and Cheavens have not published empirical results, this type of inclusion of forgiveness skills into a mainstream empirically supported psychotherapy such as DBT is promising for clinical integration.

Forgiveness in Process-Oriented Group Therapy

Only one study has examined forgiveness in process-oriented group therapy. Wade and Meyer (2009) compared a 6-hour version of the REACH Forgiveness group intervention with a short-term adaptation of Yalom and Leszcz's (2005) group therapy model in community adults. The REACH intervention focused on developing forgiveness. The group therapy condition was nondirective and focused on relational process. The treatments were equally effective on forgiveness outcomes and reducing psychological symptoms.

Blocher and Wade (2010) conducted a 2-year follow-up on this study, using 16 of the original 28 participants. They found that the treatment effects in both conditions were maintained with no significant differences. Qualitative data suggested more positive comments about the REACH Forgiveness intervention, but there was also evidence that group process factors (e.g., universality of suffering or experiencing one is not alone in suffering) were relevant in both conditions. We hesitate to infer too much from this single study, but this suggests that both (a) relational dynamics and (b) learning specific coping or emotion regulation skills are important for therapeutic healing and growth.

It is possible that future research could show advantages for longer process-oriented group therapy with some clinical issues. Process group therapy could allow more time for transforming insecure attachment templates (Marmarosh & Tasca, 2013) and also for dealing with diversity within the group in ways that increase differentiation of self.

FORGIVENESS IN SPIRITUAL AND RELIGIOUS GROUPS

Forgiveness may or may not be facilitated within various spiritual and religious groups. The empirical research in this area is limited, but the few studies available yield some interesting findings.

How Forgiveness Might Occur in Small Religious Groups

Wuthnow (2000) conducted a nationally representative survey of adults ($N = 1,379$) in the United States who were involved in religious small groups. He wanted to learn specific elements of religious small groups that might be described as helpful for forgiving others, but he also wanted to test whether positive social connection ("social capital") might cause forgiveness. Wuthnow found that it was not basic social connection that fostered forgiveness. Rather, specific group processes were helpful. These included (a) praying and studying the Bible, (b) emotional processing of personal struggles,

(c) explicit discussion of forgiveness, (d) following a 12-step format, and (e) singing together. The last process, singing together, is the most surprising finding and hard to interpret, although singing in a religious small group might suggest a heightened level of group cohesion and intimacy or stronger limbic system activation. Overall, the findings suggest that it is not simply religious affiliation but authentic socioemotional processing and connection, spiritual practice, and explicit attention to forgiveness that were helpful for practicing forgiveness. These findings suggest aspects of securely attached relational spirituality as conducive to forgiveness.

Forgiveness and Relational Spirituality Within Identification With a Religious Community

Escher (2013) also conducted a sociological study on spiritual, religion, and forgiveness using data from a nationally representative sample ($N = 1,445$) from the 1998 General Social Survey. Neither religious activity nor religious affiliation predicted forgiveness; style of relational spirituality did. More specifically, Escher found a collaborative style of relating with God, believing God forgives, and carrying one's beliefs into other parts of life were each positively associated with forgiveness.

Escher (2013) also asked about religiosity at present and at age 16 and found religious switching did not affect forgiveness. However, those who were religious at 16 but no longer considered themselves religious were less likely to forgive. It is not possible to tell what factors might have led to reductions in religiosity and forgiveness or whether one caused the other. Unresolved interpersonal conflicts in religious communities may have motivated distancing from religion and might have harmed psychological well-being (Taylor, Chatters, & Levin, 2004).

Forgiveness in the Light of Identification With a Specific Religious Group

The practice of forgiveness is certainly possible without an attachment to a spiritual or religious community. But it may become more challenging to sustain a commitment to forgiving without some healthy community connections to provide rituals and teachings that support and narrate the meaning and virtue of forgiveness. This was MacIntyre's (1984) philosophical thesis: Namely, the practice of virtue requires communal traditions to provide a narrative envelope for sustaining virtuous practices. In fact, Greer, Worthington, Van Tongeren, et al. (2014) found that group identification with a congregation mediated the relationship between trait forgiveness and forgiveness of specific offenses among Christians. Kohut (1977) suggested that people need relational connections to ideals that inspire them and bring cohesion to the self. Furthermore, adulthood requires rebuilding ideals following disappointments and the critical awareness of imperfection in one's self and one's world.

Three Examples of Spiritual Communities Facilitating Forgiveness

Three examples from qualitative studies reveal differing ritualized ways spiritual communities can facilitate forgiveness. Each of these draws from a different culture.

Forgiving Multiple Traumatic Losses in a Jewish Yizkor Service

In a qualitative family case study (Sandage, 2010), I described a family system that experienced multiple tragic and traumatic losses. "Laura" was the lone adult survivor of her nuclear family after one sister died of cancer, her father enacted suicide, and her other sister killed herself after accidently killing her mother. Laura had gained some distance from some destructive patterns in her family of origin, in part, by marrying a Jewish man and converting from Protestantism to Judaism. Her conversion was not utilitarian as part of marriage but represented a carefully considered decision in seeking a "strong religion" that she sincerely believed in. She credited her Jewish faith as one of the central resources that helped her cope with such staggering losses, describing God as benevolent and a source of hope for eventual reunion with her siblings with whom she had been deeply attached. Laura also described forgiveness as instrumental to her healing, particularly forgiveness of her parents whose severe destructive patterns had wreaked havoc on the family system. It occurred within a Yizkor service, which is part of mourning in the Jewish tradition. She described crying beyond words but then somehow experiencing the caring presence of those around her at the service even though they did not know her specific losses. Turner (1969) described this type of spontaneous solidarity and existential togetherness as *communitas*. Combined with her supportive husband and a positive relationship with a psychotherapist, Laura credited these relational resources as central to her recovery and her ability to forgive her parents. The Yizkor service, in particular, is an example of how spiritual or religious communities can help with healing and forgiveness when there are opportunities to attach for emotional processing of grief and loss.

Forgiveness Through a Communal Ritual Among Hmong Americans

An example from fieldwork with Hmong Americans reveals the power of communal ritual process to facilitate forgiveness and relational spirituality (Sandage, Hill, & Vang, 2003). Pao was a Hmong American man who divorced his wife, Kasiab, following the loss of their daughter to a rare blood disease and some affairs on his part. Of cultural importance, Pao and Kasiab divorced without family or clan approval, which caused a shaming loss of face to both families.

Through couples therapy, Kasiab and Pao decided to reconcile. But reconciling is not a simple, dyadic process in the communal context of traditional Hmong culture. Pao wanted and needed to seek forgiveness from Kasiab's parents. So the couple planned a formal ceremony with their clans. Clan leaders helped them follow cultural procedures to publicly demonstrate forgiveness and reconciliation. In Hmong culture, forgiveness is not primarily a verbal process. Conflicts are mediated more indirectly through actions and symbolic gestures. A leader from Pao's clan sacrificed a chicken and a pig to appease any ancestors who may have been offended by the divorce. Pao also washed the faces of his mother- and father-in-law as a spiritual act to transform the loss of face. Like the one above, this case involved both couples therapy and communal spiritual practices to facilitate forgiveness.

Maoris in New Zealand Use Talk Within a Sacred Space to Forgive

A qualitative study (Rata, Liu, & Hanke, 2008) explored the indigenous forgiveness perspectives of Maori adults (the indigenous Polynesian people of New Zealand). One of the themes that emerged was *Rongo*, which is a Maori concept referring to a perceptual element resulting from the restored balance of forces in nature as conflicted parties commit to restoring peace. The restoration importantly uses the *marae*, which is a sacred Maori communal meeting house. It is typically decorated with carved wood. The groups meet there to resolve conflicts, but an important protocol is the physical separation of the two groups within the meeting house. The separation has symbolic meaning combined with the gathering of both groups in the *marae*. One participant explains, "So the two parties come together on the *marae* . . . there is always that space in between . . . and the talk will begin." After some reconciliation is forged through talking, mingling can occur in the *marae*. This not only is an intriguing depiction of differentiated relational processes in rituals of forgiveness but also invites consideration of the role of sacred places in facilitating group experiences of forgiveness.

SUMMARY

We have discussed psychoeducational groups, group process groups, and community interventions. For psychoeducational groups, leaders of different levels of interpersonal and group skills can have less dramatic effects on forgiveness experienced within the groups than in freer interacting group process groups. Although slavishly working through a treatment manual can damage any psychotherapeutic process, treatment manuals do level the field across psychoeducational group leaders—to some degree. With group therapy, however, the options for doing harm are greater, given the more fragile nature of the people in group therapy and less content focus relative to most psychoeducational groups.

We conclude by summarizing key recommendations for group forgiveness interventions:

1. Screen for trauma, abuse histories, and psychopathology to make sure the intervention is an appropriate fit for the client.
2. Use a theory-driven approach that has been tested empirically.
3. Select group facilitators who have solid relational capacities (e.g., empathy, differentiation) and can handle complex issues and questions that may arise.
4. Define forgiveness early. Differentiate forgiveness and related constructs.
5. If possible, provide a minimum of 6 to 8 hours of intervention. Be clear about expectations. Outline steps participants may take to make further progress in forgiveness beyond the group experience.
6. Be clear that forgiveness is a choice and a decision. This alleviates coercive effects and highlights expectation of differentiation. Inviting participants to consider the pros and cons of forgiveness is one effective way to move into this.
7. Clarify, compassionately, some of the self-protective motives that might inhibit forgiveness, as this can foster emotional intelligence and emotional regulation.
8. Use some group time to consider differing motivations for forgiveness to enable participants to learn from one another.
9. Seek to balance emotion processing and emotion regulation in group process. Encourage participants to develop a self-soothing practice they can use to self-regulate the anxiety of unforgiveness. If participants become severely dysregulated, provide referrals and resources.
10. Emphasize the personal benefits of forgiveness, at first, to foster self-interested motives for forgiving. But spend the bulk of time cultivating empathy, gratitude, and humility in promoting emotional forgiveness.
11. Attend to attachment dynamics in the group process and recognize that group members with higher levels of insecure attachment will find it more difficult to make efficient use of the group experience (Marmarosh & Tasca, 2013).

12. Value the potential for differentiation of self for group members that could occur through diversity awareness and the reality that spiritual and cultural traditions can understand forgiveness differently. Invite participants to reflect on their own values and traditions about forgiveness and to share this with the group if they are willing. At the start of the group, take as an aim, respecting others' views.

13. Be aware that therapists' own personal spiritual commitments have predicted their use of spiritual or religious interventions in group therapy (Cornish, Wade, & Knight, 2013). Those low in spiritual commitment might underestimate the benefits and relevance of such interventions, whereas those high in spiritual commitment might overestimate the same. Group therapists need to strive toward differentiated awareness of the group process and client diversity with the help of consultation and spiritual or religious training.

14. Consider developing and testing culturally or situationally specific forgiveness interventions for a particular population: for example, group intervention for Filipino Christians (Worthington, Hunter, et al., 2010), group intervention for Arab adolescents in Israel focusing on Arab–Jewish conflicts (Shechtman, Wade, & Khoury, 2009), and age-specific group intervention for older adults (Allemand, Steiner, & Hill, 2013).

15. Look for ways to integrate forgiveness skills into groups focused on coping with various forms of transition, because transitions (a) activate attachment templates and (b) can involve increased stress, anxiety, and interpersonal conflict.

16. Suggest books and other materials that can be used for further learning and psychological and spiritual practice.

AFTERWORD

LESSONS LEARNED AND SELF-FORGIVENESS

Through living in some healing relationships, using psychotherapy, and drawing on religious and spiritual resources, people have the capacity to transcend their pasts. They don't have to hold onto grudges. They don't have to stay locked into family-of-origin patterns. We bring our journey to an end by summarizing the main lessons we have learned in this book. Psychotherapy—short-term and long-term individual psychotherapy, couples therapy, family therapy, and group treatments—aims at similar things: changing clients' maladaptive relational templates. People usually seek help when they feel that they are in a chaotic, seeking frame of mind. As helpers, we invite them into a cauldron in which they can experience the intensifying heat of reconsidering basic aspects of their lives without having to fear that we, as helpers, will influence them in ways that are not in their best interests. Over the course of psychotherapeutic

http://dx.doi.org/10.1037/14712-013
Forgiveness and Spirituality in Psychotherapy: A Relational Approach, by E. L. Worthington, Jr. and S. J. Sandage

interactions, they renarrate their personal stories into redemptive narratives. In addition to these lessons learned, we consider a new topic here: self-forgiveness. Although this book focuses on helping clients forgive others (because usually the transgressor is someone other than the client), some clients may need to forgive themselves. We discuss how the REACH forgiveness model, described earlier in this book, can be adapted to promoting self-forgiveness in clients. Furthermore, we discuss how therapists can forgive themselves.

RENARRATING PERSONAL SCRIPTS

Every person is the hero of his or her story. So, let us talk about stories for a few minutes.

Remember, Maurice Sendak's (1963) *Where the Wild Things Are?* As I (Everett Worthington) read that book repeatedly to my four children at their request, I often wondered what was appealing to a child about a naughty boy who escapes to his room and dreams about horrid monsters who "rolled their terrible eyes and gnashed their terrible teeth." How did it win the Caldecott Medal (most distinguished American picture book for children)?

The story focuses on Max, who is disciplined by his mother, who calls him a "wild thing" because of his rampage through the house dressed in his wolf suit. Max is upset and angry with his mother, who is also upset with him. He finds that his room is transformed into a jungle from which he sails to an island where the (other) wild things live. Max cannot escape, but he tames the beasts and is crowned the king of the wild things. The wild things are even upset when he decides to return home. But back home, Max discovers his supper awaiting him—"and it was still hot."

Perhaps the story captures symbolically some of the greatest fears children have, but it does so in a way that enables children to triumph over the fears (Bettelheim, 2010). Max's relationship with his mother was threatened by his acting out. That placed him in a fearful crucible of anxiety. Facing those wild things was a fearful task. One might think, though, that Max was able to face them because of the resilient (Bonanno, Brewin, Kaniasty, & La Greca, 2010), secure attachment relationships. One might infer a secure attachment between Max and his mother in the story from his still-hot supper being provided even when he felt out-of-favor with her and disappointed that he has disappointed her (the story does not tell us specifically about Max's other attachment relationships). One might suspect that he felt unforgiveness for his mother and self-condemnation for his own "wild" behavior. And he feared that his mother's unforgiveness might not be mollified and he would be banished to a lonely jungle populated by wild things that had terrible roars and worse, terrible teeth. Max had violated the sacred relationship of child and mother. That desecration set him on a path of existential loneliness and abandonment. To restore not only the spiritual balance but also the familial balance, Max had to face his wild things—alone.

Had he been uncertain of his mother's ultimate love, Max might have been stuck for years fighting those wild things in his life. He might have needed a wise guide to get him out of the jungle and back to his room.

OUR ROLE IN THE JUNGLE

In this book, we have tried to provide a blueprint for how such a wise guide might help a person with an adult version of Max's dilemma. The person would have to negotiate the jungle, find a way to tame the wild things, and get back to his or her room where there is a possibility of finding that a warm dinner might be delivered in the future.

The psychotherapist is a courageous guide through the uncharted, pathless jungles that the client is trying to negotiate. It is a scary business, in which the client is in control and the psychotherapist is trying to use his or her experience in other patches of jungle, reading of research and theory that seeks to describe how most people pass through the jungle but might fail utterly to describe how any particular client traverses it. The client is also courageous, terrified yet moving forward in spite of the terror of the unknown. He or she is terrified that you, the psychotherapist, will either get the client even more hopelessly lost and determine that life is not redeemable or that the client is doomed to unhappiness. Or, worse, the client is terrified that you will start the journey and then abandon him or her to the beasts. As the psychotherapist, you work with the particular individual, and everyone's story is different.

As scientists and theoreticians about psychotherapy, we seek to describe our best guesses, on the basis of our experiences, study, and thought, about how most clients behave. We are like the novelist who tells a particular story but hopes to touch a vast number of people, or the artist who paints a particular picture but hopes most people will be transformed by it. We are like theologians who interpret religious texts and experiences but do so to help most—but not all—people. We are aware of these limitations—that we cannot help everyone with our theorizing and our generalizing about our clinical experience—just as you as psychotherapist are aware of your limitations at helping every client. Yet, we also are aware of our responsibility to help psychotherapists guide your clients. Because of our awareness of limitations and responsibilities, we recognize—as do you—that humility is required. And, in humility, we know that we fail too frequently. And we know that we need forgiveness for those failures. In humility, then, we have tried to proceed in the tasks set before us.

SUMMARIZING OUR APPROACH

We have drawn on several theories of basic research, clinical research, and clinical experience. We have sought to provide a knowledge base from which you can work as a psychotherapist who is conducting brief psychotherapy, long-term psychotherapy, couples therapy, or group psychotherapy. We also have attempted to tie those theories together.

At the most basic level, we began with a stress-and-coping theory of forgiveness (Worthington, 2006). It is stress and the inability to cope with it that usually catapult people into psychotherapy. For most people, those stresses arise from interpersonal relationships and the fallout from earlier interpersonal relationships, which have left their marks on their internal working models of relationship. Often, people are in a place of spiritual dwelling—with attachments, regardless of how tenuous—that are at least stable. Stress, and especially traumatic stress, can propel the person into a time of spiritual seeking. Spiritual coping that is conservative (Pargament, 1997) and attempts to simply restore the previous balance has usually come up short. The person then seeks to engage in transformational coping (Pargament, 1997), a journey into the jungle with no certainty that he or she will emerge psychologically intact.

Spiritual seeking is anxiety producing, and the tendency is to escape the anxiety and find a quick route home. But when that fails to adequately quell the anxiety, the person might enter psychotherapy. In that emotion-charged, trust-building, hope-promoting relationship, the person seeks to get relief. As Sheldon Kopp (1982) described, the person's attitude is fix me but don't change me.

FORGIVENESS TREATMENTS
ACROSS TREATMENT MODALITIES

But the wise psychotherapist realizes that the person must fight those wild things if he or she is to return safely to a new place where the mother has been displeased and yet, in the end of the story, she has provided hot supper. Those wild things are found in relationships, and basic attachment relationships are some of the most important of those. Of course, how people respond to the hurts, rejections, offenses, and injuries that set them on this journey will depend or the relationship between the people who hurt them, the meaning of the hurt or offense, and the meaning of the offense to the offender. But also it will depend on the relationship between the transgression and the sacred (i.e., was it a sacred desecration or sacred loss?) and the person's perception of the relationship between the offender and the sacred (i.e., is that person religiously or spiritually similar to or different from me?). But most of the action will be in the attachment relationship of the person to the sacred. That relationship might also be influenced by early or even recent attachment experiences with family-of-origin members or other attachment figures.

Brief or long-term psychotherapy, couples therapy, family therapy, and group therapy can provide a safe haven to use as a base to fight the wild things. In the process of helping the client, the psychotherapist provides a sense of pacing and leading to move the person to consider and challenge old ways of acting, thinking, and feeling. Confronting those wild things intensifies the anxiety. The psychotherapist provides a relational crucible that can contain the heat of the battle without itself participating in the reaction and imploding or exploding. The crucible of probing critical personal issues occurs as psychotherapist and client co-construct the crucible. In that crucible, relational templates from childhood are activated, which the client keeps interposing into the psychotherapeutic relationship. The psychotherapist does not participate in the emotionality of the templates operating in important issues. Rather, the psychotherapist helps the person balance processing the meaning of the emotions with the regulation of the emotions. As the person changes into someone who is better able to act as a differentiated, mature adult, a sense of things lost occurs. Those losses must be grieved. Disappointments must be processed. Then differentiation can be enacted more consistently in more situations, which builds hope.

Forgiveness might be virtually always desirable (although we hasten to remind you that reconciliation is not always possible, prudent, or wise), but for many forgiveness will not always be possible. The wounds are too deep. The wounders are too toxic. They keep inflicting worse and worse wounds. But within the context of the person's attachment schemas and religious and spiritual commitments, the person must be helped to stay in the crucible as long as he or she can keep working productively, develop emotional regulation to sustain the work, emotionally process the issues in the present and past, cultivate a more differentiated sense of self, reprogram the basic relational templates from the past, and seek to formulate more adaptive living strategies.

SELF-FORGIVENESS

Helping Clients Forgive Themselves

As we noted briefly in the Introduction to this book, the REACH Forgiveness model has also been adapted to dealing with self-condemnation (see Worthington, n.d.). Self-condemnation can be a barrier to forgiving, reconciling, and experiencing personal well-being. Sometimes, when it is providing an obstacle to progress in psychotherapy, the psychotherapist must seek to promote self-forgiveness. As with transgressions, there are many legitimate and psychologically healthy ways to deal with self-condemnation, guilt, shame, remorse, and regret. Self-forgiveness is one effective way. One danger is trying to rush into self-forgiveness without responsibly dealing with one's own wrongdoing or one's failed expectations or failure to live up to one's moral standards. Rushing into self-forgiveness before such responsible actions has been called *pseudo–self-forgiveness*, but might better be termed *premature self-forgiveness*. Regardless of what it is called, it can impair clients' psychological development.

Responsible self-forgiveness involves six steps. These were first described as a whole treatment package in *Moving Forward: Six Steps to Forgiving Yourself and Breaking Free From the Past* (Worthington, 2013):

1. Restore a right relationship with humanity, nature, or God. This includes making things right with whatever one calls sacred— God or something nondeistic. Thus, this might be seeing one's regretted wrongdoing as a crime against humanity or against nature. One would try to do whatever is necessary to make amends in regards to the sacred.

2. Repair relationships. This is necessary because wrongdoing and even failing to live up to one's own standards usually hurt or disappoint others.

3. Rework one's unrealistic standards and reduce rumination (obsessing self-condemning thoughts and feelings). The client must consider the unrealistic nature of expectations and personal standards and try to make those more realistic. The client also must deal with negative rumination.

4. Use the REACH forgiveness steps toward forgiving the self (see above). The model is applied to clients' self-condemnation rather than to the unforgiveness of an offender.

5. Seek to accept oneself as being less perfect than one had previously felt. Often wrongdoing or failure to meet personal standards creates a loss of self-esteem and an inability to accept oneself. Rebuilding self-acceptance can be the longest step.

6. Seek not to fail in the same way again. Clients are helped to plan ways to avoid repeating wrongdoing or falling back into self-blaming patterns associated with unrealistic expectations or personal standards.

Psychotherapists' Own Forgiveness

We have mentioned the importance of managing and metabolizing one's own countertransference, especially in working with clients with insecure attachment styles. In our opinion, psychotherapists' own professional attachments and relational supports are an under-rated clinical issue. There are ethical guidelines in all the mental health professions that clinicians should seek consultation when necessary, but it is harder to find a theoretical discussion of how clinicians can create a consistent professional holding environment that enhances their own security of attachment and differentiation of self.

It may seem odd to speak of psychotherapists needing to get help in forgiving clients because even a temporary lack of forgiveness toward a client can seem too personal and highly reactive. And yet it is natural for the relational process of psychotherapy, particularly with long-term clients, to provoke various reactions in psychotherapists that can include elements of unforgiveness—anger, vengefulness, and internal avoidance or emotional cutoff. Psychotherapists serve as containers of clients' projections, and the psychotherapy process enacts various kinds of relational struggles.

In addition to wise self-care practices, we suggest that clinicians can benefit from regular participation in small consultation groups that invite support, differentiation, and mentalization related to psychotherapy. Many agencies have a clinical staff meeting at which cases get presented, but those meetings may be too large or the relational dynamics too formal to process countertransference in mentalization-based ways. The humility of mentalization described above is deeply necessary for those of us who are clinicians so we can remain differentiated in our responses to clients and sufficiently attached and supported to buffer the risk of burnout or vicarious trauma. Linehan (1993) set the wise policy that dialectical behavior therapy therapists need to be in regular consultation groups to work with clients meeting criteria for borderline personality disorder. We extend this: We believe this is a wise practice for all clinicians who conduct long-term psychotherapy

I (Steve Sandage) have been in a regular consultation group with three other psychotherapists for many years. The continuity of those relationships has not only been a great support but also has provided a context for more differentiated knowing of one another's clinical work. For example, during a recent consultation group, one member said, "I feel so frustrated with this couple that I just feel like telling them to. . . ." Another said, "I know I am sensitive to domineering males, given my older brother, so I want to factor that into how I relate to this client." These showed admirable differentiation and self-insight while allowing emotion processing and regulation.

And one said to me, "Steve, you don't usually get this agitated about a case. What do you think is provoking you so much about this couple?" This reflects the value of a differentiated relational dynamic. The group was not only supportive but also willing to offer me candid feedback and invite healthy self-confrontation that I might miss on my own. I almost always leave these meetings feeling more hopeful about doing clinical work.

We have a lot of data on how relational dynamics affect outcomes in psychotherapy but little or no data on how relational support and consultation for psychotherapists might impact outcomes. It seems like a reasonable hypothesis that this kind of securely attached and differentiated professional holding environment for psychotherapists would help metabolize emotional reactions to clients and thereby indirectly enhance the quality of psychotherapy.

YOUR ROLE AND QUALITIES AS A PSYCHOTHERAPIST

The psychotherapist is not like a Wizard of Oz, who sends Dorothy, the Scarecrow, the Tin Woodman, and the Cowardly Lion out on their own to slay the Wicked Witch. The psychotherapist is a differentiated Wizard who walks with the adventurers, on their level. This Wizard does not attempt to rescue them, fight the battles for them, or lead the hasty retreat. Rather, he or she hangs in there providing a sense of complex hope, encouragement, and gentle and timely leading through the forest.

This requires courage and insight. It requires a differentiated self that can handle ambiguity, contradiction, attack by the client whom the psychotherapist is trying to help, sensitivity, and the ability to pace treatment and to lead—at the proper moment—toward change. But more, it requires enough sense of humility and community that the psychotherapist sees himself or herself not as a vulnerable human who has his or her own struggles but is able to lay them aside to help someone who is needy. And it even requires of the psychotherapist the skill and grace to forgive others and himself or herself and to deal successfully with his or her own wanderings spiritually.

This is a noble calling for the psychotherapist. It is a calling to be part of the relational world of the clients and to help reconnect clients with the important figures in their lives and to support them in gaining the learning, wisdom, and maturity they need to succeed at getting back home once again. Yet this calling also is a great challenge. It challenges one's spirituality and one's competence. It challenges one's pride and one's humility. We hope that throughout this book, we have helped you develop more of your knowledge and capabilities, and even more, your character, to be able to deal effectively with the clients that come across your path. We hope you have more hope as you courageously guide your patients through the terrifying jungles filled with wild things.

APPENDIX: MEASURES TO ASSESS ASPECTS OF THE VICTIM–SACRED AND (VICTIM'S PERCEPTION OF) THE OFFENDER–SACRED RELATIONSHIP

ASSESSING THE VICTIM–SACRED RELATIONSHIP

Dedication to the Sacred (DS; D. E. Davis, Worthington, Hook, & Van Tongeren, 2009)

Five Items, from 1 (*strongly disagree*) to 7 (*strongly agree*)

1. My relationship with the sacred is more important to me than almost anything else in my life.
2. I want my relationship with the sacred to stay strong no matter what rough times I may encounter.
3. I like to think of the sacred and me more in terms of "us" and "we" than "me" and "him/her/it."
4. My relationship with the sacred is clearly part of my future life plans.
5. It makes me feel good to sacrifice for the sacred.

Norm group: 506 college students. Score range = 5–35; $M = 23.13$, $SD = 9.13$ (2/3 of all scores fall between 14 and 32). Christians scored higher ($M = 24.76$, $SD = 7.25$) than did those who were atheist/nonreligious ($M = 14.11$, $SD = 8.48$) and other religions ($M = 20.36$, $SD = 7.34$) ($ps < .01$). DS scores did not differ by gender or by ethnicity. Validity: Correlated with Religious Commitment Inventory—10 (RCI–10; Worthington et al., 2003) and forgiveness of a transgression but not the Similarity of the Offender's Spirituality Scale (SOS; D. E. Davis, Worthington, Hook, Van Tongeren, Green, & Jennings, 2009) or Sacred Loss and Desecration Scale (SLDS; Pargament, Magyar, Benore, & Mahoney, 2005).

Note. You have explicit permission to use these measures for clinical assessment or research.

Spiritual Humility Scale (D. E. Davis, Hook, Worthington, Van Tongeren, Gartner, & Jennings, 2010)

Four items (4), from 1 (*completely disagree*) to 5 (*completely agree*)

1. He/she accepts his/her place in relation to the sacred.
2. He/she is comfortable with his/her place in relation to the sacred.
3. He/she is humble before the sacred.
4. He/she knows his/her place in relation to nature.

Norm group: 506 college students. Score range = 4–20; M = 11.26, SD = 4.01 (2/3 of all scores fall between 7 and 15). Validity: Not correlated with RCI–10. Correlated with similarity to the offender, relational humility and trait gratitude; negatively correlated with unforgiveness of a transgression but not the SOS or SLDS.

Attitudes Toward God Scale—9 (Wood, Worthington, Exline, Yali, Aten, & McMinn, 2010)

Nine items reflecting the degree to which you currently do or feel the following about God (or whatever you call the Sacred) from 0 (*not at all*) to 10 (*extremely*)

1. I trust God to protect and care for me.
2. **I feel angry at God.**
3. **I feel that God has let me down.**
4. **I view God as unkind.**
5. I view God as all-powerful and all-knowing.
6. I feel loved by God.
7. I feel supported by God.
8. I feel nurtured or cared for by God.
9. **I feel abandoned by God.**

Note. Items in regular font compose the Positive Attitudes toward God subscale. Items in bold comprise the Disappointment and Anger With God subscale.

Norm Group: Six studies (2,992 total participants, mostly college students). Two subscales: (a) Positive Attitudes Toward God (M = 42.6; SD 11.1, five items) and (b) Disappointment and Anger With God (M = 7.3, SD = 5.8, four items). Subscale scores showed good estimated internal consistency, 2-week temporal stability, and evidence for construct and discriminant validity. Positive Attitudes Toward God correlated with measures of religiosity and conscientiousness. Women scored higher than men. Protestants scored higher than Catholics. Disappointment and Anger With God correlated with negative religious coping, lower religious participation, more distress, higher neuroticism, and entitlement. Women scored lower than men. Protestants scored lower than Catholics.

ASSESSING THE VICTIM–OTHER RELATIONSHIP

Relational Engagement of the Spiritual for a Transgression (D. E. Davis, Hook, Worthington, Van Tongeren, Gartner, Jennings, & Norton, 2010)

Four items, from 0 (*completely disagree*) to 6 (*completely agree*)

1. I tried to view him/her as a child of God.
2. I tried to pray for him/her.
3. I asked God to help me see his/her good points.
4. I believe God wants us to mend our relationship.

Norm group: Three studies of about 700 total undergraduates. Score range = 0 to 24; $M = 18.01$, $SD = 8.82$ (2/3 of participants score between 9 and 24). Scores differed by gender, women ($M = 12.35$, $SD = 7.40$) > men ($M = 9.31$, $SD = 6.31$). Scores differed by ethnicity, with Asian/Pacific Islander ($M = 10.55$, $SD = 5.46$) and Caucasian/White ($M = 9.08$, $SD = 7.08$) scores lower than African American/Black ($M = 15.44$, $SD = 5.61$). Scores differed on the basis of religious affiliation, with Christians' scores ($M = 13.80$, $SD = 6.13$) higher than those of other religious affiliations ($M = 6.88$, $SD = 5.61$) and atheists or those with no religious affiliation ($M = 5.00$, $SD = 5.86$).

Similarity of the Offender's Spirituality (D. E. Davis, Worthington, Hook, Van Tongeren, Green, & Jennings, 2009)

Nine items, from 0 (*completely disagree*) to 6 (*completely agree*)
Spiritual Similarity (SS) subscale

1. Our beliefs overlap in important ways.
2. I thought about how similar my basic religious beliefs were to his/hers.
3. I thought we are basically committed to the same belief system.
4. I recalled how similar we were in fundamental values.
5. I believe that he/she is a similar spiritual person to me.

Human Similarity (HS) subscale

6. I thought to myself that this person was a brother/sister human.
7. Even though our bond as humans was broken, I knew we were both the same under the skin.

8. I reminded myself that I was no better as a person than the one who hurt me.
9. I said to myself that he/she was no worse as a person than I am.

Norm group: Two studies of 200 and 182 undergraduates. Score range of SS = 0 to 30. SS $M = 16.24$, $SD = 8.15$ (2/3 of participants score between 8 and 30). Score range of HS = 0 to 24. HS, $M = 13.25$, $SD = 6.35$ (2/3 of participants score between 6 and 20). In the second study, people were randomly assigned to recall a hurt by one spiritually similar or different from themselves. On the SS subscale, means for the similar condition were greater ($M = 19.0$, $SD = 6.9$) than for the different condition ($M = 13.4$, $SD = 8.3$). On the HS subscale, means were not different. In the similar condition, there was less unforgiving revenge and avoidance motivation, but there was no difference in benevolence motivation.

REFERENCES

Akhtar, S. (2002). Forgiveness: Origins, dynamics, psychopathology, and technical relevance. *The Psychoanalytic Quarterly, 71*, 175–212. http://dx.doi.org/10.1002/j.2167-4086.2002.tb00010.x

Albright, C. R. (2006). Spiritual growth, cognition, complexity: Faith as a dynamic process. In J. D. Koss-Choino & P. Hefner (Eds.), *Spiritual transformation and healing: Anthropological, theological, neuroscientific, and clinical perspectives* (pp. 168–186). Lanham, MD: AltaMira.

al-Haddad, I. (2010). *Counsels of religion* (M. al-Badawi, Trans.). Louisville, KY: Fons Vitae.

Allemand, M., Steiner, M., & Hill, P. L. (2013). Effects of a forgiveness intervention for older adults. *Journal of Counseling Psychology, 60*, 279–286. http://dx.doi.org/10.1037/a0031839

Allen, J. G., Fonagy, P., & Bateman, A. W. (2008). *Mentalizing in clinical practice*. Washington, DC: American Psychiatric Publishing.

American Psychiatric Association. (2013). *Diagnostic and statistical manual of mental disorders* (5th ed.). Arlington, VA: Author.

American Psychological Association Presidential Task Force on Evidence-Based Practice. (2006). Evidence-based practice in psychology. *American Psychologist, 61*, 271–285. http://dx.doi.org/10.1037/0003-066X.61.4.271

Aten, J. D., & Leach, M. M. (2009). (Eds.). *Spirituality and the therapeutic process: A comprehensive resource from intake to termination*. Washington, DC: American Psychological Association.

Aten, J. D., McMinn, M. R., & Worthington, E. L., Jr., (Eds.). (2011). *Spiritually oriented interventions for counseling and psychotherapy*. Washington, DC: American Psychological Association. http://dx.doi.org/10.1037/12313-000

Aten, J. D., O'Grady, K. D., & Worthington, E. L., Jr., (Eds.). (2012). *The psychology of religion and spirituality for clinicians: Using research in your practice*. New York, NY: Brunner-Routledge.

Augsburger, D. W. (1996). *Helping people forgive*. Louisville, KY: Westminster John Knox Press.

Azari, N. P., Missimer, J., & Seitz, R. J. (2005). Religious experience and emotion: Evidence for distinctive cognitive neural patterns. *The International Journal for the Psychology of Religion, 15*, 263–281. http://dx.doi.org/10.1207/s15327582ijpr1504_1

Banai, E., Mikulincer, M., & Shaver, P. R. (2005). "Self–object" needs in Kohut's self psychology. *Psychoanalytic Psychology, 22*, 224–260. http://dx.doi.org/10.1037/0736-9735.22.2.224

Bartholomew, K., & Horowitz, L. M. (1991). Attachment styles among young adults: A test of a four-category model. *Journal of Personality and Social Psychology, 61*, 226–244. http://dx.doi.org/10.1037/0022-3514.61.2.226

Baskin, T. W., & Enright, R. D. (2004). Intervention studies in forgiveness: A meta-analysis. *Journal of Counseling & Development, 82,* 79–90. http://dx.doi.org/10.1002/j.1556-6678.2004.tb00288.x

Bateman, A. W., & Fonagy, P. (2004). *Psychotherapy for borderline personality disorder: Mentalization based treatment.* Oxford, England: Oxford University Press.

Bateman, A. W., & Fonagy, P. (2006). *Mentalization-based treatment for borderline personality disorder: A practical guide.* Oxford, England: Oxford University Press. http://dx.doi.org/10.1093/med/9780198570905.001.0001

Batson, C. D., Schoenrade, P., & Ventis, W. L. (1993). *Religion and the individual.* New York: Oxford University Press.

Baucom, D. H., Snyder, D. K., & Gordon, K. C. (2011). *Helping couples get past the affair: A clinician's guide.* New York, NY: Guilford Press.

Beck, A. T., & Steer, R. A. (1993). *BDI: Beck Depression Inventory.* New York, NY: Psychological Corporation.

Beck, R. (2006). God as a secure base: Attachment to God and theological exploration. *Journal of Psychology and Theology, 34,* 125–132.

Beck, R., & Jessup, R. K. (2004). The multidimensional nature of quest motivation. *Journal of Psychology and Theology, 32,* 283–294.

Benjamin, L. S. (1996). *Interpersonal diagnosis and treatment of personality disorders.* New York, NY: Guilford Press.

Benjamin, L. S. (2003). *Interpersonal reconstructive therapy: Promoting change in nonresponders.* New York, NY: Guilford Press.

Berger, P. L., Sacks, J., Martin, D., Weiming, T., Weigel, G., Davie, G., & An-Naim, A. A. (Eds.). (1999). *The desecularization of the world: Resurgent religion and world politics.* Washington, DC, and Grand Rapids, MI: Ethics and Public Policy Center and William B. Eerdmans.

Bernecker, S. L., Levy, K. N., & Ellison, W. D. (2014). A meta-analysis of the relation between patient adult attachment style and the working alliance. *Psychotherapy Research, 24,* 12–24. http://dx.doi.org/10.1080/10503307.2013.809561

Berry, J. W., & Worthington, E. L., Jr. (2001). Forgiveness, relationship quality, stress while imagining relationship events, and physical and mental health. *Journal of Counseling Psychology, 48,* 447–455.

Berry, J. W., Worthington, E. L., O'Connor, L. E., Parrott, L. III, & Wade, N. G. (2005). Forgivingness, vengeful rumination, and affective traits. *Journal of Personality, 73,* 1–43.

Besser, A., & Zeigler-Hill, V. (2010). The influence of pathological narcissism on emotional and motivational responses to negative events: The roles of visibility and concern about humiliation. *Journal of Research in Personality, 44,* 520–534. http://dx.doi.org/10.1016/j.jrp.2010.06.006

Bettelheim, B. (2010). *The uses of enchantment: The meaning and importance of fairy tales.* New York, NY: Vintage.

Bland, E. D., & Strawn, B. D. (Eds.). (2014). *Christianity & psychoanalysis: A new conversation.* Downers Grove, IL: InterVarsity Press.

Blocher, W. G., & Wade, N. G. (2010). Sustained effectiveness of two brief group interventions: Comparing an explicit forgiveness-promoting treatment with a process-oriented treatment. *Journal of Mental Health Counseling, 32,* 58–74.

Bonanno, G. A. (2005). Resilience in the face of loss and potential trauma. *Current Directions in Psychological Science, 14,* 135–138. http://dx.doi.org/10.1111/j.0963-7214.2005.00347.x

Bonanno, G. A., Brewin, C. R., Kaniasty, K., & La Greca, A. M. (2010). Weighing the costs of disaster: Consequences, risks, and resilience in individuals, families, and communities. *Psychological Science in the Public Interest, 11,* 1–49. http://dx.doi.org/10.1177/1529100610387086

Borkovec, T. D., Newman, M. G., Pincus, A. L., & Lytle, R. (2002). A component analysis of cognitive-behavioral therapy for generalized anxiety disorder and the role of interpersonal problems. *Journal of Consulting and Clinical Psychology, 70,* 288–298. http://dx.doi.org/10.1037/0022-006X.70.2.288

Boss, P. (1999). *Ambiguous loss: Learning to live with unresolved grief.* Cambridge, MA: Harvard University Press.

Boswell, J. F., Castonguay, L. G., & Wasserman, R. H. (2010). Effects of psychotherapy training and intervention use on session outcome. *Journal of Consulting and Clinical Psychology, 78,* 717–723. http://dx.doi.org/10.1037/a0020088

Boszormenyi-Nagy, I. (1984). *Invisible loyalties: Reciprocity in intergenerational family therapy.* New York, NY: Brunner-Mazel.

Bowen, M. (1985). *Family therapy in clinical practice.* New York, NY: Jason Aronson.

Bowlby, J. (1980). *Attachment and loss: Vol. 3. Loss, sadness, and depression.* New York, NY: Basic Books.

Bowlby, J. (1982). *Attachment and loss: Vol. 1. Attachment* (2nd ed.). New York, NY: Basic Books. (Original work published 1969)

Bowlby, J. (1988). *A secure base: Parent child attachment and healthy human development* New York, NY: Basic Books.

Brieger, P., Sommer, S., Blöink, F., & Marneros, A. A. (2000). The relationship between five-factor personality measurements and *ICD–10* personality disorder dimensions: Results from a sample of 229 subjects. *Journal of Personality Disorders, 14,* 282–290. http://dx.doi.org/10.1521/pedi.2000.14.3.282

Bromberg, P. M. (2011). *The shadow of the tsunami and the growth of the relational mind.* New York, NY: Routledge.

Brown, W. S., & Strawn, B. D. (2012). *The physical nature of Christian life: Neuroscience, psychology, and the church.* Cambridge, England: Cambridge University Press. http://dx.doi.org/10.1017/CBO9781139015134

Bryant-Davis, T., & Wong, E. C. (2013). Faith to move mountains: Religious coping, spirituality, and interpersonal trauma recovery. *American Psychologist, 68,* 675–684. http://dx.doi.org/10.1037/a0034380

Budden, A. (2009). The role of shame in posttraumatic stress disorder: A proposal for a socio-emotional model for *DSM–V. Social Science & Medicine, 69,* 1032–1039.

Burchard, G. A., Yarhouse, M. A., Kilian, M. K., Worthington, E. L., Jr., Berry, J. W., & Canter, D. E. (2003). A study of two marital enrichment programs and couples' quality of life. *Journal of Psychology & Theology, 31*, 240–252.

Burnette, J. L., Davis, D. E., Green, J. D., Worthington, E. L., Jr., & Bradfield, E. (2009). Insecure attachment and depressive symptoms: The mediating role of rumination, empathy and forgiveness. *Personality and Individual Differences, 46*, 276–280. http://dx.doi.org/10.1016/j.paid.2008.10.016

Burnette, J. L., McCullough, M. E., Van Tongeren, D. R., & Davis, D. E. (2012). Forgiveness results from integrating information about relationship value and exploitation risk. *Personality and Social Psychology Bulletin, 38*, 345–356. http://dx.doi.org/10.1177/0146167211424582

Burnette, J. L., Taylor, K. W., Worthington, E. L., Jr., & Forsyth, D. (2007). Attachment and trait forgivingness: The mediating role of angry rumination. *Personality and Individual Differences, 42*, 1585–1596. http://dx.doi.org/10.1016/j.paid.2006.10.033

Byrd, K. R., & Boe, A. (2001). The correspondence between attachment dimensions and prayer in college students. *The International Journal for the Psychology of Religion, 11*, 9–24. http://dx.doi.org/10.1207/S15327582IJPR1101_02

Campana, K. (2010). *Self-forgiveness interventions for women experiencing break-up.* Unpublished dissertation, Virginia Commonwealth University, Richmond.

Cashwell, C. S., Bentley, D. P., & Yarborough, P. (2007). The only way out is through: The peril of spiritual bypass. *Counseling and Values, 51*, 139–148. http://dx.doi.org/10.1002/j.2161-007X.2007.tb00071.x

Castonguay, L. G. (2013). Psychotherapy outcome: An issue worth re-revisiting 50 years later. *Psychotherapy, 50*, 52–67. http://dx.doi.org/10.1037/a0030898

Chacour, E. (2000, September). *Forgiveness.* Paper presented at the State of the World Forum, New York, NY.

Chacour, E., & Hazard, D. (1984). *Blood brothers: A Palestinian struggles for reconciliation in the Middle East.* Grand Rapids, MI: Chosen Books.

Christakis, N. A., & Fowler, J. H. (2009). *Connected: The surprising power of our social networks and how they shape our lives.* New York, NY: Little, Brown.

Cloud, H., & Townsend, J. (1992). *Boundaries: When to say yes, how to say no to take control of your life.* Grand Rapids, MI: Zondervan.

Cooper, S. H. (2000). *Objects of hope: Exploring possibility and limit in psychoanalysis.* Hillsdale, NJ: The Analytic Press.

Cornish, M. A., Wade, N. G., & Knight, M. A. (2013). Understanding group therapists' use of spiritual and religious interventions in group therapy. *International Journal of Group Psychotherapy, 63*, 572–591. http://dx.doi.org/10.1521/ijgp.2013.63.4.572

Costa, P. T., Jr., & McCrae, R. R. (1992). *Revised NEO Personality Inventory and NEO Five-Factor Inventory professional manual.* Odessa, FL: Psychological Assessment Resources.

Coyle, C. T., & Enright, R. D. (1997). Forgiveness intervention with postabortion men. *Journal of Consulting and Clinical Psychology, 65*, 1042–1046. http://dx.doi.org/10.1037/0022-006X.65.6.1042

Cozolino, L. (2006). *The neuroscience of human relationships: Attachment and the developing social brain*. New York, NY: Norton.

Davis, D. E., Hook, J. N., Van Tongeren, D. R., Gartner, A. L., & Worthington, E. L., Jr. (2012). Can religion promote virtue? A more stringent test of the model of relational spirituality and forgiveness. *The International Journal for the Psychology of Religion, 22*, 252–266. http://dx.doi.org/10.1080/10508619.2011.646229

Davis, D. E., Hook, J. N., Van Tongeren, D. R., & Worthington, E. L., Jr. (2012). Sanctification of forgiveness. *Psychology of Religion and Spirituality, 4*, 31–39. http://dx.doi.org/10.1037/a0025803

Davis, D. E., Hook, J. N., & Worthington, E. L., Jr. (2008). Relational spirituality and forgiveness: The roles of attachment to God, religious coping, and viewing the transgression as a desecration. *Journal of Psychology and Christianity, 27*, 293–301.

Davis, D. E., Hook, J. N., Worthington, E. L., Jr., Van Tongeren, D. R., Gartner, A. L., & Jennings, D. J., II. (2010). Relational spirituality and forgiveness: Development of the Spiritual Humility Scale (SHS). *Journal of Psychology and Theology, 38,* 91–100.

Davis, D. E., Hook, J. N., Worthington, E. L., Jr., Van Tongeren, D. R., Gartner, A. L., Jennings, D. J., II, & Emmons, R. A. (2011). Relational humility: Conceptualizing and measuring humility as a personality judgment. *Journal of Personality Assessment, 93*, 225–234. http://dx.doi.org/10.1080/00223891.2011.558871

Davis, D. E., Hook, J. N., Worthington, E. L., Jr., Van Tongeren, D. R., Gartner, A. L., Jennings, D. J., II, & Norton, L. (2010). Relational spirituality and dealing with transgressions: The development of the Relational Engagement of the Sacred for a Transgression (REST) scale. *The International Journal for the Psychology of Religion, 20*, 288–302. http://dx.doi.org/10.1080/10508619.2010.507699

Davis, D. E., Worthington, E. L., Jr., & Hook, J. N. (2010). Humility: Review of measurement strategies and conceptualization as personality judgment. *The Journal of Positive Psychology, 5*, 243–252. http://dx.doi.org/10.1080/17439761003791672

Davis, D. E., Worthington, E. L., Jr., Hook, J. N., Emmons, R. A., Hill, P. C., & Burnette, J. L. (2013). Humility and the development and repair of social bonds: Two longitudinal studies. *Self and Identity, 12*, 58–77.

Davis, D. E., Worthington, E. L., Jr., Hook, J. N., & Hill, P. C. (2013). Research on religion/spirituality and forgiveness: A meta-analytic review. *Psychology of Religion and Spirituality, 5*, 233–241. http://dx.doi.org/10.1037/a0033637

Davis, D. E., Worthington, E. L., Jr., Hook, J. N., & Van Tongeren, D. R. (2009). The Dedication to the Sacred (DS) Scale: Adapting a marriage measure to study relational spirituality. *Journal of Psychology and Theology, 37*, 265–275.

Davis, D. E., Worthington, E. L., Jr., Hook, J. N., Van Tongeren, D. R., Green, J. D., & Jennings, D. J., II. (2009). Relational spirituality and the development of the Similarity of the Offender's Spirituality (SOS) Scale. *Psychology of Religion and Spirituality, 1*, 249–262. http://dx.doi.org/10.1037/a0017581

Davis, E. B., Moriarty, G. L., & Mauch, J. C. (2013). God images and god concepts: Definitions, development, and dynamics. *Psychology of Religion and Spirituality, 5*, 51–60. http://dx.doi.org/10.1037/a0029289

Dekel, R. (2010). Couple forgiveness, self-differentiation and secondary traumatization among wives of former POWs. *Journal of Social and Personal Relationships, 27*, 924–937. http://dx.doi.org/10.1177/0265407510377216

Delaney, H. D., Miller, W. R., & Bisonó, A. M. (2007). Religiosity and spirituality among psychologists: A survey of clinician members of the American Psychological Association. *Professional Psychology: Research and Practice, 38*, 538–546. http://dx.doi.org/10.1037/0735-7028.38.5.538

de Reus, R. J. M., & Emmelkamp, P. M. G. (2012). Obsessive-compulsive personality disorder: A review of current empirical findings. *Personality and Mental Health, 6*, 1–21. http://dx.doi.org/10.1002/pmh.144

de Shazer, S. (1985). *Keys to solution in brief therapy*. New York, NY: Norton.

de Shazer, S. (1988). *Clues: Investigating solutions in brief therapy*. New York, NY: Norton.

Diamond, L. M., & Hicks, A. M. (2004). Psychobiological perspectives on attachment: Implications for health over the lifespan. In W. S. Rholes & J. A. Simpson (Eds.), *Adult attachment: Theory, research, and clinical implications* (pp. 240–263). New York, NY: Guilford Press.

DiBlasio, F. A. (1998). The use of decision-based forgiveness intervention within intergenerational family therapy. *Journal of Family Therapy, 20*, 77–96. http://dx.doi.org/10.1111/1467-6427.00069

DiBlasio, F. A., & Proctor, J. H. (1993). Therapists and the clinical use of forgiveness. *The American Journal of Family Therapy, 21*, 175–184. http://dx.doi.org/10.1080/01926189308250915

Diener, M. J., & Monroe, J. M. (2011). The relationship between adult attachment style and therapeutic alliance in individual psychotherapy: A meta-analytic review. *Psychotherapy, 48*, 237–248. http://dx.doi.org/10.1037/a0022425

Doblmeier, M. (Director). (2008). *The power of forgiving*. Washington, DC: Journey Films. Available from http://www.journeyfilms.com

Doehring, C. (1993). *Internal desecration: Traumatization and representations of God*. Lanham, MD: University Press of America.

Dueck, A., & Reimer, K. (2009). *A peaceable psychology: Christian therapy in a world of many cultures*. Grand Rapids, MI: Brazos Press.

Duvall, N. D. (2000, October). *Unconscious theology and spirituality*. Paper presented at the Institute for Spiritual Formation, Biola University, La Mirada, CA.

Easwaran, E. (1991). *Meditation: A simple eight-point program for translating spiritual ideals into daily life* (2nd ed.). Tomales, CA: Nilgiri Press.

Eaton, J., Struthers, C. W., & Santelli, A. G. (2006). The mediating role of perceptual validation in the repentance-forgiveness process. *Personality and Social Psychology Bulletin, 32*, 1389–1401. http://dx.doi.org/10.1177/0146167206291005

Edwards, K. J., & Hall, T. W. (2003). Illusory spiritual health: The role of defensiveness in understanding and assessing spiritual health. In T. W. Hall & M. R. McMinn (Eds.), *Spiritual formation, counseling, and psychotherapy* (pp. 261–275). New York, NY: Nova Science.

Ein-Dor, T., Mikulincer, M., & Shaver, P. R. (2011). Effective reaction to danger: Attachment insecurities predict behavioural reactions to an experimentally induced threat above and beyond general personality traits. *Social Psychological and Personality Science, 2*, 467–473.

Ellison, C. W. (1994). *Spiritual Well-Being Scale*. Nyack, NY: Life Advance.

Emmons, R. A., & McCullough, M. E. (2003). Counting blessings versus burdens: An experimental investigation of gratitude and subjective well-being in daily life. *Journal of Personality and Social Psychology, 84*, 377–389. http://dx.doi.org/10.1037/0022-3514.84.2.377

Emmons, R. A., & McCullough, M. E. (Eds.). (2004). *The psychology of gratitude*. New York, NY: Oxford University Press. http://dx.doi.org/10.1093/acprof:oso/9780195150100.001.0001

Enright, R. D. (2012). *The forgiving life: A pathway of overcoming resentment and creating a legacy of love*. Washington, DC: American Psychological Association.

Enright, R. D., & Fitzgibbons, R. P. (2000). *Helping clients forgive: An empirical guide for resolving anger and restoring hope*. Washington, DC: American Psychological Association. http://dx.doi.org/10.1037/10381-000

Enright, R. D., & Fitzgibbons, R. P. (2014). *Helping clients forgive: An empirical guide for resolving anger and restoring hope* (2nd ed.). Washington, DC: American Psychological Association.

Enright, R. D., & The Human Development Study Group. (1996). Counseling within the forgiveness triad: On forgiving, receiving forgiveness, and self-forgiveness. *Counseling and Values, 40*, 107–126. http://dx.doi.org/10.1002/j.2161-007X.1996.tb00844.x

Ephron, N., & Donner, L. S. (Producers), & Ephron, N. (Director) (1998). *You've got mail* [Motion picture]. United States: Warner Bros.

Escher, D. (2013). How does religion promote forgiveness? Linking beliefs, orientations, and practices. *Journal for the Scientific Study of Religion, 52*, 100–119. http://dx.doi.org/10.1111/jssr.12012

Exline, J. J., Baumeister, R. F., Bushman, B. J., Campbell, W. K., & Finkel, E. J. (2004). Too proud to let go: Narcissistic entitlement as a barrier to forgiveness. *Journal of Personality and Social Psychology, 87*, 894–912.

Exline, J. J., & Hill, P. C. (2012). Humility: A consistent and robust predictor of generosity. *The Journal of Positive Psychology, 7*, 208–218. http://dx.doi.org/10.1080/17439760.2012.671348

Exline, J. J., & Martin, A. (2005). Anger toward God: A new frontier in forgiveness research. In E. L. Worthington, Jr., (Ed.), *Handbook of forgiveness* (pp. 73–88). New York, NY: Brunner-Routledge.

Exline, J. J., Park, C. L., Smyth, J. M., & Carey, M. P. (2011). Anger toward God: Social-cognitive predictors, prevalence, and links with adjustment to bereavement and cancer. *Journal of Personality and Social Psychology, 100,* 129–148.

Exline, J. J., Worthington, E. L., Jr., Hill, P. C., & McCullough, M. E. (2003). Forgiveness and justice: A research agenda for social and personality psychology. *Personality and Social Psychology Review, 7,* 337–348. http://dx.doi.org/10.1207/S15327957PSPR0704_06

Exline, J. J., Yali, A. M., & Lobel, M. (1999). When god disappoints: Difficulty forgiving god and its role in negative emotion. *Journal of Health Psychology, 4,* 365–379. http://dx.doi.org/10.1177/135910539900400306

Fabricatore, A. N., Handal, P. J., Rubio, D. M., & Gilner, F. H. (2004). Stress, religion, and mental health: Religious coping in mediating and moderating roles. *The International Journal for the Psychology of Religion, 14,* 91–108. http://dx.doi.org/10.1207/s15327582ijpr1402_2

Falb, M. D., & Pargament, K. I. (2012). Relational mindfulness, spirituality, and the therapeutic bond. *Asian Journal of Psychiatry, 5,* 351–354. http://dx.doi.org/10.1016/j.ajp.2012.07.008

Farrow, T. F. D., Hunter, M. D., Wilkinson, I. D., Gouneea, C., Fawbert, D., Smith, R., . . . Woodruff, P. W. (2005). Quantifiable change in functional brain response to empathic and forgivability judgments with resolution of posttraumatic stress disorder. *Psychiatry Research: Neuroimaging, 140,* 45–53. http://dx.doi.org/10.1016/j.pscychresns.2005.05.012

Farrow, T. F. D., Zheng, Y., Wilkinson, I. D., Spence, S. A., Deakin, J. F. W., Tarrier, N., . . . Woodruff, P. W. R. (2001). Investigating the functional anatomy of empathy and forgiveness. *NeuroReport, 12,* 2433–2438. http://dx.doi.org/10.1097/00001756-200108080-00029

Fehr, R., & Gelfand, M., (2010). When apologies work: How matching apology components to victims' self-construals facilitates forgiveness. *Organizational Behavior and Human Decision Processes, 113,* 37–50. http://dx.doi.org/10.1016/j.obhdp.2010.04.002

Fernández-Montalvo, J., & Echeburúa, E. (2008). Trastornos de personalidad y psicopatía en hombres condenados por violencia grave contra la pareja [Personality disorders and psychopathy in men convicted for severe intimate partner violence]. *Psicothema, 20,* 193–198.

Finke, R., & Dougherty, K. (2002). The effects of professional training: The social and religious capital acquired in seminaries. *Journal for the Scientific Study of Religion, 41,* 103–120. http://dx.doi.org/10.1111/1468-5906.00104

Fosha, D., Siegel, D. J., & Solomon, M. (Eds.). (2009). *The healing power of emotion: Affective neuroscience, development, and clinical practice.* New York, NY: Norton.

Fowler, J. W. (1981). *Stages of faith: The psychology of human development and the quest for meaning.* San Francisco, CA: Harper & Row.

Frank, J. D., & Frank, J. B. (1993). *Persuasion and healing: A comparative study of psychotherapy* (3rd ed.). Baltimore, MD: Johns Hopkins University Press.

Fredrickson, B. L. (1998). What good are positive emotions? *Review of General Psychology, 2,* 300–319.

Freedman, S. R., & Enright, R. D. (1996). Forgiveness as an intervention goal with incest survivors. *Journal of Consulting and Clinical Psychology, 64,* 983–992. http://dx.doi.org/10.1037/0022-006X.64.5.983

Friedman, E. H. (1985). *Generation to generation: Family process in church and synagogue.* New York, NY: Guilford Press.

Gelfand, M. J., Nishii, L. H., Holcombe, K. M., Dyer, N., Ohbuchi, K. I., & Fukuno, M. (2001). Cultural influences on cognitive representations of conflict: Interpretations of conflict episodes in the United States and Japan. *Journal of Applied Psychology, 86,* 1059–1074. http://dx.doi.org/10.1037/0021-9010.86.6.1059

Gomez, R., & Fisher, J. W. (2003). Domains of spiritual well-being and development and validation of the Spiritual Well-Being Questionnaire. *Personality and Individual Differences, 35,* 1975–1991. http://dx.doi.org/10.1016/S0191-8869(03)00045-X

Gordon, K. C., Burton, S., & Porter, L. (2004). Predicting the intentions of women in domestic violence shelters to return to partners: Does forgiveness play a role? *Journal of Family Psychology, 18,* 331–338. doi:10.1037/0893-3200.18.2.331

Gore, W. L., Presnall, J. R., Miller, J. D., Lynam, D. R., & Widiger, T. A. (2012). A five-factor measure of dependent personality traits. *Journal of Personality Assessment, 94,* 488–499. doi:10.1080/00223891.2012.670681

Gottman, J. M. (1999). *The marriage clinic: A scientifically based marital therapy.* New York, NY: Norton.

Granqvist, P. (2005). Building a bridge between attachment and religious coping: Tests of moderators and mediators. *Mental Health, Religion & Culture, 8,* 35–47. http://dx.doi.org/10.1080/13674670410001666598

Granqvist, P., & Kirkpatrick, L. A. (2008). Attachment and religious representations and behavior. In J. Cassidy & P. R. Shaver (Eds.), *Handbook of attachment: Theory, research, and clinical applications* (2nd ed., pp. 906–933). New York, NY: Guilford Press.

Greenberg, L. J., Warwar, S. H., & Malcolm, W. M. (2008). Differential effects of emotion-focused therapy and psychoeducation in facilitating forgiveness and letting go of emotional injuries. *Journal of Counseling Psychology, 55,* 185–196. http://dx.doi.org/10.1037/0022-0167.55.2.185

Greenberg, L., Warwar, S., & Malcolm, W. (2010). Emotion-focused couples therapy and the facilitation of forgiveness. *Journal of Marital and Family Therapy, 36,* 28–42. http://dx.doi.org/10.1111/j.1752-0606.2009.00185.x

Greer, C. L., Worthington, E. L., Jr., Lin, Y., Lavelock, C. R., & Griffin, B. J. (2014). Efficacy of a self-directed forgiveness workbook for Christian victims of within-congregation offenders. *Spirituality in Clinical Practice, 1,* 218–230. http://dx.doi.org/10.1037/scp0000012

Greer, C. L., Worthington, E. L., Jr., Toussaint, L., Garzon, F., & Sutton, G. (2012). *Prevalence of church conflicts*. Unpublished manuscript, Department of Psychology, Spring Hill College.

Greer, C. L., Worthington, E. L., Jr., Van Tongeren, D. R., Gartner, A. L., Jennings, D. J., II, Lin, Y., . . . Ho, M. Y. (2014). Forgiveness of in-group offenders in Christian congregations. *Psychology of Religion and Spirituality, 6,* 150–161. http://dx.doi.org/10.1037/a0035186

Griffin, B. J., Worthington, E. L., Jr., & Lavelock, C. R. (2014). *Moving forward: Six steps to forgiving yourself and breaking free from the past.* Unpublished self-directed workbook, available from http://www.EvWorthington-forgiveness.com

Griffin, B. J., Worthington, E. L., Jr., Lavelock, C. R., Greer, C. L., Lin, Y., Davis, D. E., & Hook, J. N. (2015). Efficacy of a self-forgiveness workbook: A randomized controlled trial with interpersonal offenders. *Journal of Counseling Psychology.* Advance online publication. http://dx.doi.org/10.1037/cou0000060

Griffin, B. J., Worthington, E. L., Jr., Wade, N. G., Hoyt, W. T., & Davis, D. E. (in press). Forgiveness and mental health. In L. Toussaint, E. L. Worthington, Jr., & D. Williams (Eds.), *Forgiveness and health: Scientific evidence and theories relating forgiveness to better health.* New York, NY: Springer.

Griffith, J. L. (2011). *Religion that heals, religion that harms.* New York, NY: Guilford Press.

Guerin, P. J., Jr., Fogarty, T. F., Fay, L. F., & Kautto, J. G. (2010). *Working with relationship triangles: The one-two-three of psychotherapy.* New York, NY: Guilford Press.

Gutierrez, G. (2003). *We drink from our own wells: The spiritual journey of a people.* Maryknoll, NY: Orbis.

Haggerty, G., Hilsenroth, M. J., & Vala-Stewart, R. (2009). Attachment and interpersonal distress: Examining the relationship between attachment styles and interpersonal problems in a clinical population. *Clinical Psychology & Psychotherapy, 16,* 1–9. http://dx.doi.org/10.1002/cpp.596

Hall, T. W. (2004). Christian spirituality and mental health: A relational spirituality paradigm for empirical research. *Journal of Psychology and Christianity, 23,* 66–81.

Hall, T. W., Fujikawa, A., Halcrow, S. R., Hill, P. C., & Delaney, H. (2009). Attachment to God and implicit spirituality: Clarifying correspondence and compensation models. *Journal of Psychology and Theology, 37,* 227–244.

Hall, T. W., & Porter, S. L. (2004). Referential integration: An emotional information processing perspective on the process of integration. *Journal of Psychology and Theology, 32,* 167–180.

Hammer, M. R., Bennett, M. J., & Wiseman, R. (2003). Measuring intercultural sensitivity: The Intercultural Development Inventory. *International Journal of Intercultural Relations, 27,* 421–443. doi:10.1016/S0147-1767(03)00032-4

Hardy, D. S. (2000). A Winnicottian redescription of Christian spiritual direction relationships: Illustrating the potential contribution of psychology of religion to Christian spiritual practice. *Journal of Psychology and Theology, 28,* 263–275.

Harper, Q., Worthington, E. L., Jr., Griffin, B. J., Lavelock, C. R., Hook, J. N., Vrana, S. R., & Greer, C. L. (2014). Efficacy of a workbook to promote forgiveness: A randomized controlled trial with university students. *Journal of Clinical Psychology, 70,* 1158–1169. http://dx.doi.org/10.1002/jclp.22079

Hay, D., Reich, K. H., & Utsch, M. (2006). Spiritual development: Intersections and divergence with religious development. In E. C. Roehlkepartain, P. E. King, L. Wagener, & P. L. Benson (Eds.), *The handbook of spiritual development in childhood and adolescence* (pp. 46–59). Thousand Oaks, CA: Sage.

Hayes, A. M., Laurenceau, J. P., Feldman, G., Strauss, J. L., & Cardaciotto, L. (2007). Change is not always linear: The study of nonlinear and discontinuous patterns of change in psychotherapy. *Clinical Psychology Review, 27,* 715–723. http://dx.doi.org/10.1016/j.cpr.2007.01.008

Hayes, D. (2012). *Forged in the fiery furnace: African American spirituality.* Maryknoll, NY: Orbis.

Heiden Rootes, K. M., Jankowski, P. J., & Sandage, S. J. (2010). Bowen family systems theory and spirituality: Exploring the relationship between triangulation and religious questing. *Contemporary Family Therapy, 32,* 89–101. http://dx.doi.org/10.1007/s10591-009-9101-y

Herman, J. H. (1992). *Trauma and recovery: The aftermath of violence—from domestic abuse to political terror.* New York, NY: Basic Books.

Hill, P. C., & Hall, T. W. (2002). Relational schemas in processing one's image of God and self. *Journal of Psychology and Christianity, 21,* 365–373.

Hill, P. C., & Pargament, K. I. (2003). Advances in the conceptualization and measurement of religion and spirituality. Implications for physical and mental health research. *American Psychologist, 58,* 64–74. http://dx.doi.org/10.1037/0003-066X.58.1.64

Hill, P. C., Pargament, K. I., Hood, R. W., McCullough, M. E., Swyers, J. P., Larson, D. B., & Zinnbauer, B. J. (2000). Conceptualizing religion and spirituality: Points of commonality, points of departure. *Journal for the Theory of Social Behaviour, 30,* 51–77. http://dx.doi.org/10.1111/1468-5914.00119

Holeman, V. T. (1999). Mutual forgiveness: A catalyst for relationship transformation in the moral crucible of marriage. *Marriage & Family: A Christian Journal, 2,* 147–158.

Holeman, V. T. (2004). *Reconcilable differences: Hope and healing for troubled marriages.* Downers Grove, IL: InterVarsity Press.

Holm, A. L., Berg, A., & Severinsson, E. (2009). Longing for reconciliation: A challenge for women with borderline personality disorder. *Issues in Mental Health Nursing, 30,* 560–568. http://dx.doi.org/10.1080/01612840902838579

Holmes, J. (2001). *The search for the secure base: Attachment theory and psychotherapy.* London, England: Routledge.

Hook, J. N., Davis, D. E., Owen, J., Worthington, E. L., Jr., & Utsey, S. O. (2013). Cultural humility: Acknowledging limitations in one's multicultural competencies. *Journal of Counseling Psychology, 60,* 353–366.

Hook, J. N., Worthington, E. L., Jr., & Davis, D. E. (2012). Religious and spiritual psychotherapies in counseling psychology. In N. A. Fouad (Ed.), *APA handbooks in psychology: APA handbook of counseling* (Vol. 2, pp. 417–432). Washington, DC: American Psychological Association.

Hook, J. N., Worthington, E. L., Jr., Davis, D. E., Jennings, D. J., II, Gartner, A. L., & Hook, J. P. (2010). Empirically supported religious and spiritual therapies. *Journal of Clinical Psychology, 66,* 46–72.

Horvath, A. O., Del Re, A. C., Flückiger, C., & Symonds, D. (2011). Alliance in individual psychotherapy. In J. C. Norcross (Ed.), *Psychotherapy relationships that work: Evidence-based responsiveness* (pp. 25–69). New York, NY: Oxford University Press. http://dx.doi.org/10.1093/acprof:oso/9780199737208.003.0002

Ingersoll-Dayton, B., Campbell, R., & Ha, J. H. (2009). Enhancing forgiveness: A group intervention for the elderly. *Journal of Gerontological Social Work, 52,* 2–16. http://dx.doi.org/10.1080/01634370802561901

Jakubowski, S. F., Milne, E. P., Brunner, H., & Miller, R. B. (2004). A review of empirically supported marital enrichment programs. *Family Relations, 53,* 528–536. http://dx.doi.org/10.1111/j.0197-6664.2004.00062.x

James, W. (1958). *The varieties of religious experience: A study in human nature.* Cambridge, MA: Harvard University Press. (Original work published 1902)

Jankowski, P. J., & Sandage, S. J. (2011). Meditative prayer, hope, adult attachment, and forgiveness: A proposed model. *Psychology of Religion and Spirituality, 3,* 115–131. http://dx.doi.org/10.1037/a0021601

Jankowski, P. J., & Sandage, S. J. (2012). Spiritual dwelling and well-being: The mediating role of differentiation of self in a sample of distressed adults. *Mental Health, Religion & Culture, 15,* 417–434. http://dx.doi.org/10.1080/13674676.2011.579592

Jankowski, P. J., & Sandage, S. J. (2014a). Attachment to God and dispositional humility: Indirect effect and conditional effects model. *Journal of Psychology and Theology, 42,* 70–82.

Jankowski, P. J., & Sandage, S. J., (2014b). Meditative prayer and intercultural competence: Empirical test of a differentiation-based model. *Mindfulness, 4,* 360–372. http://dx.doi.org/10.1007/s12671-012-0189-z

Jankowski, P. J., Sandage, S. J., & Hill, P. C. (2013). Differentiation-based models of forgivingness, mental health and social justice commitment: Mediator effects for differentiation of self and humility. *The Journal of Positive Psychology, 8,* 412–424. http://dx.doi.org/10.1080/17439760.2013.820337

Jankowski, P. J., & Vaughn, M. (2009). Differentiation of self and spirituality: Empirical explorations. *Counseling and Values, 53,* 82–96. http://dx.doi.org/10.1002/j.2161-007X.2009.tb00116.x

Johnson, R. E., & Chang, C.-H. (2006). "I" is to continuance as "we" is to affective: The relevance of the self-concept for organizational commitment. *Journal of Organizational Behavior, 27,* 549–570. http://dx.doi.org/10.1002/job.364

Johnson, S. M. (1996). *The practice of emotionally focused marital therapy: Creating connection.* New York, NY: Brunner/Mazel.

Johnson, S. M. (2002). *Emotionally focused couple therapy with trauma survivors: Strengthening attachment bonds.* New York, NY: Guilford Press.

Jones, J. W. (2002). *Terror and transformation: The ambiguity of religion in psychoanalytic perspective*. New York, NY: Brunner-Routledge.

Jung, C. G. (1953). *Psychology and alchemy* (2nd ed.). (R. F. C. Hull, Trans.). Princeton, NJ: Princeton University Press. (Original work published 1944)

Kabat-Zinn, J. (2013). *Full catastrophe living: Using the wisdom of your body and mind to face stress, pain, and illness*. New York, NY: Bantam Books.

Kahneman, D. (2011). *Thinking, fast and slow*. New York, NY: Farrar, Straus and Giroux.

Karen, R. (2001). *The forgiving self: The road from resentment to connection*. New York, NY: Doubleday.

Kashima, Y., Yamaguchi, S., Kim, U., Choi, S.-C., Gelfand, M. J., & Yuki, M. (1995). Culture, gender, and self: A perspective from individualism–collectivism research. *Journal of Personality and Social Psychology, 69*, 925–937.

Kegan, R., & Lahey, L. L. (2009). *Immunity to change: How to overcome it and unlock the potential in yourself and your organization*. Cambridge, MA: Harvard Business Review Press.

Kernberg, O. (1991). The psychopathology of hatred. *Journal of the American Psychoanalytic Association, 39*, 209–238.

Kerr, M. E., & Bowen, M. (1988). *Family evaluation*. New York, NY: Norton.

Kiefer, R. P., Worthington, E. L., Jr., Myers, B., Kliewer, W. L., Berry, J. W., Davis, D. E., . . . Hunter, J. L. (2010). Training parents in forgiveness and reconciliation. *The American Journal of Family Therapy, 38*, 32–49. http://dx.doi.org/10.1080/01926180902945723

Kirkpatrick, L. A. (2005). *Attachment, evolution, and the psychology of religion*. New York, NY: Guilford Press.

Klein, M. (1975). *Envy and gratitude and other works, 1946–1963: Vol. 3. The writings of Melanie Klein*. New York, NY: The Free Press.

Kohut, H. (1977). *The restoration of the self*. New York, NY: International Universities Press.

Konrath, S., & Cheung, I. (2013). The fuzzy reality of perceived harms. *Behavioral and Brain Sciences, 36*, 26–27. http://dx.doi.org/10.1017/S0140525X12000416

Konstam, V., Marx, F., Schurer, J., Lombardo, N. B. E., & Harrington, A. K. (2002). Forgiveness in practice: What mental health counsellors are telling us. In S. Lamb & J. G. Murphy (Eds.), *Before forgiving: Cautionary views of forgiveness in psychotherapy* (pp. 54–71). New York, NY: Oxford University Press.

Kopp, S. (1970, March). The wizard behind the couch. *Psychology Today, 84*, 70–73.

Kopp, S. (1982). *If you meet the Buddha on the road, kill him: The pilgrimage of psychotherapy patients*. New York, NY: Bantam Books.

Krumrei, E. J., Mahoney, A., & Pargament, K. I. (2008). Turning to God: More than meets the eye. *Journal of Psychology and Christianity, 27*, 302–310.

L'Abate, L. (2009). The drama triangle: An attempt to resurrect a neglected pathogenic model in family therapy theory and practice. *The American Journal of Family Therapy, 37*, 1–11. http://dx.doi.org/10.1080/01926180701870163

Lambert, N. M., Fincham, F. D., DeWall, N. C., Pond, R., & Beach, S. R. (2013). Shifting toward cooperative tendencies and forgiveness: How partner-focused prayer transforms motivation. *Personal Relationships, 20*, 184–197. http://dx.doi.org/10.1111/j.1475-6811.2012.01411.x

Lambert, N. M., Fincham, F. D., Stillman, T. F., Graham, S. M., & Beach, S. R. H. (2010). Motivating change in relationships: Can prayer increase forgiveness? *Psychological Science, 21*, 126–132. http://dx.doi.org/10.1177/0956797609355634

Lampton, C., Oliver, G., Worthington, E. L., Jr., & Berry, J. W. (2005). Helping Christian college students become more forgiving: An intervention study to promote forgiveness as part of a program to shape Christian character. *Journal of Psychology and Theology, 33*, 278–290.

Lawler-Row, K. A., Hyatt-Edwards, L., Wuensch, K. L., & Karremans, J. C. (2011). Forgiveness and health: The role of attachment. *Personal Relationships, 18*, 170–183.

Lawler-Row, K. A., Younger, J. W., Piferi, R. L., & Jones, W. H. (2006). The role of adult attachment style in forgiveness following an interpersonal offense. *Journal of Counseling & Development, 84*, 493–502. http://dx.doi.org/10.1002/j.1556-6678.2006.tb00434.x

Lazarus, R. S. (1997). *Fifty years of the research and theory of R. S. Lazarus: An analysis of historical and perennial issues*. Mahwah, NJ: Erlbaum.

Lazarus, R. S. (1999). *Stress and emotion: A new synthesis*. New York, NY: Springer.

Lazarus, R. S. (2006). Emotions and interpersonal relationships: Toward a person-centered conceptualization of emotions and coping. *Journal of Personality, 74*, 9–46. http://dx.doi.org/10.1111/j.1467-6494.2005.00368.x

Lazarus, R. S., & Folkman, S. (1984). *Stress, appraisal, and coping*. New York, NY: Springer.

LeRoy, M. (Producer), & Fleming, V. (1939). *The Wizard of Oz* [Motion picture]. United States: Metro-Goldwyn-Mayer.

Levinas, E. (1969). *Totality and infinity: An essay on exteriority* (A. Lingis, Trans.). Pittsburgh, PA: Duquesne University Press.

Levy, K. N., Ellison, K. D., Scott, L. N., & Bernecker, S. L. (2011). Attachment style. In J. C. Norcross (Ed.), *Psychotherapy relationships that work: Evidence-based responsiveness* (2nd ed., pp. 377–401). New York, NY: Oxford University Press. http://dx.doi.org/10.1093/acprof:oso/9780199737208.003.0019

Lewis, T., Amini, F., & Lannon, R. (2000). *A general theory of love*. New York, NY: Vintage.

Lin, W. F., Mack, D., Enright, R. D., Krahn, D., & Baskin, T. W. (2004). Effects of forgiveness therapy on anger, mood, and vulnerability to substance use among inpatient substance-dependent clients. *Journal of Consulting and Clinical Psychology, 72*, 1114–1121. http://dx.doi.org/10.1037/0022-006X.72.6.1114

Linehan, M. M. (1993). *Cognitive-behavioral treatment of borderline personality disorder*. New York, NY: Guilford Press.

Loder, J. E. (1989). *The transforming moment*. Colorado Springs, CO: Helmers & Howard.

Loder, J. E. (1998). *The logic of the Spirit: Human development in theological perspective*. San Francisco, CA: Jossey-Bass.

Luskin, F. M. (2001). *Forgive for good: A proven prescription for health and happiness*. San Francisco, CA: Harper.

Lynch, T. R., & Cheavens, J. S. (2007). Dialectical behavior therapy for depression with comorbid personality disorder: An extension of standard dialectical behavior therapy with a special emphasis on the treatment of older adults. In L. A. Dimeff & K. Koerner (Eds.), *Dialectical behavior therapy in clinical practice: Applications across disorders and settings* (pp. 264–297). New York, NY: Guilford Press.

MacIntyre, A. (1984). *After virtue: A study in moral theory* (2nd ed.). South Bend, IN: University of Notre Dame Press.

Maddock, J. W., & Larson, N. R. (1995). *Incestuous families: An ecological approach to understanding and treatment*. New York, NY: Norton.

Maddock, J. W., & Larson, N. R. (2004). The ecological approach to incestuous families. In D. R. Catherall (Ed.), *Handbook of stress, trauma, and the family* (pp. 367–391). New York, NY: Brunner-Routledge.

Mahoney, A., Rye, M. S., & Pargament, K. I. (2005). When the sacred is violated: Desecration as a unique challenge to forgiveness. In E. L. Worthington, Jr., (Ed.), *Handbook of forgiveness* (pp. 57–72). New York, NY: Brunner-Routledge.

Majerus, B., & Sandage, S. J. (2010). Differentiation of self and Christian spiritual maturity: Social science and theological integration. *Journal of Psychology and Theology, 38*, 41–51.

Makinen, J. A., & Johnson, S. M. (2006). Resolving attachment injuries in couples using emotionally focused therapy: Steps toward forgiveness and reconciliation. *Journal of Consulting and Clinical Psychology, 74*, 1055–1064.

Malcolm, W. M., & Greenberg, L. S. (2000). Forgiveness as a process of change in individual psychotherapy. In M. E. McCullough, K. I. Pargament, & C. E. Thoresen (Eds.), *Forgiveness: Theory, research, and practice* (pp. 179–202). New York, NY: Guilford Press.

Malcolm, W. M., Warwar, S., & Greenberg, L. (2005). Facilitating forgiveness in individual therapy as an approach to resolving interpersonal injuries. In E. L. Worthington, Jr., (Ed.), *Handbook of forgiveness* (pp. 379–391). New York, NY: Brunner-Routledge.

Marcia, J., Waterman, A. S., Matteson, D. R., Archer, S. L., & Orlofsky, J. L. (2011). *Ego-identity: A handbook for psychosocial research*. New York, NY: Springer-Verlag.

Marmarosh, C. L., & Tasca, G. A. (2013). Adult attachment anxiety: Using group therapy to promote change. *Journal of Clinical Psychology, 69*, 1172–1182. http://dx.doi.org/10.1002/jclp.22044

Masterson, J. F. (1993). *The emerging self: A developmental, self, and object relations approach to the treatment of the closet narcissistic disorder of the self*. New York, NY: Brunner/Mazel.

McAdams, D. P. (2006). *The redemptive self: Stories Americans live by*. New York, NY: Oxford University Press. http://dx.doi.org/10.1093/acprof:oso/9780195176933.001.0001

McAdams, D. P., & de St. Aubin, E. (1992). A theory of generativity and its assessment through self-report, behavioral acts, and narrative themes in autobiography. *Journal of Personality and Social Psychology, 62*, 1003–1015. http://dx.doi.org/10.1037/0022-3514.62.6.1003

McCullough, M. E. (2008). *Beyond revenge: The evolution of the forgiveness instinct*. San Francisco, CA: Jossey-Bass.

McCullough, M. E., Bono, G., & Root, L. M. (2007). Rumination, emotion, and forgiveness: Three longitudinal studies. *Journal of Personality and Social Psychology, 92*, 490–505. http://dx.doi.org/10.1037/0022-3514.92.3.490

McCullough, M. E., Fincham, F. D., & Tsang, J.-A. (2003). Forgiveness, forbearance, and time: The temporal unfolding of transgression-related interpersonal motivations. *Journal of Personality and Social Psychology, 84*, 540–557. http://dx.doi.org/10.1037/0022-3514.84.3.540

McCullough, M. E., Luna, L. R., Berry, J. W., Tabak, B. A., & Bono, G. (2010). On the form and function of forgiving: Modeling the time-forgiveness relationship and testing the valuable relationships hypothesis. *Emotion, 10*, 358–376. http://dx.doi.org/10.1037/a0019349

McCullough, M. E., Rachal, K. C., Sandage, S. J., Worthington, E. L., Jr., Brown, S. W., & Hight, T. L. (1998). Interpersonal forgiving in close relationships: II. Theoretical elaboration and measurement. *Journal of Personality and Social Psychology, 75*, 1586–1603. http://dx.doi.org/10.1037/0022-3514.75.6.1586

McCullough, M. E., Root, L. M., & Cohen, A. D. (2006). Writing about the benefits of an interpersonal transgression facilitates forgiveness. *Journal of Consulting and Clinical Psychology, 74*, 887–897. http://dx.doi.org/10.1037/0022-006X.74.5.887

McCullough, M. E., Sandage, S. J., & Worthington, E. L., Jr. (1997). *To forgive is human: How to put your past in the past*. Downers Grove, IL: InterVarsity Press.

McCullough, M. E., Worthington, E. L., Jr., & Rachal, K. C. (1997). Interpersonal forgiving in close relationships. *Journal of Personality and Social Psychology, 73*, 321–336. http://dx.doi.org/10.1037/0022-3514.73.2.321

McHugh, R. K., & Barlow, D. H. (2010). The dissemination and implementation of evidence-based psychological treatments. A review of current efforts. *American Psychologist, 65*, 73–84. http://dx.doi.org/10.1037/a0018121

McMinn, M. R., Fervida, H., Louwerse, K. A., Pop, J. L., Thompson, R. D., Trihub, B. L., & McLeod-Harrison, S. (2008). Forgiveness and prayer. *Journal of Psychology and Christianity, 27*, 101–109.

Meichenbaum, D. (1977). *Cognitive-behavior modification: An integrative approach.* New York, NY: Springer. http://dx.doi.org/10.1007/978-1-4757-9739-8

Meyer, B., & Pilkonis, P. A. (2011). Attachment theory and narcissistic personality disorder. In W. K. Campbell & J. D. Miller (Eds.), *The handbook of narcissism and narcissistic personality disorder* (pp. 434–444). Hoboken, NJ: Wiley.

Mikulincer, M., & Shaver, P. R. (2007). *Attachment in adulthood: Structure, dynamics, and change.* New York, NY: Guilford Press.

Miller, W. R. (Ed.). (1999). *Integrating spirituality into treatment: Resources for practitioners.* Washington, DC: American Psychological Association. http://dx.doi.org/10.1037/10327-000

Miller, W. R., & C'de Baca, J. (2001). *Quantum change: When epiphanies and sudden insights transform ordinary lives.* New York, NY: Guilford Press.

Mitchell, S. A. (2000). *Relationality: From attachment to intersubjectivity.* Hillsdale, NJ: Analytic Press.

Moore, R. L. (2001). *The archetype of initiation: Sacred space, ritual process, and personal transformation.* Bloomington, IN: Xlibris.

Moore, R. L. (2003). *Facing the dragon: Confronting personal and spiritual grandiosity.* Wilmette, IL: Chiron.

Mueller, W. (1992). *Legacy of the heart: The spiritual advantages of a painful childhood.* New York, NY: Simon & Schuster.

Muñoz Sastre, T. M., Vinsonneau, G., Chabol, H., & Mullet, E. (2005). Forgiveness and the paranoid personality style. *Personality and Individual Differences, 38,* 765–772. http://dx.doi.org/10.1016/j.paid.2004.06.001

Napier, A. Y., & Whitaker, C. A. (1978). *The family crucible.* New York, NY: Harper & Row.

Nauta, R., & Derckx, L. (2007). Why sin? A test and an exploration of the social and psychological context of resentment and desire. *Pastoral Psychology, 56,* 177–188. http://dx.doi.org/10.1007/s11089-007-0097-7

Newberg, A., & Waldman, M. R. (2009). *How God changes your brain: Breakthrough findings from a leading neuroscientist.* New York, NY: Ballantine Books.

Newman, M. G., Crits-Cristoph, P., Connolly Gibbons, M. B., & Erickson, T. M. (2005). Participant factors in treating anxiety disorders. In L. G. Castonguay & L. E. Beutler (Eds.), *Principles of therapeutic change that work* (pp. 121–153). New York, NY: Oxford University Press.

Nhat Hanh, T. (2001). *A pebble in your pocket.* Delhi, India: Full Circle.

Norcross, J. C. (Ed.). (2011). *Psychotherapy relationships that work: Evidence-based responsiveness.* New York, NY: Oxford University Press. http://dx.doi.org/10.1093/acprof:oso/9780199737208.001.0001

Oman, D., Shapiro, S. L., Thoresen, C. E., Plante, T. G., & Flinders, T. (2008). Meditation lowers stress and supports forgiveness among college students: A randomized controlled trial. *Journal of American College Health, 56,* 569–578. http://dx.doi.org/10.3200/JACH.56.5.569-578

Orcutt, H. K., Pickett, S. M., & Pope, E. B. (2008). The relationship of offense-specific forgiveness to posttraumatic stress disorder symptoms in college students. *Journal of Aggression, Maltreatment & Trauma, 16,* 72–91. http://dx.doi.org/10.1080/10926770801920776

Osterndorf, C., Enright, R. D., Holter, A., & Klatt, J. (2011). Treating adult children of alcoholics through forgiveness therapy. *Alcoholism Treatment Quarterly, 29,* 274–292. http://dx.doi.org/10.1080/07347324.2011.586285

Panksepp, J. (1998). *Affective neuroscience: The foundations of human and animal emotions.* New York, NY: Oxford University Press.

Panksepp, J., & Biven, L. (2012). *The archaeology of mind: Neuroevolutionary origins of human emotions.* New York, NY: Norton.

Pargament, K. I. (1997). *The psychology of religion and coping: Theory, research, practice.* New York, NY: Guilford Press.

Pargament, K. I. (2007). *Spiritually integrated psychotherapy: Understanding and addressing the Sacred.* New York, NY: Guilford Press.

Pargament, K. I. (Ed.). (2013a). *APA handbooks in psychology: APA handbook of psychology, religion, and spirituality: Vol. 1.* Washington, DC: American Psychological Association.

Pargament, K. I. (Ed.). (2013b). *APA handbooks in psychology: APA handbook of psychology, religion, and spirituality: Vol. 2.* Washington, DC: American Psychological Association.

Pargament, K. I., Koenig, H. G., & Perez, L. (2000). The many methods of religious coping: Initial and validation of the RCOPE. *Journal of Clinical Psychology, 56,* 519–543.

Pargament, K. I., Magyar, G. M., Benore, E., & Mahoney, A. (2005). Sacrilege: A study of sacred loss and desecration and their implications for health and well-being in a community sample. *Journal for the Scientific Study of Religion, 44,* 59–78. http://dx.doi.org/10.1111/j.1468-5906.2005.00265.x

Pargament, K. I., Murray-Swank, N. A., Magyar, G. M., & Ano, G. G. (2005). Spiritual struggle: A phenomenon of interest to psychology and religion. In W. R. Miller & H. D. Delaney (Eds.), *Judeo-Christian perspectives on psychology: Human nature, motivation, and change* (pp. 245–268). Washington, DC: American Psychological Association. http://dx.doi.org/10.1037/10859-013

Paris, P. J. (1995). *The spirituality of African peoples: The search for a common moral discourse.* Minneapolis, MN: Fortress Press.

Park, C. L., & Ai, A. L. (2006). Meaning making and growth: New directions for research on survivors of trauma. *Journal of Loss and Trauma, 11,* 389–407. http://dx.doi.org/10.1080/15325020600685295

Park, C. L., & Folkman, S. (1997). Meaning in the context of stress and coping. *Review of General Psychology, 1,* 115–144. http://dx.doi.org/10.1037/1089-2680.1.2.115

The Pew Forum on Religion & Public Life. (2008). *U.S. religious landscape survey.* Washington, DC: The Pew Research Center.

Pincus, A. L., Ansell, E. B., Pimentel, C. A., Cain, N. M., Wright, A. G., & Levy, K. N. (2009). Initial construction and validation of the Pathological Narcissism Inventory. *Psychological Assessment, 21*, 365–379. http://dx.doi.org/10.1037/a0016530

Prochaska, J. O., Norcross, J. C., & DiClemente, C. C. (2007). *Changing for good: A revolutionary six-stage program for overcoming bad habits and moving your life positively forward*. New York, NY: HarperCollins.

Ra, Y. S., Cha, S. Y., Hyun, M., & Bae, S. M. (2013). The mediating effects of attribution styles on the relationship between overt-covert narcissism and forgiveness. *Social Behavior and Personality, 41*, 881–892. http://dx.doi.org/10.2224/sbp.2013.41.6.881

Rambo, L. R. (1993). *Understanding religious conversion*. New Haven, CT: Yale University Press.

Rata, A., Liu, J. H., & Hanke, K. (2008). Te Ara Hohou Rongo (The Path to Peace): Maori conceptualisations of inter-group forgiveness. *New Zealand Journal of Psychology, 37*, 18–30.

Ravitz, P., Maunder, R., Hunter, J., Sthankiya, B., & Lancee, W. (2010). Adult attachment measures: A 25-year review. *Journal of Psychosomatic Research, 69*, 419–432. http://dx.doi.org/10.1016/j.jpsychores.2009.08.006

Reed, G. L., & Enright, R. D. (2006). The effects of forgiveness therapy on depression, anxiety, and posttraumatic stress for women after spousal emotional abuse. *Journal of Consulting and Clinical Psychology, 74*, 920–929. http://dx.doi.org/10.1037/0022-006X.74.5.920

Richards, P. S., & Bergin, A. E. (1997). *A spiritual strategy for counseling and psychotherapy*. Washington, DC: American Psychological Association. http://dx.doi.org/10.1037/10241-000

Richards, P. S., & Bergin, A. E. (Eds.). (2000). *Handbook of psychotherapy and religious diversity*. Washington, DC: American Psychological Association. http://dx.doi.org/10.1037/10347-000

Richards, P. S., & Bergin, A. E. (Eds.). (2004). *Casebook for a spiritual strategy in counseling and psychotherapy*. Washington, DC: American Psychological Association. http://dx.doi.org/10.1037/10652-000

Richards, P. S., & Bergin, A. E. (2005). *A spiritual strategy for counseling and psychotherapy* (2nd ed.). Washington, DC: American Psychological Association. http://dx.doi.org/10.1037/11214-000

Richards, P. S., & Bergin, A. E. (2014). Toward religious and spiritual competency for mental health professionals. In P. S. Richards & A. E. Bergin (Eds.), *Handbook of psychotherapy and religious diversity, 2nd ed.* (pp. 3–19). Washington, DC: American Psychological Association. http://dx.doi.org/10.1037/14371-001

Riek, B. M., & Mania, E. W. (2012). The antecedents and consequences of interpersonal forgiveness: A meta-analytic review. *Personal Relationships, 19*, 304–325. http://dx.doi.org/10.1111/j.1475-6811.2011.01363.x

Ripley, J. S., & Worthington, E. L., Jr. (2002). Hope-focused and forgiveness-based group interventions to promote marital enrichment. *Journal of Counseling & Development*, *80*, 452–463. http://dx.doi.org/10.1002/j.1556-6678.2002.tb00212.x

Ripley, J. S., & Worthington, E. L., Jr. (2014). *Couple therapy: A new hope-focused approach*. Downers Grove, IL: InterVarsity Press.

Rowatt, W. C., & Kirkpatrick, L. A. (2002). Two dimensions of attachment to God and their relation to affect, religiosity, and personality constructs. *Journal for the Scientific Study of Religion*, *41*, 637–651. http://dx.doi.org/10.1111/1468-5906.00143

Rye, M. S., Fleri, A. M., Moore, C. D., Worthington, E. L., Jr., Wade, N. G., Sandage, S. J., & Cook, K. M. (2012). Evaluation of an intervention designed to help divorced parents forgive their ex-spouse. *Journal of Divorce & Remarriage*, *53*, 231–245. http://dx.doi.org/10.1080/10502556.2012.663275

Rye, M. S., Loiacono, D. M., Folck, C. D., Olszewski, B. T., Heim, T. A., & Madia, B. P. (2001). Evaluation of the psychometric properties of two forgiveness scales. *Current Psychology*, *20*, 260–277. http://dx.doi.org/10.1007/s12144-001-1011-6

Rye, M. S., & Pargament, K. I. (2002). Forgiveness and romantic relationships in college: Can it heal the wounded heart? *Journal of Clinical Psychology*, *58*, 419–441. http://dx.doi.org/10.1002/jclp.1153

Rye, M. S., Pargament, K. I., Pan, W., Yingling, D. W., Shogren, K. A., & Ito, M. (2005). Can group interventions facilitate forgiveness of an ex-spouse? A randomized clinical trial. *Journal of Consulting and Clinical Psychology*, *73*, 880–892. http://dx.doi.org/10.1037/0022-006X.73.5.880

Safran, J. D., Muran, J. C., & Eubanks-Carter, C. (2011). Repairing alliance ruptures. *Psychotherapy*, *48*, 80–87. http://dx.doi.org/10.1037/a0022140

Sandage, S. J. (1999a). The ego-humility model of forgiveness: Implications for couple and family dynamics and therapy. *Marriage and the Family: A Christian Journal*, *2*, 277–292.

Sandage, S. J. (1999b). An ego-humility model of forgiveness: Theoretical foundations. *Marriage & Family: A Christian Journal*, *2*, 259–276.

Sandage, S. J. (2010). Intergenerational suicide and family dynamics: A hermeneutic phenomenological case study. *Contemporary Family Therapy*, *32*, 209–227. doi:10.1007/s-10591-009-9102-x

Sandage, S. J., Cook, K. V., Hill, P. C., Strawn, B. D., & Reimer, K. S. (2008). Hermeneutics and psychology: A review and dialectical model. *Review of General Psychology*, *12*, 344–364. http://dx.doi.org/10.1037/1089-2680.12.4.344

Sandage, S. J., & Crabtree, S. (2012). Spiritual pathology and religious coping as predictors of forgiveness. *Mental Health, Religion & Culture*, *15*, 689–707. http://dx.doi.org/10.1080/13674676.2011.613806

Sandage, S. J., Crabtree, S., & Schweer, M. (2014). Differentiation of self and social justice commitment mediated by hope. *Journal of Counseling & Development*, *92*, 67–74. http://dx.doi.org/10.1002/j.1556-6676.2014.00131.x

Sandage, S. J., & Harden, M. G. (2011). Relational spirituality, differentiation of self, and virtue as predictors of intercultural development. *Mental Health, Religion & Culture, 14*, 819–838. http://dx.doi.org/10.1080/13674676.2010.527932

Sandage, S. J., Hill, P. C., & Vang, H. C. (2003). Toward a multicultural positive psychology: Indigenous forgiveness and Hmong culture. *The Counseling Psychologist, 31*, 564–592. http://dx.doi.org/10.1177/0011000003256350

Sandage, S. J., Hill, P. C., & Vaubel, D. C. (2011). Generativity, relational spirituality, gratitude, and mental health: Relationships and pathways. *The International Journal for the Psychology of Religion, 21*, 1–16. http://dx.doi.org/10.1080/10508619.2011.532439

Sandage, S. J., & Jankowski, P. J. (2010). Forgiveness, spiritual instability, mental health symptoms, and well-being: Mediator effects of differentiation of self. *Psychology of Religion and Spirituality, 2*, 168–180. http://dx.doi.org/10.1037/a0019124

Sandage, S. J., & Jankowski, P. J. (2013). Spirituality, social justice, and intercultural competence: Mediator effects for differentiation of self. *International Journal of Intercultural Relations, 37*, 366–374. http://dx.doi.org/10.1016/j.ijintrel.2012.11.003

Sandage, S. J., & Jensen, M. L. (2013). Relational spiritual formation: Reflective practice and research on spiritual formation in a seminary context. *Reflective Practice: Formation and Supervision in Ministry, 33*, 95–109.

Sandage, S. J., Jensen, M. L., & Jass, D. (2008). Relational spirituality and transformation: Risking intimacy and alterity. *Journal of Spiritual Formation and Soul Care, 1*, 182–206.

Sandage, S. J., Link, D. C., & Jankowski, P. J. (2010). Quest and spiritual development moderated by spiritual transformation. *Journal of Psychology and Theology, 38*, 15–31.

Sandage, S. J., & Moe, S. P. (2011). Narcissism and spirituality. In W. K., Campbell & J. Miller (Eds.), *The handbook of narcissism and narcissistic personality disorder: Theoretical approaches, empirical findings, and treatment* (pp. 410–420). New York, NY: Wiley.

Sandage, S. J., & Morgan, J. (2014). Hope and positive religious coping as predictors of social justice commitment. *Mental Health, Religion & Culture, 17*, 557–567.

Sandage, S. J., & Shults, F. L. (2007). Relational spirituality and transformation: A relational integration model. *Journal of Psychology and Christianity, 26*, 261–269.

Sandage, S. J., & Williamson, I. T. (2010). Relational spirituality and dispositional forgiveness: A structural equations model. *Journal of Psychology and Theology, 38*, 255–266.

Sandage, S. J., & Worthington, E. L., Jr. (2010). Comparison of two group interventions to promote forgiveness: Empathy as a mediator of change. *Journal of Mental Health Counseling, 32*, 35–57.

Sansone, R. A., Kelley, A. R., & Forbis, J. S. (2013). The relationship between forgiveness and borderline personality symptomatology. *Journal of Religion and Health, 52*, 974–980. http://dx.doi.org/10.1007/s10943-013-9704-3

Sapolsky, R. M. (1994). *Why zebras don't get ulcers: A guide to stress, stress-related diseases, and coping.* New York, NY: Freeman.

Sauerheber, J. D., Holeman, V. T., Dean, J. B., & Haynes, J. (2014). Perceptions of counselor educators about spiritual competencies. *Journal of Psychology and Christianity, 33,* 70–83.

Scherer, M., Worthington, E. L., Jr., Hook, J. N., & Campana, K. L. (2011). Forgiveness and the bottle: Promoting self-forgiveness in individuals who abuse alcohol. *Journal of Addictive Diseases, 30,* 382–395. http://dx.doi.org/10.1080/10550887.2011.609804

Schnarch, D. M. (1991). *Constructing the sexual crucible: An integration of sexual and marital therapy.* New York, NY: Norton.

Schnarch, D. M. (1997). *Passionate marriage: Love, sex, and intimacy in emotionally committed relationships.* New York, NY: Norton.

Schnarch, D. M. (2009). *Intimacy and desire: Awaken the passion in your relationship.* New York, NY: Beaufort Books.

Schoenleber, M., & Berenbaum, H. (2010). Shame aversion and shame-proneness in Cluster C personality disorders. *Journal of Abnormal Psychology, 119,* 197–205. http://dx.doi.org/10.1037/a0017982

Schore, A. (1994). *Affect regulation and the origin of the self: The neurobiology of emotional development.* Hillsdale, NJ: Erlbaum.

Schore, A. N. (2012). *The science and the art of psychotherapy.* New York, NY: Norton.

Searles, H. F. (1986). *My work with borderline patients.* Northvale, NJ: Jason Aronson.

Selye, H. (1956). *The stress of life.* New York, NY: McGraw-Hill.

Sendak, M. (1963). *Where the wild things are.* New York, NY: Harper & Row.

Seybold, K. S., Hill, P. C., Neumann, J. K., & Chi, D. S. (2001). Physiological and psychological correlates of forgiveness. *Journal of Psychology and Christianity, 20,* 250–259.

Shafranske, E. P. (Ed.). (1996). *Religion and clinical practice of psychology.* Washington, DC: American Psychological Association. http://dx.doi.org/10.1037/10199-000

Shaw, D. (2014). *Traumatic narcissism: Relational systems of subjugation.* New York, NY: Routledge.

Shechtman, Z., Wade, N., & Khoury, A. (2009). Effectiveness of a forgiveness program for Arab Israeli adolescents in Israel: An empirical trial. *Peace and Conflict: Journal of Peace Psychology, 15,* 415–438.

Sherry, A., Lyddon, W. J., & Henson, R. K. (2007). Adult attachment and developmental personality styles: An empirical study. *Journal of Counseling & Development, 85,* 337–348. http://dx.doi.org/10.1002/j.1556-6678.2007.tb00482.x

Shults, F. L., & Sandage, S. J. (2003). *The faces of forgiveness: Searching for wholeness and salvation.* Grand Rapids, MI: Baker Academic.

Shults, F. L., & Sandage, S. J. (2006). *Transforming spirituality: Integrating theology and psychology.* Grand Rapids, MI: Baker Academic.

Skowron, E. A. (2004). Differentiation of self, personal adjustment, problem solving, and ethnic group belonging among persons of color. *Journal of Counseling & Development, 82*, 447–456. http://dx.doi.org/10.1002/j.1556-6678.2004.tb00333.x

Skowron, E. A., & Dendy, A. K. (2004). Differentiation of self and attachment in adulthood: Relational correlates of effortful control. *Contemporary Family Therapy, 26*, 337–357. http://dx.doi.org/10.1023/B:COFT.0000037919.63750.9d

Skowron, E. A., & Schmitt, T. A. (2003). Assessing interpersonal fusion: Reliability and validity of a new DSI fusion with others subscale. *Journal of Marital and Family Therapy, 29*, 209–222. http://dx.doi.org/10.1111/j.1752-0606.2003.tb01201.x

Smit, Y., Huibers, M. J. H., Ioannidis, J. P. A., van Dyck, R., van Tilburg, W., & Arntz, A. (2012). The effectiveness of long-term psychoanalytic psychotherapy—a meta-analysis of randomized controlled trials. *Clinical Psychology Review, 32*, 81–92. http://dx.doi.org/10.1016/j.cpr.2011.11.003

Snyder, C. R. (1994). *The psychology of hope*. New York, NY: The Free Press.

Snyder, C. R., Harris, C., Anderson, J. R., Holleran, S. A., Irving, L. M., Sigmon, S. T., . . . Harney, P. (1991). The will and the ways: Development and validation of an individual-differences measure of hope. *Journal of Personality and Social Psychology, 60*, 570–585. doi:10.1037/0022–3514.60.4.570.

Soldz, S., & McCullough, L. (Eds.). (2000). *Reconciling empirical knowledge and clinical experience: The art and science of psychotherapy*. Washington, DC: American Psychological Association. http://dx.doi.org/10.1037/10567-000

Solomon, Z., Dekel, R., & Zerach, G. (2009). Posttraumatic stress disorder and marital adjustment: The mediating role of forgiveness. *Family Process, 48*, 546–558. doi:10.1111/j.1545-5300.2009.01301.x

Sorotzkin, B. (1998). Understanding and treating perfectionism in religious adolescents. *Psychotherapy: Theory, Research, Practice, Training, 35*, 87–95. http://dx.doi.org/10.1037/h0087792

Sperry, L., & Shafranske, E. P. (Eds.). (2004). *Spiritually oriented psychotherapy*. Washington, DC: American Psychological Association.

Sprenkle, D. H., Davis, S. D., & Lebow, J. L. (2009). *Common factors in couple and family therapy: The overlooked foundation for effective practices*. New York, NY: Guilford Press.

St. John of the Cross. (1990). *Dark night of the soul* (E. A. Peers, Trans. & Ed.). New York, NY: Image Books.

Stratton, S. P., Dean, J. B., Nooneman, A. J., Bode, R. A., & Worthington, E. L., Jr. (2008). Forgiveness interventions as spiritual development strategies: Workshop training, expressive writing about forgiveness, and retested controls. *Journal of Psychology and Christianity, 27*, 347–357.

Strelan, P., Acton, C., & Patrick, K. (2009). Disappointment with God and well-being: The mediating influence of relationship quality and dispositional forgiveness. *Counseling and Values, 53*, 202–213. http://dx.doi.org/10.1002/j.2161-007X.2009.tb00126.x

Strelan, P., & Covic, T. (2006). A review of forgiveness process models and a coping framework to guide future research. *Journal of Social and Clinical Psychology, 25,* 1059–1085. http://dx.doi.org/10.1521/jscp.2006.25.10.1059

Strozier, C. B. (2010). The apocalyptic other. In C. B. Strozier, D. M. Terman, & J. W. Jones (Eds.), *The fundamentalist mindset* (pp. 62–70). New York, NY: Oxford University Press. http://dx.doi.org/10.1093/acprof:oso/9780195379655.003.0006

Tabak, B. A., & McCullough, M. E. (2011). Perceived transgressor agreeableness decreases cortisol response and increases forgiveness following recent interpersonal transgressions. *Biological Psychology, 87,* 386–392. http://dx.doi.org/10.1016/j.biopsycho.2011.05.001

Taylor, R. J., Chatters, L. M., & Levin, J. (2004). *Religion in the lives of African Americans: Social, psychological, and health perspectives.* Thousand Oaks, CA: Sage.

Terman, D. M. (2010). Fundamentalism and the paranoid gestalt. In C. B. Strozier, D. M. Terman, & J. W. Jones (Eds.), *The fundamentalist mindset* (pp. 47–61). New York, NY: Oxford University Press. http://dx.doi.org/10.1093/acprof:oso/9780195379655.003.0005

Toussaint, L. L., Williams, D. R., Musick, M. A., & Everson, S. A. (2001). Forgiveness and health: Age differences in a U.S. probability sample. *Journal of Adult Development, 8,* 249–257. http://dx.doi.org/10.1023/A:1011394629736

Toussaint, L., & Zoelzer, M. (2011, April). *Learning to forgive at Luther College: A randomized, controlled trial of REACH and Forgive for Good.* Paper presented at the Christian Association for Psychological Studies national conference, Indianapolis, IN.

Tsang, J.-A., McCullough, M. E., & Hoyt, W. T. (2005). Psychometric and rationalization accounts for the religion–forgiveness discrepancy. *Journal of Social Issues, 61,* 785–805. http://dx.doi.org/10.1111/j.1540-4560.2005.00432.x

Turner, V. (1969). *The ritual process: Structure and anti-structure.* Ithaca, NY: Cornell University Press.

Tutu, D. (2013, December). Desmond Tutu on Nelson Mandela: "Prison became a crucible." *The Guardian.* Retrieved from http://www.theguardian.com/commentisfree/2013/dec/06/desmond-tutu-nelson-mandela

Tyler, L. E. (1973). Design for a hopeful psychology. *American Psychologist, 28,* 1021–1029. http://dx.doi.org/10.1037/h0036044

Unterrainer, H., Ladenhauf, K. H., Wallner-Liebmann, S., & Fink, A. (2011). Different types of religious/spiritual well-being in relation to personality and subjective well-being. *International Journal for the Psychology of Religion, 21,* 115–126. http://dx.doi.org/10.1080/10508619.2011.557003

van der Kolk, B. A., McFarlane, A. C., & Weisaeth, L. (Eds.). (1996). *Traumatic stress: The effects of overwhelming experience on mind, body, and society.* New York, NY: Guilford Press.

Van Tongeren, D. R., Burnette, J. L., O'Boyle, E., Worthington, E. L., Jr., & Forsyth, D. (2014). A meta-analysis of inter-group forgiveness. *The Journal of Positive Psychology, 9,* 81–95. http://dx.doi.org/10.1080/17439760.2013.844268

Van Tongeren, D. R., Green, J. D., Davis, D. E., Worthington, E. L., Jr., & Reid, C. A. (2013). Till death do us part: Terror management and forgiveness in close relationships. *Personal Relationships*, *20*, 755–768. http://dx.doi.org/10.1111/pere.12013

Vitz, P. C., & Mango, P. (1997a). Kernbergian psychodynamics and religious aspects of the forgiveness process. *Journal of Psychology and Theology*, *25*, 72–80.

Vitz, P. C., & Mango, P. (1997b). Kleinian psychodynamics and religious aspects of hatred as a defense mechanism. *Journal of Psychology and Theology*, *25*, 64–71.

Volf, M. (1996). *Exclusion and embrace: A theological exploration of identity, otherness, and reconciliation*. Nashville, TN: Abingdon.

Wade, N. G., Hoyt, W. T., Kidwell, J. E. M., & Worthington, E. L., Jr. (2014). Efficacy of psychotherapeutic interventions to promote forgiveness: A meta-analysis. *Journal of Consulting and Clinical Psychology*, *82*, 154–170. http://dx.doi.org/10.1037/a0035268

Wade, N. G., & Meyer, J. E. (2009). Comparison of brief group interventions to promote forgiveness: A pilot outcome study. *International Journal of Group Psychotherapy*, *59*, 199–220. http://dx.doi.org/10.1521/ijgp.2009.59.2.199

Waldron, V. R., & Kelley, D. L. (2008). *Communicating forgiveness*. Thousand Oaks, CA: Sage Publications. http://dx.doi.org/10.4135/9781483329536

Wallin, D. J. (2007). *Attachment in psychotherapy*. New York, NY: Guilford Press.

Watson, D., & Clark, L. A. (1997). Measurement and mismeasurement of mood: Recurrent and emergent issues. *Journal of Personality Assessment*, *68*, 267–296. http://dx.doi.org/10.1207/s15327752jpa6802_4

Weaver, A. J., Flannelly, K. J., Flannelly, L. T., & Oppenheimer, J. E. (2003). Collaboration between clergy and mental health professionals: A review of professional health care journals from 1980 through 1999. *Counseling and Values*, *47*, 162–171.

Webb, J. R., Phillips, T. D., Bumgarner, D., & Conway-Williams, E. (2013). Forgiveness, mindfulness, and health. *Mindfulness*, *4*, 235–245. http://dx.doi.org/10.1007/s12671-012-0119-0

Webb, M., Call, S., Chickering, S. A., Colburn, T. A., & Heisler, D. (2006). Dispositional forgiveness and adult attachment styles. *The Journal of Social Psychology*, *146*, 509–512. http://dx.doi.org/10.3200/SOCP.146.4.509-512

Webb, M., Chickering, S., Colburn, T., Heisler, D., & Call, S. (2005). Religiosity and dispositional forgiveness. *Review of Religious Research*, *46*, 355–370. http://dx.doi.org/10.2307/3512166

Weinberg, M. (2013). The bidirectional dyadic association between tendency to forgive, self-esteem, social support, and PTSD symptoms among terror-attack survivors and their spouses. *Journal of Traumatic Stress*, *26*, 744–752. http://dx.doi.org/10.1002/jts.21864

Weissman, M., Markowitz, J., & Klerman, G. L. (2007). *Clinician's quick guide to interpersonal psychotherapy*. Oxford, England: Oxford University Press.

Welwood, J. (2000). *Toward a psychology of awakening: Buddhism, psychotherapy, and the path of personal and spiritual transformation.* Boston, MA: Shambala.

Wiesel, E. (2006). *Night* (M. Wiesel, Trans.). New York, NY: Hill and Wang.

Williamson, I. T., & Sandage, S. J. (2009). Longitudinal analyses of religious and spiritual development among seminary students. *Mental Health, Religion & Culture, 12,* 787–801. http://dx.doi.org/10.1080/13674670902956604

Williamson, I. T., Sandage, S. J., & Lee, R. M. (2007). How social connectedness affects guilt and shame: Mediated by hope and differentiation of self. *Personality and Individual Differences, 43,* 2159–2170. http://dx.doi.org/10.1016/j.paid.2007.06.026

Wilson, J. P., Drozdek, B., & Turkovic, S. (2006). Posttraumatic shame and guilt. *Trauma, Violence, & Abuse, 7,* 122–141. http://dx.doi.org/10.1177/1524838005285914

Winnicott, D. W. (1986). *Holding and interpretation: Fragment of an analysis.* New York, NY: Grove Press.

Witvliet, C. V. O., Phipps, K. A., Feldman, M. E., & Beckham, J. C. (2004). Posttraumatic mental and physical health correlates of forgiveness and religious coping in military veterans. *Journal of Traumatic Stress, 17,* 269–273. http://dx.doi.org/10.1023/B:JOTS.0000029270.47848.e5

Wood, B. T., Worthington, E. L., Jr., Exline, J. J., Yali, A. M., Aten, J. D., & McMinn, M. R. (2010). Development, refinement, and psychometric properties of the Attitudes toward God Scale (ATGS–9). *Psychology of Religion and Spirituality, 2,* 148–167. http://dx.doi.org/10.1037/a0018753

Worthington, E. L. (n.d.). *Moving forward: Six steps to forgiving yourself and breaking free from the past.* Retrieved from http://ForgiveSelf.com

Worthington, E. L., Jr. (2003). *Forgiving and reconciling: Bridges to wholeness and hope.* Downers Grove, IL: InterVarsity Press.

Worthington, E. L., Jr. (2005). *Hope-focused marriage counseling: A guide to brief therapy, Revised edition.* Downers Grove, IL: InterVarsity Press.

Worthington, E. L., Jr. (2006). *Forgiveness and reconciliation: Theory and application.* New York, NY: Brunner-Routledge.

Worthington, E. L., Jr. (2009). *A just forgiveness: Responsible healing without excusing injustice.* Downers Grove, IL: InterVarsity Press.

Worthington, E. L., Jr. (2013). *Moving forward: Six steps to forgiving yourself and breaking free from the past.* Colorado Springs, CO: WaterBrook Multnomah.

Worthington, E. L., Jr., Davis, D. E., Hook, J. N., Gartner, A. L., & Jennings, D. J., II. (2009). Relational spirituality and forgiveness. In J. H. Ellens (Ed.), *The healing power of spirituality: How religion helps us* (pp. 41–58). Westport, CT: Praeger.

Worthington, E. L., Jr., & Drinkard, D. T. (2000). Promoting reconciliation through psychoeducational and therapeutic interventions. *Journal of Marital and Family Therapy, 26,* 93–101. http://dx.doi.org/10.1111/j.1752-0606.2000.tb00279.x

Worthington, E. L., Jr., Greer, C. L., Hook, J. N., Davis, D. E., Gartner, A. L., Jennings, D. J. II, . . . Toussaint, L. (2010). Relational spirituality and forgiveness in organizational life: Theory, status of research, and new ideas for discovery. *Journal of Management, Spirituality, and Religion, 7*, 119–134.

Worthington, E. L., Jr., Hook, J. N., Davis, D. E., Gartner, A. L., & Jennings, D. J., II. (2013). Conducting empirical research on religiously accommodated treatments. In Kenneth I. Pargament (Ed.-in-Chief), A. Mahoney, & E. Shafranske (Assoc. Eds.), *APA handbooks in psychology: APA handbook of psychology, religion, and spirituality* (Vol. 2, pp. 651–669). Washington, DC: American Psychological Association.

Worthington, E. L., Jr., Hook, J. N., Davis, D. E., & McDaniel, M. A. (2011). Religion and spirituality. *Journal of Clinical Psychology, 67*, 204–214. http://dx.doi.org/10.1002/jclp.20760

Worthington, E. L., Jr., Hunter, J. L., Sharp, C. B., Hook, J. N., Van Tongeren, D. R., Davis, D. E., . . . Monforte, M. V. (2010). A psychoeducational intervention to promote forgiveness in Christians in the Philippines. *Journal of Mental Health Counseling, 32*, 75–93.

Worthington, E. L., Jr., Johnson, E. L., Hook, J. N., & Aten, J. D. (Eds.). (2013). *Evidence-based practices for Christian counseling and psychotherapy.* Downers Grove, IL: InterVarsity Press.

Worthington, E. L., Jr., & Langberg, D. (2012). Religious considerations and self-forgiveness in treating trauma in present and former soldiers. *Journal of Psychology and Theology, 40*, 274–288.

Worthington, E. L., Jr., Sandage, S. J., & Berry, J. W. (2000). Group interventions to promote forgiveness: What researchers and clinicians ought to know. In M. E. McCullough, K. I. Pargament, & C. E. Thoresen (Eds.), *Forgiveness: Theory, research and practice* (pp. 228–253). New York, NY: Guilford Press.

Worthington, E. L., Jr., & Sotoohi, G. (2010). Physiological assessment of forgiveness, grudges, and revenge: Theories, research methods, and implications. *International Journal of Psychology Research, 5*, 291–316.

Worthington, E. L., Jr., Wade, N. G., Hight, T. L., Ripley, J. S., McCullough, M. E., Berry, J. W., . . . O'Connor, L. (2003). The Religious Commitment Inventory—10: Development, refinement, and validation of a brief scale for research and counseling. *Journal of Counseling Psychology, 50*, 84–96. http://dx.doi.org/10.1037/0022-0167.50.1.84

Worthington, E. L., Jr., Witvliet, C. V. O., Pietrini, P., & Miller, A. J. (2007). Forgiveness, health, and well-being: A review of evidence for emotional versus decisional forgiveness, dispositional forgivingness, and reduced unforgiveness. *Journal of Behavioral Medicine, 30*, 291–302. http://dx.doi.org/10.1007/s10865-007-9105-8

Wuthnow, R. (1998). *After heaven: Spirituality in America since the 1950s.* Berkeley: University of California Press. http://dx.doi.org/10.1525/california/9780520213968.001.0001

Wuthnow, R. (2000). How religious groups promote forgiving: A national study. *Journal for the Scientific Study of Religion, 39,* 125–139. http://dx.doi.org/10.1111/0021-8294.00011

Yalom, I. D., & Leszcz, M. (2005). *The theory and practice of group psychotherapy* (5th ed.). New York, NY: Basic Books.

Yoder, J. H. (1994). *The politics of Jesus* (2nd ed.). Grand Rapids, MI: William B. Eerdmans.

INDEX

Hill, P. C., 22, 32, 38, 39, 64, 84, 86, 106–107, 159
Hmong Americans, 262–263
Holding environments, 42
Holding onto forgiveness, 15
Holocaust, 200
Hook, J. N., 62, 100, 101, 103, 159, 256
Hope, 91–93
    in long-term psychotherapy, 189–190, 212
    in personality transformation, 127
    tension between humility and, 14
Hope-Focused Couple Approach (HFCA), 253
Horowitz, L. M., 191–192
Hoyt, W. T., 106
Hugo, Victor, 115
Human development, and relational spirituality, 41–43
Humility
    brief psychotherapy case study, 159–160
    in brief therapy, 152
    in long-term psychotherapy, 190–191, 219
    in personality transformation, 127
    tension between hope and, 14
Hyatt-Edwards, L., 46
Hyperindependence, 192
Hypothalamus–pituitary–adrenal axis, 27

Identity, 47
Illuminative way, 57
Implicit memory, 186
Independence, of self, 64
Injustice gap, 25, 30, 72
Insecure attachment templates, 187
Intercultural aspects of relational spirituality, 44–45, 94–95
Intergenerational relationship patterns, 124
Internal conflicts, 65
Internal transformations, 119
Internal working model, 29
Interpersonal conflicts, 46, 186
Interpersonal neuroscience, 41
Interreligious conflict, 74–76
Intimacy, 53
Intrinsic religious motivation, 69
Islam, 34, 74–76

James, William, 39
Jankowski, P. J., 84, 86, 91–93, 95
Johnson, S. M., 29, 107
John Templeton Foundation, 11
Jones, J. W., 51–52
Judaism, 46, 74–76, 262
Jung, C. G., 53
Justice
    and forgiveness, 23, 25
    in personality transformation, 128–131
    tension between release of resentment and, 14

Kabat-Zinn, Jon, 258–259
Karremans, J. C., 46
Kegan, R., 209
Kerr, M. E., 224
King, Martin Luther, Jr., 25, 113
Kirkpatrick, L. A., 69
Klein, M., 198
Kohut, H., 193, 213, 261–262
Kopp, Sheldon, 113, 131

Lahey, L. L., 209
Lament, 215
Lannon, R., 41
Larson, N. R., 205
Lavelock, C. R., 256
Lawler-Row, K. A., 46
Lazarus, R. S., 26, 73
Lazarus, Richard, 26
Leading, in long-term psychotherapy case study, 204–205
Les Misérables (Hugo), 115
Leszcz, M., 260
Leverage, in brief psychotherapy case study, 156–157
Levinas, Emmanuel, 44–45
Lewis, T., 41, 188
Limbic system, 30, 41, 48, 186
Loder, J. E., 51
Long-term psychotherapy, 185–202. See also Long-term psychotherapy case study
    attachment dynamics in, 187–188
    commonalities between brief and, 140–143
    defined, 185
    differences between brief and, 143–148

Offender–sacred (OS) relationships, 69–70, 73, 80, 81, 97, 98, 107, 109
  brief psychotherapy case study, 167
  in brief therapy, 152–153
  measures to assess aspect of, 276–277
Offender–transgression (OT) relationship, 67, 73
Oman, D., 259
Ontological hermeneutics, 43
Open-ended psychotherapy, brief vs., 139–140
Openness to Experience, 119
Oppression, 58
Orbitofrontal cortex, 29–30
OS relationships. *See* Offender–sacred relationships
OT relationship. *See* Offender–transgression relationship
Out-group members, generosity/compassion toward, 44
Owen, J., 159

Pacing
  in couples and family therapy, 226–227
  long-term psychotherapy case study, 204
Paranoid personality disorder, 197–198, 216
Parentification, 225
Pargament, K. I., 32, 38–40, 50, 54, 70, 73–74, 150, 200
Paris, P. J., 40
Patrick, K., 106
Payback, pursuing, 21
Personality factors, in long-term psychotherapy, 191–202
Personality transformation, 115–137
  attachment templates vs. differentiation of self in, 122–125
  case examples illustrating, 120–121, 134–137
  centrifugal conflict vs. centripetal forgiveness in, 122
  and coping skills, 117
  difficulty of, 117–118
  emotional processing/regulation in, 125–127
  evolutionary vs. revolutionary, 143

and external vs. internal transformations, 119
and forgiveness, 119–120
general strategy for, 119–121, 132–134
hope and humility in, 127
justice vs. forgiveness in, 128–131
keys to, 121–131
and personality × situation interaction, 118–119
prerequisites for, 116–119
and psychotherapy, 117
psychotherapy for, 131–134
and religion/spirituality, 117
as second-order change, 117–118
situational factors in, 118
spiritual dwelling vs. seeking in, 127–128
subjective factors in, 118
Personality × situation interaction, 118–119
Personal religion, 39
Personal scripts, 268–269
Phillips, T. D., 259
Plante, T. G., 259
The Politics of Jesus (Yoder), 42
Positive religious coping, 93–94
Power, in couples and family therapy, 226
Prayer, contemplative, 69, 91–93
Premature self-forgiveness, 272
Preoccupied/ambivalent attachment, 195–196
Problem-focused coping, 27
Process model groups, 249–250
Process-oriented group therapy, 260
Proctor, J. H., 11
Pseudoforgiveness, 195
Pseudo–self-forgiveness, 272
Psychodynamic psychotherapy, 132
Psychoeducational forgiveness groups, 249–258
Psychotherapeutic distance, 205–206
Psychotherapist(s)
  brief psychotherapy case study, 158–160
  qualities of, 274
  and religiousness of clients, 9–10
  role of, 269, 274
  skill of, at dealing with forgiveness, 11

Psychotherapy. *See also* Brief psychotherapy; Long-term psychotherapy
addressing forgiveness in, 11
as crucible, 7, 142, 151
importance of forgiveness in, 10–12
and personality transformation, 117,
131–134
for personality transformation,
131–134
and stress-and-coping theory of
forgiveness, 35
as strong situation, 131
Purgative way, 56–57
Purity, and compassion, 43–44

Quantum change, 51, 59
Questing, 90, 95
Quest motivation, 69

Racism, 52, 236
Rambo, L. R., 51
Rational emotive therapy (RET), 175
Raya, Joseph, 75
RCI–10 (Religious Commitment
Inventory—10), 161, 162
REACH forgiveness model, 15, 92, 117,
146, 147, 174, 176, 249–256,
260, 271
Reactance, 212
Recall, 15
Reconciliation, forgiveness vs., 218–219
Reframing, 142
Relational Engagement of the Spiritual
for a Transgression (REST) scale,
97, 98, 107, 276–277
Relationality
and forgiveness, 25–26, 29–35
of self, 64
Relational objects of hope, 189–190
Relational spirituality, 7–8, 32–35,
38–45. *See also* Forgiveness and
relational spirituality structural
model
in attachment phase of psychotherapy, 211
and borderline personality disorder,
199
and crucible, 208
and dependent personality, 195–196

developmental character of, 41–43
embodiedness of, 40–41
with graduate students, 82–95
hermeneutical character of, 43–44
intercultural character of, 44–45
and narcissism, 193
and OCPD, 194
and paranoid personality disorder,
198
roots of, 38–39
and spirituality vs. religion, 39–40
as term, 38, 39
and trauma, 200
and vulnerable narcissism, 196
Relational templates, 16, 29, 41
Relationship(s). *See also* Therapeutic
relationship
brief psychotherapy case study,
160–161
and differentiation of self, 124
forgiveness in, 25–26
helping, 141
internal working models of, 31–32
and personality change, 119
tension between conflict and
restoring, 13
Religion
personal, 39
and personality transformation, 117
spirituality vs., 39–40
as term, 32
utilization of, in brief psychotherapy,
149–150
Religious Commitment Inventory–10
(RCI-10), 161, 162
Religious coping, 28, 93–94
Religious groups, forgiveness therapy
with, 260–263
Religious institutions, 83
Religious motivation, intrinsic vs.
extrinsic, 69
Religiousness
and essential tensions, 14
pervasiveness of, 9, 32
Religious spirituality, 28
Resentment, tension between justice
and release of, 14
REST scale. *See* Relational Engagement
of the Spiritual for a Transgression scale

ABOUT THE AUTHORS

Everett L. Worthington, Jr., PhD, is Commonwealth Professor of Psychology at Virginia Commonwealth University (VCU). He is a licensed clinical psychologist in Virginia and has had an active private practice, directed a counseling service, and been clinical supervisor for other agencies. As a professor, he has done teaching and research at VCU since 1978. He has studied forgiveness since the 1980s, and he makes many practical resources available on his website (without cost; http://www.evworthington-forgiveness.com). In his career, he has written or edited 35 books and almost 400 articles or chapters. Dr. Worthington is regularly interviewed in media and is a frequent speaker throughout the world.

Steven J. Sandage, PhD, is the Albert and Jessie Danielsen Professor of Psychology of Religion and Theology at Boston University and the research director and senior staff psychologist at the Danielsen Institute. He is a licensed psychologist with clinical specialization in couples and family therapy. Dr. Sandage has academic appointments at Boston University in the School of Theology, the Department of Psychological and Brain Sciences, and the Graduate Division of Religious Studies and has been training clinicians for 18 years. He has previously published four books and numerous articles and chapters in the areas of positive psychology, spirituality, psychopathology, psychotherapy, and intercultural competence.